A COOK'S TOUR OF MEXICO

A Cook's Tour of Mexico

Authentic Recipes from the Country's Best
Open-Air Markets, City Fondas, and Home Kitchens

Nancy Zaslavsky

Drawings by Morris Zaslavsky
Photography by Nancy Zaslavsky

St. Martin's Press
New York

Left: Oaxaca's traffic-free "zócalo" bustles with people.

A Cook's Tour Of Mexico

Design by Ultragraphics, Venice, California

Library of Congress Cataloging-in-Publication Data
Zaslavsky, Nancy.
A cook's tour of Mexico : authentic recipes from the country's best open-air markets, city fondas, and home kitchens / Nancy Zaslavsky.
p. cm.
ISBN 0-312-13454-1
1. Cookery, Mexican. I. Title.
TX716.M4Z37 1995
641.5972— dc20 *95-32918*
CIP

First Edition: November 1995

10 9 8 7 6 5 4 3 2 1

Acknowledgments

MORRIS, THIS BOOK IS FOR YOU. My husband and sunshine, number-one supporter, traveling partner, artist extraordinaire, unflinching food taster, and unflappable driver.

GOOD FRIENDS HAVE BEEN MORE THAN GENEROUS with their time, talent, help, and spirit: Soledad López de Wittrock, Angela Rinaldi, Rosario Chávez, and Nancy Lamb, thank you so much.

Dad and Gwen, Renate and Skip, and Dad Albert, thank you for your love and encouragement.

I'm no expert on Mexico but a lover of Mexico—its food, fiestas, culture, and lifestyle. The people I interviewed for this book *are* experts, and each in his or her particular region of a large and complex land. I'd love you to meet all these people who have shared family recipes (sometimes never revealed outside their homes): from a Zapotec grandmother who lives in a pueblo outside Oaxaca; another grandmother and fonda owner in Guadalajara's bustling Mercado Juárez; and still one more grandmother living in Zinacantán, a Tzotzil village up in the clouds near San Cristóbal de las Casas, in Chiapas. Meet a flamenco-dancing cooking teacher in San Miguel de Allende who loves serving Technicolor drinks made from tropical flowers; a *cochinita pibil* (pit-cooked pork) pig farmer and underground cook in Ucu, a village of thatched-roof cottages in Yucatán; and a top female restaurateur in Mexico City. They know, too, that many traditional dishes are becoming lost in today's hectic world, and that their regional recipes need to be recorded for generations to come.

Throughout Mexico, hundreds of generous people helped this book come to life, and from the bottom of my heart I thank each and every one of you. The name above each recipe holds a fond memory for me and without these names there would be no book. I would especially like to thank: Carmen Ramírez Degollado, Mexico City; Lula Bertrán, Mexico City; Lila Lomeli, Mexico City; Roberto Santibañez, Mexico City; Marcela López Brun, Puebla; Marilyn Mayo, Pátzcuaro; Reyna Polanco Abrahams, San Miguel de Allende; Jesus A. Hernández Remos, Veracruz; Carlos Ramon Hernández Estrada,

Veracruz; Emilia Arroya de Cabrera, Oaxaca; Ita Cabrera, Oaxaca; Sylvia García de López, Oaxaca; Isis Rique León y Vélez, San Cristóbal de la Casas; Gloria Torres Alvarez, San Cristóbal de las Casas; and Adda Erosa, Mérida.

Thank you to all the helpful people at the Mexican Government Tourism Office, Los Angeles, and John O'Malley at the Mexican Ministry of Tourism, Chicago. Thank you to Freida's, Inc., Los Angeles, for the generous supply of picture-perfect fresh and dried chiles. Thank you to friend and photographer Steve Smith for the scrumptious color chile shots.

Taste testers and still friends: Gwen and Chas Garabedian, Fritzy Roeder, Tina Beesemyer, Pat Gable, Donna Vaccarino and David Denton, Shinji Isozaki, Lee Burns, Gary Praglin, Danna and Ed Ruscha, Jeanne and John Binder, Roger Hayot, Mike Perlis, Peter Strauss and Rachel Ticotin, Peggy and Ted Raess, Kim and Michael McCarty, Patricia and Franklin Melton, Anne Graham and Joe Lewis, Ruth and Ron Amen, Janie Hewson and Victor Budnik, Kathryn Peters, Liz and Peter Goulds, and Melony, Tom, and Henry Wudl.

My editor at St. Martin's Press, Barbara Anderson: Thank you for taking a chance with my concept and working enthusiastically throughout the project. Thank you to the creative team at St. Martin's Press, especially Charles Woods. Thank you to my copy editor, Joan Whitman, whose eagle eye examined every nook and cranny with diligent vigor. My assistant and computer wiz, Robin Pirog, toughed out the rough spots with good humor and sheer determination to finish on schedule. My agents, Betsy Amster in Los Angeles and Angela Miller in New York, made this book possible.

Contents

INDEX OF RECIPES

BY CATEGORY AND LISTED IN ALPHABETICAL ORDER IN ENGLISH

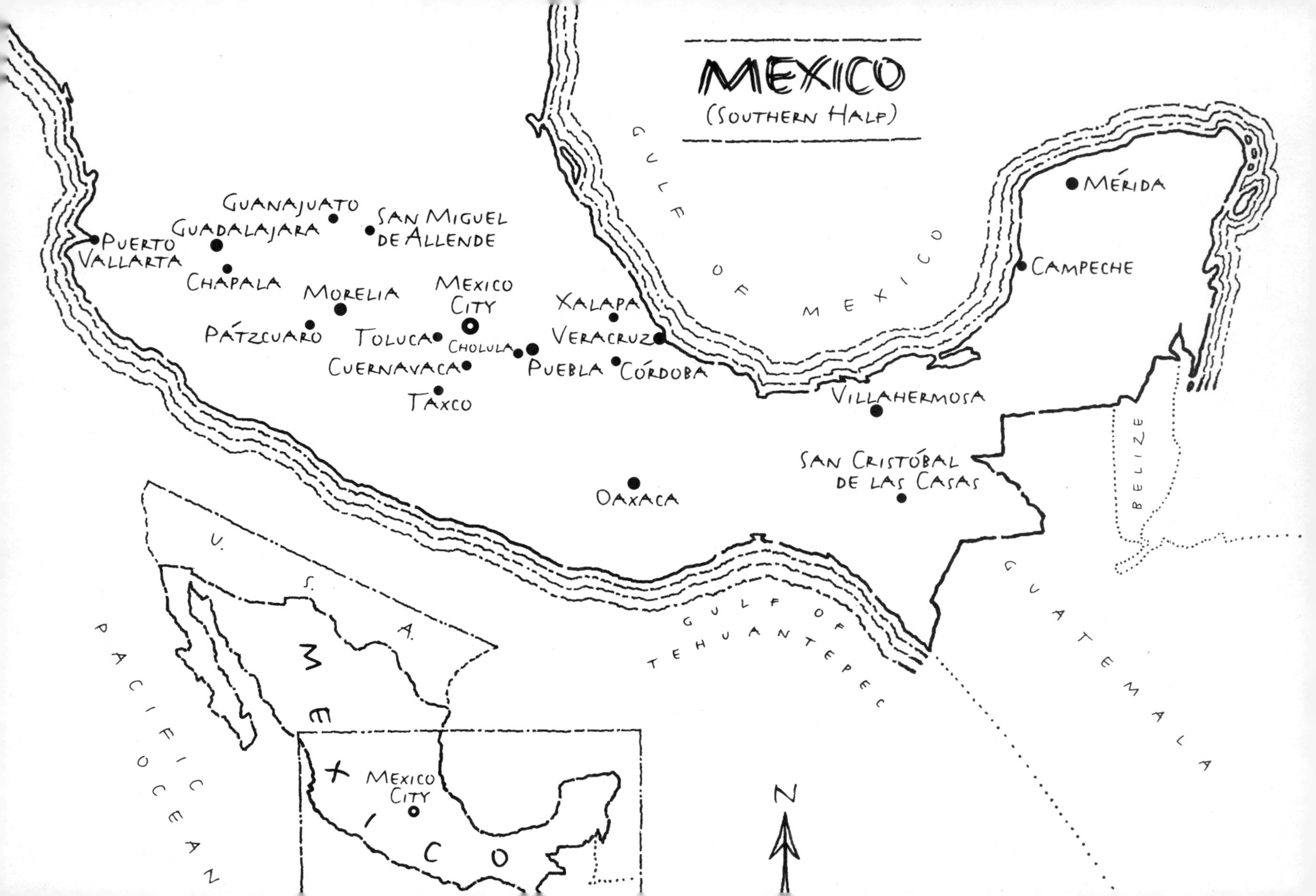
MEXICO
(Southern Half)
Gulf of Mexico
Mérida
Campeche
Puerto Vallarta
Guadalajara
Guanajuato
San Miguel de Allende
Chapala
Morelia
Mexico City
Pátzcuaro
Toluca
Cholula
Cuernavaca
Taxco
Xalapa
Veracruz
Puebla
Córdoba
Villahermosa
San Cristóbal de las Casas
Oaxaca
Belize
Guatemala
Gulf of Tehuantepec
Pacific Ocean
U.S.A.
Mexico
Mexico City
N

Introduction

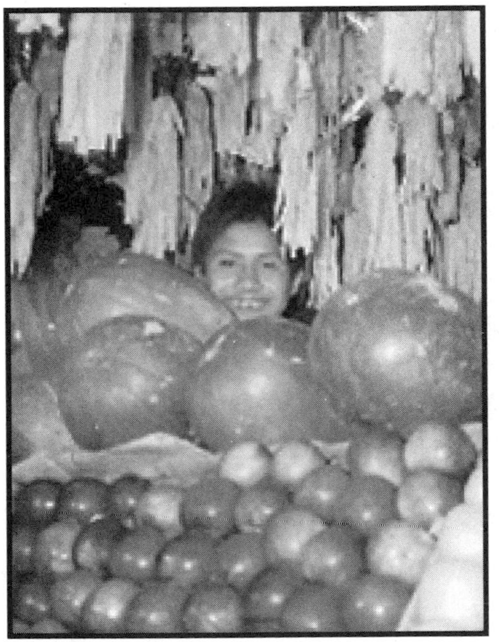

Smiles through piñata tails at Córdoba's Mercado Revolución.

FOOD AND LOVE ARE UNIVERSAL LANGUAGES. My seduction began twenty years ago on my first trip to Mexico. As a graphic designer with art history classes up to here, I intended to visit every museum and archaeological gem imprinted in my brain. I planned to roam great cities and jungle pueblos, taking slides of art world wonders. Sure. The very first day in Oaxaca changed years of day-dreams. I was mesmerized by the old Juárez market. I remember strolling through a tangle of aisles past armloads of aromatic produce being piled high into not-so-still-life master-pieces. The chile displays were so spectacular my camera worked overtime. How I wished the hotel room was a small apartment with a kitchen; I longed to prepare my very own Mexican meals. I was hooked. Thereafter, my quest in every new city and village throughout Mexico became *el mercado*.

Over the past twenty five years, my love of cooking has lured me time and time again to the marketplace, the world's greatest cooking school. In Mexico I've learned how to choose the choicest chipotle chiles (smoked jalapeños), sweetest tropical mangoes, and tastiest tortillas. Moreover, every time I've asked how to cook an unfamilar fish from the Gulf, prepare enchiladas a new way, or choose the correct pumpkin seeds for *pipián*, the fishmonger, farmer, or grower has shared family hints or personal favorites. From the covered marketplaces in major cities to once-a-week, open-air markets in small towns, markets are the hub and heartbeat of the people. The people who sell their corn husks, their tiny wild avocados, and their red-skinned bananas are proud and passionate about their work. Let's face it, they're not making a fortune. What motivates them is their love and respect for quality products, and they're determined to keep those traditional values alive in today's freeze-dried, shrink-wrapped world. So am I. My love of seasonal foods like jet black *zapotes negros* to eat with a spoon in spring; *huitlacoche*, the prized corn fungus with intense mushroom flavor in summer; *flores de calabazas,* sunny yellow pumpkin blossoms for quesadillas in early fall; and warm-your-tummy dried chiles in winter, is the *raison d'être* behind this book.

Mexican people are kind, affectionate, and generous beyond belief. Again and again I make new friends in marketplaces when I approach complete strangers, whether market workers or shoppers, and ask how they prepare the vegetables they are selling or admiring. Beyond their initial shock and amazement when this blond gringa speaks to them in some out-of-the-way open-air market, or a bustling big city market hall, everyone is so helpful I am constantly overwhelmed. True, many people are stunned that I'm interested in them, or their Indian grandmother's old recipe, but my enthusiasm and sincere interest wins them over. It would be difficult to find one person in a Mexican marketplace who doesn't like to talk about food and cooking. Everyone has an opinion, everyone has a recipe, and everyone thinks his family's is the uncompromised best. And to prove it, people invite me into their homes so I can watch them prepare dishes and taste for myself. Wielding cameras, notepads, measuring cups, and spoons, in my demand for detail I can be a pain-in-the-neck, but my unconventional behavior is taken in good humor. This diligence pays off; recipes are recorded, and in some cases written down for the first time.

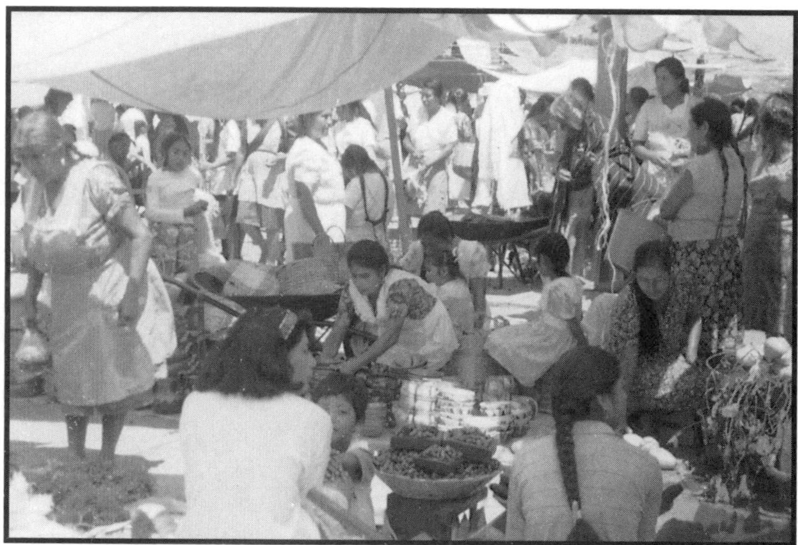

Zaachila's Thursday open-air market.

A Cook's Tour of Mexico focuses on the top market regions of central and southern Mexico: from Puerto Vallarta through Mexico City, and across to Veracruz, south, and up into Yucatán. It's broken into chapters by regions so you'll get a good idea of how flavors and dishes are unique to certain areas of the country. In 1993 my husband, Morris, a professor of art on university leave, and I drove from California down the west coast of Mexico then east to Guadalajara; the historic Colonial Circle; Mexico City; its environs of Toluca, Taxco, and Cuernavaca; then Puebla and Veracruz. Heading south, we explored Oaxaca, San Cristóbal de las Casas, Villahermosa, Campeche, Mérida, and the Yucatán. It was quite an adventure—eight months and more than ten thousand miles on the 1993 trip alone, and the basis for this book. I confess to being a fortunate person—traveling to favorite, often breathtakingly beautiful places with notebook and camera, eating exceptional food, meeting wonderful people, and then reliving all these magical moments when I write.

MEXICO'S MARKETS AND FONDAS

YOU CAN STILL FIND ANCIENT AZTEC OR MAYAN MARKETS IN MEXICO—in the same locations they occupied thousands of years ago. You will also find the same items that the ancient marketgoers enjoyed—the chiles, corn, beans, avocados, tomatoes, tomatillos, pineapples, guavas, squash, sweet potatoes, coconuts, cocoa beans, peanuts, prickly pears, and papayas that are indigenous to the country. Today, though, you will also find items that reflect the Spanish influence. In the sixteenth century, the Spaniards introduced cattle, sheep, pigs, chickens, wheat, rice, citrus, nuts, melons, onions, olives, and new herbs and spices to the Western hemisphere. Hispanic products gave a new life to Mexican cuisine and immediate excitement to the culinary culture. Mexican food became truely *mestizo*—a mixture of Indian and Spanish.

Today's markets, countrywide, also have their share of produce flown in by jet, but it's the seasonal crops and regional specialties that are their heart and soul. Because of this, the feeling of each market is different and each has a personality. Regional markets are not at all like *supermercados* which are part of a chain and look exactly alike. But these supermarkets, too, have their place in Mexico because they offer the greatest selection of paper products, canned goods, crackers, cookies, toiletries, and pet food. Despite their increasing presence all over the country, however, consider how fast weekly farmer's markets are making a grand comeback in the United States. Let's hope that Mexico can hold onto both so that comebacks aren't necessary in years to come.

Mexican regional markets are exciting, exotic, boisterous, mysterious, mystical, shocking, seductive, spiritual, clamorous, and highly aromatic. Cannibalistic-looking cauldrons bubble with pig parts in scalding fat; smoke from incense wafts through piles of medicinal herbs into aisles; mounds of *moles* are redolent with chiles and cinnamon; animal intestines hang from above to dry but seem like decorations; butchered pigs' heads appear as ornaments with herbs and fruit stuck in their mouths; dried chiles are so intense everyone sneezes as they walk past; hawkers thrust products in your face; vendors shout in your ear; live animals squawk, squeal, gobble, moo, baa, and bleat in rhythm to a blaring cassette tape seller's ranchero music.

Adding to the olfactory explosions are fondas—the counters that are owned and operated by Mexican women and offer prepared food. They are my favorite places to eat in Mexico. For the purposes of this book all fondas and *comedors* are called fondas, as they most often are throughout Mexico. Originally fondas were remodeled garages, or front rooms of homes, where women made a bit of extra money selling meals to local workers. Nowadays, neon signs scream Fonda María, Comedor Leila-Luisa, or Fonda Mama, plus the women scream for your attention, as market competion is stiff. They thrust menus in front of your face and insist you check out their daily *comida corrida* (lunch special). They even pull you over to see a good-looking fish or smell a special sauce. At the more aggressive city fondas, incessant barking forces me to relax, become a bit more Mexican in my approach, and just let the noise become ambient market sound. For the vendors, the strolling guitarists playing for pesos, the never-ending flow of handcraft sellers, and the kids selling Chiclets, this is business as usual. A fonda lunch can never be mistaken for a ladies luncheon.

Fondas are most often small counters within the large markets of cities or good-sized towns, and they are specialists. Each counter has a small menu of related items: fish and seafood; *antojitos* (*masa* snacks) in all shapes and sizes; tacos of beef, chicken, chorizo, and crisp fried pork; hominy stews; chicken-cheese quesadillas, or entire dinners; goat soup; grilled beef steaks; *moles*; sky-high sandwiches; tamales; and *pibiles*—the list goes on. They are the eating places of not only marketgoers and market workers, but also office workers, shoppers, and staff from stores throughout the neighborhood. For a fonda to survive, it has to be good. Word gets around quickly within the food community, so if a marketplace fonda serves an inferior product, it won't last long.

There's nothing quite like a fonda outside of Mexico, so be sure to visit fonda sections at markets to see what locals are preparing with regional products. This is the typical, everyday food of the people, because fondas are always the traditionalists when it comes to the preparation of regional foods. When Mexicans want fancier, nouvelle-style, or Continental-influenced food and presentation, there are restaurants especially for that purpose. It's best to eat at fondas for breakfast, or for lunch, when the food is at its freshest. General lack of refrigeration increases the chance of your having a food problem when eating at night. Of course there are places open evenings only, or weekends only, or afternoons only to further complicate your food decisions.

Smaller pueblos may have only two or three fondas in or near the marketplace. Their menu (of sorts) will have five or six items plus a daily special—usually nothing is written except a sign for the special. You'll need to look around and see what others are eating or ask what's cooking; vendors will be more than happy to recite their list. And, like everyone else, ask the price before agreeing to anything. The way people choose a fonda is simple: Those working in the markets know who makes a favorite dish on a certain day; or a man's wife will own a fonda so guess where he eats every day; men know where they can flirt with pretty countergirls; single diners sit where their favorite lunchtime soap opera is on television; or just plain superb cooking always draws aficionados.

Groupings of movable tables, grills, and instant kitchens are always set up for weekly markets. It would be unnatural for an open-air market *not* to have smoke rising from somewhere and a cloud wafting over the crowd. Mexicans, by the way, seem to eat more food while walking on the street than they do in houses. Men-or women-operated street food carts known as *cocinas callejeras* are everywhere. "Over six million people eat at one in Mexico every day," says Lula Bertrán, a Mexico City food specialist. If you're fortunate to spend time in one town, before long you'll get to know who's on what corner and when. There are morning, day, or night guys. Some have grills, other griddles, steamers, and pots of boiling oil for deep-frying. Big cities have carts on every corner near markets. Mexicans see the hot food cart as yet another opportunity to eat their favorite way—snacking.

The restaurants included in this book were chosen because they are specialists in top-quality, traditional, regional dishes. They might be as simple as a fonda, or as elegant as the dining room of a world-class hotel, but they are all my personal favorites.

There are many fine guidebooks on the subject of traveling through Mexico (such as those of Lonely Planet, Frommer's, and American Express) with up-to-date travel information, maps, hotel listings, restaurants, and rates. Most provide dining information for the average traveler—not for us. We're tired of reading about the same overpriced, gringoesque hotel dining rooms offering "safe" food. They're usually all on a tourist beach or town square, as if you wouldn't be willing to walk three blocks for something truly special. Who cares if Hilton's or Hyatt's restaurant is biggest and brightest with Continental service? Go out and find the *real* Mexico by dining on *real* Mexican food and meeting *real* Mexicans. My favorite place to start is the market—always an adventure, and always full of surprises, *never* "no surprises," as Holiday Inn's advertising loved to brag for so many years.

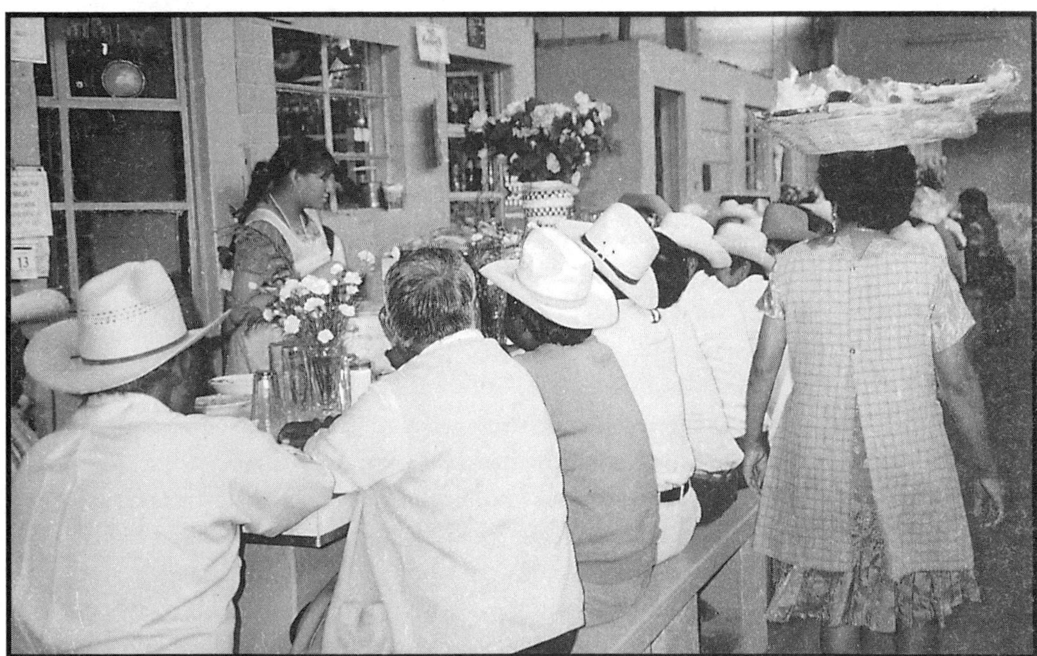

Lunchtime in Oaxaca's Mercado 20 de Noviembre fondas building.

Basics of Mexican Cooking

TODAY'S LIFESTYLES AND EATING HABITS HAVE CERTAINLY CHANGED since these traditional recipes were developed, mostly generations ago. No one ever said regional Mexican dishes, especially those from the southern half of the country, were quick to prepare. In fact, the recipes in this book are a collection for people who really love food and are willing to spend time in a kitchen preparing many of the world's great dishes. None of the recipes involves complicated or tricky techniques, but many call for a long ingredients list and a fair amount of preparation. A few sauces take a full day to make—after cleaning and toasting chiles, grinding nuts, seeds, and spices, then simmering with a homemade stock. The good news is that most of these sauces keep extremely well in the refrigerator and can be frozen. Think about making *mole* paste one weekend (store some in the refrigerator for months and freeze the rest for more than a year) and completing the dish the following week at a leisurely pace. As with all cuisines, soups, sauces, and stews taste better a few days later—it's up to your timetable. Mexico's complex sauces are always served with very simply prepared meats, vegetables, beans, rice, or tortillas, making the rest of the meal a snap.

Learning more about fats in cooking has played a major role in our eating habits lately. These recipes are, indeed, for people looking for fat-free ideas. In fact, after reading and understanding the composition of a traditional dish, lard can often be changed to vegetable oil (as is happening throughout Mexico today), and the quantity of vegetable oil can, in many cases, be cut in half, or even eliminated by exchanging fruit juice for the sautéing medium, and using nonstick skillets and pots. The flavor of southern Mexican cooking generally comes not from fats but through herbs, nuts, seeds, corn, cocoa, vine-ripened and tree-ripened fruits and vegetables, and "toasting" these flavorings on an ungreased skillet to intensify their tastes before turning them into superlative sauces. But more than any other item, it's chile that makes Mexico's cuisine come to life, and all chiles are fat-free.

Assuming you have a stove, pots and skillets, quality knives, and basic kitchen equipment, few items are necessary: a blender and *comal,* a cooking disk made from steel, cast iron, or unglazed earthenware—(see Glossary), or heavy skillet, and a tortilla press if you're interested in making your own tortillas. Traditional hand-grinding equipment produces lovely results, and the items are interesting to try if only to appreciate the fabulous textures they provide. We are living in a modern world and everyone I spoke with in Mexico knows this fact very well. Hand-ground *masa* is appreciated by villager and city slicker alike, and people are willing to spend extra money now and then to buy handmade tortillas from women who earn their livings by continuing this, and similar, time-consuming culinary traditions.

As good cooks everywhere know, the most important concept in any cuisine is using the best quality, freshest, and seasonal ingredients. If a certain produce item is out of season, change gears and choose another recipe. Mexicans have greater fruit and vegetable selections than most of us, so they're very fussy. Follow their lead and buy the best, cook with care, and you'll produce winning results.

CHILE

> *Chile, they say, is the king, the soul of the Mexicans—a nutrient, a medicine, a drug, a comfort. For many Mexicans, if it were not for the existence of chile, their national identity would begin to disappear.*
>
> —*Arturo Lomeli,* El Chile y Otros Picantes.

CHILE, GENUS *CAPSICUM*, IS MEXICAN CUISINE'S PERSONALITY STAMP. Along with beans, corn, and tortillas, chiles are the soul of the country's cooking. There are hundreds of varieties grown in Mexico today—direct descendants of those grown by ancient Aztecs and Mayans. Today, most of the world's chile crop is grown in Mexico, and most is eaten there.

Flavor (not hotness) is what puts a particular chile brand on regional Mexican cuisine. When a certain chile is called for in a recipe, it's because it provides a particular flavor necessary to duplicate a dish's authentic taste. Spiciness (the chemical, capsaicin, along with four other less-known chemicals causes this burning sensation) is synonymous with chile, often because too much is used and a chile's basic flavor is masked by fire. Generally, the smaller a chile, the hotter it is. But, there's always that one hot poblano chile in a dozen mild or a "dud" within a handful of hot habaneros. Then there's the Scoville test, which measures the strength of a chile by dilutability. A ranking of 10,000 means you can put a piece of chile in 10,000 times as much slightly sweetened water and still taste hotness. Only chile-heads concern themselves about these trendy numbers. Mexicans who care anything about food hardly ever eat chiles for heat alone (that's like drinking grain alcohol versus matching fine wine with food) and are very picky about what super-hot sauces go with what tacos, seafood cocktails, etc. There are often four or five different bottled brands on a neighborhood fast food counter.

Chiles are used both fresh and in dried forms throughout the country and usually the fresh and dried forms have completely different names. It's important not to mix and match them at whim because their flavors don't necessarily go well with one another—fresh and dried chiles are not generally used together anywhere in Mexico. If certain chiles are impossible to locate in your area, or by mail order, substituting is possible but the flavor will not be exactly traditional. Substitute a fresh green chile for another fresh green chile; tiny hot dried chiles for the like; smoky dried chiles for other smoky dried chiles; yellow for yellow. If you need a medium hot yellow chile, try a hot yellow habanero chile and yellow bell pepper, mixed, for the right heat and color. Just remember: fresh for fresh, dried for dried, heat for heat, color for color. The only canned chiles I recommend are chipotles en adobo, because good quality dried chipotles chiles are still hard to find, and pickled jalapeño chiles, because they are used religiously in Mexico as condiments.

Many people clean chiles with rubber gloves. If standard gloves make you helplessly clumsy, try thin medical gloves, available through medical supply stores (a similar version can be found in hardware and paint-supply stores), or simply wash your hands with soapy water immediately after preparing chiles. When you're cleaning a lot of chiles, wash your hands from time to time during the process. When you are cleaning especially spicy chiles, wash more often. Never touch your face, especially your eyes; they will burn and tear for hours.

To stem, seed, devein, and toast a medium to large-sized fresh chile you must first *toast* the chile to blister its skin for easy removal (tiny chiles always keep their skins, seeds, and veins). You can put the chile on a hot *comal*, or in a heavy skillet, or impale it on a fork and rotate it over an open flame on your stove. For toasting in quantity, loosely arrange fresh chiles on a baking sheet under a hot broiler, and turn them constantly as they blacken. When the skin blackens, put the toasted chile in a plastic bag to let it "sweat" for a few minutes. Remove the chile and easily peel away the loosened, blackened skin. If you have trouble with an especially uncooperative chile, peel it while running tepid water over it, but this diminishes flavor. Stem, seed, and remove any veins.

To stem, seed, devein, and toast a dried chile, first cut off the stem end just below the stem, including the hard clump of seeds. Then vertically cut open the chile from the stem to the point. Shake or scrape out the seeds. Lay the chile flat and remove the lighter colored veins running vertically on the inside—often these veins are spicier than the seeds. If you like spicy foods don't remove the veins—most Mexicans don't. Now the chile is ready to toast—a process that develops flavor and removes any bitterness—though not all dried chiles are toasted. Toast the chile on both sides in a heavy skillet until the color changes, then put it in a bowl of hot water to soften. It is now ready to be ground into a sauce. I prefer not to use the chile soaking water for the sauce because it often contains pesticide residue.

Dried chiles are superb travelers. Nothing makes a better souvenir for the adventurous cook than a selection of dried chiles from Mexico's great markets.

Mexico's best-known chiles are listed here. There are dozens more, not including still others in the United States and in other countries. Due to the wave of new immigration in the U.S. chiles are now freely available where they never saw a grocery shelf five years ago. Bottled hot sauces from chile-loving countries all over the world and fresh refrigerated salsas are everyday items today. (See color photos of fresh and dried chiles).

Fresh Chiles

de Agua. Fiery hot chile about four inches long, found only in the valley of Oaxaca. They are grilled in markets to put atop tortillas with grilled meats, and for *rajas*. Green, orange or red-ripe. Fruity flavor with a tart tomatillo-like tang.

Gordo Huachinango. Large ripe, red jalapeño with thin white veins running vertically. Dried to make the largest and most pricey chipotle chile, the meco chile. Sweet flavor.

Güero. Young Hungarian wax pepper, a.k.a. a banana chile. In Yucatán it is the xcatick or chawa chile. Called largo or carricillo chile when pickled. Waxy texture.

Jalapeño. The most widely used fresh, green (ripens to red) chile in the United States. Ripened and smoked, it becomes a chipotle chile. Solid vegetable flavor.

Habanero. Mexico's hottest. Delicate-looking green, yellow and orange "lanterns" are prized by Yucatecos for their hotter-than-Hell fire. Green are crispest, orange softest. Use a tiny, ½-inch piece the first time you cook with habanero chile—you can always add more. The special fruity flavor compliments fresh salsas made with tropical fruits.

Macho. Tiny long chiles with a macho bang. Green or red. Various regions.

Perón. A.k.a. manzano and rocoto chile. Looks like a cross between a yellow bell pepper and golden habanero. Medium to hot and at its peak of popularity in Michoacán. It has black seeds and the flower is purple. Fruity flavor with a thin flesh.

Poblano. Dark green with meaty, thick flesh. The prerequisite for Stuffed Chiles with Walnut Sauce (pages 67 and 162). Always cooked, never raw (as in fresh salsas). Dried, it's an ancho chile. (Only in California are the fresh poblano chile and the dried ancho chile both called the pasilla chile.)

Serrano. Next to the jalapeño, Mexico's most popular fresh chile; in fact, the two are often interchangeable. A thickly fleshed serrano is slightly hotter than the larger jalapeño. Dried, a serrano becomes a very hot serrano seco chile, a.k.a. morita chile in some regions.

Dried Chiles

Ancho. The most popular dried chile in Mexico and the United States. It's a dried poblano chile, and the smoky-sweet flavor accents numerous dishes. Mild spice.

Cascabel. Richly flavored, brown, round chile from central Mexico, especially Michoacán. It's also called bola chile, because of its ball shape. Flavor is nutty, slightly smoky, and acidic.

Chilcosle. Found only in Oaxaca's markets and necessary for classic yellow *mole* and some red *moles*. Also called amarillo chile. Similar to guajillo chile, but smaller and the color is much lighter. Thin fleshed with citrus flavor overtones.

Chilhuacle. Originally grown for the *moles* of Puebla, but it's not found there today. Black, red, and amber are sold in Oaxaca's markets for black, red, or amarillo *mole*. Hard to come by outside of Oaxaca. Intense flavor of dried fruits.

Chipotle. Ripened and smoked jalapeño. Fiery hot with lasting smoky flavor. Meco, the largest, is smoked in a special humid environment and has a brown, suedelike surface. Mora is cordovan-colored with a fruit-leather texture. This midsize jalapeño is lightly smoked and often used for canned chipotles en adobo (Clemente Jacques brand has the most chiles and least tomato). Morita is the last picking from the plants and always smallest, with the same characteristics as mora.

Criollo. The word translates to wild or native. It's the term for a local chile grown in any small region and generally not seen elsewhere.

de Árbol. Red, tiny (about 2 inches long), and pointed—with a searing heat. Used in bottled salsas. It's the cayenne powder chile and dried, it's de árbol seco. Thin fleshed.

Guajillo. Deep cordovan color with a thin skin. Mild heat and very popular throughout Mexico. Fresh, it's a rare pulla chile. Fruity, citrusy flavors. Substitute dried California or New Mexico chiles, in the U.S. Southwest.

Holy Trinity. You'll hear this term often when talking about black *mole*. Three dried chiles necessary for the classic sauce are: true pasilla chile (a.k.a. negro chile); mulato chile; and ancho chile (if you can't get the hard-to-find chilhuacle negro chile of Oaxaca).

Mulato. A type of dried poblano chile, similar to the ancho chile but with more smoke and anise flavor, and used to make *mole poblano*. Very dark black.

Pasilla. A.k.a. negro chile. It's raisin-black, thin, and long (about six inches by one inch), and used in *mole negro*. It is a dried chilaca chile.

Pasilla de Oaxaca. Sold by one hundred pieces (not by weight like other chiles) in various sizes, and only in Oaxaca markets. It's expensive, cordovan red, fruit leather-textured, and smoky-flavored (from smoking over beds of ferns). Not quite so hot or smoky as a chipotle chile. A.k.a. mije chile in Oaxaca.

Piquín. Very hot, small, oval, or round chiles. Thin flesh which crumbles easily. Often ground and sprinkled on grilled or boiled corn sold by street vendors. Grown primarily in northern Mexico around Monterrey, but popular throughout the country.

Chile Powder. Chile powder blends and single variety powders are available. Be sure the product is pure chile powder and not a blend of chile, salt, sugar, pepper, and paprika.

✷ CHILE SUBSTITUTIONS ✷

All fourteen of the chiles listed below are fairly common, and you should be able to find one or the other of an equivalent pair in your local supermarket or specialty store. Using a listed equivalent will alter the flavor of your dish somewhat, just as if you substituted one herb for another in a dish. For the esoteric chiles called for in some of the recipes, there are no substitutes, unfortunately. These chiles are what give the dish its unique taste and texture. If you cannot find a particular chile locally, it can almost always be obtained by mail order, through one of the stores or companies listed in the back of this book (see page 350).

Fresh Chile	Substitute
Jalapeño	Serrano
Poblano	California (Anaheim)
Güero	Yellow Hungarian, wax, or banana

Dried Chile	Substitute
Ancho	Mulato
Chipotle	Canned chipotle en adobo
de Arbol	Pequín, or any tiny, red hot chiles
Guajillo	New Mexican

CORN TORTILLAS (TORTILLAS DE MAÍZ)

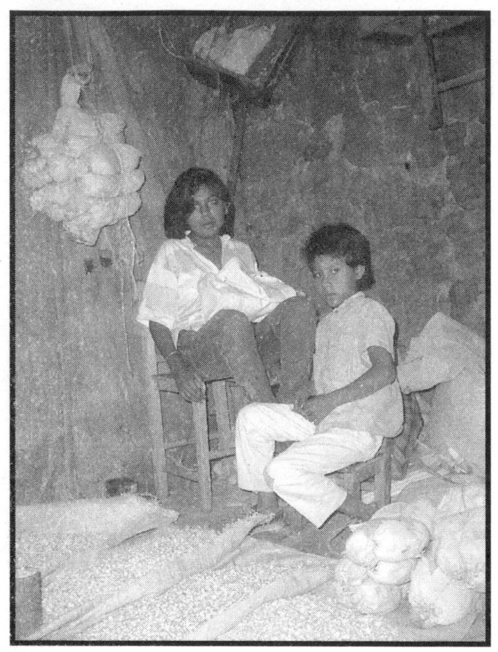
Dried corn vendors in Cuernavaca's market.

TORTILLAS ARE THE BREAD OF MEXICO. Most cities in the U.S. have Mexican populations and if you look around (five minutes with the yellow pages is all it takes), you'll probably find a tortillería, where a pound of fresh *masa* (corn dough) for twelve tortillas can be bought. You need to purchase *masa* the day you are using it, whether for tortillas, tamales, or *antojitos*, because it keeps fresh for less than six hours, unrefrigerated, before souring (refrigerated, *masa* keeps for less than two days). If this is impossible, make your own with *masa harina,* a dried, ground corn flour that gives you very acceptable, delicate tortillas and excellent *masa* for banana-leaf-wrapped tamales, where finely-textured *masa* is desired over a coarse, stone-ground-style. Don't even think about using cornmeal, it just doesn't work. Cornmeal, made by cutting corn kernels, is a totally different product from *masa,* made by grinding lime-slaked kernels. Cornmeal will make your tortillas gritty and impossible to fold or roll.

A few examples of the country's finest tortillas: *Blanditas* are Mexico's thinnest, whitest (besides northern flour tortillas), and most delicate. Handmade, they're sold by women from cloth-lined baskets in Oaxaca's markets, especially around fondas, where fonda owners buy them as needed for their customers. *Clayudas* are slightly coarser, a bit leathery, yellower, and much larger than *blanditas.* They're Oaxaca's other famous tortilla and also handmade and individually baked on special, slightly curved, clay *comales.* Sold from tall baskets, *clayudas* are the classic "plates" to pile with grill-your-own meat, chiles, and onions in Tlacolula's smoky, cavernous Sunday market building. Never fried in oil, *clayuda* chips are oven- or *comal*-roasted. *Totopos* are from Tehuantepec, on the Pacific. (Actually, the tortillas are made in nearby pueblo of San Blas, even though larger Tehuantepec generally gets all the credit.) They're thick, round, and crisply made with ground black beans in coarse *masa,* then cooked in ovens very similar to Indian tandoori ovens. *Totopos* are covered with small holes. Similar *tortillas de corrosos*, from Juquila, a tiny village east of Oaxaca City, are sweetened with *panela* and coconut. They travel well but toast *totopos* to ensure crispness. *Ordas,* Villahermosa's delicious, large, thick, handmade specimens are sold by women from cloth-lined baskets along with smaller, sweeter, tortillas *toda poste*. Blue corn tortillas are almost always handmade, and found in markets from Toluca to Oaxaca. They range in thickness from delicate to one-quarter-inch thick. Flour tortillas are eaten only in northern Mexico, Southwestern U.S. and with Tex-Mex dishes. Never serve flour tortillas with southern Mexican meals.

There is nothing quite as good smelling or tasting as hot, handmade corn tortillas—you'll be a believer after your first whiff.

> *Chemists at the U.S. Department of Agriculture say the aroma of a tortilla is mostly due to 2-amino-acetophenone, a compound which develops when corn is soaked in lime water, the traditional treatment for producing corn* masa. *Food chemists have identified more than forty flavor compounds in tortillas, but 2-amino-acetophenone was the hands-down winner as most tortilla-like, as judged by a panel of government-appointed flavor smellers.*
>
> —Bruce Henstell, *Los Angeles Times*, January 1995.

Carmelita Acosta de García's ▲▼▲

Tortillas de Maíz *Corn Tortillas*

WHEN MY FRIEND, CARMELITA ACOSTA DE GARCÍA, WAS A GIRL living on the outskirts of Morelia, in Michoacán, she made tortillas by hand with her grandmother. Dried hominy was soaked with *cal* (limestone, or calcium hydroxide) to make the skins come off the kernels easily. The skins were removed by rubbing the kernels back and forth in their hands under running water (corn is called *nixtamal* at this point). Then they hand-ground the kernels with a *metate* (lava grinding stone) and a *mano* (hand-held stone resembling a small rolling pin) before kneading it into *masa* (corn dough). Rather than using a press, Carmelita and her grandmother patted each tortilla out by hand. They repeated this process every day. Many rural cooks still make tortillas this ancient way, but like most people in urban areas, Carmelita now buys fresh *masa* at a local tortillería, then presses and cooks hers at home. If her lunch is ready and no time allows for handmade, she sends her son to get in line at the corner tortillería for a half kilo of fresh tortillas—hot and just off the clanking, squealing machine. She says an even better, although more expensive, alternative is to buy handmade tortillas (not with a press, but by the old pat-pat method) from women who sell them from cloth-lined baskets at markets.

Carmelita's tortillas are coarser than Oaxaca's *blanditas* but are still delicate. She uses a medium *masa,* which is a bit coarser than *masa harina*. Tortillas made with *masa harina* come closest to *blandita's* fine texture.

Yield: 12 tortillas, each recipe (Continued)

To make tortillas, prepare *masa* (corn dough) either the traditional or contemporary way:

Traditional method

1 pound dried hominy, field or flint corn
2 Tablespoons powdered, slaked lime (purchase 'cal' at a tortillería, or calcium hydroxide powder at a building supply store)

1. Rinse the hominy in a colander under running water to remove the chaff.

2. In a large nonreactive pot (one that won't react with acidic ingredients) made of stainless steel, enameled cast iron, lined copper, or with a nonstick surface (avoid cast iron and aluminum), bring 2 quarts water to a boil. Sprinkle the slaked lime into the boiling water and dissolve. Add the hominy (remove any floating kernels), reduce the heat, and simmer for 1 minute, then soak the kernels 8 hours or overnight, unrefrigerated.

3. Wash the kernels under running water while rubbing them against one another in your hands, washing away the hulls. Hand-grind the soaked corn (now called *nixtamal*) with *metate* and *mano,* or use a hand-powered mill set at the finest grind. (Many health food stores carry the mills for people who stone-grind their own grains.) Knead about ½ cup water into the dough to ensure smoothness. *Masa* is now ready to be made into tortillas.

Contemporary methods

2 cups "masa harina"
½ teaspoon salt
¼ cup white flour
1⅓ cups warm water

Either buy 1 pound *masa* at a tortillería, or make the *masa* using *masa harina.* Mix the *masa harina*, salt, flour, and water in a bowl, then knead together until the mixture forms a ball and is no longer sticky, about 3 minutes. Cover the bowl with a towel and let the corn dough rest for 5 minutes while you heat a *comal* or heavy skillet to very hot.

To form tortillas

tortilla press

2 Baggies, larger than the press

1. Put a plastic Baggie on the bottom of your tortilla press. The extra thickness of the bag works better than a flimsy sheet of plastic wrap.

2. Pull off a walnut-sized piece of *masa,* roll it into a ball, and center it on the Baggie. Cover the *masa* with another Baggie. Press down with your hand to flatten the *masa* a bit. Lower the top of the press and push down on the handle—less hard for thicker, smaller tortillas, or harder for larger, thinner tortillas.

3. Open the press. The tortilla will have a Baggie on the top and one on the bottom. Peel away the top plastic, then flip the tortilla over into your other hand and carefully peel that plastic away. If there are cracks along the edges, the dough is too dry and a little more water must be kneaded in.

4. Slowly lay the tortilla in the ungreased *comal* or skillet over high heat. The tortilla should make a small sizzle sound. When the edges begin to dry (about 30 seconds) turn the tortilla over and continue to cook as it begins to puff. Cook another minute more, depending upon its size and thickness. The second side should color slightly. Flip it back over to the first side—if it puffs, it was cooked perfectly. Remove the hot tortilla to a napkin-lined basket to keep warm and continue with the others. Tortillas hot off the stove, no matter how badly misshapen, taste fabulous. When serving, don't take the top tortilla, but dig down and take one from the center where they are the warmest and moistest, as all Mexicans do.

Note: Tortillas keep up to one week, refrigerated and tightly wrapped, but never taste as heavenly as freshly made. Reheat in a skillet or directly on a gas burner. You can also wrap a dozen or so in foil and bake at 375°F for about 12 minutes, or wrap a dozen in plastic, cut a small air vent, and microwave for 25 seconds on each side, turning once. With both ovens, be sure the tortillas in the middle of the pile are hot.

COOKED SALSAS (SAUCES)

REMEMBER THE FIRST TIME YOU STIR-FRIED WITH A WOK? It seemed such a foreign yet intriguing process. Now you stir-fry with your eyes closed; in fact, stir-frying is how you make those famous ten-minute dinners. Mexican cooked salsa-making is another one of those exotic cooking techniques—and unique to Mexico—in no time the process will become as natural to you as stir-frying. Its three-step process has been used for centuries to achieve the complicated, intense, and smoky-flavored sauces so strongly associated with southern Mexican dishes. First your ingredients are "toasted" to release flavors, then they're "ground" or "blended" to a liquid, finally the liquid is "fried" with hot fat before being simmered into a cooked sauce.

1. Toasting For toasting, Mexicans use a cooking disk called a *comal* which is made from steel, cast iron, or unglazed clay (the latter extremely fragile). *Comales* are heated to very hot without fat to toast chiles, onions, garlic, tomatoes, *etc.*, until their outside skins are charred. The skins are peeled and, even without their blackened skins, vegetables have a smoky, grilled flavor to enrich salsas. Tomatoes and fresh chiles are put in a plastic bag for a few minutes after toasting to "sweat" and to loosen their skins for easy peeling. Nuts and seeds are toasted until they turn light brown. Spices and herbs are toasted until they release their aromas—time varies from just seconds to one minute. Most Mexican kitchens have a black, misshapen *comal* on the stove, in a permanent position, used for the sole purpose of toasting ingredients. Toasting ruins a good pan by eventually blackening it; therefore, a heavy cast-iron skillet is the best substitute for a *comal,* but you will probably burn the outside of your hands on its high sides.

2. Grinding/Blending For centuries, Mexican cooks used *metates* and *molcajetes* (lava rock mortars) with hand-held pestles for grinding corn, nuts, seeds, and chiles into pastes that eventually were thinned and became sauces. Today, blenders are often the one electrical appliance in a poor Mexican home. At open-air weekly markets, you can't miss the blender repair section, where hundreds of blender parts, for every make and model, are on display. Purists mourn the passing of subtle, but distinct, textural qualities of certain sauces caused by newfangled blenders, but the arduous task of hand grinding is no everyday joy. Food processors don't work as well—their blades don't chop as fast as a blender's so they can't purée such hard items as nuts with toasted chiles, and processors tend to overprocess to too fine a purée. This may be fine in the U.S. where smooth sauces are preferred or when a smooth sauce is called for, but most salsas should not be smooth; perfect texture is very important in all Mexican salsas. The subtle difference is whether a seed, grain, spice, or chile is crushed between coarse rock, with the rocks grinding the juices and oils from the pulp—or sharp, tiny knives precisely cutting (chopping, mincing) through each element. Think of the textural difference between rolled (squashed) oats and steel-cut oats, or ground (squashed) corn kernels (for *masa*) versus cut cornmeal.

To achieve impeccable texture today many serious cooks take their pre-weighed ingredients to local mills for stone grinding even if they have blenders at home. Mexico's majestic *mole*, *pipián*, and *recado* pastes are excellent reasons to attain textural perfection. But, like everything else, one woman's gritty sauce is another's masterpiece.

3. Frying Sauce "frying" is unique to Mexico's cooked salsas, especially when numerous ingredients are combined, as with *moles*. To fry, heat fat to very hot in a deep pot, then add liquid from a blender (it splatters!), stir a few moments, then reduce the heat and simmer the sauce uncovered. A deep pot is mandatory even if there are only a few cups of salsa; thick sauces bubble and polka-dot your stove with terracotta chile colors.

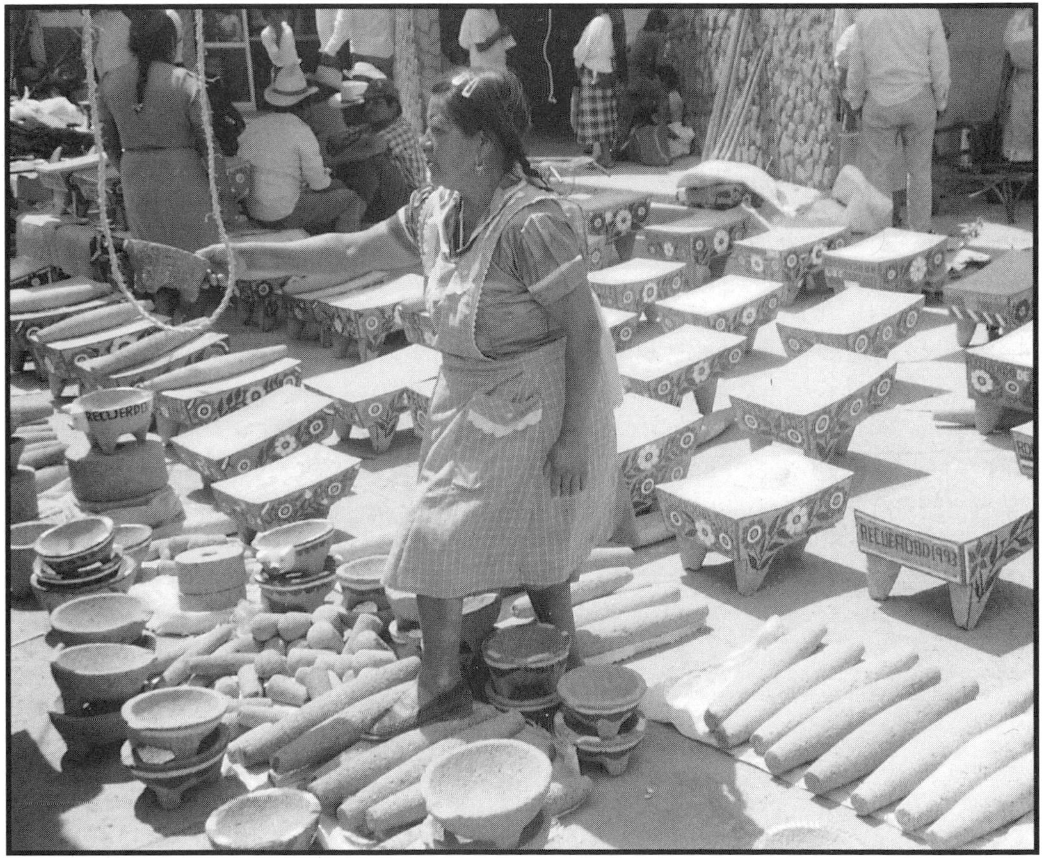

"Metates" and "molcajetes" for hand grinding are for sale in Tlacolula's Mercado Martín González.

RENDERING LARD

DON'T HAVE A FIT. Bruce Henstell wrote in the *Los Angeles Times*, April 28, 1994, "According to Dr. Jacob Exler of the USDA's Agricultural Research Service Human Nutritional Information Service, butter has about fifty percent saturated fat while lard has only thirty-nine percent. Butter is twice as high in cholesterol." Nobody is saying go out and spread lard all over your food, but certain foods cooked in small quantities of *freshly* rendered lard are tastier and healthier than when cooked in butter. And using lard is the only way to achieve a tamale's traditional taste and texture.

White, flavorless opaque lard sold in plastic buckets is nothing like freshly rendered pork fat. Mexican markets sell pigs butchered daily, and still-warm liquid lard is a staple. It's ladled from tubs into plastic bags. You can easily duplicate this fresh taste at home. When cool, the color will be similar to that sold in Mexican markets: a pale, brown-gray tint rather than preserved-snow-white as seen in tubs of hydrogenated blocks in the U.S.

While we're on the subject, now's a good time to discuss tamales and the "lard problem." Good-quality fresh lard is an integral part of traditional tamale excellence. The texture and flavor it imparts when blended into *masa* cannot be matched with butter, chicken fat, vegetable shortening or oil. But, Mexicans, too, understand health problems caused by too much dietary fat. One simple answer is to eat fewer tamales less often (most Mexicans eat them only for special occasions). Another answer is to prepare tamales with *masa harina* (per package directions), delete all fat, add baking soda, and have nonfluffy, *masa.* In fact, before the Spaniards arrived with pigs, natives moistened tamales with water or broth. The trick in preparing nonfat tamales is to be sure your *masa* is extra moist. This process works exceptionally well with banana leaves, which tend to hold moisture better than fresh corn leaves or dried corn husks.
Yield: ¾ cup liquid

Manteca *Freshly Rendered Lard*

1 pound pork fat, cold, and cut into half-inch cubes

1. In a wide skillet, sauté the pork fat at a low simmer until the fat is rendered and the cubes are crisp *chicharrones* (fried pork fat, or rind), about 45 minutes.
2. Drain the *chicharrones* on paper towels, salt lightly, and enjoy as a snack (omit this step if desired).
3. Strain the fat into a glass jar, or crockery container with a lid, or cool and use immediately. Refrigerate.

CHICKEN BROTH (CALDO [O SOPA] DE POLLO)

WHEREVER YOU GO, THERE YOU, AND CHICKEN SOUP, ARE. It's ubiquitous—found everywhere in Mexico. Mexicans in every village throughout the country insist on great chicken soup—it must run in their veins. Long-simmering market fonda stock pots are prime sources for simple chicken broth. Elaborate chicken broth-based soups such as Tortilla Soup (page 64) are usually homemade or restaurant fare. Chicken broth (called *caldo* or *sopa* in different regions) is one dish you can always count on to calm a queasy stomach. When you've had one too many meals ablaze with fiery chiles, look to fondas for a bowl of soup served with French rolls or tortillas. Locals often slurp down a "morning-after" broth as a hangover cure (similar in thought to northern Mexico's tripe soup, *menudo*).

Making Mexican chicken broth is not so time-consuming as French stock because it's not so richly reduced. You don't want to have the chicken completely fall apart in the liquid. Fonda cooks keep the cooked chickens whole, and cut off pieces as orders come in—to cover with broth for chicken soup, to shred and stuff enchiladas, or to smother chicken quarters with *mole.*

Yield: 3 quarts

Caldo de Pollo *Chicken Broth*

- 1 whole or cut-up chicken, about 5 pounds, innards removed
- 1 white onion, quartered
- 4 garlic cloves
- 10 carrots, peeled and whole
- 6 sprigs fresh cilantro (plus additional sprigs for garnish)
- 2 bay leaves
- 1 teaspoon salt
- ½ teaspoon freshly ground pepper

1. Put the chicken in a large pot with 4 quarts of water to just cover the chicken and bring it to a boil, then reduce the heat to a simmer.

2. Skim off any foam that rises to the top and add the onion, garlic, carrots, cilantro (stems tied), bay leaves, salt, and black pepper. Set cover slightly askew and continue simmering the stock for 1 hour, or until the chicken is cooked. Carefully remove the chicken and carrots to a large plate or bowl.

3. Strain the broth through a sieve. Most Mexican cooks don't skim fat off the chicken broth surface. You may want to go around the surface with a large spoon, removing as much as you can, or refrigerate the broth so that the fat will rise to the top and congeal for easy removal before reheating.

Jalisco

▼▼▼▼▼▼▼▼▼▼

Guadalajara
Lake Chapala
Pacific Coast Towns

JALISCO GROWS SOME OF THE WORLD'S FINEST mangoes. Bananas, pineapples, papayas, and coconuts are huge crops that grow in jungle clearings just south of the Tropic of Cancer and along the Pacific Coast. Mexico's best tequila comes from the town of the same name situated in picturesque hill country northwest of Guadalajara. The state leads Mexico in growing corn for torillas and for cattle. And Jaliscans love their meat dishes—some of the most popular include Carne Asada *(Marinated and Grilled Beef Steak) (page 34) and* Birria *(Kid, Lamb, or Beef with Dried Chile Broth) (pages 43 and 45).* Pozole Verde *(Hominy and Meat Soup with Green Herbs) (page 54) reaches its zenith in the states of Jalisco and Guerrero.*

Left: A Guadalajara patio garden.

◆ Guadalajara ◆

Señor Guadalupe Calvario Medina offers "pulque" at Lake Chapala.

FOUNDED IN 1542 BY SPANISH CONQUISTADORES, Guadalajara, in the state of Jalisco, high up (5,200 feet, 1,584 meters) in central-western Mexico, boasts colonial architecture, mariachis, museums, and good restaurants. Decades of retired North Americans have discovered Guadalajara's attributes, namely gorgeous, mountain-surrounded golf courses, almost perfect year-round weather, and easy-living condos within walking distance of the first tee.

As a tourist, especially without a car, you'll be pretty much confined to the city center for hotels and convenient taxi or bus transportation. No problem: Most of Guadalajara's sights are right there, almost surrounding Mercado Libertad, the city's fabulous covered food market. The market is adjacent to Plaza Tapatía, now a seven-block pedestrian walkway and people-watching mecca filled with fountains, food carts, street performers, restaurants, and assorted entertainment options for locals and travelers alike. Plaza Tapatía's focal point is Guadalajara's mighty twin-towered cathedral surrounded by four plazas. Cross Plaza de la Liberación to the historic landmark theater, Teatro Degollado, and continue walking east toward the far end and the Cabañas Cultural Institute with its world class José Clemente Orozco murals. Take the steps off to the right near Calzada Independencia Sur where you'll see the market just ahead.

* MARKET *

Mercado Libertad The huge market is located at Calzada Independencia Sur, Av. Javier Mina, and Calle Cabañas at the east end and just south of Plaza Tapatía. Hours are dawn to about 7 P.M., but midmorning until 3 P.M. is best. You can park in the market lot. Approach from the south on Independencia and turn right into the lot immediately after going under the overpass for Plaza Tapatía. This is a good place to park when visiting the Instituto Cultural Cabañas (Orozco's famous murals are on display) and the Plaza de Mariachis (one block south).

Touted as the largest enclosed market in Latin America, Guadalajara's Mercado Libertad is, certainly, large—four city blocks. The market has been remodeled in recent years and there's yet a new section being added. The upper, third floor is filled with endless hardware, clothing, leather saddles, *huaraches*, knickknacks, and household goods galore. Pre-Columbian pottery copies, faux silver, painted gourds, good- and not-so-good-quality guitars, and surrealistic booths of witch necessities are scattered about. Fresh produce, flowers, meats, and fish occupy the ground floor, along with some good cookware shops. Dried chiles to look for include guajillo, catarino (similar to guajillo), cascabel, and serrano seco. Aisles burst at their seams with chayote squash from nearby Lake Chapala. As in all markets (except new *supermercados*) in Mexico, there are no price tags on anything—bargaining is a must. When you're parched from all the haggling, walk over to the sugarcane juice bar (outside on the ground level), and throw back a glass of pure, healthful, surprisingly not-too-sweet nectar.

It's certainly not necessary to run around the city shopping to prepare a feast; everything you need is right here, at Mercado Libertad, and mostly on the ground floor. You're assaulted with sights and smells: *carnitas* and *chicharrón* counters; fresh and dried seafood; melon piles reeking of perfume overdose; and breads hot from nearby ovens. For take-out food extraordinaire, fill your containers from bubbling pots at any of the second-floor fondas.

Fondas. Hundreds of fondas fill the immense and well-lit, arenalike second floor of Mercado Libertad. My favorite way to eat here is to have a progressive lunch of sorts. Try to get food-loving friends to go along to share the very best regional specialties; otherwise, endless choices will be too frustrating. First roam around and see what's being offered, which colorful, tiled counters are crowded (a good sign), and remember where you saw that delicious-looking Guadalajaran white (versus red or green) *pozole*! Each fonda is vying for your attention, so if an enticing aroma doesn't catch your attention, an owner shouting out his specialty will certainly grab an ear. As in every Mexican market you will constantly hear, "*¿Qué va a llevar*?" (What'll you take?)

Start out with a famous Guadalajara-style shrimp cocktail (page 28) at Ricardo and Teresa López's fonda, **Pescadería**

Ricardo No. 611, then move on to **Fonda El Tapatía III** for *sopes* (small corn dough tarts, called *picaditas* here, with beans or cheese and fresh garnishes) washed down with excellent local lager, Modeno, or Negro Modeno, a dark beer. Fried whole fish, shrimp cooked any way you want, and mixed shellfish soups are only a few of the many seafood choices. Don't forget that Guadalajara is very close to the shrimping lagoons of the Pacific Coast, and truckloads of shrimp arrive daily.

Kid or Lamb Soup with Chile Seasoning (page 43) is another regional dish; here the meat soup is made with kid, in the traditional style of central-western Mexico. You'll spot *Birria* signage—goat skulls (with horns) proudly arranged on counters.

Northern-style *Carne Asada* (page 34), Jalisco's favorite meal (a thin beefsteak, marinated and grilled), is everywhere, and is typically served with Chiles Rellenos (page 77), or Quesadillas (page 114), and *Frijoles Charros* (page 31), made from local, pale terracotta-colored beans.

Butchers. On the ground floor, you'll first see the gigantic piles of pork skin cracklings keeping warm under the glow of orange heat lamps, then rows of pork, beef, and innard specialists. Plenty of thin steaks for *carne asada* fill more than one counter. Poultry butchers are on the next aisle over.

Seafood. Seafood stalls are on the ground floor near the meat and cheese counters. Look for freshness and buy only what's on ice, and early in the day. Head upstairs for prepared seafood soups to go.

Tamales. The best are sold by a vendor, mornings only, on the ground floor near the fresh sugarcane juice stall. Ask around and someone will know his location. Buy a bunch—they refrigerate well for two or three days. These northern-style tamales are small, rough corn *masa*-filled husks with a bit of chile-spiced shredded pork or chicken. The vendor sometimes has sweet, meatless tamales made with raisins or other dried fruit, or *rajas* made with lightly cooked chile strips.

Cheese. *Queso asadero* is the northwest's version of Oaxacan *quesillo*. Compare it to mozzarella or string cheese. Being so far north, Guadalajara is big on even-farther-north's Chihuahua, a mild cheddar cheese from the city of the same name. It's sold from huge wheels in all the dairy stalls. *Queso añejo* (aged cheese), a dry, salty, grating cheese from Michoacán, is a favorite of Guadalajarans as well as Mexicans all over the country. It's Mexico's Parmesan. You'll also find *Crema* (page 80) here, a close relative to France's crème fraîche. Look for various colors from white to buttercup yellow; strengths from sweetly mild to richly pungent.

Tortillas. Since Guadalajara is on the fringe of northern Mexico, flour tortillas are almost as popular here as corn tortillas. You'll find commercial tortillerías as well as women selling handmade tortillas from cloth-lined baskets on the ground floor.

Chiles. Fine Jalisco specimens of the state's most popular chiles—dried guajillos, de árboles, and fresh serranos—are arranged in huge piles for your picking. Guajillos and de árboles make perfect souvenirs, as they are dry, and permitted to cross the border (see page 349). Serranos are popular throughout the U.S.

Jícama. Jícama is a tan tuber, about six inches in diameter, with a crunchy, slightly sweet, water chestnut-like texture. At the market jícama is always sold with its leaves intact to show freshness (I've never seen jícama leaves anywhere in the U.S.). Guadalajarans know jícama's sweetness diminishes as it grows old.

Pottery and Textiles. You'll find these at super prices on the ground and third floors of the market, along with baskets, woven placemats, and napkins. Don't forget to bargain ferociously. Also, the suburbs of **Tlaquepaque** and **Tonalá**, southeast of Guadalajara's center, are renowned for quality ceramics, and the better shops will ship mugs, platters, and pitchers to restaurant-sized orders.

Desserts. Second-floor fonda's everyday-style desserts to go: *chongos*, a very sweet and immensely popular cheesy-flavored, curdled milk, caramel, and cinnamon mixture; and *jericalla*, simple baked custard in individual-sized plastic custard cups, make carry-out a cinch.

Flowers. Flowers are in abundance on the ground floor and the prices are always right. Mornings are best because the selection is greatest. Catch the scent of tuberoses the moment you enter the court-yard area from any direction.

Wine. *Atotonilco el Alto*, from the high-lands of Jalisco, is an interesting matchup to local specialties. Rojas Fábrica produces a golden orange wine, vino de Naranja, for afternoon or after-dinner sipping.

✷ PLACES TO GO AND THINGS TO EAT ✷

Plaza de los Mariachis. In a wide alley just off Calzada Independencia Sur and just south of Mercado Libertad, is the home of Guadalajara's gift to the world of music: mariachis. Plaza de los Mariachis gets going late at night with various groups playing all at once and trying to outdo one another with louder and brasssier brass (you pay by the song and price depends on the size of the group). It's an especially fun spot on warm, starry evenings. Guadalajarans meet and drink here; it's certainly not a tourist-only hangout. Similar cafés line the pedestrian street but food is secondary—go only for drinks and snacks. Try Guadalajara's Modeno beer. Claro is a new and cheaper version of Modeno and is sold in trendy, tall, clear bottles; it's the local competition for Monterrey's popular Corona.

Charreada. Campo Charro Jalisco, next to Agua Azul Park at Dr. R. Michel 577. Every Sunday at noon. A true Guadalajara tradition, *charros* are cowboys, but more horsemen than steer-roping wranglers. Their ropework is as fascinating as their silver studded costumes, which include broad-brimmed sombreros. But it's also the action in the stands that makes the experience synergistic. Swooning, screaming young female fans sit down close to get the full impact of each rider careening toward them and screeching to a dust-billowing halt at the last possible moment. Farther up in the bleachers a full mariachi band plays its heart out with various singers having a go at seat-rocking standards. Food is cold beer, chips, and tacos. Just outside the arena vendors sell lassos, sombreros, and spurs.

Carnitas. On the outskirts of town, Sunday means **Carnitas Urapán**, on highway 15 a few miles south of the Guadalajara airport on the right-hand side just past an overpass. It's packed with families munching away on every cut of *carnitas* imaginable—both innards and outards. Huge orders of the fried pork are served picnic-style on folding chairs and tables. Beans, cactus leaf salad, and fresh limes are ready to pile on hot corn tortillas with outrageously fattening, succulent pork. You positively have to try a *gordita chicharrón*, a thick, coarse *masa* tortilla that looks more like an English muffin stuffed with the crunchiest, crispest pork skin and meat bits, then toasted on a hot griddle. Be sure to wash it down with plenty of beer. All this to a live, one-man electronic band.

Birria and Barbacoa. The countryside in the hills around Guadalajara comes to life with families crowding *birrerías* and *barbacoa* tables that set up shop under shade trees every Sunday. Some places are relatively permanent; others are one-day stands. In this part of Mexico, *Birria* (page 43) and *Barbacoa* (page 137) usually mean young goat even though you'll sometimes see lamb. *Birria's* kid is submerged in a broth flavored with guajillo and de árbol chiles, the main chiles and flavors of Jalisco. In your bowl of rich broth you'll find chunks of meat falling apart with the slightest touch from your spoon, plus succulent meat clinging to tiny ribs for gnawing and sucking, and blissful bits from meat that is roasted above the broth. Jalisco's *barbacoa* cooks underground, Hawaiian luau-style, with maguey leaves used for flavor and to retain moisture. Tortillas, salsas, sodas, and beer are accompaniments and all are served at shared picnic tables covered with flower-patterned oilcloth.

TLAQUEPAQUE

Old adobe architecture, colonial antiques, famous hand-thrown pottery (along with that of nearby **Tonalá**), bubble glass manufacturers (such as **La Rosa de Cristal** on Independencia), boutiques for handwoven placemats, tablecloths, and napkins, and good restaurants make Tlaquepaque a favorite section of Guadalajara. Tree-lined streets blocked off to cars make strolling a pleasure. Just off the *zócalo* (main plaza), **El Parián** is an entire block of *portales* filled both inside and out with cafés and mariachis. You'll enjoy having a beer at one courtyard café (buy a bag of hot, handmade potato chips splashed with bottled hot sauce from a passing vendor) then moving streetside for some Guacamole (page 142) and another view before choosing yet a third location for dinner. El Parián is the place to be on Saturday night when the mariachis are at their weekly frenzied peak.

Why there aren't hotels in this lovely section of town is a mystery; you'll have to stay in the city center and take a taxi or bus. Determined to find a place in Tlaquepaque, Morris and I happened to drive right past a clean, large motel just blocks from the center. Stop! Screech! Back-up! A sweet woman showed me a spotless, round-bedded room with dark velvet draperies and a mirrored ceiling. The room rented by the hour. In other cities, Morris and I tried elsewhere as soon as we saw motels with curtains strung across parking spots for discreetness (and to think I thought they were shower curtains for car washes). Live and learn.

TEQUILA

Thirty miles west of Guadalajara is some of the most spectacular countryside in Mexico, and a town with a famous name: Tequila. Spiky blue-green agave plants (*Agave tequilana* Weber blue variety) line up like perfect soldiers in waves across rolling hills fronting majestic volcanic mountains. Juice from the plants is fermented and distilled twice before bottling, or aging in oak casks. Tequila is legally produced in only five states: Jalisco, and areas of Michoacán, Tamaulipas, Guanajuato, and Nayarit, with Jalisco's considered best, and the town of Tequila's considered the cream of the crop. Many of Tequila's world-class distilleries are open to the public for tastings, but hours are short and erratic so it's easiest to go with a group from almost any large hotel, or take a day tour out of San Francisco Park.

Below: Agave plants front "Volcán de Tequila" volcano.

Ricardo and Teresa López's

Cóctel de Camarones

Shrimp Cocktail with Shrimp Broth, Tomato Sauce, and Avocado

PESCADERÍA RICARDO #611, AT MERCADO LIBERTAD, IS AN IMMACULATELY CLEAN FONDA specializing in seafood cocktails served in old-fashioned, soda-fountain sundae glasses, the kind that are wide on top and come to a point about eight inches below, and hold twelve ounces. The glass needs to be substantial because Guadalajara-style cocktails contain sweet, liquidy sauce, unlike our shrimp cocktail with its thick blob of horseradish-flavored ketchup. The López's delicious specimens are served with a slightly warm sauce poured over iced shrimp, along with tortilla chips and saltine crackers. The fonda's seafood is not spicy. For that extra pizzazz, de Árbol Chile Hot Sauce (page 29) is always on the counter with various brands of commercial liquid devils, or Tabasco sauce may be substituted.
Yield: 8 servings

For the shrimp broth

- 1 small white onion, quartered
- 1 medium tomato, quartered
- 1 teaspoon salt
- 2½ pounds medium shrimp

1. Bring 4 quarts water to a boil. Add the onion, tomato, and salt. Cook 10 minutes.

2. Add the shrimp and cook until they turn pink, about 5 minutes. Remove them from the cooking broth and cool. Retain the broth for the sauce.

3. When the shrimp are cool enough to handle, peel and devein, then refrigerate.

For the sweet tomato sauce

- 1 cup ketchup
- 1 rounded Tablespoon "panela" or dark brown sugar
- ½ to ¾ cup Fanta or other orange soda ("Our secret ingredient," claims Teresa, "added to thin the liquid with effervecence!"—and a touch of flavor)

1. Combine ketchup and sugar in a 2-quart, nonreactive (nonaluminum) pot and bring to a simmer.

2. Add the Fanta. Stir and simmer 10 minutes.

Ricardo and Teresa López.

For the garnish

- 1 cup cilantro leaves, chopped
- 2 medium tomatoes, chopped
- 2 avocados, peeled and coarsely chopped
- 1 white onion, minced
- 8 small limes

1. In each of 8 large glasses add: 2 tablespoons cilantro, 3 tablespoons chopped tomatoes, 3 tablespoons avocado, 1 teaspoon onion, the juice of 1 small lime, about 12 cold shrimp, and ¼ cup tomato sauce.

2. Add ½ cup slighty warm shrimp broth and stir.

Teresa López's

Salsa Picante de Chile de Árbol *de Árbol Chile Hot Sauce*

MOST DISHES IN THE MARKET ARE REALLY NOT SPICY. It's the salsas and chiles that you add after the dish is served that ignite it. De árbol chile hot sauce, always on fonda counters in liter-sized bottles throughout Mexico, is the local version of Tabasco sauce. The López's Shrimp Cocktails (page 28) are jazzed up with impressive shots of this firewater. Other fondas in Mercado Libertad serving *Birria* (page 43) and *Pozole* (page 54) keep bottles of de árbol chile hot sauce within easy reach of every diner. The sauce lasts almost indefinitely.
Yield: about 2 cups

- ½ teaspoon cumin seed
- 4 allspice berries, or 1 teaspoon ground
- 3 cloves
- 1½ ounces (about 70) dried chiles de árbol or substitute tiny, hot, dried red peppers found in most grocery stores and called simply "hot chile peppers"
- 4 garlic cloves
- 2 teaspoons dried oregano
- 1 teaspoon salt
- 1 cup apple cider vinegar
- 1 cup water

1. Toast (page 16) the cumin, allspice, and cloves, stirring, until the spices give off their aromas, about 1 minute. Pulverize the spices in a spice grinder, then place in a blender (or processor) container.

2. Stem the chiles, then toast them for about 1 minute, until they change color (along with the seeds). Put in the blender with the spices.

3. Toast the garlic for 3 minutes. Put in the blender. Add the oregano, salt, and vinegar to the blender. Blend for 3 minutes, turning on and off a few times, scraping the container with a rubber spatula.

4. Strain the liquid through a fine sieve and stir in the water. Using a funnel, pour the salsa into an empty and thoroughly clean soda, wine, or long-necked beer bottle. Tightly wrap a piece of aluminum foil over the spout, or use a bottle that has a screw cap, such as Perrier or San Pellegrino water. Let stand at least 1 day before using, for the flavors to mingle.

Señora Petra Jiménez Anguiano's

Picardía *Chopped Jícama Salad with Fresh Mint Leaves*

SHOPPERS AT MERCADO LIBERTAD WOULDN'T THINK OF BUYING JÍCAMA without the tuber's leaves attached. "No leaves is the sure sign of age," claims Señora Anguiano at her stall of precisely arranged vegetables, next to a three-foot pile of freshly unearthed jícama, *Pachyrhizus erosus*, a large tuber with a sweet taste and the texture of water chestnuts. People of Jalisco eat refreshing jícama often, as a minced salsa ingredient, sliced in green salads, sliced into spears and sprinkled with chile powder, or chopped in *picardía*. Señora Anguiano's daughters, both teenagers, love huge amounts of this low-calorie, delicious, easy-to-prepare salad.
Yield: 2 cups

- 1 jícama, about 6 inches in diameter
- 3 limes
- 3 serrano chiles, or 2 jalapeño chiles
- 8 mint leaves
- lettuce leaves

1. Peel and chop the jícama and put it in a bowl.

2. Squeeze the limes and pour the juice over the jícama.

3. Stem and mince the chiles (seed if desired). Chop the mint. Mix into the jícama and lime juice. Chill and serve on lettuce leaves.

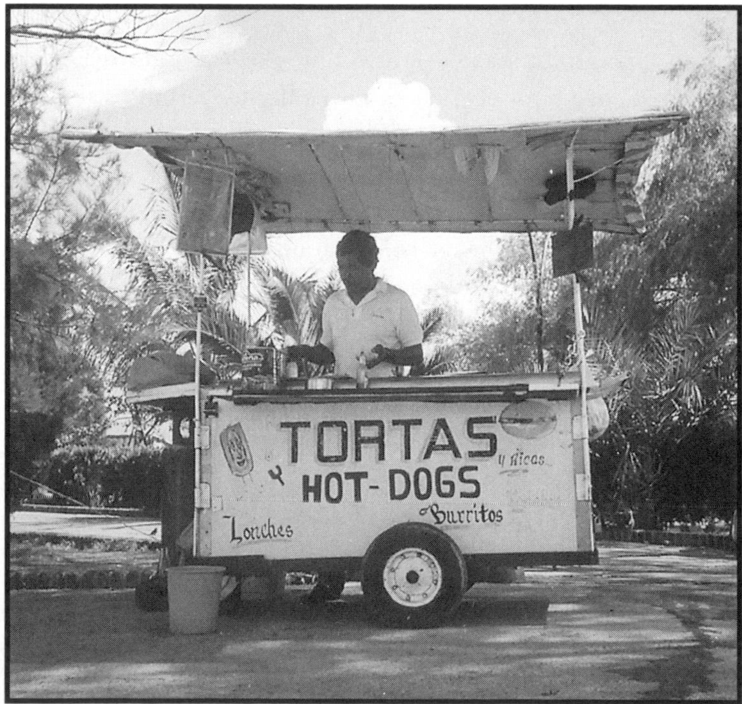

A "cocina callejera" (street food cart) offers snacks in Jalisco.

Señora Lourdes Mendoza's

Frijoles Charros de Guadalajara

Horsemen's Beans with Bacon and Chorizo

CHARROS STILL RIDE WITH FUROR AROUND CONSERVATIVE GUADALAJARA. Dressed to kill in silver-studded regalia, they're show-offs to appreciative fans who pack horsering bleachers on weekends to watch rope tricks and riding stunts. Old traditions run deep in Jalisco. These beans, which were once cooked over fires on the open range by cowboy chefs, now bubble away on innumerable stovetops throughout the region (by folks wearing fancy sombreros, one would guess).

Señora Mendoza's soupy pink beans are made with huge amounts of onion and tomatoes, and are enlivened with chorizo and serrano chile. These delicious beans are so soupy they are served in separate bowls alongside main-course plates. Her "would-be-cowboy" grandsons, two adorable six-year-old twins, eat more beans in one sitting than you could possibly imagine. They would gladly eat their hands-down favorite dish, *frijoles charros*, every day.

Yield: 2 quarts

- 1 pound pink beans
- 3 bacon slices
- 1 large white onion, chopped
- 2 fresh serrano chiles, stemmed and sliced
- 8 ounces chorizo, removed from casings
- 3 tomatoes, toasted (page 16) and peeled
- salt to taste

1. Put the beans in a nonaluminum (nonreactive) pot and cover with 3 inches of water. Bring to a boil, then lower the heat and simmer, covered.

2. Meanwhile, cook the bacon in a skillet. Remove the crisp bacon and drain on paper towels. Sauté the onion and chiles in the bacon grease until the onion is transparent. Add the chorizo and cook together with the onion mixture until the onion is light brown and the sausage is cooked through, about 5 minutes.

3. Purée the tomatoes in a blender. Add the tomato purée to the bean pot. Add the skillet ingredients and cooked and crumbled bacon and mix.

4. Cover and simmer 2 to 3 hours, or until the beans are tender. Cooking time depends on the age as much as the type of bean. When the beans have finished cooking, add salt to taste and serve in bowls with some of the cooking liquid.

A Chicken Stand Just South of Guadalajara's Parque Azul's

Pollo Adobado *Chile-Marinated and Grilled Chicken*

WEEKENDS MEAN OUTDOOR FAMILY EATING THROUGHOUT JALISCO, both in the city and in the outlying hills. Grills are set up along busy roadways, and smoke starts rising around noon for *pollo adobado*. Often a picnic table is provided and beans, tortillas, and drinks are available. At other times the chickens are strictly "to go" for your own backyard get-together.

Mexican birds are older and larger than the tender broiler-fryer chickens we're used to, but their flavor is incomparable. Most Mexican recipes call for chickens to be boiled before grilling and saucing to tenderize the tough old things. In this winning recipe the chicken is marinated overnight to tenderize and develop flavor. Serve with Refried Beans (page 47), lime wedges, fresh salsa, and corn or northern-style flour tortillas. Grilled Corn on the Cob (page 79) is a great accompaniment.

Yield: 8 servings

For the marinade

Yield: about 2 cups sauce

- 6 ancho chiles, stemmed and seeded, or a mixture of ancho and guajillo, or all New Mexico chiles (about 3 ounces total)
- 5 garlic cloves, unpeeled
- ½ teaspoon cumin seed, or powder
- 2 large bay leaves
- ½ teaspoon dried oregano
- ½ teaspoon dried thyme
- 4 Tablespoons cider vinegar
- ½ teaspoon ground cloves
- ½ teaspoon salt

1. Tear the chiles into large flat pieces and toast (page 16). Hold them down for a moment with a metal spatula until they crackle and change color. Turn them over and hold down a few seconds more. Do not allow the chiles to burn or they will become bitter. Put the chiles in a bowl and pour 1 quart hot water over them. Soak them for at least 1 hour.

2. Toast the unpeeled garlic until it's well browned, about 3 minutes. Peel when cool enough to handle.

3. Drain the chiles and put them in a blender or processor with the garlic and remaining ingredients. Blend, adding ¼ cup water at a time as needed, until the sauce becomes a smooth paste (scrape the container sides every few moments). Divide the sauce in half. Reserve half for basting while the chickens are grilling.

For the chickens

1. Remove the backbones of two 3½-pound chickens with a sharp boning knife. Butterfly each chicken by pressing down on the breast until the bone cracks and the chicken flattens. Turn the wings under so the chicken is as flat as possible (or have your butcher do it).

2. Spread half the *adobado* sauce over both chickens and marinate them for 24 hours in the refrigerator, or at least overnight, in a glass or ceramic dish or plastic bag.

For grilling and serving

- ¼ pound (1 stick) butter, clarified*
- the reserved marinade
- 20 raw white onions
- 20 radishes, sliced

1. Prepare the grill at medium heat and place the rack about 4 inches from the coals.

2. Brush clarified butter on the skin side of the chickens. Place the chickens on the grill rack, skin side down. Baste continuously and alternately with the marinade and clarified butter. Turn the chickens after 15 minutes and baste for 15 minutes on the second side. Turn the chickens again and grill, basting often, for 5 minutes on each side, 40 minutes total.

3. Cut the chickens into serving pieces and present them family style on a large platter garnished with raw onion rings and sliced radishes.

*To clarify butter, melt butter and carefully pour off the clear liquid (on top) into a small bowl. Discard the remaining cloudy residue. (Clarified butter will not burn so easily as unclarified butter.)

Juan Ríos's

Carne Asada *Marinated and Grilled Beef Steak*

WITHOUT A DOUBT CARNE ASADA IS THE MOST POPULAR DISH SERVED IN GUADALAJARA, and probably all of northern Mexico, from Tiajuana to Tampico. You'll see the name on every restaurant and fonda menu, whether grand-scale elegant or four-stool casual. *Carne asada* is never just a grilled steak, it's the classic combination plate—Mexico's interesting answer to meat and potatoes. *Carne asada* is always a thin, grilled or griddled beefsteak with a dish of soupy beans, guacamole, and either a cheese quesadilla, enchilada, scoop of *chilaquiles*, or French fries alongside, depending on the cook's whim. The platter is served with northern-style flour tortillas, grilled onions or scallions, and fresh tomato or tomatillo salsa.

Although grilling over coals is the preferred cooking method, Juan cooks his steaks at his fonda on a very hot griddle. But first, in the morning, he slices boneless beef, cut with the grain and from the loin, into slices about one-half inch thick and marinates them in freshly squeezed lime juice. By noon the steaks are marinated and ready to dry and griddle per order, along with tiny onions with their greens still attached (scallions work well). Horsemen's Beans with Bacon and Chorizo (page 31) bubble away on a back burner and a roasting pan full of *Chilaquiles* (page 286) keep warm. Chunky guacamole, made with no more than avocado, chopped white onion, and lime juice, sits waiting for the lunch bunch to arrive.

Yield: 4 servings

- 4 thin steaks cut from the loin
- 2 limes
- 12 scallions

1. Put the steaks in a dish and squeeze the lime over them, turning to be sure all the meat is covered, and marinate for 2 to 3 hours.

2. On a lightly oiled griddle, heavy skillet, or grill, cook the meat quickly to your taste. At the same time, lay the scallions on the griddle and cook, turning and brushing them with vegetable oil.

3. When the meat and scallions are done, transfer them to warm plates. Place a scoop of *chilaquiles*, an enchilada, or quesadilla on each plate. Ladle beans into 4 small bowls and serve alongside.

No Name's

Filete de Res en Aguacate *Filet Mignon in Avocado-Tomatillo Sauce*

RESTAURANT NO NAME IS A POSH RESTAURANT IN TLAQUEPAQUE, known for its lovely patio with exotic birds. Waiters pan-sauté sliced steaks, then spoon avocado-tomatillo sauce over the meat at the table. The system is successful in Mexico where medium- to well-cooked, thinly sliced beef is preferred over North America's thick, medium-rare slabs. My suggestion is to grill small, thickly cut steaks in one piece, then center the beef on a pool of delicious sauce. Fish steaks also match well with the tomatillo's slight sourness.

Yield: 4 servings

- 4 filet mignon steaks, each at least 1 inch thick and about 6 ounces

For the sauce

- 8 tomatillos, papery husks removed and washed, or one 13-ounce can, drained and rinsed (as a last resort)
- 3 fresh serrano chiles, stemmed and chopped
- 3 Tablespoons chopped white onion
- 4 sprigs fresh cilantro leaves, chopped
- ½ cup Chicken Broth (page 19)
- 1 ripe avocado, about 4 inches in length
- salt and freshly ground black pepper to taste

1. Bring salted water to a boil and boil the tomatillos for 5 minutes, or until they are barely soft throughout. Drain and put them in a blender container. If you are using canned tomatillos, put them directly into the blender after draining.

2. Add the chiles, onion, cilantro, and broth to the blender and purée.

3. Meanwhile, grill the steaks.

4. Cut the avocado in half all around from stem end to stem end. Remove the pit. Scoop out the flesh into the blender. Blend. Taste and add salt and pepper. Lime is not necessary (as with guacamole) to prevent the mixture from turning black because the tomatillos have enough acid. Pour the contents of the blender into a small pot and heat. Divide the sauce onto 4 warm plates. Lay a grilled steak in the center of each.

Bo-Bo's

World's Best Margarita *Tequila, Cointreau, and Lime Drink*

NO FALSE MODESTY HERE. The simplest and best ingredients make the World's Best Margaritas. Bo-Bo (for Bonifacio) is a Tlaquepaque bartender who knows his way around a mean margarita. He insists you forget those foamy, slushy, sugary, artificially flavored and colored headache-makers—it's time to grow up. Buy silver (clear) or aged (*añejo*) tequila (to be decadent) made from 100 percent agave tequila (no added sugars); use Cointreau; and hand-squeeze fresh limes. Don't put another thing in the glass except ice cubes. Read this: No slush allowed!
Yield: 1 drink

- lime wedges
- Kosher or sea salt
- ice cubes
- 1½ parts 100 percent tequila
- ½ part Cointreau
- 1 part freshly squeezed lime juice, if possible from Key limes

1. Rub a glass (about 4 inches high and 3 inches wide) with a lime wedge then dip the rim in coarse salt, not fine-textured table salt. Add ice cubes.
2. Mix the tequila, Cointreau, and lime juice in a pitcher, then carefully pour the mixture into the glass without messing the salted rim. Place a lime wedge on the rim. *¡Salud!*

Lazy Man's Margarita *Tequila and Lime Soda Drink*

NEXT TO BEER, THIS TEQUILA-AND-SQUIRT COMBINATION IS THE MOST POPULAR DRINK around the *portales* of Tlaquepaque's El Parián. Bo-Bo (the World's Best Margarita master) first rubs tall glass rims (preferably thick, hand-blown glasses with air bubbles, and a dark blue rim around the lip) with lime juice, then dips them in salt to offer fancy, early evening presentations. Hours later, bottles of tequila and endless bottles of Squirt crowd tables for self-service, and by then fancy salt-rimmed glasses are long forgotten. This thirstquencher, for listening to mariachis by, is a cinch to make.
Yield: 1 drink

- Kosher or sea salt
- ice cubes
- 1 lime wedge
- 1 shot 100 percent agave tequila
- fresh limes (tiny "limones" or Key limes are best)
- Squirt, Sprite, Fresca, or 7-Up soda

1. Put a few tablespoons of salt in a small dish. Moisten the rim of a tall glass (about 8 ounces) with a wedge of lime. Turn the glass over and dip it in the salt to coat the rim. Add ice cubes. Carefully pour tequila in the glass without disturbing the salt.
2. Carefully squeeze lime into the glass, being careful with the salt, fill with lemon-lime soda, and stir. Add a colorful straw.

Tlaquepaque Cantina's

Cacajuates con Chile *Spanish Peanuts with Chile Powder, Salt, and Lime*

THESE ADDICTIVE MUNCHIES ARE SERVED WITH ICY TEQUILA DRINKS and cold beers at many Tlaquepaque cafés. Warm peanuts are squirted with fresh lime then tossed in a chile-salt mixture. That's it—and little to do for something so good.
Yield: 1 cup

- 1 cup canned, roasted Spanish peanuts, in their red skins, salted or unsalted
- 1 lime quarter
- ½ teaspoon chile powder (any pure, unblended type)
- ½ teaspoon salt

1. Just before serving, heat the oven to 350°F. Put the peanuts on a baking sheet and heat for 10 minutes.
2. Put the hot peanuts in a bowl, squirt the lime juice over them, and mix.
3. If the peanuts are salted, add only chile powder. If they are unsalted, add the chile powder and salt. Mix very well and serve warm.

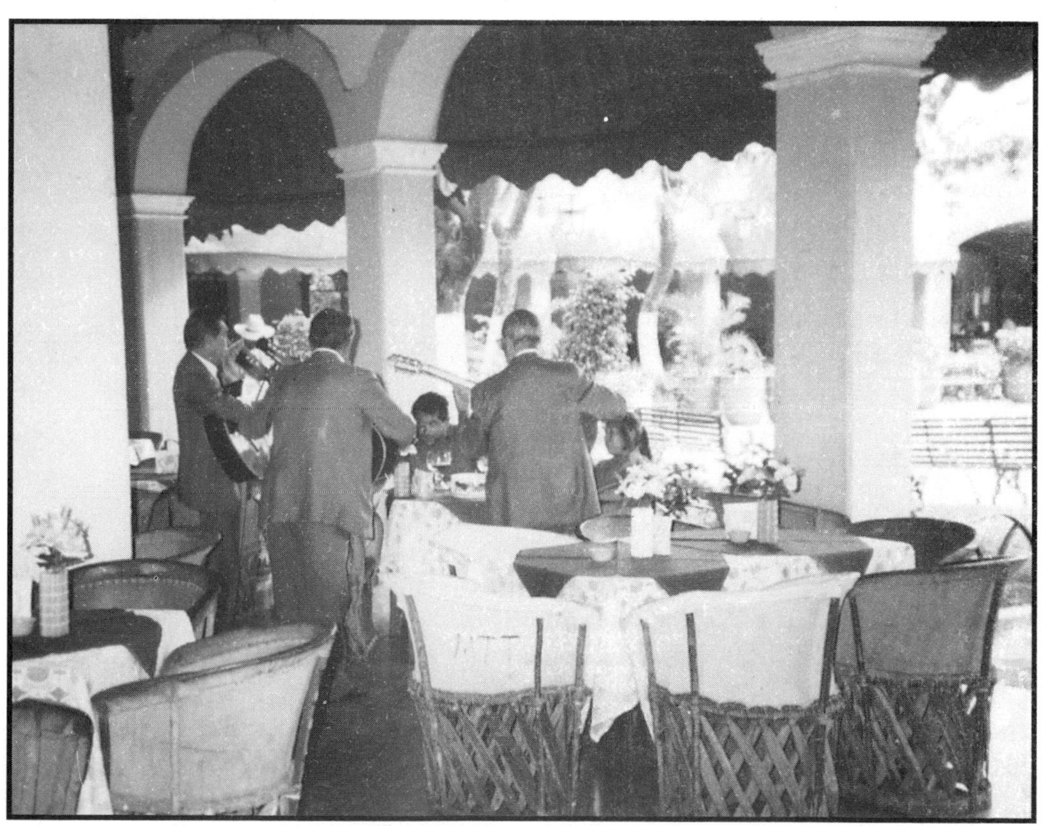

A good time is had by all at Tlaquepaque's El Parián.

◆ Lake Chapala ◆

Lake Chapala is less than an hour away from Guadalajara.

LAGUNA DE CHAPALA, 25 MILES (40 KILOMETERS) SOUTH of Guadalajara, boasts near-perfect weather year-round. It's Mexico's largest lake at 53 by 19 miles (85 by 30 km) and is surrounded by mountains and fabulous billowy clouds all summer. The lake is a popular weekend destination for Guadalajarans craving the local specialty, lake whitefish. For years Lake Chapala was polluted, then the government realized its importance as a natural resource, and now the lake is coming back to its original beauty.

Lake Chapala was discovered long ago by expatriate U.S. and Canadian retirees. Private houses have begun to dominate the landscape, with condos making an impact on the town outskirts. Even so, the Mexican character comes through loud and clear around the *zócalos* of Chapala, Ajijic, and Jocotepec.

✸ MARKETS ✸

Mercado Municipal Chapala, the lake's largest town, has two markets. The indoor market is on the *zócalo* and open every day. It's small but has a fine produce selection, butchers, chicken (fresh and rotisseried), plus a few fondas up and downstairs.

Chapala Market A weekly open-air market takes place Monday on Chapala's east side—look for the throngs and traffic on Madero, the main drag into town. Produce is sold at giveaway prices even though you'll have to hunt through rows of knickknacks to get at it. But this is a fun and social market where friends meet and bargain, trade gossip, and just hang out while enjoying the frenzied atmosphere, especially when cassette sellers decide to turn their speakers up full throttle in friendly competition. Peeled mangoes are a spring and summer treat. Get yours either impaled on a stick and cut like a flower, or sliced into a plastic bag then splashed with lime juice and chile powder. Peeled fruit and vegetables such as melon, papaya, jícama, and cucumber are always top market refreshers and usually safe to eat off clean carts.

Ajijic Market The charming Wednesday morning open-air market runs along one of Ajijic's main cobblestoned streets, downhill, toward the lake. Look for a woman selling russet-colored tamales. The *masa* inside is flavored with *panela*, and baking in coals, rather than steaming, brings out its molasses flavor. Other tamales are sold from a wheelbarrow. Chayote squash grown along the shores of Lake Chapala, set off the ground on trellises, are popular market vegetables. You'll see both smooth and spiky varieties. *Barbacoa* is sold by the kilo, or in a taco. Cactus paddles are de-thorned, trimmed, and ready for turning into soups and salads.

Jocotepec Market Jocotepec is surprisingly large but the least influenced by the U.S. of the three towns. It's situated at the western end of the lake and has a Thursday open-air market in the center. Everyday household goods make up the bulk of items sold, but small kitchen tools are fun to look for. Orange, blue, or green plastic lime presses are good buys and great gifts (but best for Mexico's tiny Key limes). *Pozole* (page 54) vendors dish up steaming bowls of the hominy and pork stew to eat on the spot, or will fill your container to carry home. Homemade jams, jellies, and preserved green and red cactus fruit glisten in jars of all sizes.

A father-son team sells tamales in Ajijic's market.

* PLACES TO GO AND THINGS TO EAT *

Charales. Along with larger lake whitefish, *charales* are the most famous food of Lake Chapala. The tiny fish, no longer than a few inches, are deep-fried before being loaded onto umbrella-topped carts to be sold along the lakefront. Lime and hot sauce are liberally squirted over the *charales*, which are served in cardboard containers. The popular snack is eaten in quantity on weekends by Guadalajarans down for the day—but remember: The lake is still polluted, so go easy on the number that you consume.

Carnitas. For carnivores, stands with Deep-Fried Pork Pieces (page 90) are set up right in the heart of town every day about noontime on the northern side of the *zócalo* right outside the market. Each vendor brings his freshly slaughtered pig that's been boiled in hot lard until crisp and tender. Every person has his favorite part: loin, leg, liver, heart, head, or hoof. A sheet of brown paper is placed on a scale and you choose the still-warm pieces to be hacked off then weighed by the kilo. Buy some handmade tortillas, *masa* shells, or rolls from women at the main entrance to the market. Lunch, as you can see by the crowd, is a cinch. Benches in the park are favorite dining spots, or take yours home and serve with guacamole, thinly sliced white onion, and fresh salsa.

Pulque. A kilometer or so after the row of lakeside restaurants, past Ajijic, on the way to Jocotepec, is a spa called San Juan Cosala. It has thermal springs, and a day pass is inexpensive. If you're lucky, immediately past the spa and on the same side, a *pulque* stand may be open under the trees. **Señor Guadalupe Calvario Medina**, a charming man who takes great pride in his slightly alcoholic drink made from maguey (a succulent plant in the agave family) served from a huge ceramic *pulque* pot (see page 22). He will gladly explain the brewing process as you sip this ancient nectar along the roadside. You'll learn that the two-to-three-day fermentation time depends upon how hot the weather is. He also has on hand a container of *agua miel* (honey water), a refreshing, unfermented, and nonalcolholic maguey juice that children enjoy. Ask for the drinks *llevar* ("to go"—in plastic cups); otherwise, you'll drink from a communal glass rinsed in a bucket of water (stomachs, beware).

If *pulque* intrigues you, Tlaxcala (in the tiny state of Tlaxcala, east of Mexico City and north of Puebla) has a museum where artisans demonstrate their crafts. There's also a *pulque* processing display, so if you're in the area stop in at **Museo de Artes Tradicionales Populares**, Avenida Emilio Sánchez Piedras, No. 1. Hours: 10 A.M. to 6 P.M. Tuesday through Sunday (less than $1 entrance).

Candy. *Dulces* (sweets) *de Chapala*, are sold on almost every street corner in town. Cellophane packages contain four to twelve candies, depending on type. Favorites are chocolate (think of excellent chocolate gumdrops, slightly squashed), citrus, tamarind, and—look out!—tamarind with chile. The sensation is sour, spicy, sweet, and a bit salty all at once. Also try toasted coconut, vanilla *jamoncillo* "fudge" with nuts, coconut, or cinnamon, and other flavors depending on the vendor's whim.

RESTAURANTS

Even though landlocked, Mexico's largest lake boasts restaurants that specialize in both fresh and saltwater fish and shellfish. With everyday flights from the Gulf and Pacific to Guadalajara, seafood is everyone's first choice on lakeside menus. It's probably not a great idea to eat the whitefish more than once, as a taste, because it's caught in the still-polluted lake. Chapala's inexpensive fish restaurants are found at the southern end of town. Go to the pier, turn left on Ramón Corona, and at the far end of the park you'll see Restaurant Güicho.

Güicho. Inexpensive. No. 20, on the corner. This restaurant serves the favorite of both locals and retired U.S. folks: mixed, spicy seafood soup. Shrimp dishes are immensely popular, too.

El Pescador. Inexpensive. A few doors closer to the lake than Güicho, El Pescador definitely has the best lakeside views, and almost identical menus to a few nearby places. Menu samplings include a slew of shrimp dishes, including butter sauce, spicy red sauce, and browned garlic sauce. Whole fish and fillets are cooked numerous ways, and seafood cocktails are available in all sorts of combinations. A local treat is Carp Roe Tacos (page 42) and the best are El Pescador's because of its Cucumber Salsa (page 42) served alongside.

A few blocks farther east there is yet another group of lakeside eateries—choose among them as the mood strikes. Musicians will eventually come by and ask if you'd like a song for a price. Dessert is local candy sold by vendors. Try a few flavors; they're all interesting and some are even addictive.

Los Naranjitos. Moderate. Located at Hidalgo No.10, just off the *zócalo* in Ajijic. Comfortable and attractive Los Naranjitos serves *Birria* made with a combination of beef and pork (page 45). The rich sauce (not a broth at all) is a fine match to the restaurant's napkin-wrapped cornbread-in-a bowl.

On the main road between Ajijic and Jocotepec there's a line-up of casual, inexpensive fish joints overlooking the water. The first is **Playa Azul**, then comes **Las Gariotas**, followed by **El Mirador** and five or six others. They all serve approximately the same dishes, their beers are all icy cold, and the wonderful, breezy views are identical. The choice is yours; easy parking may be the decisive factor on a busy Sunday afternoon.

El Pescador's

▲▼▲

Tacos de Caviar con Salsa de Pepino

Soft Tacos with Carp Roe and Cucumber Salsa

LONG BEFORE IT BECAME A RETIREMENT HAVEN FOR GRINGO MILITARY PERSONNEL, Chapala had its mark on the culinary map. The largest lake in Mexico, forty-five minutes south of Guadalajara by car, Lake Chapala supplied locals with freshwater whitefish, carp, and catfish years before expatriates and Mexicans alike discovered its gorgeous scenery and near-perfect year-round weather.

Popular with Guadalajarans, a lakeside lunch starting with a shared order of tacos with caviar can't be beat. Serve with cool, crunchy, cucumber salsa.

Yield: 4 servings

- ½ pound carp, cod, or other similar fresh roe
- 2 Tablespoons vegetable oil
- ½ small white onion, chopped
- 1 medium tomato, chopped
- 8 warm corn tortillas

1. Bring 4 cups water to a boil in a shallow pan. Add the roe and simmer for 7 to 8 minutes.

2. Remove the roe from the water with a slotted spoon and drain in a sieve for a few minutes until cool enough to handle. Remove any skin from the roe.

3. Heat the oil in a skillet. Add the onion and tomato and sauté until the onion is soft. With your fingers, crumble the roe into the onion and tomatoes. Cook a few minutes until the mixture is dry and crumbly.

4. Spoon 3 tablespoons onto a tortilla. Fold, and put the taco on a serving dish, or in a napkin-lined basket, as at El Pescador. Continue with the remaining tacos.

EL PESCADOR'S *SALSA DE PEPINO* IS A TASTY MATCH for the fish restaurant's special taco appetizers, but it's wonderful with other seafood and meat dishes, too. The flavors are similar to some Indian fresh chutneys, and hotness can vary from nice to nasty by regulating the quantity of fresh chiles.

Yield: about 2 cups

For "Salsa de Pepino" (Fresh Cucumber Salsa)

- 3 pickling cucumbers, about 5 inches
- 1 medium white onion, finely minced
- 2 serrano or jalapeño chiles
- ¼ cup chopped cilantro leaves
- 3 Tablespoons fresh lime juice
- ¼ teaspoon salt

1. Peel and finely chop the unseeded cucumbers. Stem and finely slice the chiles. Mix all ingredients in a bowl and cover with plastic wrap.

2. Let the salsa stand at least 1 hour, refrigerated, and up to 4 hours, to let the flavors mingle and develop. Serve cold.

Lupita Moreno de López's

Birria I *Kid or Lamb with Guajillo and Ancho Chile Broth*

BIRRIA IS WESTERN JALISCO AND MICHOACÁN'S ANSWER TO CENTRAL MEXICO and Oaxaca's *Barbacoa* (page 137), chile-marinated and slow-baked, super-tender, meat in broth.

One thankfully unrainy summer Sunday afternoon Morris and I were invited to join the López family's *birria* picnic along the shore of Lake Chapala, between Ajijic and Jocotepec. We spread the feast on an ancient picnic table in a field belonging to a relative, ate, drank, and watched captivating clouds mushroom all afternoon across the lake.

Being rather modern, Lupita doesn't bother with a pit lined with maguey leaves as her parents did. (Maguey leaves are the thick, spiked leaves of the agave plant, which produces pulque and mezcal throughout central Mexico and Oaxaca's countryside). True, steaming the leaves around the meat (she uses either kid or lamb) does add flavor and she uses them when she can, but Lupita makes up for their absence by including a good shot of firewater, either tequila or mezcal. She prepares the marinated meat in her kitchen a day in advance, then drives to the picnic spot where everyone helps unload a fully cooked feast from the back of her pickup. Serve with fresh limes, bottled spicy salsas, warm tortillas, and cold beers and sodas.

Yield: 12 servings

For the adobo marinade

- 2 lamb legs, or kid hindquarters, about 8 pounds total
- 10 guajillo chiles
- 6 ancho chiles
- 8 garlic cloves, peeled
- 2 tomatoes
- 1 Tablespoon black peppercorns
- ½ teaspoon cumin seed
- 4 whole cloves
- 2 large sprigs thyme, or 2 teaspoons dried
- 2 sprigs Mexican oregano, or 2 teaspoons dried
- 4 bay leaves
- 3 Tablespoons vegetable oil
- ¼ cup cider vinegar
- 1 teaspoon salt (or to taste)
- ½ cup tequila or mezcal

1. One day in advance, partially bone the kid or lamb, or have your butcher do it for you. Cut the meat into large chunks (some bone left on makes for a more tasty broth). Prick all over with a small sharp knife and put the meat into a deep, lidded roasting pan or Dutch oven.

2. Stem, and seed the chiles. Toast (page 16) until they release their scents and change color.

3. Toast the garlic cloves and the tomatoes until they become blistered and blackened. Put the tomatoes in a plasic bag for a few minutes to "sweat" and loosen their skins. Peel, then purée with the garlic in a blender container or processor.

4. Put the toasted chiles, and the peppercorns, cumin seed, cloves, thyme, oregano, and bay leaves in the blender. Add ¼ cup water and purée, scrape the sides with a rubber spatula, and continue to purée until smooth.

5. Heat the oil in a deep pot. Add the chile mixture (it splatters!), cook for 1 minute then reduce the heat, and

(Continued)

4 cups chicken or meat broth, or use Knorr chicken bouillon

simmer, uncovered for 15 minutes, until it thickens. Add 1 tablespoon of the vinegar and the salt, stirring. Continue adding the remaining vinegar plus the tequila or mezcal, blending until smooth.

6. Pour over the meat and rub in the marinade. Pour the broth around the meat. Cover and let marinate 24 hours in the refrigerator.

For steam-roasting the lamb

12 small limes, cut in half

1. Preheat the oven to 375°F.

2. Be sure the lid is secure and weight it down if necessary to keep steam from escaping. Bake for 2½ hours. Remove only the very large bones and spoon the meat into individual bowls. Ladle some broth over each portion and pass soup spoons. Serve with limes.

Ajijic is home to a weekend-only "birria" stand.

Los Naranjitos Restaurant's

Birria II *Beef and Pork in Chile Sauce*

BIRRIA JOINTS DOT THE LANDSCAPE IN JALISCO ON SUNDAY AFTERNOONS, and friends gather at the roadside stands shaded by mango trees to feast on this regional masterpiece. For a comfortable restaurant *birria*, the delightful Los Naranjitos in Ajijic serves another style of *birria* made with a combination of beef and pork. The rich, thick sauce (not a broth at all) is intensely flavorful. Today many Jaliscos prefer *birria* cooked this way—a pot roast of dreams.

Serve with Chopped Jícama Salad with Fresh Mint Leaves (page 30) and tortillas or U.S.-style corn bread, as they do at Los Naranjitos.

Yield: 10 servings

- 3 pounds pork loin or leg
- 3 pounds beef chuck
- 6 ancho chiles, stemmed and seeded
- 6 guajillo chiles, stemmed and seeded
- 1 pasilla or fresh chilaca chile, stemmed and seeded
- 8 garlic cloves, peeled
- 6 bay leaves
- 1 teaspoon cumin seed
- 6 whole cloves
- 1 Tablespoon dried Mexican oregano
- 1 Tablespoon dried thyme
- 6 Tablespoons sesame seeds
- 2 cups cider vinegar
- ¼ cup "masa," or "masa harina" mixed with water per package directions (as a thickener)
- salt

1. Cut the meat into big chunks (including bones) and put it in a Dutch oven or other big, heavy roasting pot with a lid. Pour in enough water to come to the depth of 4 fingers over the top of the meat. (This isn't very scientific but everyone I spoke with agreed with this measuring system.) Bring the water to a boil, then reduce the heat to medium, uncovered.

2. Meanwhile, bring the chiles and garlic to a boil in a pan with enough water to cover. Reduce the heat and simmer for 12 to 15 minutes, until the chiles are soft.

3. Check the water depth in the Dutch oven after cooking 1 hour. The water should be just at the top of the meat. If not, continue cooking.

4. Put the chiles, garlic, and the cooking liquid in a blender container. Add the bay leaves, cumin, cloves, oregano, thyme, sesame seeds, and vinegar to the blender, and purée. Pour the liquid into the *masa* and mix until the *masa* is a thick liquid. Pour the *masa* into the pot with the meat. Pour the chile mixture into the pot with the meat and simmer for another hour, covered.

5. Season to taste with salt. *Birria* can be cooled at this point and refrigerated before reheating. Cut the meat into portions and serve with generous spoonfuls of sauce and tortillas.

Katalina Barrajas de Gómez's

Frijoles de Olla *Beans Cooked in a Clay Pot*

KATALINA LIVES IN PICTURESQUE AJIJIC, along the shore of Mexico's largest lake, Chapala. She's a great cook, so we talked about food every day when I was fortunate enough to spend a month in the cobblestoned village. She worked in the kitchen of Chapala's Hotel Nido for many years, so she really knows her regional cooking.

When I asked her about soaking beans before cooking, Katalina said she heard about people soaking beans but never knew anyone who did, whether a restaurant chef or home cook. She has cooked beans in an *olla*, a traditional clay cooking pot, since she was a girl, but any cooking pot is fine.

Yield: 8 servings

- 1 pound dried, light pink beans, or pinto beans
- 1 medium white onion, peeled and cut in half
- salt to taste

1. Bring 3½ quarts water to a boil in an *olla*, or other large pot.

2. Pick over the beans and wash in two changes of water. Put the beans in the boiling water with the onion. Bring the water back to a boil, then reduce the heat and simmer, cover slightly askew, for about 2 hours, depending on the age of the beans. Taste a bean and check to see if it is cooked. If it's still a bit hard at the center, continue simmering for another 30 minutes and taste again.

3. Add 1 teaspoon salt (or to taste) when the beans are done. Katalina says if you salt the beans in the beginning rather than after cooking they will be tough.

See *Note* on page 47.

Katalina Barrajas de Gómez's

Frijoles Refritos *Refried Beans from Jalisco*

EVEN WITH THEIR MOTHER'S YEARS OF RESTAURANT COOKING, Katalina's kids' favorite meal is simply refried beans on hot tortillas. She laughs at the fact that they complain when she makes anything more elaborate when they come home for lunch from school. But, the budding gourmets do insist on refried beans rather than soupy *frijoles de olla* simply because the sticky beans stay put on their tortillas!

Yield: 8 servings

- 1 recipe "Frijoles de Olla" (page 46)
- ¼ cup lard or oil, plus extra

1. Heat the lard or oil in a very large skillet (or pot).

2. Add half the beans and half the bean cooking liquid to the hot oil. Mash them with a bean masher, a potato masher, or a large wooden spoon. They should be coarsely mashed, not a purée (as in the Yucatán).

3. Add the remaining beans and liquid to the skillet and continue mashing the beans into the fat, adding more fat if necessary. The process takes 10 to 15 minutes. There will be some liquid left but most will be absorbed a few minutes after the skillet is removed from the heat.

Note: Some people say soaking makes beans more digestible by dissolving gas-causing substances in the discarded soaking water. Mexicans don't presoak beans, but if you'd like, put them in a pot and cover with at least 2 inches of water (about 10 cups). Bring to a boil and boil for 5 minutes. Remove the pot from the heat and cover for 1 to 5 hours. Drain the water and add fresh water (double the amount of beans) and onion. Bring to a boil then reduce the heat and simmer for about 2 hours. Add salt or lime juice when the beans are finished cooking.

Beans can be easily and successfully cooked in slow cookers, or Crock-Pots: Put the beans, water, and onion in a pot. Turn the heat to "high" and cook for about 5 hours. Or, if more convenient, cook on "high" 1 hour, then turn to "low" and cook 8 to 10 hours, or until they are done.

◆ Pacific Coast Towns ◆

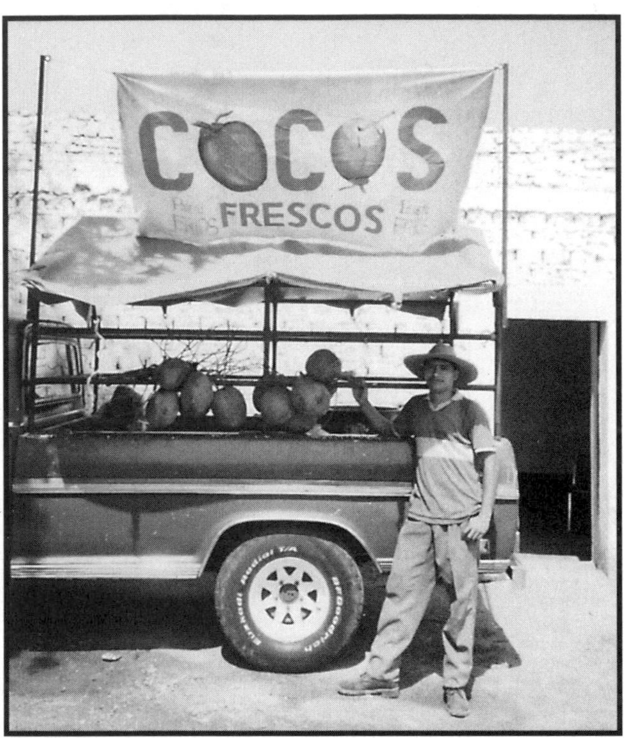

Coconut vendors open thick "cocos" with machetes to make room for your straw.

FROM JALISCO'S PUERTO VALLARTA, SOUTH to Manzanillo, Acapulco, Puerto Escondido, and all the sleepy Pacific pueblos in between, seafood is definitely Top Banana. Every beachside shack selling grilled whole fish offers what is the best eating in this part of the world. Sometimes the whole fish is cooked directly on a grill, other times it's impaled from mouth to tail on a stick and grilled over mesquite on the sand. Pacific lobsters (no claws) are split and grilled over wood, or boiled whole in seawater. Can you imagine anything better than lobster tacos? Pile lobster meat onto just-made, hot tortillas, spoon on guacamole and salsa, roll it up, and devour. All this in thatched-roofed huts on the beach while enjoying the moon's reflection on the Pacific, and lingering with a nightcap of Colima's famous coconut liquor.

Other seafood along the coast in Jalisco, Colima, Guerrero, and Oaxaca are various shrimp dishes outnumbering everything else on fonda signs. Almost all are made with shelled shrimp in a simple chile sauce, quick-griddled, then turned into soft tacos. Lime wedges, like smiles and cold beers, are everywhere.

✸ MARKETS ✸

Mercado Municipal Puerto Vallarta's market and a few upstairs fondas are located at A. Rodríguez at Insurgentes on the north bank of the Río Cuale. Hours: 7 A.M. to 8 P.M., Sunday 9 A.M. to 2 P.M. Fresh fish is the big draw early in the day. Criollo chiles (translates to very regional specimens) are fun to spot in tiny piles sold by native women. These chiles are grown in their yards and often have no specific botanical names. Look around for very tiny, tamarind- and sugar-filled sweet tamales (actually ancient sweets) from Nyarit. *Acitrón* (cactus candy) is popular—there are plenty of cactus growers in Jalisco to meet the great demand. Slip a straw in a giant, fresh green coconut (straight from a nearby plantation) for its thirst-quenching pleasure. By the way, because of Puerto Vallarta's huge tourist population, this market tends to be more expensive than just about any other market in Mexico for craft items and handwoven goods, but it's still a fun place to shop and bargain.

✸ PLACES TO GO AND THINGS TO EAT ✸

Liquor. *Raicilla*, a clear liquor made by the local Cora Indians, is said to cure seasickness. You'll see it around town along with *tuba*, a mild, fermented drink made from palm sap. Mexico's best wines like Monte Xanic Sauvignon blanc from Baja can be found in Puerto Vallarta's upscale liquor shops.

RESTAURANTS

Playa de los Muertos beach is known for food stands selling whole, skewered fish cooked over mesquite and many super-casual dining spots are scattered about on the sand. If you'd prefer a real restaurant, nearby **Daiquiri Dick's** is the ideal place for rum and fruit drinks and a place to sit (and get out of the hot sun) while eating your fish from 9 A.M. to 11 P.M. Other popular places include **La Palapa** and **El Dorado**, on the same beach. **Las Tres Huastecas** is at the corner of Olas Altas and Francisco Rodríguez.

Guillermo and Julia Pérez's

Ceviche de Jalisco *Raw Fish and Avocado Appetizer*

CEVICHE IS RAW, BUT NOT IN THE SAME WAY SASHIMI IS RAW. Twenty-four hours of marinating in lime juice "cooks" the fish and turns it opaque, just as if it were cooked over heat. Mexicans along both the Pacific and Gulf coasts enjoy ceviche made from oily fish like mackerel, but any fish that's not too soft is fine, such as yellowtail, dorado, and halibut, or a combination for textural interest. Go to your best seafood market and buy only what's super-fresh and never frozen.

Morris and I met the Pérezes at a tiny seafood joint just north of Puerto Vallarta one lunchtime. We got to talking—Morris and Guillermo about fishing, Julia and I about cooking. When Guillermo is lucky and brings home a catch, Julia makes ceviche from a kilo (two pounds) of the meat and serves it as an appetizer. The Pérezes favorite chiles for the dish are pickled, or *en escabeche*. Easily found canned, pickled jalapeño chile is fine, because it's exactly what Julia uses and any unattractive softness of canned chiles is no problem, they're finely chopped, or use finely minced fresh serrano or jalapeño chiles.

A basket of tortilla chips is wonderful, their crunchiness an ideal match. A bottle of spicy de Árbol Chile Hot Sauce (page 29) on the table is appreciated by those who like even more chile zap.

Yield: 8 servings

- 2 pounds very fresh fish fillets, cut into small pieces no more than ½-inch square
- 1½ cups fresh lime juice (about 10 limes)
- 1 white onion, finely minced
- 4 pickled jalapeño chiles, finely chopped, or fresh serrano or jalapeño chiles, if you prefer
- 2 tomatoes, chopped
- 2 avocados, diced into ½-inch cubes
- 3 Tablespoons vegetable oil
- 10 cilantro sprigs, leaves only, chopped
- ¼ teaspoon salt
- ¼ teaspoon freshly ground black pepper
- 2 limes, quartered

1. Put the cut-up fish in a ceramic or glass bowl, pour the lime juice over, and mix. Cover the bowl with plastic, pressing the plastic onto the fish to keep out air. Refrigerate for 24 hours. Stir halfway through the marinating process.

2. Immediately before serving, place the fish in a large strainer and drain. Put in a serving bowl. Mix in the onion, chiles, tomatoes, avocados, oil, cilantro, salt, and pepper.

3. Serve in goblets with a lime wedge on each rim.

Rosa Cobián Portillo's

Sopes de Colima *Masa Tartlets Filled with Pork, Potatoes, and Peas*

ROSA WAS BORN AND GREW UP IN COLIMA, a few miles inland from the Pacific Coast, south of Puerto Vallarta. This *sope* recipe is from her home town and remains her favorite light lunch or supper. Smaller versions make great cocktail snacks.
Yield: 25 sopes

For the meat filling

- 2 pounds lean pork
- ½ pound fresh peas, shelled
- 3 Tablespoons lard or vegetable oil
- 1 medium potato, peeled and diced
- 1 medium white onion
- 2 medium tomatoes, chopped
- 1 teaspoon dried Mexican oregano
- ¼ teaspoon cumin seed

1. Put the pork in a pot and cover it with water. Bring the water to a boil and boil for 30 minutes. Remove the meat, cool, and shred it with a fork, scraping with the meat's grain. Set aside.

2. In a small pot, bring 2 cups of water to a boil and add the peas. Cook until done; the time depends upon the age of the peas. Drain and set aside.

3. In a large pot, heat the lard or vegetable oil. Add the diced potato and cook until lightly brown. Chop the onion and add it to the potato. Add the tomato to the pot. Add oregano, cumin seed, and pork. Sauté for 10 minutes. Set aside.

For the shells

- 2 pounds "masa" from a tortillería, or 4 cups prepared "masa harina" per package directions
- ¼ cup water mixed with ½ teaspoon salt
- oil for frying, about 2 cups
- 1 cup shredded mozzarella
- 4 cups shredded cabbage
- 10 red radishes, sliced

1. Mix the salt water into the *masa* to make a soft dough. Pull off golf ball-sized pieces and form about 25 balls. Flatten each ball into 3-inch-diameter disks.

2. Heat an ungreased skillet and cook the disks on one side for 2 minutes. Turn over and pinch up the sides ¼ inch. The cooked side is now on the inside. Cool on a rack while finishing the rest.

3. Add ½ inch fresh oil to a cleaned pan and heat to 360°F or until it ripples. Add a few *sope* shells and cook until crisp on the outside and soft inside, about 1 minute. Remove to absorbent paper.

4. Fill each shell with some meat mixture. Top the meat with a bit of shredded cheese then a big pile of shredded cabbage, and radish slices.

Javier Martínez Orozco's

Pescado en Pepián *Whole Fish in Pumpkin Seed Sauce*

JAVIER'S WIFE, MARÍA, HAS A FONDA IN HER HOME on the outskirts of Puerto Vallarta. Her garage was transformed into a lunch spot about ten years ago and she serves about twenty lunches every day, six days a week. She sells typical favorites: enchiladas, quesadillas, fish and shrimp tacos in handmade tortillas, tortilla soup, plus a daily special.

Javier enjoys cooking weekend family feasts because he loves going to Mercado Municipal for fresh fish and gathering all the ingredients. Whenever Javier spots a particularly fine *pargo* he can't resist making his favorite, *Pescado en Pepián* (the sauce is spelled "pepián" in western states, "pipián" farther east and south). *Pargo* (Pacific rock cod) is a beautiful silvery-pink fish found all along the west coast of Mexico. Javier doesn't cook *pargo* in the sauce, but pours it over the fish after baking and cutting it into serving pieces.

This *pepián* is typical of the Jalisco region—thinned with cream rather than the less rich chicken broth typical of Chiapas, Tabasco, and Oaxaca. Their *pepián* is made coarser and less oily because unhulled seeds are used (page 284). Serve with hot corn tortillas, a simple steamed vegetable such as green beans or broccoli, and Mexican Rice Pilaf (page 66). Rather than fish, try chicken, lean pork cubes, or a vegetable mixture such as yams, squash, and string beans served with rice, which is delicious with the rich sauce.

Yield: 4 servings

For the sauce

- 1 cup raw, unsalted, pumpkin seeds ("pepitas") without hulls (they are an olive green color)
- 2 cups Chicken Broth (page 19), or 1 teaspoon Knorr chicken bouillon dissolved in 2 cups hot water
- 5 serrano chiles, sliced
- 6 sprigs cilantro, stems removed
- 1 small white onion, chopped
- 3 garlic cloves, chopped
- 2 Tablespoons vegetable oil
- 1 cup "Crema" (page 80), or sour cream
- salt (no salt if broth has salt, or if using Knorr bouillon)
- ½ teaspoon freshly ground pepper

1. Toast (page 16) the pumpkin seeds until they begin to swell and pop. Stir them often; you don't want the seeds to brown. Put them in a blender or processor container.

2. Pour the chicken broth into the blender. Put the chiles, cilantro, onion, and garlic in the blender and purée until smooth, starting and stopping the blender from time to time, pushing down the ingredients with a rubber spatula.

3. Heat the vegetable oil in a deep pot. Carefully pour the blender contents into the pot (it splatters!), add salt and pepper, reduce the heat, and simmer, stirring, for about 15 minutes. Turn off the heat. Stir in the *crema* and let the sauce sit for about 3 minutes, just for the *crema* to heat through.

For the fish

1 whole Pacific rock cod, sea bass, or similar fish, about 4 pounds, cleaned and scaled
salt and freshly ground black pepper
2 cups fresh herbs: Javier always uses a big handful of mixed fresh herbs he finds in the market to stuff the fish. He admits, however, the mixture is never the same. You may want to try a mixture of thyme, oregano, cilantro, and fresh chives. Save a few sprigs for garnish.
2 limes, cut into wedges
vegetable oil

1. Preheat the oven to 350°F.
2. Season the gutted cavity of the fish. Fill the cavity loosely with a mixture of fresh herbs—do not pack the herbs in tightly. Add 1 sliced lime on top of the herbs.
3. Rub vegetable oil over both sides of the fish and place it in an oiled roasting pan with any remaining herbs underneath the fish. Put the fish on the center shelf of the oven and roast for about 45 minutes. Test to see that it's done by making a small cut in the thickest section. Do not overcook—the fish will continue cooking a bit more when it's removed from the oven because it is still very hot.
4. Take the fish from the oven and place it on a platter or cutting board. Remove the herbs and lime slices from the cavity and discard. Carefully skin the upper side of the fish. The flesh will easily separate from the bone. Cut the top fillet in half and put each piece on a warm serving plate. Turn the fish over and repeat with the other side.
5. Spoon the sauce over the fish and accompaning rice, dividing it equally among the plates. Garnish with fresh herbs and lime wedges.

Rosa (Rosita) Cobián's

Pozole Verde *Hominy and Meat Soup with Green Herbs*

ROSITA LIVES IN OAXACA BUT COLLECTS SOUVENIR RECIPES WHEN TRAVELING. What could be a better memento of her vacation than this *pozole* recipe she hurriedly jotted down while a fonda cook rattled off ingredients and preparation over fifteen years ago in Acapulco? She still has the yellowed, *pozole*-spotted original.

Pozole is everybody's favorite dish, and to make sure they have it at least once a week, Thursday is "*Pozole* Day" in Guerrero. Fondas that don't usually serve it always have *pozole* on Thursday or customers flee! Just like roadside stands for *barbacoa* and *birria* open only on Sundays, similar *posolerías* open Thursdays for green *pozole*. A white version is Mexico's most popular *pozole*; red, colored by de árbol and guajillo chiles, is second; green, colored by herbs and vegetable leaves, is the least common, and strictly a home-style dish not often seen in restaurants, or even fondas. Traditionally the workingman's low-cost dish is made with hominy kernels, a whole pig's head, pig's feet, and soup bones. People enjoy more meat in *pozole* these days so Rosita's version provides more meaty chunks and offers plenty of flavor.

Serve in large deep bowls with crisp *tostadas* (fried, whole corn tortillas to break apart) or corn chips. Rosita says chopped white onion, radish slices, *chicharrones* (deep fried pork skin), lime wedges, and bottled hot sauce are passed at the table.
Yield: 12 servings

When using traditional dried hominy

1 pound dried hominy, field or flint corn
2 Tablespoons powdered, slaked lime (purchase "cal" at a tortillería, or calcium hydroxide powder at a building supply store)

When using reconstituted or canned hominy

4 pounds prepared hominy ("maíz para pozole"), found in refrigerated cases in Latino markets), or 4 one-pound cans hominy, drained and rinsed

1. Rinse the hominy in a colander under running water to remove the chaff.

2. In a large nonreactive pot (one that won't react with acidic ingredients—stainless steel, enameled cast iron lined copper, and nonstick; avoid cast iron and aluminum), bring 2 quarts water to a boil. Sprinkle the slaked lime into the boiling water and dissolve. Add the hominy (remove any floating kernels), reduce the heat, and simmer 15 minutes. Turn off the heat, cover the pot, and let it rest 30 minutes.

3. Dump the kernels into a colander and wash them under running water, rubbing them against one another in your hands. This motion causes the skin to slip off.

4. Remove the tiny hard germ from the base of kernel. This traditional step takes about 30 minutes, but the best *pozole* kernels must open like a flower (or popcorn) when simmered with the meats and chile, and this is guaranteed only if time is taken to follow these time-honored steps precisely.

For the meats and broth

- 2 pounds lean beef chuck or round
- 3 pounds pork leg or butt
- 2 pounds pork shin or shoulder bones
- 2 heads garlic, halved

1. In a very large pot, bring 2 gallons of water to a boil with the meat and garlic. Cook over medium heat, cover askew, for 2 hours, or until the meat is tender.
2. Remove the meat to a platter. When cool enough to handle, shred the cooled meat with the grain, in large pieces. Discard bones, fat, and gristle.
3. Skim fat from the broth's surface.

For the sauce

- ¼ cup vegetable oil
- 8 ounces raw pumpkin seeds, shelled ("pepitas")
- ¼ cup chopped cilantro leaves
- ¼ cup chopped parsley leaves
- ¼ cup chopped "epazote" leaves (if available)
- 10 small Boston lettuce leaves, or 5 large romaine leaves, chopped
- 5 large radish leaves, chopped
- 10 spinach leaves, chopped
- 2 "hoja santa" ("acuyo") leaves, chopped, if available
- 10 serrano chiles, stemmed
- 1 pound tomatillos, papery skins removed, cored, and chopped
- 1 to 1½ cups water
- ¼ cup vegetable oil

1. Heat the oil in a skillet. Add the pumpkin seeds and sauté until they are light brown and popping. Put the pumpkin seeds and oil in a blender or processor and blend. Add the remaining ingredients, except the last ¼ cup vegetable oil, and purée. You may have to do this in two batches.
2. Heat the remaining ¼ cup vegetable oil in a deep pot. Add the blended ingredients carefully (they splatter!). Simmer, stirring with a large wooden spoon, for 30 minutes, uncovered until the sauce becomes thick.
3. Add the meat, hominy, and sauce to the broth. Bring back to a boil, then simmer uncovered, for 15 minutes. Season to taste with salt and pepper.

The Colonial Circle

San Miguel de Allende
Guanajuato

MEXICO'S COLONIAL CIRCLE, roughly the mountainous area between Guadalajara and Mexico City, is blessed with old silver mining cities. Included in the architectually picture-perfect package are: Guanajuato, San Miguel de Allende, Dolores Hidalgo, and Querétaro. Just east of Guadalajara lies the vast Central Plateau, which is one of Mexico's most fertile agricultural valleys and provides Mexico City with produce and dairy products. Here food-processing plants pack the region's famous strawberry preserves, pickled chiles, cactus leaves, and tomatoes, among other seasonal items. Favorite dishes of the Colonial Circle's sophisticated palate include Salsa de Flores de Calabasa con Pollo *(Squash Blossom Sauce with Chicken)* (page 70) *and plump* Chiles Rellenos *(Cheese-Stuffed Poblano Chiles, Battered and Fried)* (page 77).

Left: A street scene in colonial San Miguel de Allende.

◆ San Miguel de Allende ◆

Strawberries and cream vendors are familiar spring sights.

A RAVISHING TOWN, SAN MIGUEL DE ALLENDE is designated a national historic monument by the Mexican government, which means it must maintain its colonial atmosphere by conforming to strict building codes. Discovered long ago by international tourists, the small hilly city has some of the finest hotels and restaurants in the country, with prices to match. A colony of retired U.S. citizens keeps growing due to San Miguel's classic beauty, cultural activities, and lovely year-round weather. If you plan to visit Mexico for the first time and want to avoid the beach resorts, San Miguel de Allende is perfect. There are plenty of English-speaking people, including the hundreds taking Spanish classes at the half-dozen schools and with additional private tutors. U.S. citizens swarm the Instituto de Allende and Belles Artes buildings taking painting, sculpture, photography, weaving, writing, crafts, dance, music, and more Spanish classes. The library is a central meeting place for North Americans because it has an enormous selection of books in English, sponsors fund-raising home tours every Sunday at 11 A.M. (an easy way to meet people), and publishes *Atención*, a weekly English newspaper which lists activities and tours, runs restaurant ads with addresses and hours, and has a classified page with furnished apartment and house rentals.

If your plans call for at least a month in town, consider staying in an apartment with your own kitchen. The markets are exciting to roam, and become even more intriguing if you can buy things. Sure, a perfect mango can be eaten on a hotel bed, but cooking a traditional dish with the proper chiles, wild herbs bought from Indian women, and a Mexican cut of meat is an experience that makes you feel as if you're living there. Two covered markets, one on the east side and one on the west, a sprawling Tuesday open-air market on the western end, two supermarkets on the *jardín* (town square), a modern Gigante supermarket on the far eastern end, and neighborhood food stores all around town make shopping in San Miguel de Allende a cinch.

✷ MARKETS ✷

Tuesday Open-Air Market Take Canal Street and go west, passing under the Canal bridge, and turn right at the second street (or just follow the crowds). The open-air market meanders through the cobblestoned streets ahead of you and surrounds the Mercado de San Juan de Dios indoor market and its fondas. Walking can be a bit treacherous on the cobblestones, especially if they're wet, so wear the right shoes. It's a country fair swap meet with everything from leaf-wrapped, handmade cheeses to tables of underwear.

Mercado Ignacio Ramírez El Nigromante The most central of markets, Ignacio Ramírez "El Nigromante" is small and easy to roam in less than an hour, including the interesting outdoor patio Indian market. It's located on Colegio, just north of Mesones, and is open every day from 7 A.M. to 8 P.M. Here, women in shawls and braids sell herbs, fruits, and vegetables they grow at home. Some sell handmade tortillas and *gorditas*. Weekends are busiest when the patio takes on a swap-meet appearance. Indoors, the center flower aisle is a great place to linger.

Fondas. The combination of *tortas* (sandwiches) and blended fruit drinks are found at four or five fondas. *Tortas* are fresh, filling, and cheap but keep away from the lettuce. Try a blended juice combo: orange, mango, papaya, and lime. **Los Farolitos**, across from the *birrería*, is good, so are the ones named **Tortas 83**, and **Local 122**.
Chicken Pollería El Gallo de Oro, stall No. 18, in back, all the way to the right before stepping into the fonda area. The best, freshest, raw chickens in town.

Mercado de San Juan de Dios Mercado de San Juan de Dios, located on the corner of San Antonio and San Rafael, near the San Juan de Dios church, is surrounded by the Tuesday open-air market, and is open 7 A.M. to 8 P.M. every day.

Carnitas. At fonda **Don Toño**, try the chopped *carnitas* piled in a French roll. This delicious and simple pork sandwich is great to wrap up and take on a picnic. It brings back memories of the day Morris and I went with Michigan friends Barbara Essick and Chic Mendez to historical Pozos, now an intriguing ghost town but at one time a hacienda-filled silver-mining town. It's home to a music museum and workshop for ancient musical instruments. Our brown-bagged lunch on the town square couldn't have been more delectable.

Quesadillas. At the fonda right next to Carnitas Don Toño, tortillas are made to order for quesadillas filled with mushrooms, *rajas*, *picadillo*, potato and onions, brains, or shredded beef.

* PLACES TO GO AND THINGS TO EAT *

Huaraches. From a stand in front of the market on Colegio, after 7 P.M. Handmade tortillas are called *huaraches* (sandals), because their long oval shape, thickness, and chewiness is like a sandal sole. They are topped with refried beans, spicy de árbol chile sauce, shredded cabbage, and cooked cactus leaves. Sit at the picnic table and enjoy a delightful, nongringo experience.

Gorditas. Under the bridge on Canal just west of Bellas Artes you'll find women selling melted cheese and mild guajillo chile-stuffed, Celaya-style *gorditas* (small, very thick tortillas), made with *maize martajado* (fresh, chewy, coarsely-crushed corn *nixtamal*). Simply sensational.

Gordita vendors waiting for customers under the Canal Street bridge.

Tamales. Street vendors are called *tamaleros(as)* and their large steamer pots are called *tamalerías.* Look for one on the corner of Mesones and Calsada de la Presa, in front of the bakery, in the morning and at night. There's another at night, after 8 P.M., on the plaza in front of Church of La Salud, off Mesones. They also sell *atole (masa* gruel*)*, for the classic, pre-Columbian combo, *tamales y atole.*

Cheese. Remo's has very clean, refrigerated cases on Codos near Zacateros and Ancha de San Antonio, tel. 2-60-780. The freshest and sweetest *Crema* (page 80) and ranchero cheese in San Miguel de Allende is here because Remo's has its own dairy and factory just east of town. If you're dying for Parmigiano-Reggiano, Gorgonzola, or Gouda, this is the place, but prices are steep for imported foods.

Basically, beware of all cheese sold in open-air and indoor markets that are not refrigerated, or buy only early in the morning while temperatures are still cool. Even Mexicans get sick from poorly handled cheeses.

Chicken. Pollería Insurgentes, Insurgentes No. 132, tel. 2-23-42, specializes in fresh and rotisseried chickens. At the intersection of Mesones and Juárez, on the north side, are two or three places that have rotisseried chickens. One block east on Colegio, a few doors down from Don Toño, is a very good place without a name.

Butchers. **Los Filetes**, Insugentes next to Pollería Insugentes. Known for quality among local good cooks.

Los Toritos, at booth No. 13 in Mercado Ignacio Ramírez, carries U.S. cuts of beef for steaks (cut across the grain). The stall has a reputation for overcharging, so watch the scale after asking the price.

Carnitas. **Apolo XI**, Mesones No. 43. A crisp-cooked pork counter is in the entrance area (admire the surprisingly ornate tile work), with plenty of tables in the skylit back room.

Don Toño, at Colegio No. 13. The original large version (a spin-off fonda is in the San José del Dios market). Plenty of tables available.

La Cruz del Perdón, at the road to Taboada Hot Springs, five miles north of town on the road to Dolores Hidalgo. Weekends only. This countryside spot is popular; by 3 P.M. they're out of *carnitas.*

Bread. Who knows why all the *bolillos* in Guanajuato are browned and crisp on the outside and yeasty and chewy on the inside, while the same French rolls in San Miguel de Allende are pale, soft, and uninteresting? Luckily, there's **La Colmena Panadería**, at Reloj No. 21, just north of the *jardín* (town square). The French bread loaves are also very good. You'll find the best *pan dulce* (sweet rolls) in town here. Selections change somewhat every day.

Wines and liquors. **La Europea**, Canal #13 (a half block off the *jardín*), tel. 2-20-03. La Europea offers the best selection of imported and domestic wines, liquors, and champagnes in town. Prices are very fair at this Mexico City chain. You'll see excellent Rioja wines from Spain.

Pulque. On Canal. Go under the bridge by the Belles Artes building (where the *gordita* sellers sit) and keep walking for about a quarter mile. You'll see the big letters "Pulquería" on the left. As in almost all *pulque* bars, the archaic macho rule applies: no women allowed. Give a male friend a container and have him get it filled. Or go during the day when no one's around except a female bartender (no comment). A word of caution: Don't shake the container. One evening, after extolling the virtues of *pulque* to friends, I decided to turn the bottle over just to mix. Fermented brew bubbled up inside and the huge glass jar looked like a time bomb ready to explode. When I unscrewed the lid, it did. Our kitchen smelled just like a *pulquería.*

Coffee. Nescafé ruined good coffee in Mexico. Years ago Mexicans were led to believe that the "new and incredibly chic" instant coffee was superior to their traditional brew. In almost every restaurant in San Miguel de Allende, there it is—the ubiquitous jar graciously placed upon layers of tablecloths, next to your cup of hot water. Thank goodness times are changing and there are now **Cappuccinos** at two locations: San Francisco No. 1 (just east of the *jardín*), and Ancha de San Antonio No. 6 (in the block with Instituto Allende). While waiting for your cup of freshly brewed espresso or cappuccino you can decide on the bean blend you want to have ground to take home.

Aguas frescas. Refreshing drinks are made with purified water (and ice) at **La Gardenia Repostería**, on the east side of the *jardín* smack in the center of the block where souvenir shops and street food vendors rule. The classics: tamarind, sweet rice, and hibiscus are usually available.

Cajeta. *Cajeta*, a specialty of the nearby city of Celaya is caramel sauce made from goat's milk, and found in traditional small wooden boxes or contemporary jars all over Mexico. The favorite use in San Miguel de Allende's restaurants is in hot crêpes, folded and sprinkled with toasted pecans. As a snack, it's eaten straight from the box with a spoon.

Linens. La Alfonsina, Hidalgo No. 36, tels. 2-14-29 and 2-15-72. Closed during lunch. Hand embroidery on hand-woven cloth. Tablecloths, napkins, placemats, cocktail and hostess napkins. Lace and handwoven fabrics are sold by the meter.

Pottery. It's best to take a tour of nearby **Dolores Hidalgo's Talavera showrooms** if you see a tour offered. You'll go into different Talavera factories, see artisans at work, and be more than pleased at the outstanding selections and prices.

Cooking classes. Reyna Polanco Abrahams, Calle Cri Cri, Nop. 25 in Colonia Guadaloupe. Reyna's Friday noon Mexican cooking class (in English) is always a hit with locals and tourists alike. Call her at 2-11-02 to find out what she's preparing, and to reserve a seat in her open-kitchen home classroom.

RESTAURANTS

Bugambilia. Moderate. Hidalgo No. 42, tel. 2-01-27, Hours: open every day noon to 11 P.M. Evenings are special at Bugambilia, when a guartarist plays and candlelight glows in the colonial building's plant-filled courtyard. Traditional dishes of Puebla are superb and hard to find elsewhere in this trendy town. Definitely try the specialty, *Chiles en Nogada* (page 67). *Tinga* is shredded pork loin with chorizo and potatoes in a tomato, onion, and chipotle chile sauce. *Pollo en pulque* is a dish made by stewing chicken in *pulque.*

Hotel Villa Santa Monica. Moderate. Baeza 22, tel. 2-04-27. Hours: The dining room is open all day, every day. Go on a chilly evening for a drink in front of the stone fireplace while snuggled in a cushy sofa. Walk through surprisingly fetching Juárez Park to the far corner and you'll see a small, pink, gem of a hotel, once a silver baron's hacienda. In fact, Juárez Park was once the entrance grounds (he liked to impress guests with this grand entranceway). The baron's clay riding paths are still maintained (joggers take note: these paths are heavensent in a town of cobblestone streets and unstable sidewalks full of what I call "gringo traps"). This charming hacienda then became the residence of notorious José Mogica, a famous gay Mexican singer and film star of the thirties who later fled the country and became a monk in Peru. Later, an American turned it into a hotel and it's a perfect setting for a quiet lunch. Something simple such as tortilla soup and quesadillas or a salad is the best choice.

El Correo. Inexpensive. Correo No. 23, tel. 2-01-51. Hours: Thursday to Tuesday 9 A.M. to 9 P.M. Breakfast, lunch, or dinner right across from the post office. Mexican and North American dishes at reasonable prices. Go ahead and have a salad; everything is washed in purified water. Try the apple fritters or *migas*, a homey scrambled egg and tortilla dish with onion, tomato, and a hint of chile. Their tortilla soup is one of the best in town, with chopped raw onion, fresh *crema,* and chipotle chiles en adobo served alongside. Good rich coffee.

El Mesón de San José. Moderate. Mesones No. 38, tel. 2-38-48. Hours: 8 A.M. to 9 P.M. Dine in a shaded courtyard surrounded by tasteful boutiques. There is live music in the evenings. All salads at El Mesón de San José are carefully washed in purified water, and the large selection is very welcome when you're craving greens in Mexico. Traditional Mexican soups are great, sandwiches big enough for two (because there are two, but you have to see this for yourself), and the homemade bread is reason enough for going in the first place. Try your hardest to leave room for Angelika Merkel's substantial Baked Corn Flan (page 74).

Dolores Hidalgo A town full of Mexican independence history, Dolores Hidalgo is a one-hour drive north of San Miguel de Allende through beautiful rolling hills dotted with natural spas. Dolores Hidalgo is known for its Talavera tiles and pottery, and you'll spot plentiful shops and ceramic studios on the way into town. After shopping for gorgeous serving platters and spectacular pitchers, and roaming through the Parroquía church and colonial public buildings, head for the opposite side of the *zócalo.* Carts on a far corner boast some of the most delicious, and different, ice creams and ices in the world. Emiliano Aguilar's sign lists such exotica as *mole, pulque,* alfalfa, *zapote negro,* cactus paddles with shrimp, *pescado* (red snapper, I swear), cheese, and the clincher: *chicharrón.* Bizarre, to be sure, but samples are generously handed out and before you know it you'll be graduating from strawberry, melon, vanilla special (with nuts and prunes), chocolate, coconut, lemon, pineapple, mango, papaya, and banana to the big kid's list.

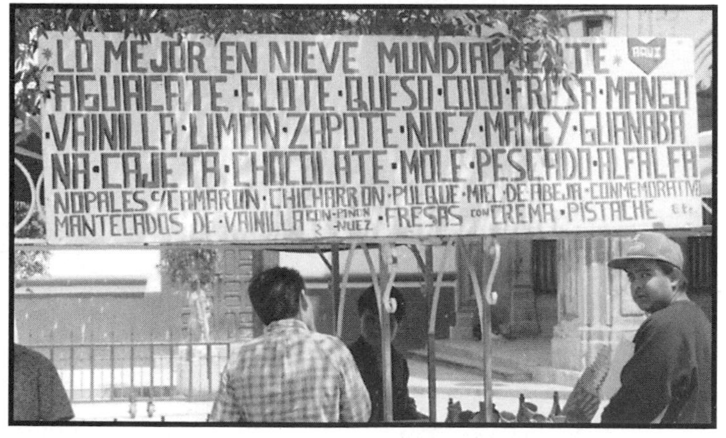

Emiliano Aguilar's exotic flavor ice cream stand in Dolores Hidalgo.

Reyna Polanco Abrahams's

▲▼▲

Sopa Azteca *Tortilla Soup with Avocado, Chile, Cheese, and Chicken*

TORTILLA SOUP, ALSO KNOWN AS *SOPA AZTECA*, IS THE CLASSIC CHICKEN SOUP found on almost every restaurant and fonda menu in Mexico. Reyna insists on starting with good Chicken Broth (page 19). Crisp, freshly fried tortilla strips, plus slices of toasted mild guajillo chile (or other dried chile depending on the region of Mexico) are imperative to this dish. Tortilla strips add flavor, but mostly they add texture. When added to the broth they keep their crunch for a few minutes, then become chewy and take on a meatlike consistency. If you're a slow eater, the strips dissolve and soften, making the broth thicker. Dried, toasted chiles are always the flavor big-hitters in tortilla soup. Add more or less depending upon your taste, but adding at least one is essential. Guajillo chile is the most commonly used chile for this soup throughout the country, but also-mild ancho chile generally prevails in Michoacán's tortilla soups; rare, smoky, Oaxacan pasilla chile adds a completely different flavor in that state; and hotter chipotle chile adds a spicy-smoky punch in Veracruz.

What makes tortilla soup special are garnishes sprinkled in and served alongside: Pieces of cooked chicken create a full meal; cubes of fresh cheese add protein and a nice texture before melting; avocado cubes are smooth and buttery; *crema* adds richness plus cuts spiciness (tortilla soup becomes a cream soup if enough is stirred in); and chopped fresh cilantro or flat-leaf parsley contribute a fresh zing. All add a personal touch. Fresh lime juice squeezed over everything is a must and completes the dish.

Yield: 4 as a full meal, or 8 as a first course

For the soup

- 3 garlic cloves
- ½ onion, peeled and cut into large chunks
- 3 ripe tomatoes
- 8 cups Chicken Broth (page 19)
- 1 Tablespoon vegetable oil
- 2 small sprigs "epazote," if available
- salt
- freshly ground black pepper

1. Toast (page 16) the garlic, onion, and tomatoes. Put the tomatoes in a plastic bag to "sweat" a few minutes, then peel and core. Put them in a blender container and purée with the garlic and onion, adding ¼ cup of the broth.

2. Heat the vegetable oil in a deep pot over high heat. Carefully (it splatters!) add the blender contents and fry the tomato purée for 2 minutes. Lower the heat and simmer, stirring, for another 5 minutes, or until the purée thickens and changes color.

3. Add the remaining chicken broth and *epazote*. Return the liquid to a boil, then lower the heat and simmer, covered, for 15 minutes. Add salt and pepper to taste.

For the chiles

4 guajillo or ancho chiles, or 2 spicier chipotle chiles
3 Tablespoons vegetable oil

For the tortillas

8 to 10 stale, day-old corn tortillas
2 cups oil for frying the tortillas

For the garnish

fried chile strips
2 cups (about ½ pound) "quesillo de Oaxaca," Monterey Jack cheese, or mozzarella cut into ½-inch cubes
1 (or 2 depending on size) avocado, diced or sliced (Reyna's hint: "Avocados may be cut ahead and wrapped in aluminum foil—the aluminum keeps them from turning black.")
½ cup "Crema" (page 80), crème fraîche, or sour cream, plus additional if desired
2 cups shredded cooked chicken, for a full meal (optional)
fried tortilla strips
¼ cup chopped cilantro or flat-leaf parsley leaves
3 limes, halved or quartered

4. Cut the chile stems and a bit of the hard area just under them off, and discard. Discard the seeds. Slice the chiles into ⅛-inch rings from the top (stem area) to the pointed bottom with a sharp knife, or I've found scissors work great.

5. Heat the oil in a large skillet over medium-high heat and add the sliced chiles. Cook, stirring for 30 seconds. Reyna says, "when you start to cough they're done." Remove the chile from the oil with a slotted spoon and drain on absorbent paper.

6. Stack the tortillas and cut in half with a large knife. Cut each pile into ¼-inch strips.

7. Heat the oil in the cleaned skillet and fry the tortilla strips until they are golden brown. Remove from the oil with a slotted spoon and drain on absorbent paper.

8. Five minutes before serving, reheat the broth.

9. Ladle broth into each bowl, add a few chile strips, cheese cubes, avocado, and a rounded tablespoon of *crema* to each bowl (and pieces of cooked chicken if you want). Top with a handful of the fried tortilla strips and sprinkle with chopped cilantro or flat leaf parsley. Pass separate bowls of lime wedges, additional *crema,* and additional chile strips.

Variation: Sopa Tarasca, from Michoacán, is similar but has more tomato purée plus cream. It's like a Mexican cream-of-tomato soup. Another delicious variation incorporates puréed pink beans with the creamy tomato soup.

Variation: The Yucatán's famous *Sopa de Lima* is basically tortilla soup cooked with a piece of habanero chile and a generous squirt of the peninsula's sour lime.

Graciela's

Arroz Mexicano

Mexican Rice Pilaf with Sautéed Onion, Chile, and Broth

EXCEPT ALONG THE EASTERN COAST OF MEXICO, WHERE STEAMED WHITE RICE IS PREFERRED, pilaf-style rice dishes—whether made with olive oil, vegetable oil, lard, or butter, or with onion, garlic, chiles, tomatoes, or herbs—are all flavored with broths. When Mexicans don't have homemade chicken broth (French reduced stock is much richer) they use Knorr chicken bouillon powder, made by the Swiss company (there's a jar in every kitchen). Mexicans hardly ever use canned broths. The Knorr product may seem pedestrian to some of you, but it's a popular taste and enjoyed country-wide. Many people cook with it rather than with salt.

On Tuesdays, San Miguel de Allende's open-air market, surrounding the Mercado de San Juan de Dios building, next to San Juan de Dios church, is definitely the place to be. On other days the neighborhood indoor market is a fun shopping spot in a non-touristy area of town. Fondas, like the one where Graciela works, serve chicken dishes smothered in sauces and served with a rice that seems to be the preferred local version. It's simple and tasty thanks to a kick from fresh chiles. Sit down at an appealing counter (notice no other gringos in the house) and ask what's cooking today. You won't be disappointed if you ask the price first, as do all Mexicans.

Yield: 4 servings

1½ Tablespoons vegetable oil
1 small white onion, finely chopped
1 garlic clove, minced
1 cup long-grain white rice
1 whole jalapeño chile washed, stemmed, and slit down the length, leaving the seeds intact
2 cups Chicken Broth (page 19), or 2 teaspoons Knorr powdered chicken bouillon dissolved in 2 cups simmering water
1 sprig "epazote," if available

1. Heat the oil in a saucepan over medium heat. Add the onion and garlic and cook until the vegetables are transparent. Add the rice and stir until the rice and vegetables are light brown.

2. Add the chile to the rice, stirring for 30 seconds.

3. Add the broth and optional *epazote*. Reduce the heat, cover, and simmer for 25 minutes. Remove the pot from the heat and leave the cover on for an additional 10 minutes to let the rice absorb all the moisture. Fluff the rice with a fork so all the grains are separate. Remove the chile before serving.

Mercedes Arteaga Tovar's

Chiles en Nogada I

Stuffed Chiles with Walnut Sauce, San Miguel de Allende Style

THE COLONIAL BUILDING THAT HOUSES THE RESTAURANT BUGAMBILIA encircles a gorgeous but unpretentious patio lit with flickering candlelight in the evenings, when a classical guitarist turns the setting magical. All this and affordable, fabulous food. No wonder snagging executive chef-owner Mercedes Arteaga Tovar's recipe for *chiles en nogada* was a priority during my month's stay in the hill town. Too often grease levels are unbearable from deep-fried battered chiles that haven't been drained. These non-greasy gems are simply fabulous. The old San Miguel de Allende family's recipes are rarely given out, and I won mine through perseverance. I scheduled countless appointments with Señora Tovar, only to have her postpone them at the last moment. Finally I was told the recipe was ready. Expecting to pick up a piece of paper on the way back from a trip to Querétero, I asked Morris to wait in the car. It's a good thing I married a patient man. Señora Tovar recited from memory her *Chiles en Nogada* (also see page 162) recipe of fresh green poblano chiles stuffed with *picadillo* (a lucious mixture including beef, nuts, candied fruit, and *canela*), covered with walnut cream sauce, then sprinkled with red pomegranate seeds.
Yield: 12 servings

For the chiles

12 plump, fresh poblano chiles
1 cup vegetable oil

1. Clean the chiles with a damp towel and dry.
2. Heat the oil in a wide pot and fry the chiles in two batches until their skins turn white and blister. Drain the chiles and put them in a plastic bag, closed, for 5 minutes to "sweat" and loosen their skins.
3. Cool and carefully peel the chiles. Cut a slit down the side of each, vertically, from the stem end almost to the pointed end. Remove all the seeds and any large veins, leaving the stem attached.
(Continued)

For the optional marinade

- 6 cups water
- 1 cup white vinegar
- 2 Tablespoons salt
- 1 garlic head (at least 12 unpeeled cloves, separated)
- 1 onion
- 12 bay leaves
- 6 black peppercorns
- ½ teaspoon dried thyme leaves, or 1 large fresh sprig
- ½ teaspoon dried Mexican oregano leaves, or 1 large fresh sprig

You may prepare the chiles ahead: Put the used chile frying oil and these ingredients in a large glass jar to soak until you are ready to use, up to one week in advance. Remove from the liquid and dry each chile before filling.

For the picadillo stuffing

- ¼ cup vegetable oil
- 1 medium white onion, peeled and minced
- 4 garlic cloves, peeled and minced
- 2 pounds lean beef chuck, ground or finely chopped
- 2 pounds tomatoes (about 6), boiled for 5 minutes, peeled, puréed, and strained
- 1 teaspoon salt, or to taste
- ½ teaspoon freshly ground pepper
- ½ cup almonds, blanched and sliced vertically into slivers
- ½ cup chopped walnuts
- ½ cup raisins
- ½ cup candied fruit, candied barrel cactus if available, chopped (not citrus). Dried papaya or mango spears found in health food stores work wonderfully
- 1 four-inch canela stick, or two-inch cinnamon stick
- 6 bay leaves
- 1 large fresh thyme sprig, or ½ teaspoon dried thyme

1. Heat the oil in a heavy skillet. Add the onion and garlic and brown lightly. Add the beef and cook over medium heat, stirring and breaking up any lumps, until it is well done.

2. Stir in the tomato purée. Season with salt and pepper to taste.

3. Add the nuts, raisins, candied fruit, *canela*, and herbs. Reduce the heat to a strong simmer, stirring occasionally, for 30 minutes. Remove the *canela* stick and bay leaves. The *picadillo* may be cooled and refrigerated at this point up to 48 hours.

For the walnut sauce

- 1 cup very finely chopped walnuts, not a paste, the nuts must have some texture
- 2 cups "Crema" (page 80), crème fraîche, or sour cream
- 1 Tablespoon Worcestershire sauce
- 1 teaspoon Maggi seasoning sauce (a U.S. gravy-flavoring product popular in Mexico)
- 2 garlic cloves, peeled and finely chopped
- ¼ teaspoon freshly ground pepper
- ½ teaspoon salt, or to taste

Mix all the ingredients together with a wooden spoon in a large ceramic or glass bowl until they are well blended. The sauce may be prepared up to 24 hours in advance and refrigerated.

For the garnish

- 1 small head iceberg lettuce, finely shredded
- 12 red radishes, thinly sliced
- 1 fresh pomegranate, peeled and seeded (reserve the seeds)
- ½ cup coarsely chopped walnuts

1. Reheat the beef mixture if necessary.

2. Dry the chiles. When the beef mixture is hot, fill the chiles.

3. Place the shredded lettuce on a serving platter. Decorate with radish slices. Place the filled chiles in the center, on top of the lettuce and radishes. Just before serving, at the last possible moment, cover the chiles with walnut sauce (if you do this step too far ahead, the sauce will liquefy on the hot chiles). Sprinkle with pomegranate seeds and chopped walnuts and serve at once. The chiles may also be served at room temperature for a spectacular buffet dish.

Note: Pomegranate red skin is peeled away to reveal a pale yellow soft pith, which holds the edible seeds. To peel, cut a one-inch vertical slit into the red skin. Break the fruit in half and separate the seeds from the yellow pith. Put the ruby-red seeds in a bowl and discard the pith and skin. The tart seeds are sweeter than cranberries, and have a definite crunch to their bite. Beware: The red seeds stain like crazy.

Reyna Polanco Abrahams's

Salsa de Flores de Calabaza con Pollo

Squash Blossom Sauce with Chicken

REYNA POLANCO ABRAHAMS IS SAN MIGUEL DE ALLENDE'S premier cooking teacher. Her bubbly personality (she's Veracruzana; Mexicans tell me that says it all) and knowledge of traditional Mexican dishes are what keep her students coming back. Along with this recipe, one group learned that Reyna's true love, next to her husband and cooking, is flamenco dancing. Olé.

Reyna says squash blossom sauce develops more flavor when prepared a day or two in advance. It's classically poured over hot, boiled chicken parts, allowing the sauce to cook a bit more while it penetrates the hot poultry flesh. Its intense, golden color is brilliant when presented on a brightly colored platter. Try to get pumpkin flowers and not the greenish-orange zucchini blossoms, which make a less colorful sauce. Garnish with a whole blossom and serve with rice and plenty of tortillas. It's not traditional, but I love serving this sauce with bright yellow Yucatán Rice (page 307).

Speaking of yellow, Mexicans like their chickens and eggs a rich golden color, and to achieve this chickens are systematically fed marigold flowers. When you drive through beautiful farmland country east of Morelia, on the way to Mexico City, and as you pass field after field of bright orange flowers, think not of bouquets but of Reyna's Squash Blossom Sauce. Lamenting colorless U.S. chickens, Reyna jokes, "Chickens in the U.S. are white because they're gringas."

Yield: 4 servings

Reyna Polanco Abrahams in one of her popular Friday noon cooking classes.

- 1 pound pumpkin blossoms (about 25)
- 2 Tablespoons vegetable oil
- 1 medium white onion, finely chopped
- 4 garlic cloves, peeled and finely chopped
- 1 cup Chicken Broth (page 19), or 1 teaspoon Knorr chicken bouillon dissolved in 1 cup hot water
- 1 cup "Crema" (page 80), crème fraîche, or sour cream
- ½ teaspoon freshly ground white pepper, or to taste
- salt to taste (none if using Knorr bouillon)

1. Wash and drain the blossoms. Remove the stems and the small, spiky, cuplike section that connects the stem and the blossom, and discard. Set aside.

2. Heat the oil in a deep skillet. Sauté the onion and garlic until lightly brown. Add the chicken broth and cook over medium heat for 2 minutes. Remove the pan from the stove and cool for 3 minutes, so the *crema* won't curdle as you add it to the hot ingredients. Add the *crema.*

3. Put a handful of the whole blossoms in a blender container with ½ cup *crema* liquid and purée. Add another handful of blossoms and add ¼ cup water slowly, stopping the blender, pushing down on the ingredients, and blending again. Repeat, adding additional water as needed, until all the blossoms are puréed. Add the purée to the cream sauce. Add white pepper and salt.

The chicken

- 1 chicken, 4 pounds, cut into pieces
- 1 Tablespoon Knorr chicken bouillon

4. In a large pot (with cover) place chicken parts and water to cover. Add the bouillon and stir. Bring the water to a boil. Reduce the heat and simmer the chicken for 40 minutes with the cover slightly askew, or until no red shows when you cut a slit in a thigh section.

5. Remove the chicken from the pot with a slotted spoon to drain off any water. Remove the skin. Add the chicken to the sauce and simmer 5 minutes longer.

Note: Small broiler-fryer chickens take less well to boiling than do Mexican chickens. Try grilling, broiling, or baking a small chicken, then spooning sauce onto plates and placing a crisp piece of chicken on top of the sauce.

Salsa de Flores de Calabaza is the highlight of numerous regional vegetarian dishes when made with vegetable broth.

Josefina Murillo and Christina Hernández's

Mole de Almendras *Red Chile Sauce with Almonds*

CHRISTINA IS A LANGUAGE TEACHER AT CENTRO MEXICANO DE LENGUA Y CULTURA de San Miguel de Allende. It was there she introduced me to her mother, a fabulous cook who was once a private chef to wealthy families in town. Señora Murillo guided her daughters in the kitchen, and now Christina is as accomplished a cook as she is a language teacher, thanks to her mother's devotion to regional cooking and her extensive recipe collection.

Their delicious recipe for *mole de almendras* is made with both fresh poblano chile and its dried version, the ancho chile, which is unusual. Throughout Mexico fresh and dried chiles are used separately, seldom together. In those few instances where they are, like this, the fresh and dried versions of the same chile are used. Señora Murillo suggests slicing a baked pork roast or large chicken and spooning the sauce over (the aroma is intoxicating). Serve with Mexican Rice Pilaf (page 66) and a crunchy salad. The sauce can be made up to a week ahead and kept refrigerated, to be reheated at serving time. It freezes indefinitely.
Yield: 8 servings

- 4 poblano chiles
- 4 ancho chiles, stemmed and seeded
- 2 Tablespoons vegetable oil
- ½ pound almonds, blanched and skins removed
- 4 whole cloves
- 4 black peppercorns
- ¼ teaspoon freshly ground black pepper
- 2 bay leaves
- 1 medium onion, chopped
- ½ teaspoon cumin seeds
- 3 cups water
- 3 Tablespoons lard, or vegetable oil

1. Toast (page 16) the poblano chiles. Put them in a plastic bag to "sweat" for a few minutes to loosen their skins. Peel, seed, and stem.

2. Stem and seed the ancho chiles. Soak for at least 20 minutes in hot water until soft.

3. Heat the 2 tablespoons of oil in a skillet, add the almonds, cloves, peppercorns, pepper, bay leaves, onion, and cumin and cook for about 5 minutes, until the color changes and the perfume from the spices is released. The onion and almonds should be golden. Put in a blender container and blend.

4. Add the poblano and ancho chiles and 2 cups water to the blender and purée. Then purée again adding ¼ cup water. Stir down and purée again, adding another ¼ cup water. Continue until all 3 cups of water are incorporated and the ingredients are finely textured. (There will be some texture from the almonds; this is not a completely smooth sauce.)

5. Heat the 3 tablespoons of oil in a deep pot. Pour the blender contents into the hot fat (it splatters!) and cook 1 minute, then reduce the heat and simmer, cover askew, for 1 hour.

Reyna Polanco Abrahams's and Ana Patricia Ruiz's

▲▼▲

Aguas Frescas *Violet Bougainvillea Drink or Ruby Red Hibiscus Drink*

AGUA FRESCA, OR FRESH WATER, IS THE NAME FOR MEXICO'S FLAVORED WATER DRINKS. If you have access to bougainvillea flowers, unusual *agua de buganvilia*, is sunshine in a glass. The color is positively neon and the taste refreshingly delicate. The only drawback, Reyna says, is that the drink can be made with only one color bougainvillea. Look for fluorescent purple *Bougainvillaea brasiliensis*. It covers garages and backyard fences all over the Southwest. Red and magenta bougainvillea flowers, such as Barbara Karst and James Walker varieties, as well as orange and pink versions just don't have enough color electricity to make the drink so visually exciting.

Ana's recipe for *agua de jamaica* is brewed from dried hibiscus-family flower-coverings, found in Latino markets. The flowers impart a sour taste and make a tart, refreshing drink not unlike cranberry juice cocktail (*jamaica* is an ingredient of Red Zinger tea). In many Mexican markets the popular garnet-colored liquid is served from huge, clear glass jars to show off its brilliance, as at Ana's fonda.

An unbeatable combination for mild party drinks is a clear glass pitcher each of violet *agua de buganvilia*; ruby *agua de jamiaca;* and chartreuse *Agua de Limón* (page 267) prepared with alcohol. Mix one bottle white wine to 2 quarts *agua fresca*. For a stronger *Refresca de tequila* pour any *agua fresca* into a clear glass with ice cubes. Add one jigger clear (not gold) 100 percent agave tequila to each glass and stir.

Yield: 2 quarts

- 2 quarts water
- 6 cups lightly packed, washed bougainvillea flowers (the purple part, not the tiny, white true flowers) or 2 cups dried "jamaica" flowers
- ½ to ¾ cup sugar, or to taste
- 3 limes (with bright green skins), cut into round slices, as garnish for the glass rims

1. Bring the water to a boil in a large pot. Add the flowers, reduce the heat and simmer, with the cover slightly askew, for 15 minutes.

2. Remove from heat. Cool for 15 minutes. Strain the bougainvillea flower liquid, pressing down on the flowers, into a pitcher or bowl. Or, strain *jamaica* liquid through a sieve lined with cheesecloth or a coffee filter to trap any possible sediment. While still warm, add the sugar and stir to dissolve. Refrigerate.

3. Serve in tall, clear glasses to flaunt the vibrant color, and put a slice of bright green lime on each glass rim. To turn into a party drink, go for color overkill and add a bright plastic straw.

Angelika Merkel's

Flan de Elote *Baked Corn Flan with Corn Kernel Texture*

ANGELIKA MERKEL'S COMBINATION MEXICAN-GERMAN MENU at El Mesón de San José is a joy, *i.e.*, potato pancakes with applesauce as a starter, then on to a big bowl of traditional Mexican soup. *Flan de elote* is a grand Indian-Spanish recipe, a European baked custard, with New World corn flavor and texture. It's best a day or two after it's made, served cold. *Yield: 12 servings*

- 12 large eggs
- 2 fourteen-ounce cans sweetened, condensed milk
- 3 cups milk (approximately)
- 1 Tablespoon vanilla extract
- 1 teaspoon ground cinnamon
- 2 cups fresh, tender corn kernels, or 2 cups frozen

1. Put the eggs and condensed milk in a large measuring bowl. Add enough milk (about 3 cups) to total 2 quarts. Add the vanilla and cinnamon. Pour into a blender container, in batches, and blend until foamy. Remove to a large bowl.

2. Put the corn kernels in the blender and blend just enough to break them up, keeping some texture. Mix into the egg mixture.

Caramelizing the baking pan

- 1½ cups sugar
- 9 Tablespoons water
- a round baking dish, 12 inches across and 2 inches deep

1. Put the sugar in a heavy-bottomed pot with a lid. Add the water and swirl the pan, by its handle (do not stir with a spoon) over medium-high heat until the syrup comes to a boil and turns clear.

2. Cover the pot and raise the heat for about 6 minutes, or until the sugar is caramel brown. Immediately pour the caramel into the baking dish. Swirl the syrup around quickly to cover the entire bottom of the dish.

3. Pour the egg and corn mixture over the caramel.

4. Preheat the oven to 325° F. Make a *bain marie* (water bath) by placing the baking dish in a larger baking pan. Pour boiling water into the larger pan, about 1 inch up the sides of the flan dish.

5. Place the *bain marie* in the center of your oven and bake for 1 to 2 hours. When the top becomes medium brown, put a toothpick in the flan. If it comes out clean, the flan is done. If there are bits of flan adhering, continue baking. Cool to room temperature, then refrigerate before serving. To serve, cut a wedge (like a pie) and spoon some of the caramel sauce over.

◆ Guanajuato ◆

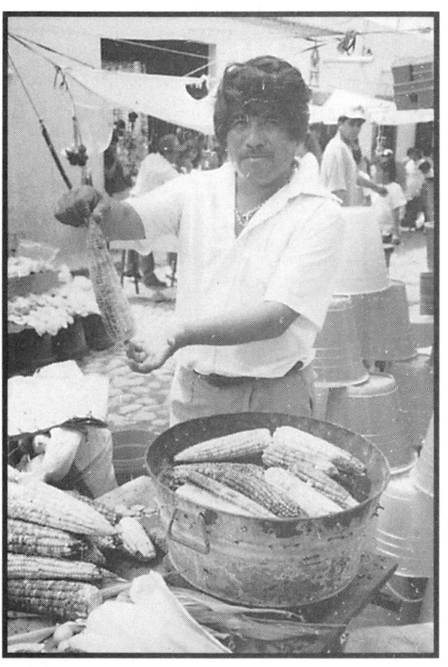

Grilled market corn rubbed with lime and chile powder.

GUANAJUATO, WITH ITS STEEP, WINDING, NARROW, cobblestoned streets; beautiful colonial architecture; and plaza upon plaza in the city center, could easily be mistaken for a European hilltop village. Guanajuato's immediate impact is stunning—exactly what money from one-time rich silver mines could do for a city. For almost two centuries after 1559, thirty-five percent of all the world's silver was mined here. One ride through a maze of underground tunnels and you know this is no typical town; indeed, it is best known for mummies, in Museo de las Mómias, at the cemetery. But gorgeous Guanajuato, located 50 miles (82 kilometers) west of San Miguel de Allende, has more to offer, including an exciting indoor market.

✸ MARKET ✸

Mercado Hidalgo Guanajuato's main market, Mercado Hidalgo, is open every day from morning to night. Located at Avenida Juárez at Mendizabal, it's a cavernous, cast-iron structure with a second floor mezzanine running completely around the huge market's circumference. Mostly full of too-cute tourist items, the mezzanine does offer great bustling market views. The ground floor's abundance of produce, pottery, basketry, meats, fabulous French rolls, hot flour tortillas, and nut and pumpkin seed candies sweetened with honey and sugar, will certainly awaken your taste buds. All the way to the left as you enter the market are *carnitas* stands that make the tastiest sandwiches on fabulous rolls this side of pig heaven. Try one with salsa and raw onion slices for about a dollar. Then go out the nearest door and cross the patio to find fondas selling *barbacoa*, *pozole*, rotisseried chickens, tacos, sandwiches, and tostados. Pull up a stool at a clean, busy counter and dig into local versions of traditional Mexican dishes.

Bread. Some of the best French breads and most fabulous *bolillos* in Mexico are sold from baskets near the main market entrance on Juárez. The reason Guanajuato's breads are so good is they are made from unprocessed hard wheat and baked in old, wood-burning, brick and clay ovens.

Strawberries. In the spring and early summer you'll see strawberries from the nearby town of Irapuato, famous throughout Mexico for its vast strawberry fields. In fact, when driving toward Irapuato from any direction, you pass kilometer after kilometer of fields with stands selling buckets of beauties with fresh *crema*.

Herbs. A knock-out assortment is sold by Indian women to the right of the market and just outside the side door. Wild and cultivated, fresh and dried. Wild mushrooms, too, in the summer rainy months.

Candy. As you enter the market's main entrance, off Juárez, you'll see tables crowding the center aisle. At first you'll think the figures are cellophane-wrapped dolls, but on closer inspection these bizarre faces and figures reveal themselves as a Guanajuato specialty: *Mómias de Charamuzcas,* representing the mummies of Guanajuato. These are equally as odd as the cemetery's real things. Rather plain, but colorful sugar figures are wrapped six to a package. Larger, intricate figures carry tiny bottles of tequila and may be smoking a cigarette. Ingredients: sugar, water, citric acid, flavorings, with raisin eyes.

Tortillas. To the left from the main entrance you'll find one of Mexico's most southern *tortillerías* making the northern Mexico favorite, flour tortillas. Just listen for the familiar clanking tortilla machine. Fresh and hot, they're wonderful to fill with warm *carnitas* from counters a few steps away.

* PLACES TO GO AND THINGS TO EAT *

RESTAURANTS

Besides the market fondas on the patio, everyone's favorite place to eat is at one of the cafés around the *Jardín de la Unión*, across from Teatro Juárez. Musicians hang out here and a mariachi group is always playing; on weekends, there are often three or four at once. Stick to simple fare and you won't go wrong.

Other outdoor cafés across from the Basilica, on Plaza de la Paz, are outstanding people-watching locations. An attractive Spanish restaurant, **Tasca de los Santos,** can be very good. Have a plate of their hand-sliced Spanish Serrano ham served with Guanajuato's excellent, chewy *bolillos* (French rolls).

Rosalita's

▲▼▲

Chiles Rellenos *Cheese-Stuffed Poblano Chiles, Battered and Fried*

CHEESE-STUFFED, BATTERED, AND GOLDEN-FRIED RELLENO CHILES are one of Mexico's glories when made with care. Sparsely filled canned chiles, fried in too-old (and too-cold) oil, left to resoak their own grease on holding plates, are sad examples of what's often seen these days. Fondas just across the patio from Guanajuato's market sell the real thing; plump poblano chiles generously stuffed with cheese, fried in delicate batter, and served piping hot with tomato sauce seasoned with Mexican oregano.

Rosalita says that when you make your own, care should be taken not to tear the delicate chiles. Egg batter is an excellent sealer only if tears aren't huge. But for large holes, toothpicks are used to close any gaps before dipping in the batter. At home, chiles can be prepared and stuffed a day in advance, then tightly covered with plastic wrap, and refrigerated. Batter and fry the chiles just before serving. Rosalita prepares fresh *chiles rellenos* every day and serves them with Red Rice (page 114).

Yield: 6 servings

For the chiles

- 6 poblano chiles, plump and heavy for their size, or Anaheim chiles
- 6 pieces quesillo de Oaxaca, mozzarella, or Monterey Jack cheese, 3 inches long by ½-inch thick
- 3 eggs, separated
- ⅓ cup white flour
- 2 cups vegetable oil

1. Toast (see page 16) the chiles. Put one in a plastic bag for the skin to sweat, and continue with the others. When all the chiles have sweated for at least 2 minutes, peel them. Cut open one side, vertically, below the stem area and remove the seeds and veins, keeping the stem attached. Insert a piece of cheese in each opening and set aside. If making the chiles in advance, refrigerate.

2. Beat the egg whites until they form stiff peaks. Stir the yolks into the whites one at a time until blended. Spread the flour on a plate and roll a chile in it to coat lightly. Dip the chile in the beaten eggs and coat the chile completely.

3. Heat the oil in a skillet to 375°F and fry one chile at a time, frying until each is golden brown. Drain immediately on paper towels. Finish with all the chiles, wait a few minutes, then change to fresh paper towels, or the chiles will re-soak their own grease. The chiles may be kept warm on a cookie sheet lined with paper towels in a 300°F oven for 20 minutes.

For the tomato sauce

- 3 tomatoes
- 1 small onion, coarsely chopped
- 3 garlic cloves, coarsely chopped
- 1 Tablespoon vegetable oil
- 1 teaspoon dried Mexican oregano
- salt, freshly ground black pepper, and sugar to taste

1. Stem and core the tomatoes and put them in a blender container with the onion and garlic.

2. Heat the oil in a small deep pot. Pour the blender ingredients into the hot oil (it splatters!) and sauté. Add the oregano, lower the heat, and simmer for 10 minutes, uncovered. Taste and add salt and pepper. If the tomatoes are acidic, add ½ teaspoon sugar. Simmer 5 minutes longer. Pour around the *chiles rellenos*.

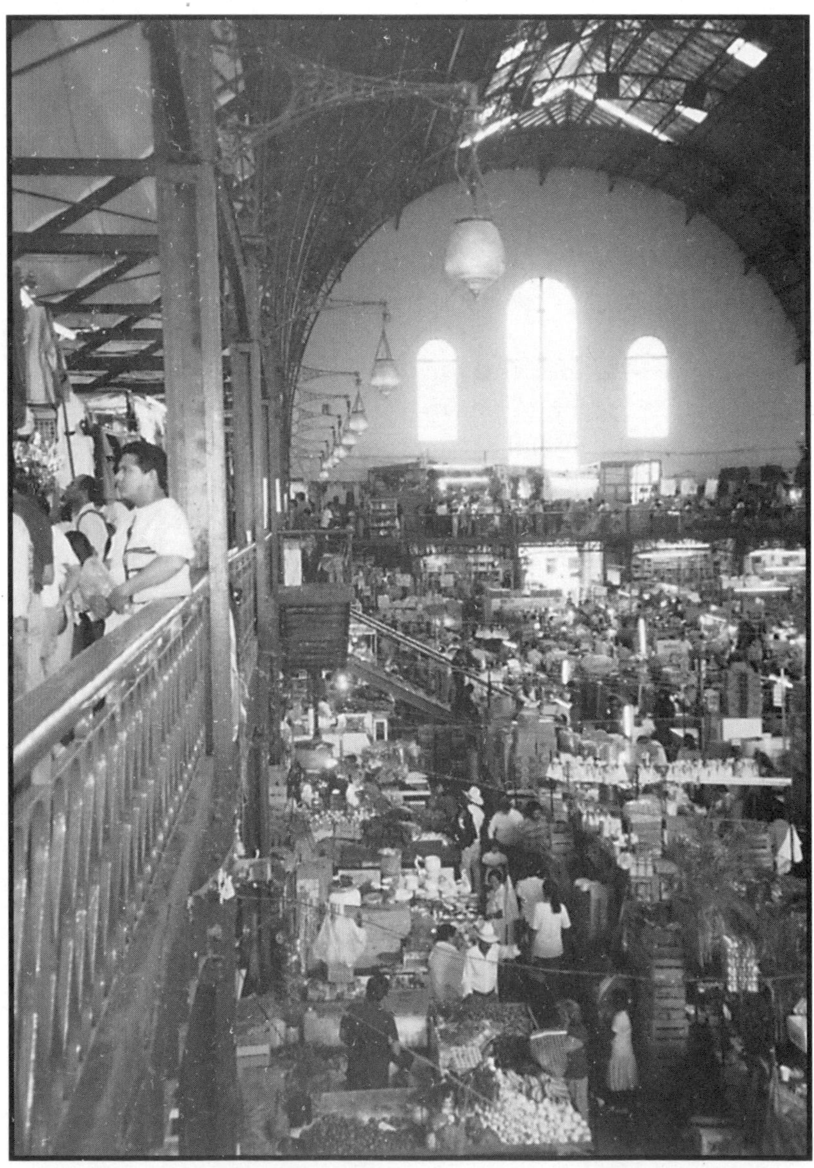

Guanajuato's exciting indoor market, Mercado Hidalgo.

A Mercado Hidalgo Vendor's

Elotes *Boiled or Grilled Corn, Street Vendor Style*

EARS OF FRESH, COOKED CORN ARE SOLD THROUGHOUT MEXICO by street vendors. There are two types in the central states—boiled and grilled—and both are immensely popular. Guanajuato has more than its share of carts, and all seem to enjoy a brisk business, especially those near the capital city's market and university.

The boiled version is slathered with mayonnaise, coated with shredded grated cheese, and finally sprinkled with chile powder. A half lime dipped in chile powder is rubbed on corn grilled over mesquite. Both versions are served piping hot on a corn leaf "plate" or impaled on a wooden stick to eat popsicle style.

Corn in Mexico is much more mature than the delicate, very sweet types preferred in the U.S. Big yellow kernels that look like burro's teeth are very chewy (especially the grilled corn), but so satisfying you'll grow fond of them and may eventually prefer them to smaller kernels.

Yield: 4 servings

For the boiled version

- 2 sprigs fresh "epazote" in the boiling water, if available
- 4 ears fresh corn on the cob, leaves intact
- 1 Tablespoon salt
- ¼ cup mayonnaise
- ½ cup "queso añejo" or Parmesan cheese
- 1 Tablespoon chile powder

1. In a large pot, bring 8 quarts of water with the *epazote* to a boil. Shuck the corn, reserving 4 to 8 large leaves. Boil the corn for about 5 minutes (time varies depending upon its size and age), or until tender.

2. Dissolve the salt in another gallon of hot water and dip the corn into the salted water (hold the corn by its thick end with a towel, market-style, or, better yet, with corn holders). Spread with 1 tablespoon of the mayonnaise.

3. Sprinkle 2 tablespoons of the cheese over the corn and pat to adhere. Finally, sprinkle with the chile powder (to taste) and serve on a reserved leaf "dish."

For the grilled version

- 4 ears fresh corn on the cob, leaves intact
- 1 Tablespoon salt
- 2 fresh limes, cut in halves
- 1 Tablespoon chile powder, on a small dish

1. Place the grill 4 inches over the coals and heat to hot. Shuck the corn, reserving 4 large leaves. Place on grill and cook, turning, for about 10 minutes.

2. Dissolve the salt in 1 gallon of hot water. Dip each ear of corn into the salted water just before serving.

3. Holding each ear of corn by its thick end with a towel or with corn holders, dip a lime half into the chile powder, then rub the corn with it, squeezing the juice. Serve on a reserved leaf "dish."

Amalia Rulfo de Fernández's

Crema *Slightly Sour, Thick Cream*

CREMA, MEXICO'S VERSION OF SOUR CREAM, OR FRENCH CRÈME FRAÎCHE, is beloved all over the country and is used daily on enchiladas, in *chilaquiles*, with plantains, over tamales, and mixed with fresh fruit. It's a natural chile-heat neutralizer, so a spoonful on any dish containing a spicy sauce is more often seen than not. Market stalls offer buckets filled with different variations of sourness and density, but you can make your own version using heavy (whipping) cream and sour cream. As with everything else in cooking, buy the best cream possible and the results will make your effort well worth any extra expense.

As with crème fraîche, *crema* is a cultured (not acidified) dairy product that's made from thick, full-fat cream. North American sour cream is not full fat, and contains stabilizers to keep the mixture from separating. Sour cream can't be boiled because it curdles, so heat this *crema* recipe to no more than a simmer. The final result is extremely similar to the *crema* Amalia serves with her bread pudding, *Capirotada* (see page 81). When she visited the U.S. recently we tested the recipe together to achieve this, Amelia's favorite version.
Yield: 2 cups

1 cup heavy cream
1 cup sour cream

Combine the heavy cream with sour cream in a jar. Place jar on your counter and let it sit at room temperature for 3 to 4 hours, covered. It will thicken and turn a bit more sour. Refrigerate for up to one week. The exact taste, texture, and thickness of the *crema* will be determined by the quality of the creams used.

Amalia Rulfo de Fernández's

Capirotada *Mexican Bread Pudding*

BREAD PUDDING IS A CHEAP COMFORT FOOD and adored by both young and old. It's a cinch to make using stale French bread, and any sweeteners that happen to be around—*panela*, brown sugar, sugar, honey, fresh fruit, or fruit juice. Fancier versions, traditionally served during Lent, include nuts, dried fruit, cheese, tomatoes, and onions, also in sugar syrup.

Mexicans always fry stale bread first for bread pudding. A good alternative is to brush the bread with minimal butter and toast it in the oven. Amalia's mother varied her family recipe after sampling bread pudding on a trip to Texas about forty years ago. She loved the custard-packed pudding her hosts offered and she still adds milk and eggs to her Mexican standby today. She also boils the syrup a full fifteen minutes until it turns to caramel and hardens when poured over the bread. It adds a delicious, crunchy texture. A traditional *capirotada* would have a greased casserole lined with tortillas (which are usually not eaten). The liquid sugar syrup is absorbed into the bread, so don't boil it down. Pass a small pitcher of *Crema* (page 80).

Yield: 8 servings

- 2 cups "panela," or brown sugar
- 1 cup water
- 1 three-inch piece of "canela," or two-inch piece of stick cinnamon
- 8 Tablespoons (1 stick) butter
- 3 Tablespoons vegetable oil
- 1 pound good-quality stale white bread torn into chunks
- 2 Tablespoons butter for the pan
- 1 cup chopped pecans
- 3 ounces raisins
- ½ cup ranchero cheese or farmer cheese
- ⅓ cup shredded mozzarella
- 3 eggs
- 1 quart milk
- 2 teaspoons vanilla extract

1. Preheat the oven to 350°F.

2. Boil the sugar and water with the *canela* for 5 minutes, until it is a syrup and caramel colored.

3. Melt the butter in a medium-sized pot and add the oil. Heat thoroughly and keep it warm. Break up the bread and spread it on a cookie sheet. Brush the bread with half the butter-oil mixture and brown in the oven.

4. Butter a 12 x 8 x 2-inch baking dish.

5. In a large bowl, mix the nuts, raisins, cheeses and toasted bread.

6. Arrange the bread mixture in the baking pan. Drizzle the syrup, and the remaining butter-oil mixture evenly over the bread. Bake for 30 minutes.

7. Beat the eggs and add milk and vanilla. Remove the *capirotada* from the oven and pour the egg-milk mixture over the bread in the baking pan. Return to the oven for about 40 minutes, until the top is brown.

Mountainous Michoacán

Morelia
Pátzcuaro

HOME TO THE PURÉPECHA (ALSO CALLED TARASCAN) INDIANS, Michoacán is a majestically mountainous state west of Mexico City, passing through Sierra Madre Occidental Mountains, down to the Pacific Ocean. High-elevation avocado ranches, peach groves, and apple orchards, as well as sweltering coconut plantations near the coast, are but an accent to the state's natural lushness. Thanks to the work of the state's first bishop, Vasco de Quiroga, an internationally esteemed crafts culture was established and today Indian works from the region are highly collectible.

Michoacán's cuisine, like that of most alpine regions around the world, is filled with nonspicy soups and stews that enjoy long simmering. Hot chiles are not a big part of this area's food repertoire, except down at sea level on the West Coast. Throughout the world the general rule of thumb is the closer to sea level and the closer to the equator (i.e., the hotter the climate), the spicier the cooking.

Left: Dining in a Morelia colonial hacienda garden.

◆ Morelia ◆

Tortillas and herbs for sale at Mercado Independencia.

MORELIA, MICHOACÁN'S CAPITAL, is architecturally one of the most beautiful cities in Mexico. Her center bursts with colonial jewels at every corner: the post office is covered with Talavera tiles; a newspaper building boasts a Churrigueresque façade; a bank branch is simply overwhelming in detail. The city, founded in 1541, is almost a museum. Many lovely buildings have been preserved and Plaza de Las Armas, the *zócalo*, is filled with exquisite samples. Morelia is 192 miles (315 kilometers) west of Mexico City.

✱ MARKET ✱

Mercado Independencia Mercado Independencia, located on the corner of Ana María Gallaga and Vicente Santa María, is open every day, from 7 A.M. to 8 P.M. and has the best selection and prices of all the city-center markets. Perones chiles are at their brightest gold and outshine all others, here, in their regional headquarters. Piles of Morelia chiles are destined for their starring roles in the city's famous chile sauce for *Pollo Plaza con Enchiladas* (page 88). Strawberries from Irapuato perfume the air; butchers are in one section of the market, fresh fish in another; piles of dried beans spill over twin aisles: clothing, hardware, saddlery. It's all in one building.

Fondas. Food counters are lined up around the market's perimeter. Most are rather run-of-the-mill, with seafood cocktail places the exception. Wonderfully hokey signage escalates a few to very-special-place status. *Torta* (sandwich) counters are fully packed at lunchtime, as is the shrimp cocktail place right next to the fresh fish stalls. Look for *chongos*, a popular fonda dessert or sweet snack made in much the same way as cottage cheese. Cubes of cream cheese-textured custard float in sweet syrup flavored with cinnamon.

Licuados. A fruit juice bar across the building from the seafood cocktail counters has the greatest graphics in the market. Order a frothy mango-orange-pineapple combo and stare at the wall. Eat (rather, drink) your heart out, Diego Rivera.

Other city markets are **Mercado Nicolás Bravo** on Nicolás Bravo between Guerrero and Corregidora, and **Mercado Municipal Revolución** on Revolución at Plan de Ayala. All three offer similar products and fondas; go to the most convenient location.

Mercado de Dulces On the west side of Palacio Clavijero, at Valentín Gómez Faríasates, is Morelia's famous arcade called Market of Sweets. Hours: 8 A.M. to about 10 P.M. every day. Open late, this is a fun place to meander in the evening. You'll see tiny bees buzzing around piles of coconut macaroons; *cocadas* (ever present variety of coconut candies); *pirulis* (cone-shaped multi-colored lollipops); *pepitorías* (thin, pumpkin seed brittle rounds); *morelianas de cacahuate* (peanut brittle rounds); loads of *cajeta* (goat milk caramel) in traditional wooden boxes from nearby Celaya; *sevillanas con cajeta* are paper-thin disks of *cajeta* sandwiched between tissue-thin disks of flour wafers; *picones de camote* made from sweet potato; the largest selection of candied fruit anywhere, including preserved-fruit-happy Puebla; and various locally made sweets sold by the kilo, or tiny bite.

✷ PLACES TO GO AND THINGS TO EAT ✷

Bakery. Trico, Av. Ventura Puente 1044, at Rafael García de León. A second store is now in the city center off the corner of the cathedral leading to Plaza Valladolid. Pastry, cookies, sweet breads, breads, and French loaves. The attached gourmet market offers a cornucopia of delicacies.

Pollo Plaza. On Plaza Valladolid, near Casa de Artesanías, and open in the evening after 7 P.M. This is the classic outdoor dining experience of Morelia. Griddled Chile-Basted Chicken with Tortillas in Enchilada Sauce (page 252) draws people in from all over Mexico like a gigantic magnet. How could something so simple be this delicious?

Tortillas and Gorditas. Find these just outside both Mercado Independencia and Mercado San Juan. Handmade, coarse *masa* tortillas are sold by women from baskets covered with lovely embroidered cloths.

Butcher. La Sabileña on Madrigal de las Altas Torres, behind the cathedral, sells all cuts of meats and three types of homemade sausage: *roja* (red); *verde* (green); and *rosa* (rose-colored, with pine nuts). Fresh and smoked chicken.

Carnitas. Cooked-pork vendors pop up on Sunday, then disappear the rest of the week. It's hard to give exact locations because they often change, but stands are found on country roads near Morelia and throughout Michoacán, the state known throughout Mexico for excellent pork and especially *carnitas.* Freshly slaughtered pigs are fried in huge copper cauldrons (manufactured in nearby Santa Clara del Cobre) and you choose any cut, part, or mixture by the kilo for take-out, or by the portion—a plate loaded with meat, tortillas, and salsa for on-the-spot dining, usually at a shared picnic table under a tree.

Folk Arts and Crafts. Casa de las Artesanías, in the beautiful Ex-Convento de San Francisco, attached to the Templo de San Francisco, three blocks east of the *zócalo* at Calle Vasco de Quiroga. Hours: every day from 9A.M. to 8P.M. Probably the finest selection of top-quality Michoacán crafts and handmade household products under one roof. Upstairs is a row of rooms where individual towns of Michoacán are represented by their unique crafts. Artists often give demonstrations of copperware, guitar-making, ceramics, and basketweaving on the mezzanine, near the shops.

RESTAURANTS

Mesón San Diego. Moderate to expensive. Calzada Fray Antonio de San Miguel, No. 344. Tel. 451-2-43-04. Patrick Palmer and chef Roberto Rodríquez Mireles own this colonial mansion restored into the town's poshest restaurant on Morelia's loveliest street, a block north of the breathtaking Sanctuary of Guadalupe. Dine under an awning poolside on regional food with Continental and North American touches. Roberto buys the thickest, sweetest *crema* available in Mexico (Lyncott brand). Try any of Mesón San Diego's dishes with a cream sauce to savor the luxury (they also use it for homemade ice creams, or try a dollop on berries). Chocoholics listen up: Save room for a bittersweet chocolate-almond torte surrounded by thick, luscious blackberry sauce made with fruit from neighbor José Cacho's mountain-high, avocado-blackberry ranch's berries.

Fonda Las Mercedes. Moderate. León Guzmán, No. 47. Tel. 2-61-13. Decadently rich Fresh Cream of Corn Soup (page 87) starts any meal off with a luxurious touch. Specialties are traditional Mexican dishes with an international flair. The interior is not to be missed; come in if just for a beer at the bar and to see the place.

El Rey Tacamba. Inexpensive. Portal Galeana, No. 577. On the north side of the Plaza de Armas. Check out the bilingual menu, in Spanish and Purépecha. There's something for everyone, at affordable prices.

Monterrey Cabrito al Pastor Restaurant. Inexpensive to moderate. Directly across from the cathedral, under the *portales.* Enter the courtyard of the wonderful colonial building and you'll see its sign directly in front. The specialty here is roasted kid cooked over hot coals and impaled on stakes *al pastor* (shepard style). The succulent meat is served with northern Mexican flour tortillas and good, fresh and cooked salsas.

Sergio Herrera's

▲▼▲

Sopa Milpera *Fresh Cream of Corn Soup*

THE MOMENT YOU ENTER MORELIA'S FONDA LAS MERCEDES you know you're in for something different. Sergio Herrera, owner and interior decorator, put together an eclectic decor, beginning with the restaurant's official greeter—a larger-than-life skeleton of a woman made by Lake Pátzcuaro sculptor Mario López from reed growing in the lake. The cozy bar is a must see—peek in at the vaulted ceiling and walls covered with terracotta pots handsomely embedded in stucco. The central courtyard plus three other dining rooms are galleries of artworks and crafts from Michoacán and Guanajuato.

Sergio's outrageously rich cream of corn soup is one of the restaurant's signature dishes. More than one person has been known to order a second bowl and cancel his entrée selection. *Yield: 6 servings*

- 6 ears of tender corn
- 4 poblano chiles
- 4 Tablespoons butter
- 1 cup heavy cream
- 1 eight-ounce package cream cheese
- 3 cups milk
- salt
- freshly ground white pepper

1. Scrape the corn kernels off the cobs into a bowl, reserving ½ cup. Cook the kernels (except the reserved) in salted, boiling water for 3 minutes. Remove from heat and drain.

2. Toast (page 16), peel, seed, and devein the chiles, and cut them into quarter-inch strips, reserving ¼ cup.

3. In a small sauté pan, melt the butter over medium heat and cook the reserved corn kernels with the reserved chile strips for 5 minutes.

4. Put the boiled corn, toasted chile strips, cream, cream cheese, and about 1 cup milk into a blender and blend. Pour the blended mixture into a large pot and add the sautéed vegetables. Bring the mixture to a simmer over medium heat. Turn down the heat and add the remainder of the milk. Bring back to a simmer for 2 minutes. Season to taste with salt and pepper. You may reheat the soup at a later time, being sure never to bring it to boil or the milk will curdle.

Ramona's

Pollo Plaza con Enchiladas

Griddled Chile-Basted Chicken, with Tortillas in Enchilada Sauce

SOME OF MEXICO'S BEST STREET FOOD COMES OFF GRIDDLES next to Casa de las Artesanías, at Plaza Valladolid's Ex-Convento de San Francisco, which is attached to the Templo de San Francisco. The fabulous crafts store, Casa de las Artesanías, is open until 8P.M., so the question of where to have dinner is an easy one to answer. Various stands sell this age-old specialty—look for a clean, popular place and pull up a bench. The combination of sizzling hot chicken, vegetables, and enchiladas makes for an unforgettable meal while sitting at a picnic table in the dark of evening with a naked bulb or two hanging from overhead for light, and smoke billowing off the griddle. You'll enjoy a truly traditional Mexican eating experience while sharing the table with other fans of fine food.

Cooking is done in huge, four-foot-diameter metal *comales*, with indented one-foot circles in the center to hold fresh, hot oil for each order. Unfilled enchiladas are constantly being made and stacked for immediate reheating along an edge of the *comal*. Enchiladas with cheese or shredded chicken fillings are also available. Cooked carrots, potatoes, and onions are kept along another edge. Large chicken quarters (request either leg or breast) are half-cooked and form a line along the final third of the *comal's* circumference. A chicken quarter is finished off when an order comes in, as are vegetables and enchiladas. The plate comes garnished with radish slices and shredded cabbage. As usual with street food, don't eat washed, uncooked vegetables because washing water is 99 percent unpurified. The nonspicy dish is easy to make at home (and you can eat the garnish); it's always a hit with guests, kids, and adults alike. Double or triple the recipe for a crowd and serve with a separate green salad (red radish slices look good with the chicken), and a fresh tomato salsa.

Yield: 4 servings

For the chicken

- 1 four-pound chicken, quartered
- 1 white onion, quartered
- 4 garlic cloves
- 3 bay leaves

1. Heat 3 quarts water with the chicken, onion, garlic, and bay leaves and bring to a boil.

2. Reduce the heat and maintain at a strong simmer, uncovered, for 50 minutes. Remove the chicken and set aside. Strain the (weak) broth and keep for another use.

For the enchilada sauce

- 5 Morelia or ancho chiles, stemmed, seeded, and opened flat
- 5 garlic cloves
- 1 white onion, quartered
- ¼ teaspoon dried thyme
- ¼ teaspoon dried Mexican oregano
- ¼ teaspoon cumin seed
- 2 Tablespoons cider vinegar
- 1 cup water

1. Toast (see page 16) the chiles, garlic, and onion. Put them in a blender container with the thyme, oregano, cumin, and vinegar. Purée, adding the water ¼ cup at a time.
2. Pour the sauce into a wide soup bowl, big enough to dip tortillas.

For the vegetables

- 2 potatoes, peeled and very coarsely chopped
- 6 carrots, peeled and very coarsely chopped
- 2 Tablespoons vegetable oil
- 1 white onion, chopped

1. Heat 2 quarts salted water in a pot and add the potatoes and carrots. Boil 10 minutes with the lid askew. Drain the water and set the undercooked vegetables aside.
2. In the same pot, heat the oil. Add the onion and sauté until transparent. Add the potatoes and carrots and continue to sauté, until the vegetables brown. Remove to a side bowl.

For the enchiladas

- vegetable oil
- 12 corn tortillas
- optional: shredded "quesillo de Oaxaca," string cheese, or mozzarella
- 4 radishes, sliced
- 2 cups shredded cabbage

1. Heat ⅛ inch oil to 365° F, or until the surface ripples, in a skillet.
2. Dip each tortilla in the enchilada sauce, and let the excess drip off.
3. Slip the tortilla into the hot oil for 30 seconds. Remove from the oil. Add the optional cheese before folding the tortilla in half, and replace in the oil for the cheese to melt and until the tortilla is chewy but not crisp, about 60 seconds. With tongs, pick up the tortilla, letting oil drip back into the pot, and put it in a dish lined with paper towels. Place in a warm (300° F) oven. Continue with the remaining tortillas, adding more oil to the pot, if necessary.
4. Rub the remaining enchilada sauce over the chicken pieces. Heat the chicken in the enchilada-cooking oil and brown until the skin is crisp and the thigh meat completely cooked, about 10 minutes.
5. Put a piece of chicken on a plate. Add 3 enchiladas and a quarter of the vegetables. Repeat with the remaining three portions. Garnish with radishes and shredded cabbage.

Ricardo Aburto de Rivera's

Carnitas *Deep Fried Pork Pieces*

YOU CAN ORDER *CARNITAS* BY THE PLATE, BY THE KILO (two pounds), and by your favorite morsel. Just remember: Every last part of the pig is fried. Innards are top choices, *chicharrones*, hunks of shoulders, ribs, lean loins and legs, ears to tails, anything you can think of, is an option but nothing goes on your plate that you don't order. Ordering a tiny piece of this and that, with and without bones, some crisp skin, some fat, some lean, is what makes *carnitas* special. The word *carnitas* translates to "little meats" because the pork is so tender it breaks into little pieces, or can be shredded for tacos in a flash.

Truly, nothing can beat the real thing, especially eating at a roadside cookery, but it is possible to make your own (minus a three-foot-diameter cauldron of boiling fat) and here's how. One Sunday Ricardo, a friend-of-a-friend and fonda owner, drove Morris and me to his favorite *carnitas* spot south of town where we sat at a picnic table spread with crisp chunks of pork and came up with this make-at-home recipe. We later tried it at home on Ricardo's kids, with great success. The simple secret is to cover pork with hot lard and simmer for an hour before raising the heat to brown and crisp the whole batch. Many U.S. cookbooks recommend boiling the meat in water, then later browning it in a hot oven. This isn't *carnitas*, guys. For fabulous taste and texture you really have to cook the pork in lard. Pork doesn't absorb lard, in fact pork fat melts in hot fat and becomes lard. After you remove the crisp pork you'll see there's more fat in the pot than when you started. Be sure to drain the meat well.

Serve with loads of warm tortillas, Fresh Tomato Salsa (page 143), Guacamole (page 142), a pot of *Frijoles de Olla* (page 46), and an assortment of ice-cold Mexican beers.
Yield: 12 servings

- 6 to 8 cups lard, or enough to cover the meat (see page 18)
- 5 pounds pork shoulder, cut into 6 to 8 chunks
- 4 racks of pork ribs, each cut into 2-rib pieces, or 4 pounds country-style ribs
- zest from 2 oranges
- salt
- 1 red onion, sliced
- 1 bunch cilantro stems, washed, dried, and left whole

1. Heat the lard in a large, very deep pot. When it just begins to simmer, add the pork and zest. Bring the lard back to a strong simmer with constant small bubbles over medium heat. This step is to cook the meat, not to brown it. Continue cooking at this temperature for 1 hour, checking often to be sure the lard is not boiling.

2. After 1 hour, raise the heat and boil for another 20 to 30 minutes. When the meats are brown, remove them from the fat and drain on layers of brown bags opened flat and covered with paper towels. Separate the pork into smaller chunks if you'd like. Sprinkle with salt while the meat is still bubbling, and serve on a huge platter. Pass bowls of red onion slices and cilantro sprigs for make-your-own soft tacos.

Robert Rodríguez Mireles's

Lomo de Cerdo con Hojas de Aguacate

Pork Loin with Avocado Leaves

MORELIA IS THE HOME OF A DELIGHTFUL RESTAURANT, MESÓN SAN DIEGO, on one of the most beautiful streets in Mexico, the sixteenth century Calzada Fray Antonio de San Miguel. The street is so ravishing that the city has turned it into a pedestrian street. It's lined with colonial buildings and ends with Morelia's logo—the Tarascan Fountain. Mesón San Diego is owned by Robert Rodríguez Mireles, chef, and Patrick Palmer, from the U.S. Patrick said Morelia is famous for pork, avocados, and molasses. These ingredients are included in this recipe, developed by Robert and inspired by an old, yellowed and stained dog-eared cookbook, *Manual de Cocina Michoacana*, by Vicenta T. de Rubio, 1896, that was his grandmother's.

Don't be shocked by Robert's use of Worcestershire sauce—it has been popular in Mexico for generations. Serve the pork loin with steamed rice. A green salad with avocado is a good match. *Yield: 6 servings*

For the sauce

- ½ cup molasses
- ½ cup orange juice
- ½ cup minced white onion
- 1 garlic clove, minced
- 1 Tablespoon olive oil
- ¼ teaspoon salt
- ¼ teaspoon Tabasco sauce
- 2 teaspoons Worcestershire sauce
- ⅓ cup ketchup
- ¼ teaspoon ground cloves
- 3 Tablespoons wine vinegar
- 1 Tablespoon Dijon mustard
- ¼ teaspoon freshly ground pepper

Mix all the ingredients in a saucepan and bring to a boil for 5 minutes.

Note: The sauce keeps, refrigerated, for one week.

For the pork and leaves

- 2 Tablespoons vegetable oil
- 2¼ pounds lean, boneless pork loin, thinly sliced (6 ounces per person)
- 30 small anise-flavored avocado leaves, if possible

1. Heat the oil in a large skillet and sauté the pork. When it is almost done (about 5 minutes on each side), add the sauce, bring to a boil, and then turn off the heat.

2. Rub the leaves with oil and place them in a hot, large skillet and toast them for a few seconds on each side. The plate, when served, looks like a flower, shiny leaves on the outside, and pork and steamed rice on the inside.

◆ Pátzcuaro ◆

"Birria" tacos on the Plaza Chica.

HIGH UP IN THE MICHOACÁN MOUNTAINS (2,170 meters, 7,135 feet) about an hour west of Morelia, Pátzcuaro has all the charm you long for in a Mexican town. Recognized for its classic beauty, Pátzcuaro has strict building codes maintaining its colonial, small-town atmosphere. It's far enough away from airports to not be overrun with tourists, but still has plenty of comfortable hotels. Cool, crisp mountain air stimulates your appetite for regional dishes found along charming streets lined with whitewashed adobe buildings and red tile roofs. The two plazas, luscious Plaza Vasco de Quiroga (known as the Plaza Grande) and lively Plaza Gertrudis Bocanegra (the Plaza Chica) are the town's focal points where you'll eventually find yourself sitting under *portales* drinking cold beer or hot chocolate.

Crafts of Lake Pátzcuaro are celebrated throughout the country, and each village around the lake specializes in a different item. Pátzcuaro's Indian crafts are world famous, second in Mexico only to Oaxaca's in quantity.

✷ MARKETS ✷

Mercado Municipal Pátzcuaro's indoor-outdoor market, on the west side of Plaza Gertrudis Bocanegra (Plaza Chica)—including Calle Libertad and the surrounding streets, is a must for *molinillos* (hand-carved beaters for hot chocolate) and carved wooden spoons. Handwoven woolen *rebozos* (shawls) are exceptionally soft and warm. Various bread shapes not seen in other towns take on exotic appeal. On tables you'll find volumes of sweets—from cookies to tiny hand-painted crocks of sweet chile-tamarind pastes to brush over chicken or meats before roasting. Summer corn is especially succulent, almost as deliciously sweet as August mangoes trucked up the mountain from tropical climates.

Fondas. On the east and west sides of Plaza Chica, Griddled Chile-Basted Chicken with Tortillas in Enchilada Sauce (page 88), in the evenings after 6 P.M., is absolutely not to be missed. *Birria* (made with beef) carts, for lunch-time tacos and bowls of meat with steaming broth, are at the entrance to the market on Plaza Chica, just where the *portales* end.

Indian Market Friday mornings, an Indian market in the Jardín Revolución, at Plaza San Francisco, one block west of Plaza Grande, is a "must" stop even if you can't possibly carry back one more piece of pottery. This extraordinarily picturesque market is teeming with Purépecha women dressed in handwoven shawls, bright blouses, and long skirts, and selling ceramics, handwork, and flowers at rock-bottom prices. Because people come into town to sell their wares on Friday, the Mercado Municipal is extra full and busy this day.

You should consider the lead content of Mexican pottery on a pueblo-by-pueblo, often artisan-by-artisan basis. Many (but not most) glazes contain enough lead to make them unsafe for serving hot food. Often it's the brightly colored flowers painted on top of glazes, usually on the outsides of bowls, that are harmful. Easy-to-use lead testing kits are availables at many U.S. hardware stores for less than ten dollars.

Pátzcuaro's Friday morning Indian market.

⁕ PLACES TO GO AND THINGS TO EAT ⁕

Tamales. Exceptional tamales are found around the Plaza Chica in the morning, or in the evening after 8P.M. , and on the Basílica grounds in the morning. Be sure to drink *atole* with your tamales for the classic combo. After 7P.M. under the *portales* and across from Plaza San Francisco, try unusual *atole de chaqueta*, called "jacket" because it's made with charred cocoa bean husks and the resulting color is black, as the sometimes-crabby elderly vendor says, "like black leather jackets." Tamale vendors sell husks filled with pork or chicken and red sauce; *corundas* are Michoacán's famous pyramid-shaped tamales made with ashes in the *masa*, then wrapped in fresh, green corn leaves; *uchepos* are also wrapped in fresh green leaves, around sweet corn custard (page 102); tamales *dulces* (sweet, with dried fruit) are wrapped in dried husks; *trigos* are made with wheat and *panela*, wrapped in burgundy-colored corn husks, the steamed *masa* is medium brown, sweet, and molasses-tasting; *atole de zarzamora* are made with blackberries and a fine cornstarch *masa* with an almost gelatin texture, wrapped in corn husks then steamed. Buy a selection and take them to a table underneath one of the plaza *portales.* Order a hot drink from the waiter and dig into your tamales, no one will mind. Peel back the leaves to use as "dishes" then enjoy the warm stuffings.

Atole. *Atole de grano* is sold on the southeast corner of the Plaza Chica in the evening. A small chunk of corn-on-the-cob is put into a bowl, then covered with broth made from freshly scraped-off-the-cob corn. The nonsweet *atole* broth is a pale green color from fresh, wild fennel (anise). Unthickened liquid is eaten like soup with a spoon, rather than drunk. As with all street foods, it's best to ask for the *atole de grano* to go, served with your own plastic cup and spoon. Morris became positively addicted to *atole de grano*; the delighted vendor would probably still recognize the face of her devoted gringo fan even today, years later.

Tacos. At night, on the southeast corner of the Plaza Chica, you'll find soft beef, chorizo, and innards tacos served on two small tortillas. There's always a huge crowd at the cheap and delicious stand-up taco cart.

Cheese. Prov. de Lacteos y Carnes Frias, Inturbe No. 9, tel. 2-03-96. Just off the Plaza Grande. A couple of good-looking guys were working behind the counter the first time I set foot in the spotless shop. After selecting *ranchero*, *añejo*, a leaf-wrapped fresh cheese, yogurt, and *crema* I asked, "*¿tienen huevos?*"—(literally, do you have eggs?). Within seconds my friend, Marilyn, and the young men were just about on the floor, dying of laughter. After their eyes dried and the choking stopped I found out I asked the guys if they had balls.

Butchers. Everything you need is at the indoor market. But when butchers around town hang out a red flag it means they have slaughtered that day. There are at least three fresh chicken stalls in the covered market and all are good.

Fish. Lake whitefish and *charales* (tiny as whitebait) are usually panfried and served whole, *charales* in a pile, along the lakeside. *Trucha ahumada* (smoked trout) is a specialty of a trout farm selling both fresh and delicious smoked trout. Look for a large two-story, Tudor-style house, with a red roof on the lake side of Carretera Pátzcuaro-Erongarícuaro Km. 14, Aróсutin, about 15 minutes west of Pátzcuaro, on the lakeside. A sign is painted on the entrance wall.

Carnitas. Carnitas las Plazas, Inturbe No.18, begins selling crisp pork tacos and meat by the kilo about 2 P.M. every day but Monday. You'll know when they open; the line is slightly smaller as people file inside.

Empanadas dulces. Huge, ten-inch sweet turnovers filled with *ates* (fruit pastes) are sold by Indian women just to the right of the Hotel de la Concordia and left of the *birria* carts on the Plaza Chica.

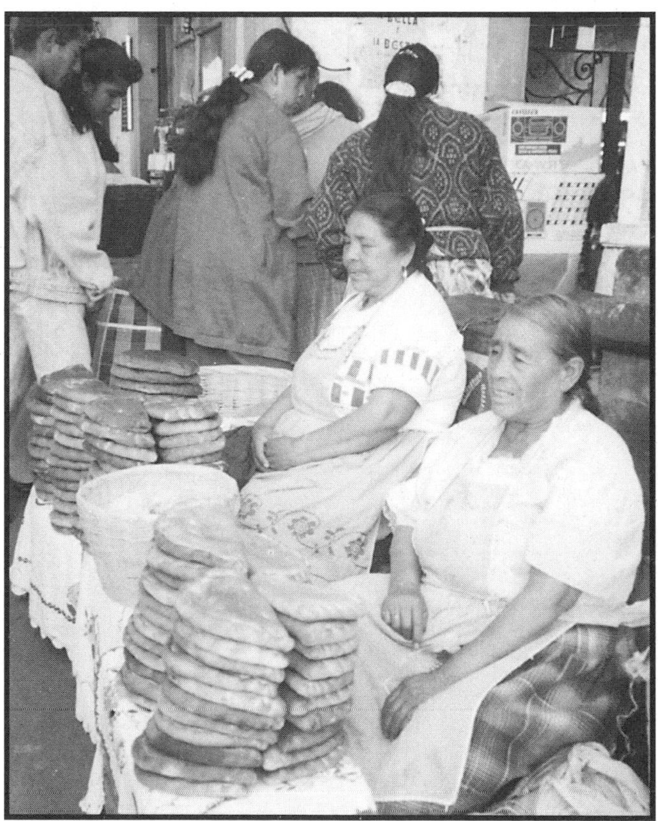

"Empanadas dulces" are sold in Pátzcuaro.

Bread. Rogelio Rodríguez, Araceli Morales, and their son, Juan Vasco Rodríguez, bake the town's best *bolillos* at **Panadero de Las Tres R's**, Independencia No. 35, Tel. 2-01-09. The bakery bakes for wholesale clients but will sell retail; in fact, you can order either *dorado* (crisp crust) or *blando* (soft) special orders a day ahead (they will consider six rolls an order). The family bakes in an old wood-burning clay oven. If you want to try their rolls first, go to the restaurant of Los Escudos Hotel, or to El Patio Restaurant.

The following breads are known as *pan de ranchero* and are sold on the west side of the Plaza Chica: *pan de nata* is made with the milk skin that forms atop boiled milk and the sweet round loaf is sold warm, from baskets, in the early evening; *sema* is a small, beautiful whole wheat loaf with light-colored stripes running lengthwise along the flat, oval shape; *picada* is an eight-inch round, flat white loaf with an alligator skin pattern carved into the top; *mollete* is a small white loaf with an odd, curved shape—it starts out raw, as a rectangle, then three slashes are cut into one side and bent into a curve before baking.

Cookies. There's an always changing assortment of cookies sold from baskets and folding tables on Plaza Grande, in front of Los Escudos Hotel. Try the fresh coconut macaroons (you'll recognize them by the attraction of teeny bees everyone mistakenly first figures to be flies), but any are delectable along with a cup of hot chocolate under the *portales*, on either square.

Guadalupe García López makes heavenly hot chocolate.

Wines and liquors. There's a good selection at **Centro Abarrotero** supermarket, Inturbe No. 43. Look over the selection of *Charanda*, an inexpensive liquor made in Michoacán and sold in an assortment of unusually decorated (some rather funny) bottles. A different gift idea.

Chocolate. For Mexican chocolate, don't miss **Joaquinita Chocolate Supremo**, Enseñanza No. 38, in an entrance to a private home (across from the folk art museum and diagonal to the Basilica). Darkly roasted, excellent Mexican chocolate tablets have been handmade here since 1898 for delicious Hot Chocolate (page 103). Guadalupe García López also sells cocoa powder.

Sweets. *Ate* pastes are sold on the west side of Plaza Chica all day, made with reduced fruit purées such as quince, guava, and pear. Serve *ate* sliced, with fresh, soft cheese or cream cheese, and sweet crackers, as a regional dessert.

Ice cream. *Pasta helado* is at its best from October through February when topped with black *zapote* fruit sauce. Stands front the Los Escudos Hotel, on the south side of the Plaza Grande. Weekend lines can be long.

Table linens. Mantas Típicas, Dr. Coss No. 5. Tel. 2-13-24. The shop is just off the southeast corner of Plaza Grande at the bottom of "Eleven Patios." Handwoven *cambaya* tablecloths and napkins plus yardgoods in both cotton and acrylic.

Mantas y Manteles, Casa 11 Patios Altos Local No. 1. Tel. 2-21-43. Up a few steps from Mantas Tipas, Mantas y Manteles's generously oversized *cambaya* cloth napkins used for lining tortilla baskets are fabulous. Get a dozen in different colors for your next barbeque.

Tour guide. Marilyn Mayo's, **"Su Casa,"** Apdo 416, 61600 Pátzcuaro, Michoacán, Mexico. Tel. 524-311-0803, Fax 524-342-2756. Marilyn's guest house, which she rents, is a three-bedroom, three-bath contemporary packed with folk art. It's on a hilltop with a picture-postcard lake view. An experienced tour guide, Marilyn takes groups to studios of artisans all around the lake. She knows everbody and gets travelers into places they dream about.

RESTAURANTS

Don Alfredo Pollos al Pastor. Inexpensive. Located at the Tanganxuan intersection on the Periférico. The dirt-floored, tin-roofed roadside building opens for business at 2 P.M. and closes about 5 P.M. Chicken and baby lamb are cooked on sticks over wood. Before serving, a sour orange is squeezed over the still-bubbling-hot meat. Tortillas are patted out by hand and are replenished before your basket empties. Orange juice, onion, perón chile, and vinegar salsa comes with the chicken. Red tomato salsa is served with the lamb. Go with a group and order both chicken and lamb—having to choose would be torture.

El Patio. Moderate. Portal Aldama 9, on the south side of Plaza Vasco de Quiroga (Plaza Grande). The mixed green and vegetable salad is a work of art to the salad-starved. It's a full meal with a bowl of El Patio's excellent soup, *sopa tarasca* (see page 65). Have the coarsely textured flan for dessert, or *ate* with cheese.

Los Escudos Hotel's dining room. Inexpensive to moderate. Portal Hidalgo 73, on the west side of Plaza Grande. Ask for the chicken and bean tostadas (you get two). The dish is not on the menu; it's for regulars who know one of the best cheap-eats deals in town. Notice the alpine feeling of the room's interior design and all the blond wood.

El Granero de Sanabria. Inexpensive to moderate. Km 6 Carretera Pátzcuaro-Quiroga, on the way to the pyramids in Tzintzuntzán. Open daily from 10 A.M. to 6 P.M. for breakfast and the lunch special in a huge, restored barn with one end opened up with glass to take advantage of the pasture-land scenery. The family-run operation is proud of its spotless, open-to-view kitchen.

Lake Zirahuén Freshwater fish is becoming scarce today due to lake pollution throughout Mexico. Lakes Pátzcuaro and Chapala, long renowned for their delicate whitefish, are still serving up fried platters at lakeside restaurants but travelers shouldn't eat much of the fish even though the lakes are cleaner than they have been for years. If you'd like to try whitefish from an unpolluted and knock-out-gorgeous lake, visit a waterside joint along untouristy Lake Zirahuén, an enchanting thirty-minute ride from

Pátzcuaro. Go out to the lakeside where there are very low-key fish shacks with dirt floors, picnic tables, and delectable *charales* (tiny deep-fried, finger-sized fish). Recommended is **Doña Paz's** place.

Santa Clara del Cobre This village, located an easy, mountainous, thirty-mile ride from Pátzcuaro, is known for its copper pots, pans, plates, paella pans, candlesticks, bowls, and more, plus prices that can't be beat anywhere else in Mexico. Buses run regularly and taxis are cheap. Just remember to work out a price with the taxi driver before zooming off. Once in the village, go directly to the copper museum and see examples of Santa Clara del Cobre's finest work. August is when the week-long annual copper fair takes place, and it's usually held during the first half of the month. Check with Morelia's or Pátzcuaro's tourist information centers for exact dates. All the year's prizewinning entries are on dislpay.

Galería Tiamuri, Piño Suárez, No. 110. The outlet for the school that is revolutionizing copper working in Santa Clara. Heavy, well made, and as of now, the only place in town with tin-lined cookware. It's on the road just to the right of the copper museum. Walk a few blocks up and you'll see it, on a corner, on the left side. Other good shops on the same block are **Casa Paz Sanabria** and **El Portón**.

Cazos are fabulous huge, deep, hand-hammered, copper preserving pots with two handles. Sizes varying from one-foot to four-feet are sold throughout town for your very own *carnitas* cauldron.

Hotel Camino Real's dining room. Inexpensive. The hotel's restaurant (not a part of the chain) is on Santa Clara's main street near the south end of town. Their bargain 4-course lunches are outstanding; breakfasts with cappuccino are a find; and all meals are served by true professionals.

Tacambaro About forty-five minutes from Santa Clara del Cobre on Rt. 41, Tacambaro is known for great scenery, almost perfect year-round weather, lush vegetation, a charming *zócalo*, and very good restaurants. A volcanic mountain range forms vistas from every vantage point in town—and they seem to go on forever. Layers upon layers, lakes, rivers, waterfalls . . . .

El Tejabán (The Shed). Moderate. The restaurant is on the road into town, on the left side. Tables in the upstairs dining room offer great views. Snacks such a *sopes*, guacamole and chips, salsas, and *flautas* arrive before you order. *Carne Asada* (page 34) plus other grilled meats and quail are good entrée selections.

Tzintuntzán Located on the eastern shore of Lake Pátzcuaro, home of five *yacatas*, or rounded pyramids of the Purépecha Indians built in the thirteenth-century, Tzintuntzán is renowned for its sixteenth-century monastery and Don Vasco de Quiroga's olive trees. See the workshop of potter **Manuel Morales**, on Calle Tariacuri, off a church courtyard, if you're interested in pottery with contemporary motifs. Local cream-colored pottery decorated with fish and birds is popular and found around town.

José Cacho's

Salsa de Naranja y Chile Perón

Fresh Orange and Perón Chile Sauce

HIGH IN THE MOUNTAINS IN THE STATE OF MICHOACÁN, near the pueblo of Ario de Rosales, stands José Cacho's "La Rosalia," the highest-altitude avocado ranch in Mexico (Michoacán is the largest producer in the world of avocados). Morris and I were invited to join a group of friends for a Sunday afternoon outdoor lunch featuring grilled chicken, salsas, cheese quesadillas, tostadas, tortillas, beer, tequila, and, of course, lots of sliced avocados. After horseback riding through the orchards, everyone piled into four-wheel drives for the ride up into the clouds and the welcoming aroma of chicken grilling in the open air.

José's salsa idea comes from roadside chicken stands around Pátzcuaro, where they not only serve a similar fresh salsa but also squeeze sour oranges over grilled chickens as soon as they come sizzling off the coals. At the ranch, we tore hot chicken off bones and placed hunks of it on freshly cooked corn tortillas with a few slices of avocado and a spoonful of this delicious and colorful salsa. Perón chile (also known as manzano), which is a medium-to-hot chile, is used exclusively in Michoacán, but you may substitute another that's similar to the bright orange-yellow color. The combination of fiercely hot, ripe habanero chile and mild yellow bell peppers would be a good solution, for example. A recent discovery is to add a cup of mashed ranch-grown blackberries to the salsa. Wow.

Yield: about 2 cups

- 4 juice oranges
- 2 limes
- 1 medium onion, finely chopped
- 1 perón chile (also called manzana chile), stemmed, seeded, and finely chopped
- 2 Tablespoons white vinegar

1. Squeeze the orange and lime juice into a bowl. Add the onion, chile, and vinegar.

2. Let the salsa rest and the flavors mingle at room temperature for at least 2 hours before serving.

Doña Esperancita de Sepúlveda's

Posolillo *Fresh Corn Soup with Smoked Meats and Ancho Chile*

ESPERANCITA IS A JOY. HER INFECTIOUS LOVE OF LIFE IS APPARENT whenever one of her ten children or twenty-six grandchildren cruises through the Pátzcuaro hacienda looking for her and to see what's cooking. She has lived in Michoacán her entire life and has amassed a formidable collection of recipes, which she was eager to share.

Spaniards brought pigs and chickens to the New World, and their classic dish of pork, chicken, garlic, and onions was enlivened with Mexico's superstars: corn and chile. *Posolillo*, a hybridized mixture of Indian and Spanish, is true *mestizo* (mixed blood) and has been a favorite of Michoacán for generations, and Esperancita's rendition is classic. Unlike *Pozole* (page 54), which uses dried hominy as its base, *posolillo* is a summer dish made when fresh corn is sweet and tender. You wouldn't think so, but during summer's rainy season, evenings get damp and jacket-cold in high-elevation Pátzcuaro, and a good soup is welcome. Serve in soup bowls and pass bottled hot sauce, a basket of warm tortillas or fried corn chips, and lime wedges.

Yield: 8 generous servings

- 3 ancho chiles
- 3 garlic cloves
- 1 white onion
- 12 ears of tender corn (about 10 cups kernels)
- ½ pound chorizo, meat removed from casing
- ½ pound pork loin meat, diced
- 1 four-pound chicken, cut into parts
- 4 ounces ham, baked or boiled, chopped
- 1 Tablespoon dried Mexican oregano
- salt and freshly ground pepper to taste

1. Stem and seed the chiles. Soak them in hot water at least 30 minutes. Put the chiles, garlic, and onion in a blender container and purée with ¼ cup water.

2. Scrape the kernels off the corn ears. A heavy knife over a large surface or wide container is best, because the kernels tend to fly off in all directions.

3. Remove the chorizo meat from the casing and fry it in a deep pot for 5 minutes. Add the pork, chicken, and ham and brown in the chorizo fat. Add the corn kernels, stirring, then add the chile mixture.

4. Add about 3 quarts water so all the ingredients are covered. Bring to a boil, add the oregano, then cover and simmer for 1 hour, stirring the ingredients from time to time. Taste first before adding salt and pepper—the ham and chorizo are salty and sometimes peppery. The soup may be cooled then refrigerated, or frozen at this point for reheating.

Note: Posolillo is easier to eat if the chicken is replaced with 6 skinless, boneless chicken breast halves, cut into 1-inch pieces.

Doña Esperancita de Sepúlveda's

Postre de Elote o Uchepos de Leche

Corn Custard, or Sweet Corn Tamales

ANOTHER OF ESPERANCITA'S TRADITIONAL MICHOACÁN DISHES is this sweet corn custard dessert guaranteed to be your new favorite comfort food. The recipe also makes *uchepos de leche*, famous Michoacán sweet tamales wrapped with fresh, green corn leaves rather than corn husks. Unlike traditional tamales, the smooth custard is not cooked after filling.

Use only mature and starchy corn for the custard; if new corn is used the custard will not have enough natural starch to hold together. Most end-of-season corn is old and starchy, and therefore suitable for this dish. The cooked, set custard is spooned onto leaves for *uchepos*, which are then folded, tied, and chilled. *Uchepos* make a fabulous buffet dessert because each delightful portion is individually wrapped.

Yield: approximately 1 quart custard or about 20 tamales

For Postre de Elote

- 3 ears very mature corn
- 1 quart milk
- 1 three-inch piece "canela," or two-inch stick cinnamon
- 2 cups sugar

1. Scrape the corn off the cobs and put the kernels in a blender. Cover the corn with water and purée. Strain the corn and water through a sieve into a large pot. Discard any corn kernels left in the strainer.

2. Add the milk, *canela*, and sugar to the pot. Heat over medium heat, stirring constantly with a wooden spoon to keep the liguid from sticking and burning. Keep stirring until the sauce thickens like a custard and you can see the bottom of the pan when stirring, and the liquid coats the spoon, about 20 minutes. Discard the *canela.*

3. Immediately empty the custard onto a shallow platter with raised sides. Cool the mixture to room temperature, or chill, before serving.

Note: If the custard doesn't set, it's because the corn wasn't old and starchy enough. You can rescue it by dissolving 2 tablespoons cornstarch in ¼ cup warm milk. Put the custard in a bowl, add the cornstarch and milk, and mix. Pour back onto the platter. Cool again.

(Continued)

Esperancita is one of Pátzcuaro's premier home cooks.

For Tamales

1. Save the fresh, green leaves from the corn by cutting clear through an ear, just above the base where the ear is thickest. Keep the largest leaves and wash them carefully, trying to keep each leaf whole. You may need additional leaves from other ears. Remove the silk.
2. Prepare the custard recipe as directed above. When the custard is set and cool, begin assembling the *uchepos.*
3. Cut 20 strips from the small leaves into "ribbons" about ¼ inch by 6 inches long, with the grain.
4. Place 2 to 3 tablespoons custard on the inside of each leaf (the leaf naturally curls inward). Fold the sides of the leaf over the filling, then fold over the pointed end. Fold the wider end over the pointed end.
5. Tie one "ribbon" around each package so the tamales do not open. Arrange on a platter, in a shallow basket, or other attractive container. Chill.

Note: Some cooks mix quickly steamed corn kernels into the custard before forming *uchepos* for texture.

Plaza Vasco de Quiroga, Pátzcuaro.

María Guadalupe García López's

Chocolate *Hot Mexican Chocolate*

JOAQUINITA CHOCOLATE SUPREMO CASERO TABLETS HAVE BEEN HOMEMADE by Lupe's family since 1898 and are famous throughout the state of Michoacán. The rich, powerful flavor of the well-toasted cocoa beans used to make the tablets is intensely sublime. As with Mexican hot chocolate everywhere, full-fat, low-fat, and nonfat milk, or water, may be used with equal success; the richness is up to you. If you are fortunate to be in Pátzcuaro, stop at Lupe's house-front shop and take home as many chocolate tablets as you can carry.

Fewer things in life can beat sitting in Lupe's kitchen sipping her just-made hot chocolate during an August thunderstorm. The mountains surrounding Lake Pátzcuaro get chilly after late afternoon rains and her frothy cup of nectar from the thunder gods couldn't be more perfect.

Yield: 4 one-cup servings

2 Joaquinita chocolate tablets
1 quart milk (or water)

1. Heat 1 cup milk (or water) over a medium flame in a traditional *jarro de barro* (clay pot) that's round on the bottom and slopes in toward the top to keep chocolate from splashing out, and has a pouring spout, or a pot with deep sides.
2. Add the chocolate tablets, broken-up, when the milk is warm. Stir with a traditional *molinillo*, or a wooden spoon, until the chocolate is melted. Add the remaining milk, reduce the heat to a low simmer, and simmer for about 2 minutes. If you own a decorative Mexican *jarro de barro* not for stove use, add the hot liquid at this point.
3. Remove the pot from the heat and, using a *molinillo*, quickly rub the handle back and forth between your palms. A thick foam will form from the churning action. Lacking a *molinillo*, whip the chocolate with an egg beater, whisk, or electric hand-held mixer. Serve immediately in cups or mugs with some foam for each.

Note: If you cannot obtain Joaquinita chocolate tablets, substitute Mexican chocolate tablets such as Ibarra or Abuelita or the U.S. brand, Gazella.

Mexico City and Environs

Mexico City
Toluca
Cuernavaca
Taxco

CENTRAL MEXICO, THE REGION IMMEDIATELY SURROUNDING MEXICO CITY, is one of the country's most stunning, and offers various landscapes and climates. The nation's capital is located on a high plateau, known as the Altiplano, between the Sierra Madre Occidental and Oriental ranges. Cascading down both sides are jagged peaks, raging rivers, and rugged woods that meld into lush valleys overgrown with tropical flower vines. Pre-Columbian ruins dot hills and plains; resorts encircle the city-center and offer weekend reprises to harried city dwellers; the world's silver center is considered to be Mexico's loveliest town; the country's highest-elevation market, up in the clouds, is Mexico's biggest market.

Left: An elegant Mexico City dining room.

◆ Mexico City ◆

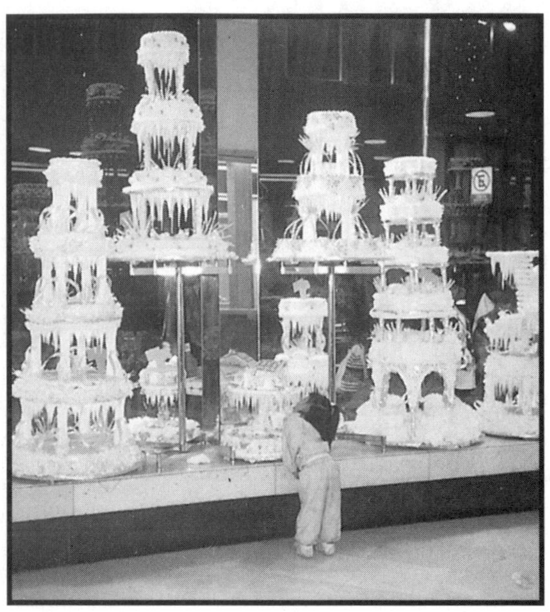

Awesome cakes at El Ideal bakery.

TWENTY-SOMETHING MILLION AND COUNTING—this is one hellava city. Sure, there is nightmarish traffic, smog you can cut with a knife, noise at a screaming pitch, and rampant crime thanks to urban guerrilla gangs. Nobody calls Mexico City charming—and probably no one ever has (the Aztecs called it Tenochtitlán—Place of the Cactus). It's a mind-blowing, action-packed whirlwind day and night. Yet people are compelled to visit and experience all this for themselves.

There are many rewards for the intrepid visitor. For example: trekking around an ancient pyramid in the morning, then eating pre-Columbian specialties such as armadillo or iguana in the afternoon; hearing ancient music played on traditional instruments, then dancing the night away to pounding Latin rhythms; sampling indigenous corn gruel at an open-air fonda, then dining on world-class delicacies after dark; visiting the world's second largest (after Moscow's Red Square) *zócalo* (main plaza), once the grounds of an Aztec empire but now home to sixteenth-century Spanish churches. Wealth and poverty, beauty and ghastly ugliness, pristineness and filth, sophistication and illiteracy—these are the elements that make up the City of Contrasts.

Mexico City is a microcosm of the country. Products from every region are trucked, trained, and jetted to its markets: tropical fruits, cocoa, and chiles from Chiapas, Tabasco, and Yucatán; seafood, vanilla, and coffee from Veracruz; mangoes, seafood, and tequila from Jalisco; pork, coconuts, avocados, and exotic wild mushrooms from Michoacán. It's all here and yours for the asking.

Mexico City grows on you. Once you get your bearings and have a sense of its scope and spread, the city's immenseness is not unlike that of Los Angeles with once-outlying towns now part of the sprawl. Try not to drive, and have a blast.

✷ MARKETS ✷

Mercado de Merced East of the city center and just east of Santo Tomás de la Palma church. Metro stop is Merced. Open every day 6 A.M. to 6 P.M. The huge wholesale and retail market is housed in a series of airplane-hangar-sized buildings, one for meats, sausages, seafood, cheeses, *moles*, and prepared food items; another for produce—cartons of fruit piled sky high and vegetables in quantities you've never seen except on a farm. Another building houses more produce plus miles of crêpe-paper piñatas. Still another mammoth building is under construction. Choices are outstanding—there must be two dozen people selling nothing but tomatoes; another two dozen hawking sacks of onions (each onion lovingly cleaned by hand then stacked in pyramids with thousands more); the same number of vendors offering photogenic garlic bunches, each tied with a piece of garlic green; and yet another twenty with only fresh cactus paddles stacked symmetrically in burlap sacks. Purple tomatillos are sweeter and more flavorful than the standard green variety; *miltomates* are tiny tomatillos with concentrated flavor that often grow wild in cornfields. Aisles formed by fruit crates teem with buyers and sellers pushing loaded dollies in every direction. Seasonal fruits such as summer strawberries take up two complete aisles of their own—it's a jam maker's heaven with boxes and buckets of vine-ripened morsels at rock-bottom prices. Ah, the perfume!

Fondas. They are located all around market buildings and offer simple breakfasts and lunches. Scout about for a clean-looking counter, and order a big bowl of homemade soup with tortillas for a few pesos. If you get hungry anywhere near the Eje 1 (street running perpendicular) entrance, look around for a group of women making *tlacoyos* on unoiled *comales*. These hand-patted blue corn *masa* ovals with pointed ends are stuffed with fava or garbanzo bean paste cooked with onion and *epazote*, or refried beans and cheese. Dab on a cooked red salsa made with de árbol chile, tomatoes, onion, and garlic. One *comal* over are *memelas*, slightly larger and thinner corn dough ovals without pointed ends. (Documenting the subtleties of *masa antojitos* [snacks] and their regional changing names would be a lifelong project.) Nearby, Indian women offer *cocoles*, anise-flavored rolls made in the high plains areas around Mexico City, which are typically eaten for *mierenda* with tea, or at night by children who wash them down with a glass of milk. Merced is so big that unless you live nearby, or it's that time of year to make your favorite preserves, the bustle may just be too much. But you have to experience it at least once. Can you believe this isn't even the city's largest market? That's La Central de Abastos, and strictly wholesale.

Mercado de Dulce Directly behind La Merced, Mercado de Dulce (sweet market) is an annex of yet another city block of stands offering every kind of commercial candy in Mexico. Many traditional *dulces* are offered especially around holidays, as are nuts, pinenuts, candied fruit, coconut candies, tamarind sweets, and more.

Mercado de Sonora Across the main street, Fray Servando Teresa de Mier, from Merced is the old Mercado de Sonora, Mexico City's main source of witchcraft supplies. Okay, not everyone who shops here is a *bruja* (witch), but anybody can get anything in the way of other-wordly materials. It's the Magical Mystery Tour for herbalists (not exactly culinary, but the culinary selection is fabulous) and *curanderos* (healers) who find dried leaves and barks from around the globe for their teas and rituals. My friend and unlikely guide, Roberto Santibáñez, the elegant and charming chef-owner of Mexico City's La Circunstancia Restaurant (*the* hottest place to be at night, just off Plaza Garibaldi), admitted he enjoys prowling the mystical labyrinths after a *tlacoyo* breakfast at Merced, "I could eat these every morning—what a great way to start the day!"

Sorcery specials, such as hummingbird wings, dried snake and skunk skins, assorted iguana parts, monkey bones, armadillo pieces, creature skulls, skeletons, claws, tendrils, teeth, and horns, are meticulously displayed. Everyday items such as mosquito eggs are only an aisle away. It's said that Mercado de Sonora is the black market for exotic animals; if you've got the money, here's the place to order a jaguar, and we're not talking cars. Suspected endangered animals of all sorts including Technicolor parrots, toucans, adult and baby owls, and falcons (wearing medieval-looking hoods) are yours for the cash.

Mercado San Juan Pugibet at Luis Moya in the central area. Open 6 A.M. to 6 P.M.Open every day. Mercado San Juan carries Mexico City's best retail seafood selection—glistening trophies from both coasts lavishly displayed on icy mounds. Live snails slide over one another in a giant box with a screen lid. Gourmet meats such as lamb, kid, rabbit, and suckling pig are available every day, not just for holidays. Poultry tables include stewing hens, capons, tiny chickens, different types of duck, quail, pigeon, and pheasant. Fancy expensive fruits are beautifully displayed, including imported beauties destined for cellophane-wrapped gift baskets. Wild mushrooms galore during the summer rainy season are sold from picture-perfect, cloth-lined baskets. *Huitlacoche* (corn fungus), too. **Los Güeros**, a smoked-meat counter with a constant line in front, sells lean, smoked pork loins, sliced hams, salamis, wursts, and various chorizos from Mexico and South America.

Mercado Jamaica Located in the southern area of the city, Mercado Jamaica is an open-air wholesale flower market. Sweet corn; *enchilados* (meaty, shockingly vermilion wild mushrooms), and morels cheap enough to buy dozens, in summer; fruits sold from the backs of farm trucks; pyramids of chiles both fresh and dried; and every seasonal herb you could ever want. Women sell buckets of *quelite*, a leaf cooked like spinach that comes in subtle color variations of red through green and is more herb-flavored. *Quelite* are also sold cooked with chopped onion and chile ready for market vendors to wrap in tortillas for stand-up tacos. Try **El Cuñado**, the *barbacoa* counter for tacos made from delectable lamb baked in maguey-lined pits. My friend, Lila Lomeli, seafood expert, cookbook author, and market guide *extraordinaria*, chooses the same selection of innards for her taco every time she shops Mercado Jamaica, usually Saturday mornings for flowers. As with *carnitas*, you choose your cut and they chop and pile it over warm tortillas. Salsas are lined up on the table—a quick, perfect market munch.

A few traditional fondas are indoors with sandwich counters, cheeses, and meats, but the building mostly contains household products.

If you have a kitchen in Mexico, a mushroom vendor with the most gorgeous morels I've ever seen gave me her recipe:

1. Open large, fresh morels and loosely fill with a mild, melting cheese.
2. Cover with egg batter and pan fry.
3. Serve with tangy tomatillo salsa.

✱ PLACES TO GO AND THINGS TO EAT ✱

Bakeries. El Ideal, 16 de Septiembre (near Lázaro Cárdenas), tel. 566-90-15. Hours: 7 A.M. to 9 P.M. every day. El Ideal has been a *pan dulce* (sweet roll) department store since the 1920s. The chandelier-lit ground floor is still a madhouse in mornings and again around 5 P.M., when the throngs are buying sweet rolls for *merienda* (Mexican-style late afternoon tea). Upstairs, you'll find wedding, fifteenth birthday (a big deal in Mexico—bigger than sweet sixteen in the U.S.), anniversary, and party cakes with so many tiers you can barely see the tops through the trees.

El Molino, 16 de Septiembre No. 37 (near Bolívar), tel. 512-31-14 and 521-04-84. Hours: 7 A.M. to 9 P.M. every day. Pastries, cakes, and a separate fancy candy counter. A few tables are available for an on-the-spot sweet fix. At least twelve other locations around the city and Mexico; call for addresses.

El Globo. The original is at Avenida Popocatepetl No. 526, tel. 605-42-16 or 605-42-82. Neighborhood branches at Periferico Sur No. 4690-F-272, tel. 665-90-20; Prado Sur 120, tel. 52- 36-96; Londres No. 256, tel. 207-94-86; and Revolución 494, tel. 272-10-42. El Globo is an institution (open since 1884), with a sweet roll, bread, or pastry for every taste.

Candy. Dulcería Celaya, Cinco de Mayo No. 39, Centro Histórico (near the cathedral). Tel. 521-17-87. This exquisite Art Nouveau landmark has been Mexico City's premier sweet shop since 1874. Coconut confections, chocolate bonbons, and candied fruits for indulgences. Newer branches are at Insurgentes Sur No, 273-A (between Álvaro Obregón y Yucatán), tel. 574-45-48; and Colima 43-A, Casi Esquina Calle de Córdoba, Colonia Roma, tel. 207-58-58.

Hot Chocolate and *Churros*. El Moro Churrería, Eje Lázaro Cárdenas No. 42, tel. 512-08-98. Open daily, 24 hours. A Mexico City institution and a "must go" in the downtown area of classic thirties-forties restaurants, bars, and clubs (the zoot suit set ate here). It's like nothing else, anywhere. Hot *churros* (ribbed donuts about ten inches long and one-half inch thick) are sugared then rushed to your table with one of four styles of hot chocolate made with milk and Mexico's Carlos V brand of chocolate. The four styles are *Francés*, a classic, silky hot chocolate; *Mexicana*, which contains more milk than Francés; *Español*, the darkest, richest, and sweetest; and *Especial*, which has the least sugar and a bittersweet flavor. All El Moro Churrería's chocolate drinks are foamed by hand with a *molinillo* as they were since opening day in 1935. The waitresses are as sweet as their products and try their best to please first-timers. The *churro* take-out line can be long in afternoons, but it's worth the wait if you're on the go.

A waitress foams hot chocolate with a "molinillo" at Mexico City's El Moro Churrería.

Gourmet Shops, Fancy Imported Foods, Florists, Elegant Linens. Items for the good life: along Masaryk in the Polanco area of town, north of Chapultepec Park. Cream of the produce crop is sold alongside designer caviar at this yuppie Rodeo Drive-ish street. Try **Saint-Honoré** for impressive gifts to give to Mexico City friends, Masaryk 341-A. Tel. 254-65-07. Hours: 10 A.M. to 7:30 P.M. The restaurant stays open later, its hours: 1 P.M. to 10 P.M.

Crafts, Gift Items, Frames, Pottery. Mercado de Artesanías de Insurgentes, Londres 154, downtown. Hours: Monday through Saturday 8 A.M. to 7:30 P.M., Sunday 8 A.M. to 4 P.M. Various merchants sell their wares from stalls, where bargaining is the norm and prices are competitive.

Traditional Kitchen Items, Linens, Pottery, Baskets. Bazaar del Sábado, on the *zócalo* in Colonia San Ángel, a charming suburb south of the city center, sells highly selected handmade items from throughout Mexico. Open only on Saturday when there's also an open-air Indian crafts market (great baskets), until 7 P.M. Inside, ask for **Victoria de la Parra**, an elegant English-speaking woman with incredible weavings, *huipiles* (traditional blouses), tablecloths, and napkins.

La Paraita, Calle Francisco Sosa (near Avenida Universidad) in lovely Colonia Coyocán. A good selection of linens, hand weavings, and embroideries, plus kitchen and home products.

RESTAURANTS

Café de Tacuba. Inexpensive. Tacuba No. 28 (near Allende), Centro Histórico. Tel. 518-49-50; also a new café at Newton No. 88 in Polanco. Tel. 2-50-26-33. Hours: 8 A.M. to 11:30 P.M. Full menu all day, every day. Since opening day in 1912 (just in time for the Mexican Revolution), Café de Tacuba has been a favorite eatery. Its physical beauty alone—original Puebla tile, luscious murals, paintings, and grand ceilings—is reason enough to stop in for coffee. The menu (translated to English) is loaded with enticing breakfast plates. A tempting sweet roll tray, passed around by waitresses in immaculately starched whites, is hard to resist in the morning. Four types of tamales are offered all day; chicken is cooked seven ways; fish fillets cooked four; steaks; chops; enchiladas; and nighttime-only *pozole*. Café de Tacuba is a perfect destination before or after ballet folklórico performances at nearby Palacio de Bellas Artes.

El Bajío. Moderate. Cuitláhuac 2709, Colonia Obrero Popular (a quick taxi ride north of the city center—Mariano Escobedo changes to Cuitláhuac just past Chapultepec Park). Hours: 8 A.M. to 7 P.M. Tel. 341-9889. Carmen Ramírez Degallado's restaurant is the best place in Mexico City for *atole* and *tamales*, or *envuelto* (omelet in banana leaves) breakfasts; snacks like her recipe for *Gorditas de Frijol* (page 215), *sopes*, and tostadas; truly top-notch *carnitas* (or to-go from a take-out window); *barbacoa*; *Mole Verde* (page 122), or full lunches with delicious changing specials such as an amazing "fresh tuna-stuffed poblano chile in *escabeche*" the last time I was there. If *mole de xico* is on the menu absolutely try it, the rich sauce from Veracruz is made from black mulato chile, prunes, and plantains. There's a full bar but order a refreshing chile-quencher, *Agua Fresca de Pepino* (page 126) with lunch. Carmen's collection of contemporary paintings and exceptional folk art adds wonders to El Bajío's all-around charm. Be sure to say "hi" to Carmen and her look-alike daughter, María del Carmen. Both speak English and are eager to guide first-timers through their menu.

Fonda el Refugio. Expensive. Liverpool No. 166, in Zona Rosa (between Florencia and Amberes). Reservations tel. 528-58-23. Lunch and dinner. Closed Sunday. Not at all what you'd expect on first sight as one of Mexico City's premier restaurants—an old house converted to multiple-level dining rooms. Once inside, its charm emerges and whitewashed rooms actually glow with warmth from old copper. Fabulous service has been a highlight since Señora Judith Martínez Ortega de van Beuren opened Fonda el Refugio in 1954; Daniela Van Beuren, her granddaughter, runs the show today. Seasonal quesadillas with either squash blossoms or *huitlacoche* are fabulous appetizers; traditional family recipes such as Beef Filet with Onion, Potato, and Chile (page 125), and *dulce de zapote negro* (an exotic, pitch black, glistening tropical fruit dessert that looks like puréed patent leather) finish a memorable meal.

Don Chón. Moderate. Calle Regina 159 (at Jesus María). No reservations. Hours: 10 A.M. to 7 P.M. every day. Basically a long lunch spot with casual, family-style decor. Over forty years serving pre-Columbian cuisine, Don Chón is located in Mexico City's fascinating downtown thirties-forties area. Sample ant roe (a Mexican delicacy), armadillo *mole*, and various iguana presentations from a menu that changes daily. Chef Florencio's meatballs in chrysanthemum petals is an ancient recipe. Here's a restaurant calling itself a fonda to imply casualness and home cooking, albeit truly fascinating home cooking for the adventurous diner.

Casa Merlos. Inexpensive to moderate. Lucila Molina de Merlos's restaurant is at Victoriano Zepeda No. 80, Colonia Observatorio (south of the city center), tel. 516-40-17 or 277-43-60. Be sure to reserve a table for Sunday afternoons because long lines of large families form at 2 P.M. Traditional favorite dishes from Mexico City and Puebla start with squash blossom soup, then go on to a delectable order of three *chiles rellenos* stuffed with squash blossoms, soft cheese, and *picadillo*. *Carne a la poblana* (grilled beef) comes with two *chalupas*, refried beans, and sautéed chile strips—it's authentic Poblano regional cooking if you're not visiting Puebla, a two-hour drive away. Lucila also prepares *mole poblano*, *pepián verde*, and *chiles en nogada* (in season, late summer-fall). Dessert puddings include rice, bread, and pine nut custard.

Restaurant Danubio. Moderate. Uruguay No. 3 (at Avenida Lázaro Cárdenas). Tel. 518-12-05, 512-09-12, and 521-09-76. Hours: 1 P.M. to midnight every day. Mexico City's best seafood restaurant and downtown classic, Danubio is around the corner from a couple of other stand-bys, El Moro Churrería and Don Chón. A huge selection of fish and shellfish from both coasts awaits you: pompano, grouper, red snapper, and shrimp from the Gulf; more shrimp, lobsters, langostinos, swordfish, yellowtail, and dorado from the Pacific. The set price meal with its five or six courses is a bargain and is served for lunch or dinner. Danubio was first recommended to me by Lila Lomeli, the highly regarded Mexico City food consultant and author who has written five seafood cookbooks.

Marita Reyes de Rodrigo's

Sopa de Nopales *Cactus Paddle Soup*

MERCADO MERCED HAS AN AISLE DEVOTED TO NOTHING BUT EDIBLE CACTUS. *Opuntia* cactus leaves (or actual flat stems) are from the same plant that produces the prickly pear fruit called *tuna* in Mexico. Cactus leaves (also called paddles) are sold from burlap sacks cut away to reveal four-foot-high cylinders of neatly arranged paddles. Strolling down market aisles you'll understand the importance of cactus as a food to Mexicans. If you have no access to fresh *nopales*, jarred or canned without vinegar will do. Just don't cook them, as they are precooked, simply drain and rinse.
Yield: 6 servings

For the "nopales"

- 4 fresh cactus leaves (about 4 inches by 8 inches)
- 1 white onion, cut in half
- 6 garlic cloves, smashed

1. Using a sharp knife, shave off the bumps that contain the paddle's cactus thorns, but not the entire skin. Cut off the base and trim the edge all around.
2. In a large pot, bring 4 quarts of water to a boil. Add the *nopales*, onion, and garlic. Boil for 5 minutes. Drain and rinse with cold water to remove the okra-like substance. Add another 4 quarts water to the pot and bring it to a boil. Add the cactus and cook for about 10 minutes longer or until tender. Drain and once more rinse with cold water.

Assembling the soup

- 1 pound tomatoes (about 3)
- 4 garlic cloves
- 2 canned chipotle chiles en adobo
- 1 Tablespoon vegetable oil
- 6 cups Chicken Broth (page 19)
- 3 Tablespoons chopped cilantro
- salt to taste
- 1 cup ranchero cheese, dry cottage cheese, or farmer cheese

1. Toast (page 16) the tomatoes and put them in a plastic bag to "sweat" for a few minutes. Toast the garlic, remove the skins, and put the vegetables in a blender. Add chipotles en adobo without sauce. Purée.
2. Heat the oil in a pot. Carefully pour in the tomato purée (it splatters!). Add the broth and cilantro. Bring the liquid back to a boil, then reduce the heat to a simmer.
3. Chop the cactus leaves then add them to the liquid and simmer 5 minutes uncovered. Salt to taste. Serve in wide, flat bowls sprinkled with ranchero cheese. Pass a basket of corn chips or tortillas.

Ana Castro de Méndez's

Arroz Rojo *Red Rice*

THE OLD STANDBY, *ARROZ ROJO*, IS SERVED EVERY DAY IN FONDAS across the country. It's the classic "cheap eats" special—rice, beans, tortillas, plus a spoonful of salsa—that costs almost nothing at market counters and even less to make at home. Red rice is a standard breakfast, lunch, or light supper bed for fried eggs. Fresh food is not cheap in Mexico; you'll discover this when shopping in markets or eating in restaurants. Very poor families throughout the country still get by on rice, beans, and tortillas on a daily basis.

At Mercado de Merced, the series of market buildings that are larger than a football field, rice and beans are sold at every fonda. Market workers hunt for bargain lunches; if a fonda is known to have excellent red rice and pink beans (whether soupy or refried) there's always a wait. At the fonda where Ana cooks there's always a line. The reason, says Ana, is the rice. It's made with care and fresh ingredients—homemade chicken stock, no canned tomatoes, and definitely no frozen vegetables.

Yield: 8 servings

- 4 ripe plum tomatoes, or 2 large tomatoes
- 1 small white onion, peeled and coarsely chopped
- 2 garlic cloves, chopped
- 2 cups long grain white rice
- 2 Tablespoons vegetable oil
- salt and pepper to taste
- ½ cup diced (¼-inch cubes) carrots
- ½ cup fresh peas (baby peas or frozen will become hopelessly overcooked)
- 4 cups hot homemade Chicken Broth (page 19)

1. Toast the tomatoes. Purée in a blender container with the onion and garlic.

2. Put the rice in a strainer and let water run over it for at least 2 minutes (this process takes longer in Mexico because of the rice) to get rid of any milky residue and to ensure that the rice grains separate after cooking. Dry the rice by shaking the strainer over the sink.

3. Heat the oil in a large saucepan (with cover), add the rice, and sauté, stirring constantly for 5 minutes, until it turns translucent then becomes golden. Add the tomato purée to the sizzling rice. Add the salt and pepper, carrots, and peas, stirring only a moment. Add the hot chicken stock, bring to a boil, then lower the heat. Cover the pot and simmer 25 minutes.

4. Remove the pot from the heat and let the rice rest for 5 to 10 minutes without removing the lid. Fluff the rice with a fork to separate the grains, and serve.

Mercado de Merced Fonda's

Quesadillas *Filled Tortilla Turnovers*

QUESADILLAS ARE PROBABLY EVERYONE'S FAVORITE STREET AND MARKET FOOD. Filling is spooned onto a tortilla, then the tortilla is folded in half and it's cooked in a little oil until it's wonderfully chewy-crisp and golden.

Quesillo de Oaxaca is the cheese everyone loves for quesadillas. Mozzarella, string cheese, or Monterey Jack cheeses are good substitutes in the U.S., but the taste won't be quite so tangy. Poblano chile, or spicier jalapeño chile strips, are sautéed with onion, spooned onto a tortilla, topped with shredded cheese, then cooked until the cheese is melted. In the U.S., a flour tortilla covered with processed orange cheese squirted from an aerosol can, and then microwaved, is sometimes called a quesadilla, but is strictly north-of-the-border kid's stuff.

Here are the easiest and most delicious *antojitos*, or margarita snacks, since potato chips and pretzels. Serve with a spicy salsa, either fresh or cooked.

Yield: 4 quesadillas

- 2 Tablespoons vegetable oil (additional, if needed)
- 1 small white onion, chopped
- 2 poblano chiles, charred, skinned, stemmed, seeded, deveined, and cut into thin vertical strips
- 4 corn tortillas
- ¾ cup "quesillo de Oaxaca," mozzarella cheese, string cheese, or Monterey Jack cheese

1. Heat the oil in a skillet. Add the onion and chile strips and sauté until lightly brown. Remove to a small bowl. There should be remaining oil in the skillet, if not, add 1 tablespoon and heat.

2. Add 1 tortilla, cook 30 seconds, and turn it over. Put a quarter of the onion-chile mixture on the tortilla, add a quarter of the cheese, and fold, spreading the filling and pressing the edges closed. Move the quesadilla to the side and continue with the other three tortillas, overlapping the folded quesadillas as finished.

3. Cook, turning to cook both sides. Quesadillas should be golden and a little crisp, but not so crisp as deep-fried, a chewy texture is very important in Mexico.

(Continued)

Variation: Cheese, Chile, Squash Blossom, and *Epazote*

This combination may appear elegant, but it's one of the most typical quesadillas around. Pumpkin blossoms add flavor and texture to the delectable morsels—*epazote*, the classic southern Mexico taste.

8 pumpkin blossoms, cleaned
4 "epazote" leaves, or 1 teaspoon dried, if possible

1. Prepare quesadillas as above but add pumpkin blossoms to the onion-chile mixture before cooking. You may omit the chile, but be sure to pass salsa at the table.
2. Before folding, add a shredded *epazote* leaf to each quesadilla. Continue with the recipe.

Lula Bertrán's

Tamales de Elote Entomatados

Fresh Corn and Tomato Mini-Tamales

LULA BERTRÁN IS ONE OF MEXICO'S BEST KNOWN FOOD WRITERS. She is editor-consultant of the three major food magazines and food editor of a fourth in Mexico City. Lula brought French cuisine into Mexico City homes years ago; lately she's a consultant to U.S. companies through her firm, Cocina Mexicana, and writing her own cookbooks. Her style is pure elegance—Mexican with classical French overtones—and her dishes are always designed with visual presentation in mind.

Fresh corn and tomato mini-tamales are from her grandmother's file of old recipes. Lula says, "It's a not-often-seen recipe that's served as a side dish. Small bits of chicken, pork, fish, or *rajas* may be used as an optional filling."

Don't be surprised by the small amount of *masa*; its role is simply to bind the kernels together. Make the tamales in summer when corn is at its sweetest and tomatoes taste the way they're supposed to—any filling is extraneous. (Fillings are more welcome off-season when fresh kernels can use a flavor boost.) With *Crema* (page 80), fresh tomato salsa, and traditionally, *Frijoles de Olla* (page 46), the tiny bundles are a child's joy and adult's delight.
Yield: 12 to 20 mini-tamales

- ¼ cup fresh lard (page 18), or butter
- ¼ cup finely chopped white onion
- 3 dark, red-ripe tomatoes, puréed in a blender to make 1 cup
- ¼ cup fresh "masa," or 3 Tablespoons flour and ¼ cup "masa harina" mixed with ¼ cup water
- ¼ teaspoon salt
- 2 cups raw corn kernels, scraped from cobs (about 5)
- Optional filling
- 20 tender, fresh corn leaves (not dried husks), washed and soaked in hot water, plus 5 or 6 extra to make "ribbons" (about ¼ inch wide and 6 inches long) to tie the tamales closed

1. Heat the lard or butter in a medium-sized, non-aluminum pot. Add the onion and sauté until golden. Add the tomato purée and cook until the mixture is almost dry, about 10 minutes.

2. In a large bowl, add the tomato mixture to the *masa* and salt, and mix well with your hand until the mixture is evenly salmon colored, about 5 minutes. Add the corn kernels and mix another minute.

3. Take a small portion (about 2 tablespoons) of the mixture and flatten it in your palm. Top with a bit of optional filling and surround the filling with the mixture into a shape and size of a thumb (or the same amount of unfilled mixture) and center it on the inside of a small corn leaf. Flap the top over and bring the sides inward (the top does not tuck under). If the sides cannot flap inward, there's too much mixture—remove a teaspoon. Tie with a "ribbon." Repeat with the remaining leaves, mixture, and optional filling.

4. Bring water to a boil in a tamale steamer (see Glossary), vegetable steamer, or even a Chinese bamboo steamer, and steam until they are cooked, about 30 minutes. You'll know they're done when you open a tamale and the *masa* separates easily from the leaf wrapping. To eat, unwrap the fresh leaf (carefully, it's hot) and discard.

Maru López Brun's

Enchiladas Blancas *Chile-Stuffed Rolled Enchiladas in White Cheese Sauce*

MARU, ORIGINALLY FROM PUEBLA, NOW RESIDES IN MEXICO CITY. Her recipe for *enchiladas blancas* is made with a few of Mexico's favorite rich ingredients—cheese and cream—but these days Maru uses milk. Poblano chiles, onions, and freshly ground white pepper add flavor to familiar filled, rolled, and sauced-style enchiladas (versus the folded style of Oaxaca).

Yield: 6 servings

- 2 Tablespoons butter
- 3 Tablespoons white flour
- 1 quart whole milk
- ½ teaspoon salt
- ½ teaspoon freshly ground white pepper
- 1 pound plump poblano chiles, stemmed and seeded
- ½ pound queso fresco, dry cottage cheese, or farmer cheese, crumbled
- 1 Tablespoon vegetable oil
- ½ cup finely chopped white onion
- ½ cup vegetable oil
- 12 corn tortillas
- ¼ cup chopped flat-leaf parsley, for garnish

1. Make a white sauce (béchamel): Heat the butter in a saucepan and, when bubbling, add the flour, stirring with a wooden spoon. Lower the heat to a simmer and cook for a minute just to cook the flour before it changes color. Add the milk slowly and simmer, stirring, for 5 minutes. Remove the saucepan from the heat and stir in salt and white pepper.

2. Wash the chiles and purée them in a blender. Add the crumbled cheese and blend with the chiles.

3. Heat 1 tablespoon oil in a deep pot and sauté the onion until it turns golden. Carefully add the chile sauce (it splatters!) and fry the sauce a minute, then turn down the heat to a low simmer.

4. Return the béchamel to low heat.

5. Heat the ½ cup oil in a skillet and fry a tortilla for about 15 seconds, shake off extra oil, then dip it in the béchamel. Put it on a plate and top with a few spoonfuls of the chile sauce. Roll the tortilla to form an enchilada. Continue with another on the same plate and top the two with additional sauce. Garnish with chopped parsley. Continue with the other 10 tortillas.

Lula Bertrán's

▲▼▲

Arroz en Adobo *Red Rice with Meat*

LULA BERTRÁN IS ONE OF MEXICO CITY'S REIGNING FOOD AUTHORITIES. Her classic French cooking background reflects Mexican touches in recipes she develops for Mexico's premier food magazines. A bit out of character from her usually elegant dishes, this traditional Mexican main course recipe for daily *comida corrida* is from Lula's grandmother. It tastes exactly like rice dishes in countless fondas and small restaurants throughout the city—waves of nostalgia hit every time you prepare this simple dish at home. "Many other ingredients can be used with, or instead of, the pork. This dish is similar to Spanish paella—you add what you have on hand," says Lula. It's delicious prepared with either chicken or strips of turkey breast. For a vegetarian meal, use large chunks of squash, whole mushrooms, yams, or carrots.

Yield: 4 servings

- 4 Tablespoons fresh lard (page 18), or vegetable oil
- 1 pound pork loin (or other meat), cut into small dice
- 1 ancho chile, washed and soaked in hot water for 30 minutes
- 2 garlic cloves, peeled
- ½ small white onion, cut in half
- ½ cup water
- 2 cups boiling water
- 1 cup long-grain white rice, washed until the water runs clear
- 2 Tablespoons large capers
- 1 Tablespoon dried Mexican oregano
- ¼ teaspoon salt

1. Heat the lard or oil and fry the meat in a deep pot until it browns. Remove the meat with a slotted spoon to a dish. Reserve the oil in the pot.

2. Stem and seed the chile. Put it in a blender container with the garlic, onion, and ½ cup water. Purée until smooth, scraping down the sides of the blender with a rubber spatula.

3. Reheat the oil in the pot, carefully add the blender ingredients (it splatters!) and fry the sauce. Cook, stirring, for 2 minutes.

4. Add 2 cups boiling water and the reserved meat to the pot. Bring it back to a boil. Add the rice, capers, oregano, and salt. Mix well, then lower the heat to the lowest simmer and cover. Cook until the rice is cooked and the meat tender, about 25 minutes. More water may be added little by little, if needed. When cooked, the rice should be a bit moist—not too dry.

Mercado de Merced Fonda's

Tortas *Overstuffed Sandwiches on French Rolls*

THERE ARE SANDWICHES AND THEN THERE ARE MEXICAN *TORTAS*. *Tortas* are the furthest thing from pretty, crustless, English tea sandwiches you can imagine. Huge, chewy French rolls, called *bolillos* (about six inches by four inches) are sliced horizontally, then their soft centers are pulled out to make room for sky-high layers of fillings. The whole thing is flopped on a grill, pressed with a spatula, flipped over to grill on side two, half-wrapped in paper, and handed over in less time than you can say "Where's the salsa?"

These recipes are a selection from watching countless examples being made at fondas in and near Mexico City markets. *Torta* varieties are endless; these are a few classics. Use whatever's in your refrigerator topped with a handful of shredded lettuce and pickled vegetables. *Yield: 1* torta

Milanese (Breaded and Sautéed Beef)

- 1 thin slice beef, about 3 inches by 4 inches and ⅛-inch thick, pounded to flatten
- 1 egg, beaten in a small bowl
- ¼ cup dry bread crumbs
- 2 Tablespoons vegetable oil
- 1 "bolillo"
- 2 teaspoons mayonnaise and/or mustard to taste
- ½ avocado
- ½ tomato
- ¼ cup shredded iceberg lettuce or cabbage
- 4 raw onion rings
- 1 sliced pickled chile

1. Dip the beef in beaten egg then bread crumbs. Sauté the meat in hot oil in a skillet until the crumbs are browned on both sides. Slice into ½-inch strips.

2. Cut a *bolillo* or French roll in half lengthwise and pull out the soft center from both sides. Place it in the skillet, cut side down, for 1 minute. Remove from the skillet. Flip the roll over and cover the bottom side with mayonnaise and the beef strips.

3. Cut 4 ripe avocado slices onto the other bread half and spread, like thick butter. Arrange 3 or 4 tomato slices on top of the beef and cover with a mound of shredded lettuce or cabbage. Add the onion rings and pickled chile.

4. Flip the meat side onto the avocado half with a spatula, put back in the skillet and continue to brown the roll while pressing down with the spatula. Flip the *torta* over again and continue pressing into the pan for final browning, another 30 seconds.

(Continued)

Puerco (Cold Pork Roast)

1. For leftover pork roast, cut a *bolillo* or French roll in half lengthwise, scoop out the inside of the roll, and heat it in a large skillet with a bit of oil, cut side down. Remove.
2. Thinly slice lean, leftover roast pork and quickly heat it in the skillet.
3. Spread both sides of the roll with mayonnaise and/or mustard. Arrange the pork on one half. Top with thinly sliced raw onions and Vinegared Chile Strips, and Carrots (page 245), or canned pickled jalapeño chiles.
4. Top the other half with shredded cabbage. Flip the meat side onto the cabbage half with a spatula and continue to brown the roll while pressing down with the spatula. Flip over again and continue pressing into the skillet for final browning, another 30 seconds.

Jamón y Queso (Ham and Cheese)

1. Cut a *bolillo* or French roll in half lengthwise, scoop out the inside of the roll, and heat in a skillet with a bit of oil, cut side down.
2. Flip the roll over and spread the bottom side with a layer of refried beans. Top with thinly sliced boiled ham and shredded string cheese or mozzarella. Add some sliced raw onions, a handful of shredded lettuce, and a few vinegared chiles.
3. Spread mustard on the inside top half and close the sandwich. Continue to brown the roll while pressing down with a spatula. Flip over again and continue pressing into the skillet for final browning, another 30 seconds.

Huevos con Chorizo (Scrambled Eggs and Chorizo)

1. Cut a *bolillo* or French roll in half lengthwise, scoop out the inside of the roll, and heat in a skillet with a bit of oil, cut side down.
2. Scramble eggs with cooked and crumbled chorizo. Flip over the roll and fill with the egg mixture. Top with thickly sliced tomatoes, chopped pickled chile, and shredded lettuce.
3. Spread mayonnaise on the inside top half and close the sandwich. Continue to brown the roll while pressing down with a spatula. Flip over again and continue pressing into the skillet for final browning, another 30 seconds.

Carmen Ramírez Degollado's

Mole Verde *Green* Mole *with Corn Dough Dumplings*

CARMEN'S DELICIOUS MEXICO CITY SPECIALTY IS INTERESTING TO COMPARE with Ana Marina (Anita) Silva Bohorquez's *Mole Amarillo con Chochoyones* (Yellow Mole with *Masa* Dumplings), from Oaxaca (page 242) . Both recipes offer a choice of meats—Carmen's more vegetables and greens for color, Anita's potatoes and cloves plus dried chiles. Anita also likes a denser liquid so she adds *masa* to the broth, plus her potatoes break down and act as a thickener. Both recipes add *masa* dumplings formed by making an indentation with a finger in tiny *masa* balls (the shape of Italian pasta, orecchiette, or "little ears," comes to mind), only here the *masa* is thicker.

Yield: 8 servings

- 6 cups water
- 3 garlic cloves
- ½ white onion
- 1 teaspoon salt
- 2 pounds pork shoulder or beef chuck with some bone, cut into 1-inch cubes
- 3 chayotes or other summer squash
- ½ pound green beans
- ½ pound fresh peas
- ½ pound tender fresh beans such as fava or lima
- ½ teaspoon salt
- 3 small sweet, cooking pumpkins (not the jack-o'-lantern variety), or acorn or butternut squash
- 1 onion
- 1 pound tomatillos
- 6 jalapeño chiles, stemmed
- ¼ teaspoon cumin seed
- 6 cilantro springs, leaves only
- 1 "epazote" sprig
- 2 tender green lettuce leaves
- 10 squash leaves, if available or substitute lettuce
- 2 Tablespoons lard or vegetable oil

1. In a clay or other pot boil the water and add 1 garlic clove, onion, and salt. When it returns to a full boil, add the meat and simmer for 1 hour with the cover askew, or until it is cooked (no pink shows when cut open). Remove the cooked meat from the broth and cut it into pieces. Retain the broth for cooking the dumplings.

2. Cut the chayotes into ½-inch cubes, cut the green beans in half crosswise, shell the peas and fresh beans, and cook in another pot of boiling water for 15 minutes with ½ teaspoon salt.

3. Cut the pumpkins into quarters and put them in yet another pot of boiling water and boil until tender, about 30 minutes.

4. Toast (page 16) the onion, tomatillos, chiles, and cumin seed and put them in a blender container and blend. Add the cilantro, *epazote*, lettuce, and squash leaves and purée.

5. Heat the lard or oil in a deep pot and carefully pour in the sauce from the blender (it splatters!). Fry the sauce for 2 minutes, stirring. Lower the heat and simmer for 15 minutes, uncovered. Add the meat, and cooked vegetables and season to taste.

(Continued)

For the corn dough dumplings

- 8 ounces "masa," or "masa harina" prepared per package instructions (1 cup)
- 3 Tablespoons lard or vegetable shortening
- pinch of salt

1. Mix the *masa* well with the lard or vegetable shortening and salt, until it is light.
2. Form balls ½ inch in diameter and, with a finger, press the ball to form a concave side, "so they look like little *cazuelas*" (earthenware cooking pots with rounded bottoms), says Carmen.

Finishing the dish

1. Skim fat from the surface, then heat the meat cooking broth to a simmer and carefully drop a few dumplings at a time into the just slightly bubbling broth. Remove when they are cooked, about 10 minutes.
2. Arrange a piece of meat and vegetables in each bowl with some dumplings and add a ladle of broth.

Carmen Ramírez Degollado at her El Bajío restaurant.

Martha Figueroa de Dueñas's

Pato Salvaje con Chocolate, Pasas y Manzanas

Wild Duck with Ancho Chile, Dried Fruit, and Chocolate

CARMEN RAMÍREZ DEGOLLADO, OF MEXICO CITY'S EL BAJÍO RESTAURANT, invited Morris and me to dinner in Puebla when we were living in that city for a month. Her culinary society was presenting a series of great Mexican chefs. Martha Figueroa de Dueñas was chef the evening of our dinner, and her dishes were outstanding. When she finally had a chance to sit and relax after the feast, she mentioned that her new cookbook, *Xocoatl: El Chocolate la Aportación de México al Mundo* (*Chocolate: Mexico's Contribution to the World*), was a collection of recipes all incorporating chocolate. I begged for a recipe right there on the spot. Martha's wild duck recipe is her grandmother's, and I'm sure the long-deceased woman would be thrilled even if you made it with a domestic duck.

Yield: 2 to 3 servings

- 8 pitted prunes
- ¼ cup raisins
- ⅓ cup rum
- 1 wild, or 5-pound domestic duck
- 3 ancho chiles, stemmed and seeded
- 2 garlic cloves
- 2 teaspoons cocoa
- 1 three-inch "canela" stick, or 1 two-inch cinnamon stick
- 1 small onion
- 2 apples, peeled, cored, and sliced
- ½ teaspoon salt and a few grinds of black pepper
- 1 slice bacon

1. Marinate the prunes and raisins in half the rum for at least 2 and up to 24 hours. Clean the duck, remove any extra fat, and prick the skin all over. Place it in a glass or ceramic casserole and marinate in the remaining rum, refrigerated.

2. Preheat the oven to 350° F.

3. Toast (page 16) the chiles and garlic. Soak the chiles in hot water for 20 minutes. Purée the soaked chiles and garlic in a blender with 1 teaspoon cocoa and 1 tablespoon water.

4. Mix the prunes, raisins, remaining cocoa, *canela*, onion, apples, and salt and pepper, and stuff the duck cavity loosely. Place the bacon slice on the duck breast, lengthwise. Truss the bird with kitchen string to keep the bacon, wings, and legs in place while roasting. Spread the blended chile paste over the duck. Place the duck on a rack in a roasting pan, breast side down. Add any remaining prune mixture to the pan.

5. Roast 50 minutes for a small, wild bird, or 1½ hours for a domestic duck, turning it breast side up 20 minutes before it is finished. Remove rendered fat from the pan with a bulb baster from time to time.

Fonda El Refugio's

Filete de Carne *Beef Filet with Onion, Potato, and Serrano Chile*

FONDA EL REFUGIO IS ONE OF MEXICO CITY'S TOP RESTAURANTS FOR TRADITIONAL FOOD. Its lovely, simple, multi-floored building is in the Zona Rosa, Mexico City's premier dining and nightlife area, which puts it within walking distance of most hotels. This restaurant is on everyone's "best" list—you probably have it on your "must go" list already—and don't miss the opportunity to taste regional cooking at its most refined. Daniela van Beuren, general manager, told me that her grandmother (Fonda El Refugio's founder) put this dish on the restaurant's menu when it opened in 1954.

Double or quadruple the ingredients for a quick, flavorful, and classically Mexican beef dinner. Serve with Tomatillo Salsa (page 244).

Yield: 1 serving

- 1 seven-ounce beef filet, butterflied and pounded at the "hinge" so the steak is uniformly thick
- ¼ cup olive oil
- 3 garlic cloves, smashed
- salt and freshly ground black pepper
- 1 small red potato, cut into cubes
- 3 "cebollitas de cambray" (tiny onions with their green tops), or whole scallions, cut into 1-inch pieces
- 3 or 4 serrano chiles, stemmed and chopped

1. Marinate the beef filet in oil, garlic, salt, and pepper for 1 hour, unrefrigerated, or for 4 hours, refrigerated.

2. Steam the potato cubes until tender when tested with a fork (about 20 minutes).

3. Heat 2 tablespoons vegetable oil and sauté the onions and chile until they turn brown.

4. Meanwhile, grill the beef to the doneness you prefer. Put the steak on a warm plate and surround it with potatoes, onions, and chile.

María del Carmen Ramírez Degollado's

Agua Fresca de Pepino *Cold Cucumber Drink*

THROUGH THE AGES CUCUMBER HAS BEEN KNOWN TO BE COOLING AND HEALING—as a drink it's both. It's simple to make and cucumbers are available year-round. Cold cucumber drink should not be sweet—it's more refreshing without too much sugar. María del Carmen, one of Carmen Ramírez Degollado's two chef daughters, enjoys serving a pitcher of it when guests eat too much of her incredible chipotle chile and garlic salsa, which arrives with *gordita* appetizers at El Bajío Restaurant.
Yield: 3 quarts

- 3 large cucumbers, peeled and coarsely sliced
- 7 limes, juiced (½ cup)
- 3 quarts water
- ¼ to ½ cup sugar

1. Put ½ cup water in a blender container with 1 cup sliced cucumbers. Blend. Add more cucumbers and blend. Continue until the cucumbers are all blended.
2. Strain the cucumber juice of its seeds into a very large pitcher or container. Add the water and lime juice. Add sugar to taste and chill before serving, stirring well.

Lina Hermila López de Reyes's

Atole *Hot* Masa-*Based Drinks*

TAMALES AND *ATOLE* GO TOGETHER LIKE BURGERS AND COKE, but the difference is that tamales and *atole* have been a classic combination since pre-Hispanic times. In fact, corn gruel was the basis of the Mesoamerican diet before 500 B.C. and *atole* is thinned corn gruel. Variations are limitless because the nourishing drink is enjoyed throughout the country and regional touches are a fact of life. Texture can vary tremendously, too, depending on the *masa's* grind or if the liquid is thickened with smooth cornstarch. Flavorings include chocolate, vanilla, fruit of all types, juices, nuts, seeds, rice, fresh corn, and chile.

You'd be hard-pressed to find a traditional market without an *atole* counter anywhere in Mexico. Morning and nighttime tamale-*atole* vendors are easy to spot on street corners by the steam rising from their portable stands. Lina, a friend met at Mercado San Juan while we were both admiring a basket of incredible wild mushrooms, graciously agreed to accompany me on a morning *atole*-tamale breakfast sampling. We hit her favorite street corner locations first, then explored places suggested by her friends, usually inside, or just outside market buuildings.
Yield: about 1 quart

Atole de Leche (Milk with Masa Drink)

- 7 ounces fresh "masa," or use "masa harina"
- 1½ quarts water
- 3 cups milk
- 8 ounces "panela" (broken up) or dark brown sugar
- 1 teaspoon vanilla extract
- 1 four-inch "canela" stick, or two-inch cinnamon stick

1. Dissolve *masa* in 1 quart water, then strain the water into a saucepan (throw away the *masa*). Boil until it is thick, stirring with a wooden spoon, about 15 minutes.

2. Add the milk, *panela*, vanilla, and *canela*.

3. Bring the liquid back to a simmer, stirring often, to thicken. This step takes from 45 to 60 minutes—keep the heat at its lowest so the milk doesn't curdle. Remove the *canela* stick before serving.

Champurrado (Chocolate with Masa Drink)

- 6 ounces fresh extra finely ground "masa," or "masa harina"
- 1 quart water
- 2 cups milk
- 8 ounces "panela" (broken up) or dark brown sugar
- 1 two-inch "canela" stick, or ¼ teaspoon ground cinnamon
- 4 ounces Mexican chocolate tablet, broken up
- 4 aniseed, crushed (optional)

1. Dissolve the fresh *masa* in 1 quart water, then strain the water into a saucepan (throw away the *masa*). Boil until it is thick, stirring with a wooden spoon, about 15 minutes. Add the milk, *panela*, *canela*, chocolate and optional aniseed.

2. Bring the liquid back to a simmer, then stir often with a wooden spoon to thicken. This step takes 45 to 60 minutes—keep the heat at its lowest so the milk doesn't curdle.

3. Strain. Right before serving, using a *molinillo* or a hand mixer, whip the *champurrado* until a foam covers the top.

Atole de Fruta (Fruit with Masa Drink)

- 4 ounces cornstarch
- 2 cups water
- 1 quart plus 1 cup milk
- 2 cups sugar ("panela" is seldom used with fruit "atoles")
- 1 to 2 pounds very ripe fruit such as berries, peaches, or mangoes

1. Dissolve the cornstarch in the water and heat it in a medium pot. When the cornstarch water begins to thicken, reduce the heat to a simmer, add 1 quart milk and the sugar, stir, and remove the pot from the heat.

2. Clean the fruit and purée in a blender. Strain the fruit if necessary. Add the additional cup of milk to the fruit and blend. Add the blender ingredients to the pot and reheat the mixture, stirring. Do not boil the mixture; bring it only to the simmer. Serve immediately.

◆ Toluca ◆

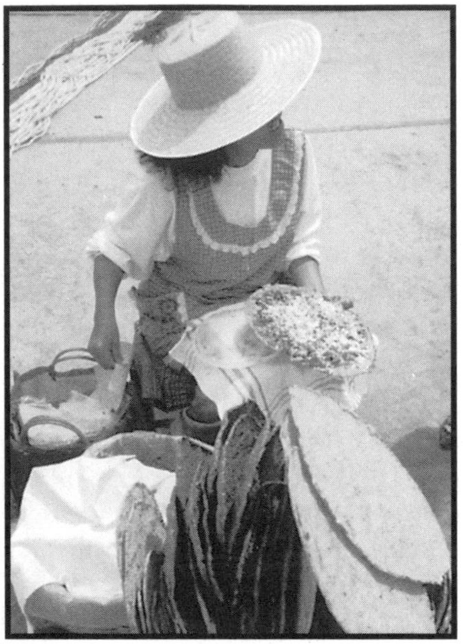

Toluca's version of "huaraches" at Mercado Juárez.

TOLUCA, LOCATED AN HOUR'S DRIVE WEST of Mexico City high up in the surrounding volcanic mountain range, usually not thought of as a tourist stop because it's a rather industrial city, is known for chorizo (sausage). Sometimes-snow-capped Nevada de Toluca, an extinct volcano, towers over the city. The city center's attractive Plaza de los Mártires, with its innumerable kiosks selling Mexican sweets of all kinds, can undo any sugar freak. Kiosk after kiosk sells more or less exactly the same products—from delightful traditional coconut confections to artificially flavored, colored, cellophane-wrapped sugar squares that melt in your hand, not in your mouth.

✷ MARKET ✷

Mercado Juárez Located at Cinco de Mayo and Isidro Fabela (just south of the city center near the bus station), and touted as the highest-altitude market in Mexico at 8,760 feet, Juárez is a nationally known mecca for Mexican foodies: Here you'll find world-class chorizo, excellent fresh and aged cheeses from cows fed in high-altitude pastures, and *crema* that seems just a bit thicker than anywhere else. As with Guadalajara's Mercado Libertad (page 23), everything you could possibly ever need can be found at this huge indoor marketplace. On Friday, the big shopping day, the entire plaza, its surrounding streets, plus every nook and cranny of outdoor space, becomes a *tianguis*, an Indian market, a frenzy of energy and visual stimulation. Many people claim Toluca's Friday market to be the biggest in Mexico. Vendors arrive before light to stake their claims for space to sell home-grown produce, baskets, wild herbs, hand-sewn items, *rebozos*, *serapes*, homemade cheeses, live poultry and pigs, pottery, tortillas, tamales, *tlacoyos*, and pottery from the nearby towns of Metepec and Uetepec. Hard bargaining is a given here. Every day is market day to the vendors at the stalls inside the three huge market buildings filled with produce, fondas, or household goods and clothing. Behind these buildings and extending for a few more blocks is yet more wholesale market space. Walk till you drop—it's exciting and like nothing at home.

Fondas. Try a sandwich of *chorizo verde* (green sausage, made with fresh herbs, chiles, and pine nuts), with sliced avocado, raw onion, and pickled vegetables. Sit right down at one of the fondas selling both raw chorizo and sandwiches, in the fondas building. You'll know you're at the right place when you see a counter piled with French rolls and sandwich fixings under strings of multicolored sausages.

Pozole, *birria*, and chicken soup variations are all served in steaming bowls, from early in the morning for market workers to about 7 P.M. Since many fondas offer the long-simmering specialties, look for a clean, crowded counter and sit down with the locals.

Tlacoyos. Outside entrances to the fondas building on the plaza, women sell *tlacoyos*, handmade, oval, blue corn tortillas folded over lengthwise and filled with such gourmet temptations as *huitlachoche* and squash blossoms. Another variation is what market women call *ava* (pronounced aba), but that is also known as *tlacoyos de dos masas*—yellow corn *masa* within a thick blue *masa* oval—cooked on an ungreased clay *comal,* then topped with tomatillo salsa.

Huaraches. In the main plaza between market buildings, other women sell an unusual variation of *huaraches*: huge 12-inch by 8-inch oval, very coarsely ground, crisp and chewy, thin, blue corn tortillas. (It's the same name as San Miguel de Allende's version, but different tortilla texture, thickness, and size.) Here they are topped with cooked salsa, shredded cheese, and pickled chiles. These platter-sized snacks are fun but almost impossible to eat if you want to end up with a clean shirt.

Chicken. Finding "chicken row" is a cinch. Toward the rear of the produce building you'll see **La Favorita** No. 502; **Pollerías Cárdenas** No. 505; or **Pollería el Gallo de Oro** No. 573, among others.

Chorizo. **Salchichonería La Flor de Toluca**, located at the very end across from the row of chicken stalls in the produce building, has a good selection besides excellent quality sausage items. Among the tempting varieties are *chorizo rojo* (ancho chile is the primary and most important chile) with almonds or peanuts; spicy chorizo (or *longaniza verde*) made with or without pine nuts; and deliciously sweet chorizo with raisins. Chorizo is everywhere in the market in the city famous for its sausage. Also look for *queso de puerco envuelto en petate*—locally made head cheese prepared in a handsome raffia wrapping.

Dairy. You'll find huge rounds of Tolucan cheeses in the produce building. Local, fresh, extra-thick *crema* (oh, to be in Toluca during strawberry season!) is a well-known specialty and a delight. Freshly churned butter is wrapped in green corn leaves. As always, buy only dairy products sold from refrigerated cases.

Wild Mushrooms. Wild mushrooms are sold by Indian women outside the main entrance (closest to the street) to the indoor produce building in the summer rainy season. A row of at least twenty people spread out their wares to entice you to try a fabulous assortment of wild beauties. Especially tasty are *arbollitos* (golden, coral-shaped mounds); *clavitos* (beige-tan clusters); *trompas* (trumpet-shaped, orange-red, thick and meaty); huge puffed *yemas*; and affordable morels and champignons.

Juice Bar. At **Juguería Paraiso**, located at the back entrance of the fondas building, try a blended combo of orange, banana, melon, and pineapple (no sugar, no water). Milk-based fruit drinks seem to be popular here, such as *mamey* fruit or papaya with protein powder. The stall is covered with palm leaves and decorated with fruit.

Hot Drinks. At a tiny, four- or five-seat, drinks-only fonda way back in the left corner of the fondas building, you can sample *atole con arroz*, made with rice meal, sugar, and *canela*. The drink has a nice rice texture, and will remind you of a hot *Horchata* (page 287). *Champurrado* and hot coffee are the only other items offered here, mornings only.

* PLACES TO GO AND THINGS TO EAT *

Sweets. Not in the market but in Toluca's central area, next to and behind the cathedral and government buildings, surrounding the *portales*, you'll find attractive kiosks selling candies and candied fruit. Most have exactly the same items, but look around and you'll see some unusual, traditional sweets worth trying. *Plananquintas* (domes of *panela* and nuts); amaranto seeds toasted and pressed with honey into light, crunchy blocks; *calaveras de azúcar* (decorated sugar skulls for Day of the Dead); and enough *jamoncillo* (milk-based candy) for the entire nation. Almost directly behind the cathedral and to the east, on Hidalgo, is a candy store packed to the rafters with sweets of all kinds, candied fruits galore, boxed cookies, and chocolates. Upon entering you'll get a tray and prongs to collect your own selections (as in Mexican bakeries). Choose a basket from overhead and make your own gift basket, which the store will arrange, wrap in cellophane, and tie with a bow.

Gorditas. Tolucan *gorditas* are a completely different animal than their namesakes in other regions. Here, silver dollar-sized pancakes are surprisingly sweet and light. They're prepared with white flour and sugar, not *masa* and salt, on tiny charcoal-heated griddles by women in Toluca's central plazas. You'll find them every evening in front of El Carmen church and around the cathedral.

Pottery and Weavings. Casart, located one block north of Mercado Juárez, on Paseo Tollocán, offers higher-quality merchandise than what is available at the market. Because this is a State-of-Mexico store, the prices are fixed.

Santiago Tianguistengo Opposite in feel from the cavernous buildings forming Toluca's market, Santiago Tianguistengo's Tuesday market is mostly open-air. In the early morning hours, the market attracts serious shoppers who swap and barter with an urgency bordering on frenzy. Later in the day the market becomes more laid back. The market is located in the high Toluca Valley, southeast of Toluca. Breakfast-only stands offer *barbacoa*, *chilaquiles*, or tamales with steaming *atole* for those setting up booths in the darkness before dawn. Lunch fondas include tacos made with everything imaginable. Big favorites are *tacos placeros*, giant tacos loaded with chopped pork cooked with chiles and garlic, raw onion, shredded cheese, shredded cabbage, guacamole, tomato slices, cactus paddle salsa, and the whole sprinkled with fresh herbs. Potato tacos with or without chorizo are fabulous street food temptations as are the same excellent blue corn *tlacoyos* stuffed or smeared with pink-, garbanzo-, or lima-bean paste, sold by Indian women at Toluca's market.

Besides the prepared-food stalls and fondas, the amount of fresh produce is mind-boggling. Bartering and selling right alongside commercial producers are hundreds of local farmers with their truck-loads of fruit or vegetables. It's not uncommon to see ten different vendors all lined up in a row and across from one another, selling exactly the same type of pear, for example, and nothing else. Assorted aromatic melons emit more perfume than the fragrance department at Bloomingdale's. Piles of golden perón (manzano) chiles, the regional favorite, have constant flurries of buying activity around them.

Santo Tianguistengo is known for serapes, and you'll see hundreds to choose from. Tough bargaining will get phenomenal prices when buying in quantity. Good quality, locally made pottery has its own look thanks to the glazes it wears—*cazuelas* (clay cooking pots) are especially handsome and are sold at bargain basement prices. Other areas (as at most open-air markets) are nothing more than swap meets of tacky plastic goods, tackier clothing, copied cassettes, and poorly made, cheap toys. Knives, bull whips, machetes, and gun holsters galore are available for *los machos.*

Tenancingo South of Toluca, on highway 55, Tenancingo is famous for extra-finely woven *rebozos* (shawls) and unusual fruit liquors from the surrounding countryside's orchards.

Almoloya between Toluca and Tenancingo, is noted for tablecloths.

Estela, Gloria, and Lupe's

▲▼▲

Tamales con Chorizo

Tolucan Sausage Tamales with Garlic, Almonds, and Raisins

When I first eyed Estela at one of Mercado Libertad's chorizo counters, she was so involved with a butcher about what herbs he uses in one of his sausages, I knew she just had to become one of my book's stars. Estela drives about a half hour to Mercado Juárez to her favorite chorizo maker and is very specific as to the age (three days, air-dried), how finely the pork is chopped (never ground), and exact spices for her tamales. She often orders chorizo in advance, made to her demanding specifications.

Estela's family enjoys tamales on Sunday and this has become a tradition at her home once a month. Her two sisters live in the same area and the three women get together and prepare tamales the evening before, then reheat them after church in the morning. Of course, they would love to share a recipe. The problem is, which? What filling? What chorizo? Too many decisions—simply too many choices. Finally a consensus is reached: a traditional corn-husk-wrapped tamale made with medium-grind *masa* (not too fine nor coarse); coarsely chopped red chorizo with ancho chile, cumin, coriander seeds, oregano, and paprika; lots of garlic; *canela*; and almonds and raisins.

If you have access to good, coarsely chopped chorizo made by a butcher who knows what he or she is doing, this recipe will be easy to duplicate. If you live near a tortillería, by all means buy *masa* there.

Yield: 30 tamales

For the chorizo (3 days ahead, if making your own)

- 4 ancho chiles
- ½ teaspoon coriander seeds
- 4 garlic cloves
- 1 one-inch "canela" stick, or ¼ teaspoon ground cinnamon
- 1 teaspoon dried Mexican oregano
- 2 Tablespoons sweet paprika
- ¼ teaspoon powdered cloves
- 1 teaspoon salt
- ¼ cup cider vinegar
- 1 pound lean pork loin or leg meat
- 6 ounces pork fat

Purchase 1½ pounds chorizo (air-dried for 3 days is best) and remove and discard the casings. Add chopped almonds and raisins if you'd like. Or, make your own:

1. Stem, seed, and toast (page 16) the chiles, opening them out flat and pressing them down with a metal spatula until they change color. Crumble them into a blender container or processor.

2. Toast the coriander seeds and garlic cloves (the seeds take only seconds). Put in the blender and blend. Add the *canela*, oregano, paprika, cloves, and salt. Add the vinegar and purée until smooth.

3. Coarsely chop the pork and pork fat together. Put the meat in a mixing bowl and add the spice ingredients.

- ¼ cup toasted and chopped blanched almonds or pine nuts
- ¼ cup raisins, chopped

Add the chopped nuts and raisins and blend everything together with your hands. Cover the bowl, and refrigerate for 3 days, stirring each day.

For the corn husks

- 1 eight-ounce package dried corn husks (found in many supermarkets, Latino markets, or by mail order)

1. Cover the husks with water and simmer, uncovered, for 10 minutes. Put a cover on the pot and turn off the heat. Let the husks soak for 2 hours until they are pliable.
2. Use the largest leaves for tamales. If you don't have enough, overlap 2 smaller leaves and "glue" them together with a bit of *masa*.

For the "masa"

- ½ pound pork lard (not liquid), or vegetable shortening
- 1 teaspoon salt
- 2 pounds "masa" for tamales from a tortillería, or 4 cups prepared "masa harina"
- 1¾ cups Chicken Broth (page 19)
- 1½ teaspoons baking powder

1. Beat the lard with an electric mixer for 2 minutes, until it becomes light. Add the salt and continue beating a minute longer. Add half the *masa* and mix until well blended. Add half the broth in a slow stream while mixing. Continue adding *masa* and broth with the baking powder.
2. To test if the mixture is light enough, ½ teaspoon should float when placed in a glass of cool water.

To assemble

1. Set up a tamale steamer (see Glossary).
2. Pick out the largest husks and set them aside for the tamales. There should be 30 (plus a few for emergencies). Cut or tear at least 60 "ribbons" to tie the tamale ends, about 5 inches by ¼ inch. Line the steamer rack with the remaining husks.
3. Lengthwise, center about 3 tablespoons *masa* on the inside of a husk and flatten it a bit. Spread a generous tablespoon of chorizo filling over the *masa*. Roll up the sides around the *masa* and filling. Tie each end with a "ribbon."
4. Lay the tamales on the steamer rack, overlapping so steam will move easily all around. Bring the water to a boil and cook for 1 to 1¼ hours. Check the water level after 45 minutes. To eat, each diner unties the "ribbon" at each end, unfolds and discards the husk (carefully—it is hot), and eats the stuffing topped with a choice of salsas.

Alejandra's

Tacos de Res, o Tacos de Papa con Chorizo

Griddled Beef Tacos and Potato-Chorizo Tacos

TWO OVERLAPPING WARM TORTILLAS ARE TOPPED WITH GRIDDLE-COOKED SAVORIES then folded, and voilá! Open-air, market-munching *supremo. Carnitas* (deep-fried pork), *barbacoa* (pit-cooked lamb or kid), and fried *charales* (tiny lake fish) are all wrapped in tortillas and gulped down at Santiago Tianguistengo. You'll do a lot of stand-up dining here while dripping salsa over your shoes. Since cooking aromas float at nose level in Santiago Tianguistengo, it's impossible to pass up exotic, smoky perfumed concoctions being brewed in *cazuelas* over wood fires. Other spots offer combinations of beef innards (like wildly popular *tacos de cabeza* made with meat from beef head) chopped with onion and chile, griddled on huge clay *comales*, then piled on tortillas almost as fast as the hungry mob is fed (no structured queues here, *amigos*).

Alejandra's *taquería* (taco stand) alternates between massive piles of beef or potato tacos, with or without chorizo as her mood strikes.

Yield: 8 beef or potato tacos

For beef tacos

2 Tablespoons vegetable oil
1 pound beef steak, thinly cut
1 large white onion, chopped
4 garlic cloves, finely chopped
3 jalapeño chiles (both green and red, if possible for color), stemmed and sliced across the grain (seeded, if you wish to cut the heat)
16 small, warm, corn tortillas (about 4 inches in diameter)

1. Heat oil in a skillet and add the beef, cooking until done. Remove the beef and put it on the side. Cook the onion, garlic, and chiles in the drippings until they are limp and just beginning to brown.

2. Chop or cut the beef into bite-sized pieces. Add the beef to the vegetables and cook, turning, just to heat the beef and brown the onions.

3. Put 2 overlapping tortillas (almost, but not quite over each other) on a plate. Spoon an eighth of the mixture onto the center of the tortillas. Serve immediately. To eat: Pick up both tortillas, fold, and bite.

For potato tacos

- ½ pound chorizo, removed from the casing (omit if you want a vegetarian taco)
- 2 large white onions, chopped
- 8 garlic cloves, finely chopped
- 3 jalapeño chiles (both green and red, if possible, for color), stemmed and sliced across the grain (seeded, if you wish to cut the heat)
- 2 large potatoes (about 1 pound total), peeled, quartered, and boiled 30 minutes, or until done
- 16 small, warm, corn tortillas (about 4 inches in diameter)
- 8 cilantro sprigs

1. If you are using chorizo, heat it in a skillet, cooking until brown. Remove and put it on the side. In the drippings (or 2 tablespoons oil, if chorizo is omitted) cook the onion and garlic until they are limp, then add the chile.

2. On a wood chopping board, dice the cooked potatoes. Add the potato to the vegetables and cook, turning, to brown the potato. When potatoes are light brown, add the chorizo (if using) and cook until the potatoes are medium brown, a few minutes more.

3. Put 2 closely overlapping tortillas (almost, but not quite over each other) on a plate. Spoon an eighth of the mixture onto the center of the tortillas. Add a cilantro sprig and serve immediately. To eat: Pick up both tortillas, fold, and bite.

Guadalupe del Inez Medina's

Sopa de Frijol y Chorizo *Tolucan Bean and Chorizo Soup*

GUADALUPE RUNS A POPULAR FONDA in Toluca's Mercado Juárez. Lupe's recipe for bean and sausage soup came from her mother, who for twenty-seven years had a fonda in another Tolucan market. Lupe's recipe uses *peruanos*, the pale pink beans that are loved in Mexico's central-western states, and copious quantities of spicy, garlicky chorizo, the taste that made Toluca famous. A long siesta is mandatory after a lunch of Lupe's "simple soup," served in enormous bowls at her tiny, five-stool counter (where every seat is usually taken).

The mouth-warming, stick-to-your-ribs dish is perfect after a day of cold-weather activity such as sledding or skiing (although many Mexicans find the heat-producing chiles to be comforting on hot days). It keeps well and is even better when reheated. Serve with lots of excellent bread, or tortillas and corn chips. Crisp carrot sticks and jícama slices sprinkled with chile powder are first-rate accompaniments.

Yield: 8 servings

(Continued)

- 1 pound dried pink beans, rinsed
- 1 white onion, cut in half
- 6 garlic cloves
- 2 tomatoes
- 4 guajillo chiles, stemmed, seeded, and opened flat
- 2 ancho chiles, stemmed, seeded, and opened flat
- 4 dried de árbol chiles
- 2 Tablespoons vegetable oil
- 1½ quarts Chicken Broth (page 19)
- 1 pound chorizo
- 1 cup "Crema" (page 80), crème fraîche, or sour cream

1. Put the beans in a large pot with the onion, add 4 quarts water, and bring to a boil. Reduce the heat and simmer the beans, covered, for 2 hours, or until they are tender. Remove the pot from the heat and cool.

2. Transfer the beans with their juice to a blender container (in batches) and purée. Remove and set aside.

3. Toast (page 16) the garlic, tomatoes, guajillo and ancho chiles. Put the tomatoes in a plastic bag to "sweat" a few minutes. Peel the tomatoes and transfer these four ingredients to a blender with ½ cup water. Toast the de árbol chiles for a few seconds until they change color. Add them to the other ingredients in the blender and purée.

4. Heat the oil in a deep pot and carefully pour in the blender ingredients (they splatter!). Stir for a minute. Reduce the heat and simmer, uncovered. After 10 minutes, add the cooked beans and chicken broth and continue simmering.

5. Remove the casings from the chorizo and put the sausage meat in a skillet. Fry until the chorizo is completely cooked, then drain the grease. Add the chorizo to the soup and continue simmering for 20 more minutes. Tolucan bean and chorizo soup is even better a day or two after it's made, and the soup freezes well. Serve garnished with a spoonful of *crema*.

Pedro Aburto Castillo's

Barbacoa *Oven-Baked Lamb in Maguey Leaves (or Marinated in Mezcal)*

THERE'S A FINE LINE BETWEEN *BARBACOA*, *MIXIOTES*, AND *BIRRIA* in the highlands around Mexico City. Traditionally, *barbacoa* is pit-baked meat wrapped in maguey leaves of the plant that produces *pulque* and *mezcal*. Maguey-wrapped meat is placed on a cooking rack (in a huge metal container to catch all the cooking juices), then the whole thing is lowered into the ground and pit-cooked for hours. *Mixiotes* are individual serving packages of maguey-wrapped meat baked in a pit or steamed in large casseroles. *Birria* (page 43) is meat marinated overnight in *adobo* made from guajillo chile, then cooked with broth and also flavored with maguey. The distinctions are fine ones, made more confusing by the fact that many home cooks use the word *barbacoa* to describe oven-baked, or stove-top-cooked, chile-flavored beef and chicken combos.

For Pedro's commercial *barbacoa* he pit-cooks his lamb overnight, then removes the meat at about 4 A.M. His drive to Santiago Tianguistengo takes almost an hour and he still has to set up his stand to be ready for the breakfast crowd shortly after dawn. Most people don't have underground baking pits in their backyards so they either buy *barbacoa* by the kilo at a market booth like Pedro's, or eat at roadside stands for the Sunday-only specialty.

Barbacoa takes on different flavorings depending on which region of Mexico you are visiting. Farther south, in Oaxaca, maguey leaves are replaced with avocado leaves for the region's preference for a slight anise taste. Exotic local chiles are added, but the general process is the same. The Yucatán offers its famous *barbacoa* called *Pibil* (pages 320 and 322), made with pork or chicken, pit- (here called *pib-*) cooked, and wrapped in flavor-loaded banana leaves and Yucatecan chiles for the southern state's flavor fingerprint.

Yield: 8 to 12 servings, depending on whether you are serving barbacoa *with broth and beans, or shredded in tacos*

- 8 to 10 maguey leaves, pointed tips removed, toasted or charred over a flame to soften, and peeled. (If maguey leaves are not available, marinate the meat in 2 cups mezcal or tequila for 2 hours before wrapping the meat in romaine lettuce leaves)
- 1 ten-pound young goat or lamb, or 2 small legs or shoulders of lamb
- salt and freshly ground pepper

1. Preheat the oven to 350° F. In a Dutch oven with a rack, lay maguey leaves over the rack, letting them reach over the top of the pot. Put the meat on top of the leaves. Season with salt and pepper. Cover with more leaves, wrapping them around the meat. Stuff any remaining leaves around the meat in the pot.

2. Bake 3 to 4 hours, until the meat falls off the bone and is fork tender. Test by pulling back a few leaves.

3. Serve with tortillas, salsas, and a big pot of your favorite beans. Skim fat off the broth and discard. Serve the broth with some meat in a bowl, or shredded, as tacos.

María Menéndez de Ramiro's

◆I◆I◆I◆I◆I◆I◆I◆I◆I◆I◆I◆I◆I◆I◆I◆I◆I◆I◆I◆I◆I◆I◆I◆I◆I◆I◆I◆I◆I◆I◆I◆I◆I◆I◆I◆I◆I◆I◆I◆I

Licuado de Agua *Fresh Fruit Blender Drink*

YOU'LL SPOT *LICUADO* (called *preparado* in the north) bars in every market throughout Mexico. Beautifully arranged tropical fruit will catch your eye before you see the *liquadoras* (blenders) lined up behind counters. Gigantic Mexican gold or orange (called Cuban) papayas are favorites, but mangoes compete for the number one spot in summer. Cantaloupes and watermelons are year-round standbys. Also common are guanábanas, guavas, and bananas of various hues—all ready to be twirled into tropical nectar. María's favorite combination is orange, mango, and lime. She puts half fruit chunks and half orange juice in a blender, adds sugar and a squirt of lime juice, then blends, and strains the foamy liquid gold into a tall glass. Orange juice as the liquid base, rather than water, is a wise decision. Most places use only bottled water these days, and purified water for blender washing, but always ask. Be sure the glass is dry or ask for your drink "to go" in a plastic cup.
Yield: 1 drink

- 1 cup very ripe, chopped mixed fruit
- 1 cup freshly sqeezed orange juice or water
- 1 small Mexican lime, juiced, or half a U.S. lime, juiced
- 1 Tablespoon sugar

1. Put the fruit (watermelon, cantaloupe, honeydew, papaya, mango, banana, strawberries, pineapple, or most tropical fruits), orange juice, lime juice, and sugar in a blender container and blend until foamy.
2. Pour the liquid through a strainer into a tall glass and serve at once with a brightly colored straw.

Variation: **Licuado de Leche** *Fresh Fruit Blender Drink with Milk*

Milk, rather than water or orange juice, is the difference between *licuado de leche* and *licuado de agua*. Whole milk turns the fruit into a rich and filling drink. The addition of protein powder turns a milk-based *licuado* into a protein-rich breakfast. As in frozen yogurt shops in the U.S., you choose toppings: chopped fruit, nuts, seeds, dried fruit, coconut, and granola to mix in or float atop your milk-based fruit shake.
Yield: 1 drink

- 1 cup very ripe, chopped, mixed fruit
- 1 cup cold milk
- 1 Tablespoon sugar

1. Put the fruit (watermelon, cantaloupe, honeydew, papaya, mango, banana, strawberries, pineapple, or most tropical fruits), milk, and sugar in a blender container and blend until foamy.
2. Pour the liquid through a strainer into a tall glass and serve at once with a brightly colored straw.

♦ Cuernavaca ♦

A Mercado Central "mascot."

THE ONE-AND-A-HALF-HOUR DRIVE SOUTH to Cuernavaca from Mexico City offers an exciting surprise: You're shocked to see Cuernavaca's valley stretched far below as you emerge from a pine forest as high as in a plane. The city is well-known among North American linguists, who study at Cuernavaca's innumerable language schools. Cuernavaca claims to have the world's best weather, but lately smog has laid its ugly blanket over Mecca. Even so, the city is still a weekend playground to Mexico City's wealthy, and their homes are encased behind twelve-foot walls with shards of security glass stuccoed along the tops.

In the city center, Cuernavaca's San Francisco Cathedral, at Hidalgo and Morelos, offers more than interesting inspirational music. An eleven o'clock mass every Sunday morning is accompanied by horn-rich mariachis. Another spiritual location, although a bit of a pilgrimage, is in the tiny village of Tepoztlán, northeast of Cuernavaca. Here you'll find a pyramid to the god of *pulque* (alcoholic drink made from maguey cactus) high up a remote mountainside.

✷ MARKET ✷

Mercado Central An airline hangar-sized building, plus extensions, houses Cuernavaca's market. It has everything; whatever can't fit inside fills outdoor walkways, steps, and plazas. Gorgeous-colored *mole* pastes piled three feet high in plastic buckets; *bruja* (witch) and *curandero* (healer) supplies galore; *barbacoa* fondas; overhead party piñatas; junky clothing and cheap shoes; beautifully glazed *cazuelas* with sturdy handles; and nonstop flowers making everything seem so special.

Fondas. My favorite place for a snack is at one of the fondas in the flower market surrounded by the aroma of tuberoses. The flower market is to the left of the indoor market and under the huge shade trees, which provide a cool repose from the hectic bustle inside. The big fonda, just as you enter, has very good sandwiches. Others offer breakfast specialties, various *moles,* hearty soups, stews simmering in *cazuelas* to be piled on tortillas for soft tacos, hot drinks, and *comida corrida* at bargain prices.

Chicken and Eggs. "Chicken row" is near the main entrance to the indoor market. Egg stalls surround the chicken places, and eggs are sold by weight, as everywhere in Mexico. When you ask for a kilo, for example, that's what you'll get, in wildly varying sizes. You might want to shop last for eggs because they're gingerly placed in a plastic bag and it's up to you to figure out how to get the time bomb home.

Produce. As usual, best buys are at the *tianguis*, the Indian market cascading over and around the patios and surrounding streets. Bargaining is expected, especially if you purchase anything in quantity.

Meats. Fondas selling goat *barbacoa* are surrounded by hanging intestines, as if for decoration, but actually to dry.

Moles. To the left of the main entrance is a row of stalls that displays buckets piled sky high with *mole* pastes of varying colors and textures. Classics such as *poblano* and *roja* are represented at every one—look for the individual's specialties and try *pipián* (pumpkin seed), peanut, or one that looks like dark bittersweet chocolate loaded with pale sesame seeds. Take some souvenir *mole* paste back home; it travels well. Get each selection double-wrapped in two plastic bags. Or, better yet, plan ahead and travel with zip-type heavy freezer bags for this purpose.

Pottery. Upstairs and behind the main market are huge clay pots and cauldrons for serious cooking. In fact, everything seems to be restaurant-sized from braziers, *comales*, to shovel-sized spoons.

* PLACES TO GO AND THINGS TO EAT *

RESTAURANT

Las Mañanitas. Expensive. Ricardo Linares No. 107. Tel. 73-12-46-46. Las Mañanitas is my favorite special-occasion restaurant/hotel in Mexico. It's definitely a "worth-the-drive" experience. Exceptional rooms are situated around an old hacienda, with some walls over two feet thick. Suites come with private patios and fountains, huge fireplaces, and elegant furnishings. It's the kind of place you'd expect to see on "Lifestyles of the Rich and Famous." The restaurant should be on your priority list if just for a drink. The grounds are spectacular, with cascading lawns and larger-than-life Zúñiga sculptures gracing the greens. Drinks can be had on sofas on covered patios, or on chairs set up at your favorite spot on the lawn. Prancing by are peacocks and various other long-legged (feathered) beauties. Dinner is candlelit under the stars. Luxury is the theme, service is tops, food is Mexican-Continental, and very good, indeed. Yes, you can drink the water.

Rosa Pérez de Torres's

Salsa de Nopales *Fresh Cactus Paddle Salsa*

THROUGHOUT THE NORTHERN TWO-THIRDS OF MEXICO, salsas and condiments made with *nopales* (*Opuntia* cactus paddles) are everyday table and fonda items. Cactus mixed with chiles, onions, and tomatoes takes the place of salad in the region, not because Mexicans don't like salads (as many guidebook and cookbook writers would have us think), but Mexicans prefer pickled vegetables, shredded lettuce and cabbage, chopped tomatoes, radishes, and sliced avocado as garnishes served on the same plate as the piece of meat, fish, or *antojito*. Rather than oily dressings, nutritious salsas are spooned onto the vegetables just as, say, a chutney is used in India.

Cleaning a cactus leaf that still has its prickers attached is no fun. The very sharp, mean, tiny needles stick to and stay in your skin, and can be extremely irritating. Purchase paddles that have been cleaned and scraped (as most are). Remove the tough outside edge all around the paddle if this hasn't been done. Canned versions are available, and, as with everything else, some brands are better than others (I recommend canned as a last resort). Experiment. The taste of cactus leaves will grow on you and in no time you'll be hunting down fresh paddles. *Yield: about 2 cups*

- 1 teaspoon baking soda
- 1 teaspoon salt
- 4 to 6 medium-sized (about 6 inches long) fresh "nopales," cleaned (or, canned and rinsed; do not cook)
- 3 ripe tomatoes, finely chopped
- 2 to 3 jalapeño chiles, stemmed, seeded if desired, and finely chopped
- 1 small white onion, finely chopped
- ¼ cup chopped cilantro leaves
- salt and freshly ground black pepper to taste

1. Bring 1 gallon water to a boil in a large pot. Add baking soda and salt.

2. Cut the *nopales* across the grain into ¼-inch strips, then cut these into ½-inch pieces. Add the *nopales* to the boiling water. When they are soft and still green, after about 15 minutes (if you cook them too much they start turning brown), drain and run cold water over them, while still in the pot, to stop the cooking process. This step (along with cooking in copper) retains the green color so important to the dish. Rinse the *nopales* in a strainer, then shake out as much moisture as possible.

3. Put the *nopales* in a bowl and add the tomato, chiles, onion, cilantro, salt, and pepper. Mix to combine. Serve at room temperature.

Estela Armas de Ruiz's

Guacamole y Tostaditas *Mashed Avocado with Tortilla Chips*

THE CUERNAVACA ARTIST ENJOYS SERVING THIS EASY-TO-PREPARE AVOCADO DIP to her clients and friends, along with *Aguas Frescas* (brightly colored flavored waters mixed with clear tequila, or sugarcane alcohol). Estela's guacamole, the simplest and most avocado-tasting possible, is a constant sensation. She serves it with Fresh Tomato Salsa (page 143), placing each condiment in its own rustic, hand-thrown bowl, and centers the bowls on a bright turquoise-glazed platter surrounded by hot, fresh *tostaditas* sprinkled with lime juice and salt.

Yield: 6 servings

For the guacamole

- 2 or 3 (depending on size) very ripe, soft, avocados
- 1 or 2 limes, juiced

1. Cut the avocados in half, remove the pits, and scoop the flesh into a bowl.

2. With a fork, mash the avocado so it's a bit lumpy—not a purée. Add the lime juice and mix lightly.

For the "tostaditas" (tortilla chips)

- vegetable oil for frying
- 12 day-old corn tortillas (fresh will do but they absorb more fat and take longer to fry).
- 1 lime
- salt to taste

1. Heat ½ inch of oil in a large skillet to 365° F, or until the surface ripples.

2. Stack 6 tortillas on top of one another and cut the pile into eighths, as though you were slicing a pie. Repeat with the others.

3. Drop a handful of the tortilla pieces into the hot oil and cook until crisp. Remove to paper towels to drain and continue until all the pieces are fried.

4. While the *tostaditas* are still warm, sprinkle with lime juice. Salt to taste.

To assemble

1. Put the guacamole and salsa bowls next to each other on a large platter.

2. At the last moment, arrange the hot chips around the bowls, covering the platter. Serve at once while the chips are hot.

Estela Armas de Ruiz's

Salsa Cruda *Fresh Tomato Salsa*

SALSA CRUDA, ALSO CALLED *SALSA FRESCA* (fresh, or uncooked table salsa), is the classic partner to guacamole, and Estela's is just about the best version around. She doesn't care for much spice in the mashed avocado, so she loads up on chiles in her salsa—choose mild or spicy for yours. Estela uses plum tomatoes, but the type of tomato doesn't really matter. What's important is that they're ripe to the point they are dark red. The salsa should be spicy—add another chile if you'd like, just before serving.
Yield: about 2 cups

- 6 very ripe plum tomatoes
- 1 medium white onion, finely chopped
- ¼ cup chopped cilantro leaves
- 3 jalapeño chiles, stem removed, chopped
- 2 limes, juiced
- 2 garlic cloves, finely chopped

1. Chop the tomatoes, skin on, and put in a bowl. Add the onion, cilantro, chile, and lime juice.

2. Using a garlic press, squeeze the garlic into the bowl. Mix thoroughly and set aside, unrefrigerated, for at least 2 hours (up to 4) for the flavors to mingle and mellow.

Variations: To use dried chiles, soak them in hot water for 30 minutes to soften before blending. To experiment with different fresh and dried chiles in *Salsa Cruda* is an excellent way to recognize various chile flavors. For a Veracruz-Puebla version, exchange the fresh chiles with canned chipotle chiles en adobo. Taste, and add more adobo sauce, or even another chile if you'd like the salsa spicier. For a Yucatecan version, exchange the fresh chiles with half a toasted (page 16) habanero chile, or to taste. Or try a bottled habanero hot sauce if fresh chiles are unavailable.

Rosa Pérez de Torres's

Tostaditas y Huevos

Scrambled Eggs with Tomato Sauce and Fried Tortilla Chips

IT'S SUCH A PLEASURE TO SIT DOWN AFTER SHOPPING and have a quick meal or drink while savoring kitchen smells and aromas from billowing bouquets. The spicy, cinnamon scent of carnations lingers and competes with sautéing garlic, bubbling pots of chicken soup, and toasting *bolillos* destined for thick sandwiches. The first time I had *tostaditas y huevos* was in the fonda where Rosa works. Surrounded by the sweet smell of flowers from the adjacent flower stalls, breakfast was a delight. *Tostaditas y huevos* is a dish similar to *Chilaquiles* (page 285), but with scrambled eggs cooked into tortilla chips and a simple sauce. (In the north, the same dish called *migas*, is often made from stale tortilla strips or stale French rolls.) It's quick and easy to make for a few, or a crowd. Like *chilaquiles* and some enchilada dishes, the tortillas are fried first so they have a satisfying, chewy texture rather than dissolving in the liquid.

Yield: 4 servings

For the "tostaditas" (fried tortilla chips)

- vegetable oil for deep-frying
- 8 day-old tortillas (fresh absorbs more fat and take longer to fry)

1. Heat ½ inch of oil in a large skillet to 360°F, or until the surface ripples.
2. Stack corn tortillas on top of one another and cut the pile into eighths, as though you were slicing a pie.
3. Drop a handful of the tortilla pieces into the hot oil and cook until not quite crisp to ensure a chewy texture when the tortillas are cooked with sauce—they should not disintegrate in liquid. Remove to paper towels to drain, and continue until all the pieces are fried.

For the sauce

- 2 Tablespoons vegetable oil
- 1 white onion, chopped
- 2 garlic cloves, minced
- 2 tomatoes, chopped
- 3 jalapeño chiles

1. Heat the oil in a large skillet and sauté the onion until it is transparent.
2. Add the garlic and cook a minute longer before adding the tomato and chile. Reduce the heat and simmer, stirring, for another 5 minutes.

To assemble

- 8 eggs
- salt and pepper to taste
- ¼ cup "queso añejo" or Parmesan cheese

1. Beat the eggs together in a large bowl with salt and pepper. Delicately fold in the *tostaditas*.
2. Pour the egg mixture into the skillet, then cook, stirring and scraping, until the eggs are just set. Add the sauce and stir in the eggs. Sprinkle with cheese. Serve hot.

◆ Taxco ◆

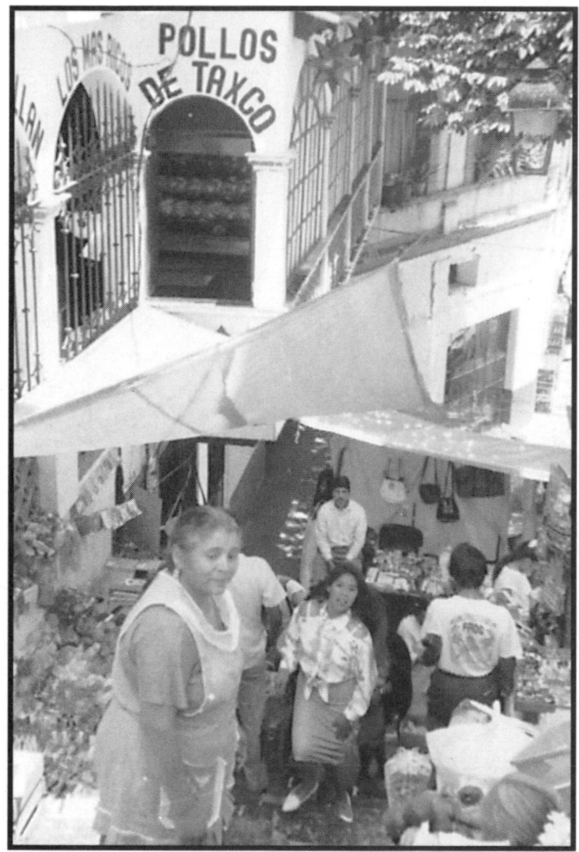

An entrance to Taxco's market—a jumble of exciting, picturesque walkways.

YOUR FIRST GLIMPSE OF TAXCO is breathtaking. Like Guanajuato, it clings to a cliff and runs up and down a mountainside, underneath which at one time ran several rich silver mines. Driving in Taxco is a challenge; proceed only if you have an excellent map and precise directions to your destination because most streets are steep, one way, and alley sized. Morris will never forget backing down one of these curving alleys after he slammed on the brakes when the cobblestoned passageway turned into a staircase. For reassurance, before entering from the north end of town (via Mexico City and Cuernavaca) stop at the tourist office, located in the Centro Convenciones de Taxco building, just as you see the old aqueduct pass over the road. Also at the entrance to town there's an aerial tramway to the Hotel Monte Taxco. Take the trip and go for a drink; the view provides a great perspective on Taxco's layout.

Taxco is designated one of three national city landmarks by the Mexican government, along with San Miguel de Allende and Oaxaca. Having been built on silver, Taxco was prosperous during the sixteenth and seventeenth centuries; the mines are not bearing as they once were, but the town thrives today on tourism and silversmithing. Artisans are everywhere; you'll find it impossible to leave without mementos. Taxco is the undisputed silver capital of the world. If you can't find what you want here, it probably doesn't exist (but any number of artisans will gladly make it for you).

* MARKET *

Mercado Municipal Located behind Calles Cuauhtémoc and Hidalgo, Taxco's market is a jumble of maze-like passageways going up, down, over, under, in, out, around, and through. Winding and hilly stairways beckon you to enter steep, ancient walkways lined with native women selling home-grown produce and homemade products, herbs, and caged parrots collected in the wild. Surprisingly, it's right in the town center hidden behind fancy silver shops and restaurants. The indoor market area houses a few fondas serving hot, cheap *comidas corridas*.

Antojitos. Within the market passageways are women selling squash blossom quesadillas with a real chile kick. Other women sell *tlacoyos*, and unlike the blue corn version found in Toluca, these are yellow. One delectable variation includes bits of *carnitas* mixed into the *masa* before griddling. If you want a bean filling, for example, they break open a *tlacoyo* and spoon in beans and salsa then pop it on a *comal* a moment longer. Taxco market vendors always offer a choice of red or green spicy salsa.

Butchers, Dairy. Pollería las Delicias is in the indoor market. Behind the stall there's an aisle of other chicken counters with a few *Tasajo* (page 262) butchers thrown in. Along with eggs, butter, *crema*, and yogurt, cheese counters are here. Try *queso criollo*—which is similar to Muenster cheese, even down to the orange outer coating. Ranchero cheese is fresh and perfect for picnics; all from refrigerated cases.

Mushrooms. Wild summer mushrooms include the *hongo azul*, a very definitely blue mushroom. Look around for vendors selling from baskets, on cloths spread on the ground, or along the edges of steps during the summer rainy months.

* PLACES TO GO AND THINGS TO EAT *

Bakery. Panadería Esmeralda is near the plaza side of the market entrance. A variety of still-warm breads, sweet rolls, and pastries for your morning coffee.

Silver. Flatware, bowls, pitchers, and platters are showcased at famous **Los Castillo**, Plazuela Bernal No. 10. The store has the most exciting designs and elegant offerings in Taxco, including tea sets for serious imbibers. For bargain shopping (mostly jewelry) go to what are locally known as *tianguis*, where groups of artisans get together and rent stalls in one building and sell at wholesale prices. There are a few down the hill from Hotel los Arcos and Hotel Posada de los Castillos on the right side. Silver napkin rings and serving spoons from different patterns are elegant, excellent buys.

Baskets and woven placemats. Crafts are found around the *zócalo* and along Cuauhtémoc, from Indian vendors. Look for tortilla baskets in bright colors with fun stripes (they really do look better once you get them home and away from the other three hundred).

RESTAURANTS

Paco's Bar Grill. Moderate. Plaza Border No. 12. Tel. 2-00-64. Go at sunset for a view of Santa Prisca from Paco's second-floor balcony. Sure, it's a touristy place and, sure, the food is mediocre, but the expensive beer is cold, and the view of the lit churrigueresque façade is very fine.

Pizza Pazza. Inexpensive. Another great view of the *zócalo* and surrounding hillsides is upstairs and to the right of, as you're facing, Santa Prisca. The pizza is good—just remember that *chorizo*—not *salchicha*—means sausage in Spanish. *Salchichas* are hot dogs and hot dog pizza is, well, hot dog pizza. Anyway, someone's mother makes good gringo-style fresh fruit pies in the summer months. Strawberry and mango (if your mother ever made mango pie) are the favorites.

Restaurant Santa Fe. Inexpensive. Hidalgo No. 2, Tel. 2-11-70. Open every day. Excellent breakfast, *comida corrida*, and dinner served in a homey, comfortable room. Many egg dishes, pancakes, plus tamales and *champurrado* (chocolate *atole*) are offered in the morning along with marinated beef or shredded pork enchiladas. Many locals like this place, and it's not overrun with tourists as most places are.

Alicia María Pedroza de Hernández's

▲▼▲

Sopa de Hongos Salvajes *Wild Mushroom Soup with Chipotle Chiles*

WHILE TASTING BLUE CORN TORTILLAS ON TAXCO'S MARKET STEPS, I froze, open-mouthed, when I spotted Alicia's array of exquisite, dew-spotted wild mushrooms. Colors? We're talking jungle parrots: glistening gold, red-orange vermilion, marine blue, bright white, plus sand with a blush of pink. It's too bad they don't keep up their looks once boiled, but who would?

All across the central states, Mexican mountains supply boletus fans with wild mushrooms during the summer rainy season from June through September. Familiar chanterelles and morels are actually plentiful (and cheap enough) to turn into soup. U.S. farmer's markets offer interesting alternatives to supermarket mushrooms, but if that's all you have, make the recipe and throw in an ounce of dried and soaked (add the strained soaking liquid) porcinis or shiitakes. Alicia turns the recipe into a cream soup by adding the optional *crema* at the end, which is an ambrosial match with chipotle chiles.

Yield: 6 servings

- 3 garlic cloves
- 1 small, white onion, halved
- 2 tomatoes
- 2 chipotle chiles, stemmed and seeded, or canned chipotle chiles en adobo without sauce
- 2 Tablespoons vegetable oil
- 1 pound wild mushrooms, cleaned and thickly sliced
- 1 "epazote" sprig, if available
- 6 cups Chicken Broth (page 19), or 6 cups water for a vegetarian soup
- salt to taste
- Optional: 1 cup "Crema" (page 80), crème fraîche, or sour cream

1. Toast (page 16) the garlic, onion, tomatoes, and dried chipotle chiles. Put the chiles in a bowl of hot water to soak for 15 minutes (canned chiles go directly into the blender). Peel the garlic and tomatoes. Put the soaked chiles, garlic, onion, and tomatoes in a blender container and purée, adding water if necessary.

2. In a pot, heat the oil and add the cleaned, sliced mushrooms. Sauté 5 minutes, until they are cooked, but not brown. Pour the chile mixture into the mushrooms. Add the *epazote* and broth and simmer, uncovered, for 20 minutes. Remove the *epazote* sprig. Add salt to taste. The soup may be cooled and refrigerated to be reheated within a few days.

3. Optional: Put the *crema* in a blender, add 1 cup cooled soup liquid (no mushrooms), and blend. Pour the mixture into the soup. Bring the soup back to a simmer (do not boil, sour cream curdles) and serve.

María-Luisa Méndez's

Sopa de Fideos *Chicken Soup with Thin Pasta*

FINDING FONDAS IN TAXCO'S HILLSIDE MARKET MAZE IS SUCH A JOY! Go a bit early so you can get "lost" climbing up and down stairway aisles before exploring the small, covered market building. You'll eventually spot some fondas on the northeast side; María-Luisa cooks at one with an oilcloth-covered counter and specials written on a blue board in different colored paints.

There are two important variations on the *sopa* (soup) theme all over Mexico, and Taxco's fondas serve them both. One (this recipe) contains thin pasta simmered in chicken broth. The other is *sopa seca*, or dry soup—in which dry pasta is sautéed in oil and then cooked with broth. It is a sauced, albeit non-al dente, spaghetti of sorts. Mexicans like their traditional pasta overcooked because they want it—like rice—to absorb all the flavorful liquid. See *Sopa Yucateca* (page 65).

María-Luisa always prepares her *sopa de fideos* with homemade broth, then sprinkles each bowl with grated hard cheese. She serves the soup with French rolls, a classic combo in central Mexico.

Yield: 6 servings

- 4 Tablespoons vegetable oil
- 4 ounces dry pasta, preferably "fideos" (nests; "fidelini" in Italian) found in Mexican markets
- 2 additional Tablespoons vegetable oil
- 1 small white onion, finely chopped
- 2 garlic cloves, put through a garlic press, or very finely minced
- 4 tomatoes, toasted (page 16), skins removed, and chopped
- 8 cups Chicken Broth (page 19)
- 2 fresh jalapeño chiles, slit down one side, seeds intact
- 8 cilantro sprigs, tied together
- salt and pepper to taste
- ½ cup "queso añejo" or Parmesan cheese

1. Heat the 4 tablespoons oil. Break the *fideo* twists and brown them until golden, about 5 minutes. Drain on paper towels.

2. Heat the 2 tablespoons oil in a large pot and sauté the onion, garlic, and tomatoes over medium heat for 2 minutes. Pour in the broth. Add the chile and cilantro. Add the pasta, and bring the liquid to a boil. Reduce the heat and simmer for 20 minutes. Salt and pepper to taste.

3. Ladle into large, low soup plates and sprinkle with cheese.

The Land of Volcanoes and Talavera Tiles

Puebla
Cholula

A scenically spectacular region directly east of Mexico City showcases one of the most characteristically Spanish cities in the country—Puebla. It lies in a fertile valley surrounded by volcanoes—Popocatépetl (active in 1995), Iztaccíhuatl, Malinche, and Citlaltépetl (also known as Volcán Orizaba). Nearby orchards produce plums, peaches, and summer fruits to preserve in sugar syrup beloved by Poblanos (natives of Puebla), while winters are cool enough for apples and pears. Maguey is grown in the northern part of the state for pulque, *the mildly alcoholic liquor that played a key role in Aztec rituals. Corn, bean, chile, and tomato fields dot the landscape and are a constant reminder of the ancient heritage of those foods.* Mole Poblano *(pages 158 and 160) is Puebla's honored special occasion treat.*

Left: Colonial architecture is part of Puebla's charm.

◆ Puebla ◆

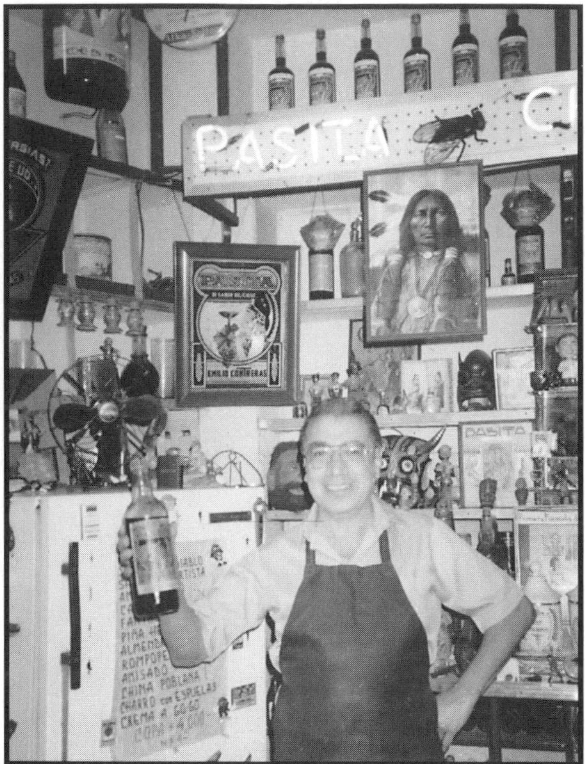

La Pasita is the place to try regional liquor specialties.

ELEGANT PUEBLA IS BEST KNOWN FOR CLASSIC SPANISH-MOORISH BUILDINGS faced with dazzling Talavera tiles, *mole poblano*, and *chiles en nogada*. The high-altitude, (7,049 feet, 2,162 meters) colonial city is very Spanish, especially its majestic *zócalo* area. Long an international business center noted for textile mills and, later, automobile manufacturing, Puebla is quite the sophisticate and less than two hours east of Mexico City by car. Plan a stroll around Callejón de los Sapos, a closed-to-traffic art and antiques quarter, four blocks behind Puebla's cathedral, in the evening when mariachis play. Another not-to-be-missed sight in the heart of Puebla is the original kitchen in the old Santa Rosa Convent, now part of the Museo de Artesanías, about five blocks north of the *zócalo* at 12 Poniente and Calle 5 Norte (the entrance is on 12 Poniente through the parking lot). The lusciously tiled, handsome room claims to be the kitchen where nuns first prepared Mexico's esteemed *mole poblano*.

Puebla's Victorian glass market building, Mercado Victoria, has been closed for "remodeling" since 1987, and people in the know say it's not coming back. To compensate, there are now smaller city-center, traditional markets each with its own personality and specialties. On weekends especially, Puebla's Nahua Indians sell their pottery, embroidered blouses, and weavings in the city. Saturday's open-air market, just off highway 131 (the road to Tehuacán) on the city's eastern fringe, bursts at its seams with their bargains.

✷ MARKETS ✷

Mercado Venustiano Carranza Mercado Venustiano Carranza is located at 11 Norte and 4 Poniente, in the central area. Puebla's oldest city-center market (since 1910) has certainly seen better days. It's rather run down and dark, but still has a few interesting aspects. As soon as you enter from the 11 Norte side your gaze will go up to piñatas hanging everywhere from crisscrossed ropes and wires, brightly decorated or skeletonlike in their newspaper underwear. You can buy everything from dimensional glittery stars to Donald Ducks to futuristic spacemen, or special-order anything your heart desires. Toward the market's 13 Norte side, the fondas glitter. Fluorescent-lit counters selling *cemitas* are incredibly popular lunch hangouts. Try the huge, clean counter on the 4 Poniente side, **El As de Oros**. Toward the center of the building, fondas dish up long-simmering *moles*, soups, and stews. Yet farther back are tiny, one-table affairs selling tortillas, rice, and beans and not much more. In the late afternoon women walk up and down the market aisles selling a spicy version of *atole* (page 126) and all the merchants dig into the cheap, pre-Hispanic *masa* brew.

Mercado Cinco de Mayo Mercado Cinco de Mayo, located at 18 Poniente at 5 Norte, in the central area, focuses on meats. The building is packed with butchers selling every cut imaginable. Some seafood is sold (the market is right across the street from **La Almeja**, Puebla's best seafood store). A sprinkling of produce, including dried chiles, fresh corn, dark red tomatoes, medicinal herbs, fresh *moles*, household products, and a few fondas specializing in meat dishes (of course) round out this neighborhood's enclosed market.

Mercado Carmen Serdan Acocota Mercado Carmen Serdan Acocota is situated between 4 and 6 Oriente and 18 and 20 Sur, in Puebla's eastern district, across Boulevard Héroes del 5 de Mayo. The bread selection is great here: Toward the eastern part of the market women sell *chanclas*, Irish soda bread-like rolls dusted with flour, crisp *cemitas*, and excellent, chewy, French-type rolls *pan de agua* (water bread) sold from baskets. The friendly *señoras* are glad to give tastes—in fact, don't be shy about asking for a taste of anything, anywhere in Mexico, including at the *mole* paste counters here. Simply ask, "*¿puedo probar?*" (May I taste?) with a smile. A tiny, wild mushroom called *hongo toltoxcan* from the surrounding country-side is a prized summer market find. Yet nearby is a booth selling nothing but used jars (washed, with their lids, but still, used jars). As at most every other market in Mexico, there's a chicken aisle; check stalls for refrigeration and/or fresh-looking birds (and, as always, buy your bird in the morning). This market has a good selection of regional pottery at rock-bottom prices, sold both inside and outside along the street.

Fonda. Try **Fonda Cemitas Poblana** for the usual sandwich selections, but instead of a *bolillo*, you'll get a *cemita*, the sesame-seeded round roll of the region. It'll be your lucky day if a woman is panfrying plantains when you stop by for lunch. Most fondas are at the opposite, rather dark, western edge of the market building. If you're looking for a hot meal, scan around for a clean, crowded place with bubbling pots. Soups are favorites here.

Mercado Central de Abastos Mercado Central de Abastos is located on the northern outskirts of the city, on the way to Tlaxcala. It's open every day, but Saturday and Sunday are best. This is Puebla's big wholesale market. People drive out here on weekends to buy in huge quantities for families to share crates of produce: vegetables, chiles, fruit, meats, and some fish. Fondas are scattered about, and instant kitchens with folding tables are set up to sell grilled chicken, *carnitas*, and quesadillas cooked on *comales* set over wood-burning braziers. On weekends, the atmosphere changes dramatically from serious business to bazaar.

* PLACES TO GO AND THINGS TO EAT *

Seafood. La Almeja. 16 Poniente No. 301, across the street from Mercado Cinco de Mayo. Tels. 32-46-69, 42-52-45, fax 32-51-58. Hours 6:30 A.M. to 4 P.M. every day. Simply the best in Puebla. An enormous selection and everything on ice. La Almeja opens at dawn for the city's top restaurants and best cooks to grab the finest selections. Before shopping, stop in next door at Marisquería la Almeja for a breakfast shrimp cocktail.

Carnitas. Los Arcos. Two shops, the old and the new, are within half a block of each other on 19 Sur Nos. 1103 and 1302. Hours: 10 A.M. to 5:30 P.M. every day. The new (No. 1103) two story, and fancy for a *carnitas* joint, is a comfortable place to sit and relax while munching tacos or sandwiches, but you can also get food to go at a large window. The original spot is equally popular but is strictly take-out.

Carnitas Ely. 4 Oriente No. 1613, tel. 36-00-71. Hours: Open every day from 9 A.M. to 5 P.M. The clean shop is right across the street from Mercado Acocota. Simple tables and chairs are provided to facilitate on-the-spot chowing down of a *carnitas* sandwich. Carnitas Ely griddle-toasts a *cemita* (sesame seed roll) first before filling it with lean (ask for *sin grasa*, without fat) pieces of pork. With a choice of three salsas, it's just *too* good.

Tacos al Pastor. Throughout Puebla, storefronts sell this relatively newfangled (possibly fifty years old) Mexican taco, thanks to Puebla's large Lebanese population. Originating in Beirut and known as *schwarma*, a vertical column of revolving sliced meat cooks as it passes a flame. Slices are taken from the outer edges to fill tortillas, or *cemitas.* With a squirt of lime and a bit of salsa, these make good, cheap lunches.

Bakery. Gigante, an aptly named superstore located in the Galería las Ánimas shopping center, has Puebla's best bread selection and Mexican pastries. The store carries all the staples: cereals; pastas; canned goods; juices; meats and poultry; a fully stocked deli with sliced meats, chorizo, cheeses, and *moles* (don't buy anything from the open bins; people love to dip their fingers in for tastes); below-average-looking fresh produce; a convenient drug and toiletries section with pharmacy; household goods and clothing to automobile accessories, Gigante has it all.

Mole pastes. Most candy shops along 6 Poniente, between 5 de Mayo and 2 Sur, sell liter containers of *mole poblano* paste packed in plastic tubs to carry back home. No refrigeration is necessary until the seal is broken. **Gigante** *supermercado* carries, as do most other large markets, the favorite packaged *mole* of Puebla, jars of Santa Mónica brand. In the city's traditional markets, such as Mercado Carmen Serdan Acocota, *mole* paste is sold by the scoop and put in plastic bags. Refrigerate these pastes once you get home, but they'll still keep for months and months, and can be frozen. Naturally, cooks everywhere doctor the pastes according to their own secret formulas by using fresh and dried fruit purées, seed pastes, sugar, tomatoes, chocolate, chiles—the list goes on.

Juice. Jugos de Cana. Maximino Ávila Camacho No. 212. Hours: 8:30 A.M. to 8:30 P.M. every day. Freshly squeezed *cana* (sugarcane juice) with a squirt of lime not only tastes great but also is claimed to have healthful properties. Sit at the clean, four-person counter and watch what seems like the world's biggest vegetable juicer grind out nectar. The bar is very clean and no water is used—it's all pure juice.

Ice cream. Topolino Plaza Express. 34 Poniente 2907 Local V-24, tel. 50-9-72. Hours 11 A.M. to 8 P.M. Open every day. An Italian family-run dairy blossomed into a thriving gelato-style ice cream business with franchised shops throughout the area. This store, and the one in Atlixco at Libramiento a Atlixco S/N, in front of El Cristo, tel. 5-09-72, are still run by the family. Exquisite gelatos and pastries made by Pilar Minutti, are just the thing when you're craving an afternoon espresso in the middle of Mexico. Notice that the gelato is served from Italian freezer cases in the immaculately clean shops. Refrigerators are full with butter, cheeses (including Villa Nolasco brand French-style sheep's milk cheese), and thick *crema* and sweet cream from the family dairy.

Regional liquor. La Pasita, near the antiques area and Los Sapos, at 5 Oriente 602, tel. 55-5-55. Hours: 12:30 P.M. to 5:30 P.M. every day. *Pasita,* raisin liqueur, the bar's specialty from opening day in 1916, is still a crowd pleaser. Two raisins and a teeny square of salty cheese stuck on a toothpick are added to a tall shot glass with *pasita*. The combination is a fun way to start a day in Puebla. Or try the garnet red, *jamaica*/raspberry liqueur with a few salty peanuts floating in it. About a dozen other unusual flavors make up La Pasita's list of drinks. The tiny, charming old building with its funky bar memorabilia shouldn't be missed, and it's right off delightful Callejón de los Sapos, a closed-to-traffic antiques quarter, behind the cathedral.

Coffee. Café Aroma, 3 Poniente No. 520, tel 32-60-77. Open for a morning cappuccino jolt to late evening sipping. Café Aroma also sells whole and freshly ground beans.

Candy. 6 Poniente, between 5 de Mayo and 2 Sur, is definitely Sweet Street. Every other shop is a *dulce* (sweet) shop specializing in the Santa Clara treat, called *Camotes* (page 167), a Puebla tradition. They're made from sweet potato and lots of sugar. *Camotes* are cigar-shaped and individually wrapped in thin paper, not unlike salt water taffy, then arranged in boxes of various sizes. **Yolanda** is my favorite shop at 6 Oriente No. 14, tel. 46-13-40, fax 49-60-32, Hours: 9 A.M. to 8 P.M. every day. Almost next door is **Dulcería la Poblanita. La Colonial** and **La Colonial Moderna** are all on the same side of the street. Across 6 Oriente are **Capilla del Rosario** and **Camotería Mary,** both having more gift items than candy but traditional *dulces* are still popular. Also, look for *polvorones sevillanos* (nut shortbread) and *jamoncillo*, a creamy milk fudge made with pumpkin seeds or nuts at all these shops.

Pottery. La Talavera de Puebla S.A. de C.V., 4 Poniente 911, tels. 42-29-43, 32-15-98, fax 42-29-43. Open Monday through Saturday 10:30 A.M. to 6:30 P.M. and Sunday 11 A.M. to 3 P.M., in the city center. Before entering the showroom you know you're in the right place. One of the most beautifully tile-decorated building façades in Puebla makes you feel welcome. Step into the court of the hacienda and you're greeted with even more tile fantasies. The salesroom is staffed with English-speaking personnel. Every day but Sunday you can see artisans at work in Puebla's best-quality Talavera shop offering platters, bowls, pitchers, urns, vases, and tiles.

Bazar la Reja, 5 Oriente No. 404 across from Plazuela de Los Sapos, tel. 35-84-05. Hours: 11 A.M. to 4 P.M. every day. New frames made from old, wonderfully worm-eaten wood (or, fakes so good they look old). These frames are inexpensive. Take home as many as you can carry and frame lovely embroidered cloths you pick up for a song from local Indian women.

RESTAURANTS

Mercado El Alto. One block behind the Church of San Francisco, the onetime market building is home to dozens of inexpensive fondas in their newly remodeled and tiled, very clean building interior (the wonderful exterior hasn't been touched). *Cemitas*, soups, and *mole poblano* are favorites. Look around for an enticing spot, pull up a stool, and dig in to some cheap, very traditional, regional dishes.

La Selva. Inexpensive. 10 Norte frente al 1410, tel. 35-90-68. One of an old-time group of open-air fondas in the park just north of the Church of San Francisco that have grown up to become casual, almost-open-air restaurants. Its specialty is *chalupas*, but La Selva also dishes out copious quantities of *mole poblano*, rice, and *Frijoles de Olla* (page 46) to the weekend crowds. Chewy, excellent *pan de agua* (water rolls) sop up the *mole*.

Bola Roja. Moderate. Three locations: 17 Sur No. 1305, tel. 43-70-51; Plaza Dorada, Zaragoza No. 266, tel. 40-75-82; and Plaza Loreto, Cinco de Mayo No. 3510, tel. 36-14-22. All locations are open 10 A.M. to 8 P.M. every day. Here's your chance to try traditional Poblana foods in comfortable settings with professional waiter service. A full bar and pitchers of *Agua Fresca* (page 73) will cure your thirst. Starters include an assorted *Chalupas* (page 171) plate. At least six soups are on the menu. Main courses include pumpkin seed sauce poured over a perfectly cooked, moist, chicken breast; *mole poblano*; *Tinga* (page 164); and *Chiles en Nogada* (pages 67 and 162). Puebla's second most popular dish, after *mole poblano*, *chiles en nogada* is served in September, in celebration of Mexican Independence with colors of the flag: poblano chile-green, walnut sauce-white, and pomegranate seed-red. Beware, in many other restaurants huge amounts of beloved candied fruit overwhelm restaurant stuffings; other times grease levels are unbearable from deep-fried, battered chiles that haven't been drained; there are silly walnut sauces not tasting of walnuts; sugary, stringy beef stuffings bordering on inedible are everyday encounters.

Fonda Santa Clara. Moderate. Two locations, both on Avenida 3 Poniente: No. 307, tel. 42-26-59, closed Monday; and No. 920, tel. 46-19-19, closed Tuesday. Both locations are favorite lunch spots of local businessmen, who insist the *mole poblano* is next best to homemade, so be sure to try it.

Pollo Quemado. Inexpensive. Calzada Zaualeta No. 96, tel. 84-53-19. Hours: Monday to Friday 9 A.M. to 6:30 P.M., Saturday and Sunday 9 A.M. to 7:30 P.M. Just off the Puebla *rectro* (fast road) from Cholula. Watch for the sign to Atlixco and Oaxaca, exit, and in a minute you'll see Pollo Quemado on the right side. The no-frills dining room and patio are furnished with ubiquitous metal tables and chairs painted with beer and soda company logos. Even so, Gaby Amador, the friendly owner, and her waitresses will make you feel right at home. Butterflied, marinated, then grilled chicken is served with an abundance of hot, handmade tortillas, salsa, and limes. *Memelas* are handmade, thick, oval tortillas stuffed with black bean purée. Gaby's bean purée is refried with minced onions, and seasoned with avocado leaves. In summer months grease-free *huitlacoche* quesadillas, *comal*-grilled and piping hot, are a delight.

Restaurante Las Bodegas del Molino. Expensive. Puente de México s/n, Col. Molino San José del Puente, reservations tel. 48-22-62. Hours: Monday through Saturday 1 P.M. to 11 P.M., Sunday 1 P.M. to 5 P.M. Mexican-Continental. Whole baked fish, rotisseried meats, some traditional Mexican dishes. Avoid pastas and fussy-sounding appetizers. Upon arrival, ask for a tour of the old hacienda gardens and mill (now a cavelike bar) after dining. Upstairs is a private club and dining rooms, gallery, ballroom, and yes, theater.

Adela Dávila's

Mole Poblano I *Mole from Puebla I*

MOLE POBLANO IS ONE OF MEXICO'S GREATEST DISHES. It's known throughout the world and people travel to Puebla specifically to eat the city's *mole*. One of the very first assignments I gave myself when we reached town was to find Puebla's most accomplished *mole* makers. Morris and I ate the dish in various traditional restaurants, but it was the special, accomplished home recipe I was determined to uncover. Then I heard about Adela Dávila, last year's grand winner of Puebla's annual *Mole Poblano* Contest. Through trial and error (ahh, those errors) I found her. After she interviewed *me* and decided to share her recipe, I tasted the real thing in her kitchen. Señora Dávila is usually secretive about the recipe, made primarily of mulato chiles, because she makes it for one of Puebla's hottest restaurants. *Yield: about 20 pounds (this commercial-sized recipe may be cut in half)*

For "mole" paste

- 1½ pounds mulato chiles
- 2 ounces ancho chiles
- 4 ounces pasilla chiles
- 1 ounce chipotle chiles
- 1 cup vegetable oil (more, if needed)
- 8 pounds plantains, very ripe and black, peeled
- 1 pound almonds, blanched
- 4 pounds raisins
- 1 pound peanuts, shelled and skinned
- 2 pounds white sesame seeds
- 4 garlic heads
- 1 Tablespoon fennel seeds
- 1 eight-inch "canela" stick, or 1 four-inch cinnamon stick
- 3 cloves
- 7 Mexican chocolate tablets, broken and chopped
- 10 tortillas, burnt to black
- 25 black peppercorns
- ½ pound white sugar

1. Keeping in mind that the full recipe makes 20 pounds of paste, get out your very largest, restaurant-sized pots and bowls. Stem, seed, and devein the chiles. Put ½ cup of the oil in a skillet and brown the chiles uniformly. Remove from the oil with a slotted spoon and put the chiles in your largest bowl (or stock pot).

2. Slice the plantains into large slices and cook in the same oil until they are light brown, then put in the bowl with the chiles. Fry the almonds, raisins, peanuts, sesame seeds, and garlic separately in the oil, adding more if needed. Put everything into the bowl.

3. Mix the fennel seeds, *canela*, cloves, chocolate, tortillas, peppercorns, and sugar. Grind the entire amount with *metate* and *mano* as Señora Dávila does or use an electric grinder, or blend in a blender, in batches. Add water, little by little, but just enough to blend the ingredients. Pour the blender ingredients into a bowl and mix.

4. To make the paste, add a few cups of the mixture to the blender and purée with a little water until it is the consistency of peanut butter. Empty into another large bowl or pot. Continue with the entire bowl of ingredients, puréeing a few cups at a time.

5. Heat ¼ cup oil in a huge, deep pot and fry the paste (it splatters!) for 15 minutes. Reduce the heat and simmer at the very lowest possible heat, stirring, for 3 hours. Señora Dávila says it takes a full 3 hours for her paste to "season" and stay smooth. The paste may be made ahead and refrigerated for months, or frozen.

For "mole" sauce and poultry

Yield: 8 servings

- 1 Tablespoon lard or oil
- 2 cups "mole" paste
- 2 quarts (approximately) Chicken Broth (page 19). Reserve the cooked chicken (or turkey) used to make the broth
- ½ cup almonds, blanched, toasted (page 16), and ground
- ¼ cup sesame seeds, toasted

1. Melt the fat over a very low simmer. Add the paste and stir. Add the chicken broth (or broth from a turkey you have cooked for the meal) little by little. Simmer, cover askew, for 1 hour.

2. Put poultry pieces on individual plates or a huge platter. Sprinkle with toasted, ground almonds. Cover generously with sauce, and finally sprinkle with toasted sesame seeds.

Adela Dávila with her prize-winning "Mole Poblano."

Graciela Ponce's

Mole Poblano II *Mole from Puebla II*

BLENDS OF CHILES GIVE *MOLE* PASTE ITS WARMTH; fruits soften and mellow the chiles; nuts and seeds give flavor, body, and protein; spices add perfume and depth; vegetables supply flavor balance and volume. Chocolate is the regal touch (it was originally food for Aztec gods and kings) and blesses the dish with character. *Mole* comes from the Nahuatl (Aztec language) word for sauce, *mulli*. As the story goes, back in the seventeenth century a Poblana nun named sister Andrea invented a chocolate-laced chile, nut, and seed sauce to impress visiting dignitaries. To say the least it was a huge success and everyone lived happily ever after. Today, you can visit Sister Andrea's exceptional tiled kitchen in the Museo de Artesanías. Graciela, who works at the tourist information office in Puebla (the building itself a Talavera-tiled colonial classic, and almost next door to the cathedral) can give you walking directions to the famous kitchen, about ten blocks away. She shared her family recipe for *mole poblano*.

Yield: about 10 pounds (the recipe may be cut in half)

For "mole" paste

- 30 mulato chiles
- 16 ancho chiles
- 4 chipotle chiles
- 1 pound lard (page 18), or 2 cups vegetable oil
- 2 large white onions, coarsely chopped
- 8 garlic cloves, peeled
- 1½ pounds white sesame seeds
- 1½ pounds almonds, blanched
- 1½ pounds peanuts, shelled and skinned
- 1½ pounds raisins
- 2 plantains, ripe and black, peeled and sliced
- 1 teaspoon coriander seeds
- ½ teaspoon fennel seeds
- 1 four-inch "canela" stick, or 1 two-inch cinnamon stick
- 1 white onion, quartered
- 1 garlic head, halved

1. Stem and seed the chiles. Toast the chiles, in batches, until they change color (page 16). Remove to a bowl of hot water and soak for at least 30 minutes, then drain.

2. Heat 3 tablespoons of the fat in a skillet and sauté the chopped onions until they are transparent. Add the peeled garlic cloves and sauté until everything is lightly browned. Add to the drained chiles in a huge bowl.

3. Heat 3 tablespoons fresh fat and sauté the sesame seeds until lightly brown (about 30 seconds). Remove with a slotted spoon to the chiles. Sauté the almonds and peanuts in the same oil until light brown; add to the chiles.

4. Clean out the old fat and add fresh oil to the pan. Fry the raisins and plantain slices until the plantains are golden brown. Add to the chile mixture. Fry the coriander seeds, fennel seeds, and *canela*. Add to the chiles.

5. Toast the quartered onion, halved garlic head, and tomato. Remove to a blender container. Char the tortillas over an open flame, until they are quite black; crumble them in the blender. Purée with water to form a sauce. Strain the ingredients into a very large pot or bowl.

- 1 tomato
- 3 burnt tortillas (charcoal-black)
- 1 small onion, sliced
- 2 cups sugar
- 4 Mexican chocolate tablets, broken and chopped
- salt to taste

6. Put the chile mixture in the blender, in batches, with water or broth as needed, and purée to form a paste. Add to the tomato mixture.

7. Put the remaining oil in your largest, deepest pot, add the onion slices, and sauté until dark brown. Discard the onion. Heat to high and carefully add the blended ingredients (they splatter!). Add the sugar and chocolate. Lower the heat to a low simmer. Stir occasionally with a wooden spoon for about 2 hours, until a smooth paste is formed. Add salt to taste. The paste is now finished and all or some may be made into sauce, or it may be refrigerated, or frozen.

For *mole poblano* (sauce and poultry): See directions on page 159.

Adela Dávila's

Chiles en Nogada II *Stuffed Chiles with Walnut Sauce, Puebla Style*

GOOD HOME COOKS, AS EVERYWHERE, DO MAGICAL THINGS with Puebla's specialty when walnuts, poblano chiles, and pomegranates all reach peaks of perfection in late summer. As a tourist you'll never get a whiff of award-winning recipes like Señora Dávila's. Apart from the recent coveted title of Puebla's Best *Mole Poblano*, Señora Dávila won the city's Best *Chiles en Nogada* contest the previous year. Her recipe contains copious amounts of the locally adored candied fruit, which can be found everywhere, at any hour of the day or night, on every street corner, and in certainly every market. In the U.S., try to find at least two fruits—the assortment doesn't have to be so enormous as that in Señora Dávila's prizewinner. Latino markets are excellent sources for candied cactus and fruit, and health food stores carry naturally dried mango and papaya spears, plus rounds of dried pineapple, which work well in the sweet, room-temperature-with-cold-sauce dish.
Yield: 12 servings

For the walnut sauce

- 50 whole walnuts
- 1 cup cold milk
- ½ can (14 ounces) condensed milk
- ⅛ teaspoon ground cloves
- ⅛ teaspoon ground cinnamon
- 2 teaspoons sugar
- 4 ounces mild goat cheese or nonsalty feta cheese
- ¼ cup red wine

1. Heat water to a boil in a large pot. Add the whole walnuts and cover. When the water boils again, turn off the heat and remove the lid. Leave the nuts in the hot water for 5 minutes. Drain the water.

2. Peel the walnuts immediately and put the nut meats in the cold milk so they don't blacken. Put the nuts and milk in a blender container with the condensed milk, cloves, cinnamon, sugar, cheese, and wine. Grind, but not to a fine sauce—this is definitely not a smooth purée—the nut texture must be noticeable in the sauce. Refrigerate.

For the picadillo stuffing

- 2 pounds tomatoes
- 1 large white onion
- 5 garlic cloves
- 1 Tablespoon vegetable oil
- 2 pounds pork leg or loin meat
- 1 Tablespoon butter
- 3 tiny candied pears, cored; 3 small candied apples, cored; 3 ounces candied pineapple; 2 tiny candied peaches; or 2 pieces candied cactus, about 4 x 1-inch (1 to 1½ cups total, finely diced)
- ½ cup almonds, blanched and sliced vertically
- ½ cup raisins
- 1 large plantain, ripe-black, peeled and chopped
- ½ teaspoon ground cloves
- ½ teaspoon ground cinnamon
- salt and pepper to taste

1. Blanch the tomatoes in boiling water for 3 minutes; peel, then chop. Finely chop the onion, reserving one quarter, and 4 garlic cloves. Heat 1 tablespoon oil in a saucepan and sauté the onion. When it is transparent, add the chopped garlic and sauté until light brown. Add the tomatoes and simmer 15 minutes longer, reducing the liquid.

2. Chop the raw pork fine. In a large pot, bring 2 cups water to a boil with the remaining garlic clove, chopped, ¼ chopped onion, and chopped meat. Continue boiling until the water has evaporated. Add the butter and sauté 1 minute. Add the tomato mixture and stir. Simmer for about 10 minutes to reduce any remaining liquid.

3. Chop the candied fruit and add it to the pot, along with the almonds, raisins, and plantain. Add the cloves and cinnamon. Mix everything well, but do not beat the *picadillo* mixture. It is important to see pieces of fruit. Add salt and pepper to taste, but "don't use too much salt because this is a sweet dish," says Señora Dávila.

For the chiles and assembly

- 12 plump poblano chiles
- 1 Tablespoon flour
- ½ cup wine (any type, red or white, sweet or dry)
- 8 eggs
- ¼ cup white flour
- ¼ teaspoon salt
- 2 cups vegetable oil for frying
- ¼ cup flat-leaf parsley leaves
- seeds of 1 large pomegranate

1. Toast (page 16) the chiles. Put them in a plastic bag to "sweat" for a few minutes, then peel them. Keeping the stem attached, cut a slit down the side of each and remove the seeds very carefully. Stuff each chile with *picadillo*, then place it in a dish. Mix 1 tablespoon flour into the wine and sprinkle over the chiles. You may close each chile with a toothpick.

2. Separate the eggs and stiffly beat the whites. Add the yolks to the whites. Combine the ¼ cup flour with salt and sprinkle over the eggs, then gently mix.

3. In a wide skillet, heat the oil to 360°F, or until the surface ripples. Dip each chile in the egg mixture, then place it in the hot oil. Fry both sides until golden brown. Remove to paper towels to drain excess oil. When all are finished, change the towels so the oil is not reabsorbed into the chiles.

4. To serve, center a chile on a plate and generously pour over it the room-temperature sauce. Garnish with chopped parsley and pomegranate seeds.

María del Socorro Brun de López's

Tinga Poblana *Shredded Pork with Tomatoes and Chipotle Chiles*

HERE'S AN OLD FAVORITE PUEBLA RECIPE FROM MARÍA DEL SOCORRO BRUN DE LÓPEZ, who was born in Mexico City but moved to Puebla as a child. She cooks pork with chorizo, tomatoes, and chipotle chiles for her classic *tinga* with incomparable flavor. The meat may be cubed, chopped, or shredded. Classically, cubed pork is preferred when the dish is served on a plate and eaten with knife and fork. Shredded pork is the choice for *antojitos*, and these self-service, home-style tacos. Serve with various salsas.
Yield: 6 servings

- 2 pounds pork leg, loin, or shoulder meat
- 1 white onion, quartered
- 2 pounds tomatoes (about 6)
- ½ pound chorizo, casing removed
- 2 white onions, chopped
- 4 garlic cloves, finely chopped
- ¼ cup chopped flat-leaf parsley leaves
- 4 canned chipotle chiles en adobo, chopped, plus 4 Tablespoons sauce
- salt and freshly ground black pepper
- 2 large avocados
- ½ pound ranchero cheese, dry cottage cheese, or farmer cheese
- tortillas

1. Bring 3 quarts of water to a boil and add the pork and quartered onion. Simmer the meat for 1 hour, or until no pink shows when cut open. Remove the meat from the liquid and cool. When the pork is cool enough to handle, shred the meat using a fork, scraping with the grain.

2. Toast (page 16) the tomatoes. Put them in a plastic bag to "sweat" for a few minutes so that their skins will loosen. Peel, core, and chop.

3. Sauté the sausage for 5 minutes in the wiped-dry meat-cooking pot. Add the chopped onions, garlic, and parsley and cook, stirring, for 5 minutes. Add the pork, tomatoes, chipotle chiles and vinegar sauce. Simmer 10 minutes, uncovered.

4. Season with salt and pepper to taste. Serve with avocado slices, a small bowl of crumbled cheese, and a pile of hot tortillas for self-service tacos.

Pamen Santiesteban Llaguno's

Chilahuates

Banana-Leaf-Wrapped Tamales Filled with Masa, *Black Beans, and Vegetables*

PAMEN IS AN EXCEPTIONAL COOK LIVING IN PICTURESQUE NORTHERN PUEBLA, just northwest of Xalapa, Veracruz. Northern Puebla, known as the Sierra Norte de Puebla, has a completely different feel from the rest of the state. Its largely remote areas are mainly populated by Nahua and Totonac Indians; their basketry and weavings can be found in Teziutlán's market.

Chilahuates, meatless tamales, wrapped in banana leaves, are from an old family recipe of Pamen's, and you can make them completely vegetarian by using vegetable shortening and vegetable broth. Serve with Tomatillo Salsa made with chipotle chiles (page 213), and drink *Atole* (page 126) for authenticity.

Yield: about 20 tamales

- 1 cup black beans
- 2 pounds "masa" from a tortillería, or 4 cups prepared "masa harina"
- ½ pound lard (page 18) or vegetable shortening
- 2 cups Chicken Broth (page 19), or vegetable broth, lukewarm
- 1 teaspoon salt
- 1 teaspoon baking powder
- 3 banana leaves
- ¼ cup vegetable oil
- 1 garlic clove, finely chopped
- ½ cup finely chopped scallions
- 1 chayote or other summer squash, finely chopped
- 3 zucchini, finely chopped
- 4 to 8 jalapeño chiles, stemmed and finely chopped
- ½ cup blanched and finely chopped almonds
- ¼ cup chopped cilantro leaves
- salt to taste

1. Prepare the black beans as Refried Beans (page 250).

2. In a mixing bowl, beat the *masa* with the lard, alternating with the broth, little by little, until it is light, about 10 minutes. Add the salt and baking powder. Beat 2 minutes more.

3. Clean and boil or char the banana leaves (if not prepared). Trim out the hard veins and cut the leaves into approximately 10-inch squares.

4. Heat the oil in a skillet and sauté the garlic and scallions until they are golden. Add the chayote, zucchini, chiles, almonds, cilantro, and refried beans. Mix completely, stirring and cooking everything together. Season to taste.

5. Prepare the tamales like *Vaporcitos* (page 313), either using the tortilla method or pressing the *masa* into a circle on the banana leaf with your hands. Fill with beans and vegetables. Steam like *Vaporcitos* for 1 hour, checking the water level after 45 minutes. As with all tamales, peel away the leaf and discard before eating the stuffing.

Antonia Villanueva's

Calabaza en Tacha *Pumpkin Stewed in Syrup*

EATEN THROUGHOUT MEXICO, Pumpkin Stewed in Syrup is said to have originated in Michoacán during pre-Hispanic days using honey, but today is considered a specialty of Puebla. Chunks of the glistening, *panela*-soaked enticement seems to be in every market around town, and people constantly buy *calabaza en tacha* to take home and put in bowls, pour milk over, and eat as a snack. It's also lip-smacking on its own, snacked on the spot, as are so many market delicacies. Antonia's *calabaza* is delectable—just remember to take along moist towels. Sticky fingers are torture at Mercado Carmen Serdan Acocota! Or try *calabaza en tacha* warm, scraped from the skin, with a scoop of coffee ice cream for dessert.
Yield: 6 servings

- 1 four-pound eating pumpkin (not a jack-o'-lantern carving type), you'll find many varieties at farmer's markets during the autumn
- 3 six-inch "canela" sticks, or 3 three-inch cinnamon sticks
- 2 pounds "panela," or dark brown sugar
- 1 orange, juiced

1. Cut off the top section of the pumpkin to form a bowl shape. Scrape out the seeds and pith. Make incisions down the outsides and into the skin, without cutting through the flesh. There should be about five vertical cuts to let the syrup permeate.

2. Put 4 cups water in a pot and add the *canela*, *panela*, and orange juice. Place the pumpkin upside down in the liquid.

3. Bring the liquid to a boil, cover the pot, reduce the heat, and simmer for about 45 minutes. When it is ready, the pumpkin will look glazed. Take the pot off the heat and let the pumpkin cool in the liquid.

Note: When cooking larger pumpkins, as market vendors do, cook them twice with a cooling period between. This system permits an even absorption of syrup and leaves the pumpkin moist.

Marcela López Brun's

Camotes *Sweet Potato Candy*

CAMOTES ARE SUCH AN IMPORTANT FOOD in Puebla that there's actually a "Sweet Street" made famous by this candy. It's lined with shops selling all sorts of goodies but *camotes* are, unquestionably, the celebrities. By the way, the word *camotes* means "sweet potatoes," and is also the name of these sweet potato candies.

Marcela, a Puebla art dealer, learned how to make this dish from her mother when she was a girl in Puebla. Pale yellow yams are the main ingredient, with colorings and flavorings added. The paper-wrapped enticements are reminiscent of the way old-fashioned salt water taffy once looked. Delightfully gift-boxed, they are every Poblano's favorite treat.
Yield: about 4 pounds, or approximately 25 pieces

- 2 pounds light yellow yams or sweet potatoes
- 2 pounds sugar
- 1 quart water
- 5 drops lemon flavoring
- 1 drop yellow vegetable coloring
- 5 drops orange flavoring
- 1 drop orange vegetable coloring
- 1 cup white sugar

1. Put the yams in boiling water and cook until they are soft, about 30 minutes. Remove from the water, cool, and peel. Mash the yams to form a smooth paste.
2. Dissolve the sugar in 2 cups water, heat to a simmer, and boil to make a syrup (do not brown or color). Pour the syrup into the sweet potato paste, then pass the mixture through a sieve. Empty into a pot and heat, stirring with a wooden spoon, until it becomes a thick paste, about 15 minutes.
3. Divide the paste into 2 bowls. Add the flavorings and colorings: one batch lemon with yellow (or green for lime), another batch orange with orange. Stir well to completely incorporate the flavors and colorings.
4. Spread out the pastes on separate baking sheets, and refrigerate. When cold, form the *camotes* with your hands into cigar shapes, using ⅓ cup dough, about 4 inches x ¾ inch thick.
5. Roll each in white sugar, then set aside until all are finished and dry.
6. Count the *camotes* and cut an equal amount of 6-inch squares of waxed paper. Center a *camote* on a sheet of paper and roll the paper around the candy, twisting each end closed. Continue with the rest.

Marcela López Brun still loves her favorite childhood sweet, "Camotes."

◆ Cholula ◆

Popocatépetl volcano behind Tepanapa pyramid.

SITUATED IN FRONT OF, and twelve kilometers closer than Puebla to wondrous Popocatépetl and Iztaccíhuatl volcanoes, Cholula is a vision, especially when you drive into town on Highway 150, from Puebla. In fact, it's one of the most dramatic sights in Mexico even without "Popo" erupting. Tepanapa pyramid, topped by an eighteenth-century church, sits impressively before the two snow-capped (year-round) volcanoes. Tepanapa pyramid is far from fully excavated; it remains a mound covered with soil and plant growth, but endless underground passageways are open to the public. Cholula boasts its pyramid as the biggest ancient pyramid in the Americas.

✸ MARKET ✸

Mercado Municipal Not more than a dozen blocks north of the pyramid is the enclosed Mercado Municipal, between Avenida Hidalgo and 2 Poniente, and Calle 3 Norte and Calle 4 Norte (one block behind the *portales* of the *zócalo*). It's open every day, early morning to about 8 P.M. Cholula's big market day is Wednesday, when the city center's streets become an open-air Indian market packed with vendors from surrounding villages. Women wrapped in traditional shawls sell carved wooden spoons, pottery, myriad home-grown chiles, fruit, and vegetables (including the tinest baby summer squash imaginable), gourmet wild mushrooms and herbs, brown sugar breads, and chewy sweets made from toasted coconut.

Fondas. There are many fondas in Cholula's market and most cater to market merchants. Specialties are *cemitas* (sandwiches), *moles*, and grilled, salted, stringy beef on handmade tortillas with salsa. Soups and stews made mostly of vegetables are popular, especially in the morning, which is actually lunch hour to the early birds who set up stalls with fresh produce.

Chilaquiles are in demand, along with steaming mugs of sweetened black coffee or *atole* in various flavors.

Butcher. Cholula Super Mercado de Carnes is in the northwest corner of the market. The very clean, refrigerated stall offers top-quality fresh beef and pork. The friendly butchers enjoy North American customers who request different cuts, and they try their hardest to please. **Fritz** pork products is right next to Cholula Super Mercado de Carnes. Fritz sells chorizos, *longaniza,* ham, bacon, and very lean smoked loins.

Bread. *Cemita* is the same name for the region's version of Mexico's beloved sandwich and the roll it's made on. Excellent warm *cemitas* (rolls) are sold from huge baskets at the Calle 3 Norte and Avenida 2 Poniente corner of the market in the evening, about 6:30 P.M.

✷ PLACES TO GO AND THINGS TO EAT ✷

Cemitas. In Cholula, *cemitas* (sandwiches) are made on a round, sesame-seed-topped, chewy roll (also called *cemita*) rather than on the more standard *bolillo* (French roll). They are always heaped with shredded *quesillo de Oaxaca*, pickled vegetables, raw onions, sliced avocados, and are spritzed with oil and vinegar. One distinction is the addition of an herby, fresh leaf, *papalo*. *Cemitas* can be found all around town at stands, fondas, and coffee shops. At the town's annual fiesta, *cemitas* sold from fair booths are especially fabulous. Heat alert: When a kind, elderly woman asked if we'd like chipotle chiles, she really meant it. Being generous to vistors, she had put seven chiles on one roll. Yabba dabba doooo.

Chalupas. *Chalupas*, tiny, three-inch tortillas, are quickly fried in oil (not crisp), smeared with a spoonful of salsa (red or green), and sprinkled with a bit of dry cheese. Tiny, tasty, and cheap, *chalupas* are popular at Cholula's big fiesta held the week before Mexican Independence Day, September 15.

Bakery. Panificadora La Blanca, located at 111 Avenida Hidalgo, tel. 47-00-20. Hours: 6 A.M. to 10 P.M. every day. Sweet rolls, *cemitas*, and flour-dusted rolls (similar to Irish soda bread in looks and texture) warm in the morning and evening.

Fiesta drink. Women set up tables at the fair for huge ceramic pots containing *tacao*, a cool, frothy drink containing chocolate, water, and sugar (no milk or corn, as for *atole*), and similar to Oaxaca's *texate*. The icy cold liquid is constantly beaten with a *molinillo* to keep its frothy, foamy head. *Tacao* is traditionally served in brightly painted dried gourd halves rinsed in a bucket of cold water between imbibers. Beware. Get yours in a not-so-traditional plastic cup, and as always, be sure it's made with purified water.

Coffee. There's good cappuccino on the plaza, at the cafés on either end of the Portal Guerrero. Cholula's interesting, two-block-long lineup of *portales* is an excellent people-watching spot on Sunday. During the week it's pretty quiet.

RESTAURANTS

La Fonda. Inexpensive. 3 Norte No. 601. Hours: 7 A.M. to 10 P.M. every day. A true fonda where a woman/owner turned her once-living-room into a restaurant by removing the sofa and TV and replacing them with six tables. Tacos are prepared to order five ways, all with grilled meats. Side dish cactus and cucumber salads pair well with the tacos.

La Casona. Moderate. 3 Oriente No. 9, Tel. 47-27-76. Open for lunch and dinner every day. Tables are set under an overhang facing a patio, or in handsome dining rooms. *Gorditas* and quesadillas with poblano chile and *epazote,* are choice appetizers. Homemade soups are on the menu every day. *Manchamanteles* with either chicken or pork is the area's noted "tablecloth stainer," here a sweet-sour chile sauce; chicken breast with various sauces; enchiladas with either chicken or shredded pork and dried fruit with *mole*; and pumpkin seed sauce with either chicken or pork, are all good choices. Dessert flan is soothing—try to save room.

Huejotzingo Being 26 kilometers closer to the two looming volcanoes (on the road to San Martín Texmelucan) than Cholula, Huejotzingo's views are nothing short of staggering. Go for the exciting Saturday *tianguis*—it's an open-air market. Great bargains in local pottery are hard-to-resist temptations and people drive from all around to gather prized *cazuelas.*

There must be a dozen bubbling caldrons for *chicharrónes* and *carnitas* made from freshly slaughtered pigs. Can all this pork possibly be bought and consumed? Buy a few warm and crunchy *cemitas* and have a *carnitas* vendor cut a hunk of still-bubbling meat, chop it, and stuff your rolls. Lamb *barbacoa* is another favorite, here pit-baked in maguey leaves with lots of fresh herbs. Women sell scoops of *quelite*, a spinachlike green but with an herbier taste; they chop it fine with onion and chile—a favorite of shoppers to spread on bits of cooked meat from the *carnitas* or *barbacoa* vendors, or to roll a tortilla around. Typical Saturday offerings include homegrown tiny yellow peaches, tiny brown Bosc-like pears, apricots, figs, the season's first apples, slightly alcoholic cider for which Huejotzingo is famous, or sparkling apple juice, small piles of white (for *pipián*) and unusual black (for eating alone, raw or roasted) pumpkin seeds, and raw bean mixtures in astonishing colors. Cows, bulls, oxen, squealing baby piglets, goats, lambs—you name it—a full menagerie is sold from the back of pickups conveniently situated on the way back to your car.

Rosalia López-Gómez's

▲▼▲

Chalupas de Cholula *Tiny Tortilla Snacks*

THREE-INCH TORTILLAS MADE ESPECIALLY FOR *CHALUPAS* are sold at tortillerías all around town. Corner stands do a brisk business with *chalupas*, the most popular street food in Cholula. Rosalia griddle-fries tortillas in oil until a bit crisp, but not crackling (they need to cook and absorb a small amount of oil in order not to fall apart when salsa is spread over them). Then she spreads either *tomatillo salsa*, or a cooked tomato salsa over the surface and sprinkles on a smidgeon of shredded cheese. Rarely does she add shredded chicken or pork.

Chalupas are meager, cheap, snacks—no more than flavored tortillas. They are favorite appetizers in traditional Mexican restaurants in Cholula and nearby Puebla. They also make great snacks with tequila drinks, or beer, and sometimes they're topped with lettuce and onions. San Cristóbal de las Casas, in the state of Chiapas, enjoys its version with a completely different approach. The only similarity between it and Cholula's *chalupa* is the tiny three-inch tortilla base. There, they're piled with refried black beans, sliced pork, cooked carrots, shredded cabbage, and a red salsa made with the tiny, hot de tuxtla chile.
Yield: 8 chalupas

- ½ cup vegetable oil
- 8 three-inch tortillas, handmade or store-bought, trimmed to size
- ½ cup Salsa de Tomatillo (page 244)
- ½ cup crumbled "queso añejo" or Parmesan cheese

1. Heat the oil on a large griddle or in a large skillet to medium-hot. Cook a few tortillas at a time until they have absorbed some oil and are throughly heated but still pliable, not snap-crisp. Drain on paper towels and fry the rest.

2. Spread with spicy salsa. Top with a light sprinkle of cheese, and an optional smidgen of cooked meat if you want to be decadent.

Señora Méndez del Ruíz y Señora Bertha del María Juárez's

Mamelas y Memenas *Thick, Oval Tortillas*

MAMELAS AND *MEMENAS* ARE NOT SOLD TOGETHER OFF THE SAME GRIDDLE, but both are found around Cholula, Puebla, and Mexico City. *Mamelas* are thick, blue-corn *masa*, oval tortillas, *comal*-cooked then topped with beans, *epazote* leaves, and shredded cheese. *Mamelas* are never filled, as are Mexico City's *tlacoyos*, which are also made from blue corn exclusively, except when stuffed with yellow corn *masa* and called *tlacoyos de dos masas* (with two *masas*). [You'll see *tlacoyos* all over Mexico's central states, but great examples are found on the winding stairways at Taxco's open-air market, the evening vendor's at San Miguel de Allende's Mercado El Nigromante, and those on the plaza at Toluca's Friday market (and called by different names). Big cities' ovals are often changed to faster-to-pat-out circles when there's a crowd.]

Cholula's *memenas* are made by forming a medium coarse blue-corn *masa* into a ball, making a hole and filling it with puréed black beans before patting it out to a bean-filled 5 by 10-inch oval. They're different from *huaraches*, which are usually made from coarse yellow *masa (*and are a specialty at Mexico City's Mercado de Jamaica), and are never filled with black beans. *Huaraches* (the word translates to "sandals" because of the oval shapes) can be seen from Guadalajara to Mexico City, and like shoes, come in various sizes. *Tlacoyos* are never filled with black beans; the standard is refried pink beans or garbanzos.

All this is to show you just how confusing one relatively small area of *antojitos* (snacks) is. Names vary by region, or by minute differences. It's best to ask names, when the tortillas are hot on the *comal*, right in front of your nose. The most important aspect of these *antojitos* is the use of coarsely ground *masa*. The dough must be as coarse as tamale *masa*, but not quite so extra-coarse as for *gorditas*, which are even thicker tortillas, like those sold on the street in San Miguel de Allende. Veracruzana *Gorditas* (page 215) are yet another story. Serve *mamelas* and *memenas* with spicy salsa.

Yield: 4 servings

For mamelas

- 3 Tablespoons lard or vegetable oil
- 2 cups coarsly ground blue-corn "masa" for tamales
- 1 cup Refried Beans (page 251)
- 1 cup shredded "quesillo de Oaxaca," string cheese, or mozzarella
- 4 "epazote" leaves, shredded

1. Heat the oil on a griddle or in a large skillet.

2. Form ½ cup *masa* into an oval and pat it out to 5 x 8 inches. Fry in hot oil until cooked, about 2 minutes on each side.

3. Top each tortilla with refried black beans, shredded cheese, and *epazote*.

For memenas

- 3 Tablespoons lard or vegetable oil
- 2 cups coarsly ground blue-corn "masa" for tamales
- 1 cup Refried Black Beans (page 250)

1. Heat the oil on a griddle or in a large skillet.

2. Form ½ cup *masa* into a ball. Poke a hole in the center and fill with refried black beans. Pat out into a 5 x 10-inch oval. Fry in hot fat until cooked, about 2 minutes on each side.

Hermina's

Vinagre de Piña y Manzana *Pineapple-Apple Vinegar*

FRUIT VINEGAR IS MADE AROUND THE CHOLULA AREA in apple orchard country. Starting with apple vinegar, fresh apples and pineapple are added so the final vinegar has a more fruity, aggressive flavor than mild pineapple-only vinegar popular in Veracruz. Home-brewed bottles of pineapple vinegar can be spotted south of Veracruz City, in La Laguna in thatched-roof pineapple stands decorated with fresh fruit. Sometimes the bottles are corked with corn cobs. In winter months apple stands line roadways up in Puebla and you'll see cider vinegar sold from one-time soda and beer bottles. Huejotzingo, with its charming Saturday country market (plus exhilarating volcano views), offers bottles of apple vinegar alongside apple cider, for which the town is famous.

Hermina likes this classic fruit combination for her vegetables in *escabeche*.

Yield: about 1 quart

- 1 quart apple cider vinegar
- 2 small sour apples, such as pippin
- 1 small pineapple, the rind scrubbed clean and rinsed thoroughly (organic, if possible)
- 6 ounces "panela" or dark brown sugar

1. Cut the apples into halves. Peel the pineapple and save the fruit for another use.

2. Place the *panela*, apples, pineapple rind, and vinegar in a glass bowl, crock, or jar (nonaluminum) and cover. Allow the mixture to ferment for 15 days before passing through a fine sieve and funneling into bottles. I use Perrier or San Pellegrino glass bottles with screw tops. Store where you keep other vinegar.

The State of Veracruz

Veracruz
Córdoba
Xalapa

THE STATE OF VERACRUZ IS A FUSION OF MISTY HILLS neatly planted with rows of coffee trees, of bougainvillea-lined waterways linked with sugar-cane and tobacco fields, of throbbingly sweaty jungles, and of coconut palm-patched plantain and pineapple plantations abruptly ending in the Gulf of Mexico. It's an entrancing mix of quaint pueblos and exuberant markets with miles and miles of lush tropical vegetation still enveloping much of the state's most interesting archaeological sites. Once home to the Olmecs, Mexico's most ancient civilization, then the Huastecs and Totonacs (who left El Tajín), Veracruz is an archaeologist's or anthropologist's dream state. Other indigenous groups still live in the north, and still others in dramatic Sierra Madre Oriental with snow-capped peaks. Xalapa's anthropology museum draws people from all over the world before they trek into the wilds and make discoveries on their own.

Left: Music under the "portales" in Veracruz.

◆ Veracruz ◆

María Alejandra Molena de Rivera of La Cría.

SINCE THE SPANIARDS ARRIVED AT the old seaport in 1519, the inhabitants of Veracruz City have been looking toward the future. Today, new building is a fact of life on every block of Veracruz, just as superhighways link once-isolated villages in the countryside. But, more than any other Mexican city, Veracruz exists for itself, and this nonconformist attitude is reflected in its cuisine. Like New Orleans, Veracruz is Creole—a mix of Spanish and French. And, again like New Orleans, it features seafood from the Gulf of Mexico.

Famous Veracruzana dishes include: *Pescado a la Veracruzana* (Fish with Tomatoes, Capers, Olives and Onions) (page 203); *Filetes de Pescados al Mojo de Ajo* (Fish Fillets in Garlic Sauce) (page 198); *Camarones Enchipolado* (Shrimp in Smoky Chile Sauce) (page 204); and *Toro* (Milk, Fruit, and Sugarcane Alcohol Drink) (page 210).

"People say it's a mental hospital with an ocean view" says my friend Jesús (Chucho) Hernández Ramos about Veracruz City. It's one of the least Catholic cities in the country and rather hedonistic. It boasts a *zócalo* scene unsurpassed anywhere in the country. Afternoons become all-night marimba magic where *Jarochos* (Veracruzanas) think nothing of dancing by themselves, then stay awake, watch the dawn, and listen to more music with breakfast. Once a year, before Lent, Veracruz's Carnival, surpassed in size and excitement only by the carnivals of Rio de Janiero and New Orleans, turns the city into a feeding frenzy of excitement.

Anytime of year pull up a chair at one of the cafés under the *portales* on Plaza de las Armas, next to city hall, for a ringside seat at a Felliniesque sideshow. There's nothing quite like it. Lean back and puff away on a huge Cuban cigar while wearing your darkest shades. Try an aged rum with club soda and swirl your swizzle stick to a military band playing rhumbas (or even older, *danzón*). Oldsters wearing whites and Panama hats, or sequined dresses, dance to tunes straight out of the last century. Meanwhile, surrounding you under the *portales*, marimba bands with their xylophones-on-wheels, exuberant *Jarocho* musicians, and mariachi groups try to outdo one another. Add, still, a vending swarm hawking everything from hammocks, huge sailing ship models, Cuban cigars, copied cassettes, steamed shrimp, assorted nuts, fried plantain chips, vanilla pods sold by Papantlans in traditional dress, to kids with Chiclets and squeaking toys—and you have an unforgettable entertainment spectacle.

About those ever-present street vendors: Don't "Just Say No." In fact, don't say anything. The Mexican way to handle unsolicitated salespeople is never to look them in the eye and never to speak. Shake your head back and forth very slightly (almost imperceptively) only twice. If that doesn't work, hold up an index finger and move it sideways, twice, slowly. Subtlety is the key, and it always works. For those who think this is cruel, just wait until your dinner-under-the-stars is bombarded with sharks and urchins who just happen to be the best actors this side of Broadway.

* MARKETS *

Mercado Hidalgo Mercado Hidalgo's building is between Cortés and Soto, Madero and Hidalgo, about a dozen blocks southwest of the *zócalo*. This bustling section of town swirls with motion—no park-bench daydreaming here. Absolutely peerless produce is displayed in styles ranging from grand presentations to grab-it-from-the-crate curbside vendors. Winter introduces *crucetas*, a type of cactus (like ever-present *nopales*) but in a long, unusual shape. Medicinal herbs play a big part in the market; vendors with fresh, dried, and powdered concoctions, candles, incense, animal bones, snake skins, etc., sit back and look for the right disease to stroll by. Bottles of Comercial Cava sugarcane and pineapple vinegars are fun to take home: You'll spot the red fly logo. Another bottled preparation is *miel de cana* found at sugarcane vendors. The sugarcane syrup is used in cooking and on pancakes. Blanketing everything is a party-decorated ceiling of crêpe paper piñatas. Don't be surprised when a marimba band starts up—it's part of Veracruz's all-encompassing celebration of life on an ongoing basis. Care to dance?

Chiles. The largest chipotle chiles (mecos) are in the market toward the end of January, so buy yours in the winter for the entire season and keep them in a freezer. The market's unrivaled selection makes choosing fun. Huge, extra thick, and meaty ancho chiles are also remarkable souvenirs.

Herbs. *Acuyo* (known in other parts of Mexico as *hoja santa,* and *momo*) leaves are sold in the market, fresh, and rolled in bundles of ten or so. To dry, lay the large heart-shaped leaves out flat so they don't curl, then turn every day for four or five days. Stack or crumble in a plastic bag and take back home (fresh leaves and plants can't be taken across the border).

Butchers. Meat counters take up a good portion of the building, next to the seafood. All the butchers are in one section and most specialize in either beef or pork. The largest array of calf's heads for tacos (cheek, tongue, brains, or eyeballs?) I've ever seen is right here.

Seafood. The fish selection is just as quintessential as in the old seafood market, possibly even more so. The array of impeccably iced specimens is positively outstanding. I've been told seafood here arrives from boats that dock in Alvarado, just to the south of the city, and the fish at the old seafood market is from boats that dock in Veracruz. Since there's not much difference in distance as far as the size of the Gulf, the separation is probably due to political, or trucking logistics. The vendors are seafood experts, one and all.

Seafood Cocktail Bars. Most are open 7 A.M. to 7 P.M. every day. Smack in the center of Mercado Hidalgo are **Mandinga, Gloria, Tampico**, and **Plaza Azul**. Choose one that's crowded and looks clean and you won't go wrong with shrimp, crab (usually with a bit too much shell left on), octopus, snail, clam, or a combination served with avocado chunks, the usual saltines, and bottles of hot sauce on the side. Since these counters are very popular you may have to wait for a seat. You'll notice that prices are slightly lower than in the seafood market, but that's because tiny crabs are used (but you don't know this since crabmeat is all you see) and portions are fractionally smaller—a better buy for market workers.

Barbacoa. Also near the center of the ground floor is a meat place doing a brisk business with the take-out crowd. **El Poblanito** specializes in lamb *barbacoa* and people line up for different cuts to be weighed by the kilo. There's a small counter for *barbacoa* tacos and it's the easiest way to taste the delicious meat.

Stuffed Chipotle Chiles. Next to El Poblanito, **Taco Paco's** has a reputation for *chipotles rellenos*, so popular that by 1 P.M. they're all gone. Taco Paco's reply of "secret ingredients, sorry" when I asked for the recipe was not unexpected, but my tasting perseverance paid off and the recipe (page 196) comes mighty close. Shredded beef with onion, raisins, and *panela* makes a splendid complement to the spicy, smoky chile that's battered and deep-fried. Try the unsauced *rellenos* topped with a spoonful of guacamole.

Pineapple juice. Swivel your stool around and order a fresh and foamy pineapple juice at the booth across the aisle and behind you. Don't worry, they'll be glad to serve you, and Taco Paco's wants you to be happy if soda's not your thing.

Fondas. A few more fondas with seafood and meat lunch specials are upstairs on the mezzanine. They're basic places serving cheap eats to market workers. A favorite plate here is *arroz a la tumbada*, Veracruz's version of Chinese fried rice made with any seafood mixture on hand.

Mercado Unidad Veracruzana Across Soto is the even older Mercado Unidad Veracruzana building with more of the same but at slightly less expensive prices, for it is, as I was told, less "fancy." Spilling out, especially more southwesterly, is a warren of hand-built, tin-roofed shacks that long ago took over an adjoining park to become a natural extension of the market building. You'll love this place. Meandering through is an adventure not to be found much anymore in Mexico's big cities. Welcome to the "back room," a definitely nontouristy, dark maze of tiny fondas and food stalls open every day from 6:30 A.M. to 8 P.M. A naked lightbulb hangs here; a stream of daylight beams there, over an oilcloth-covered counter. Enter between fresh-poultry sellers, whose menagerie is bound by legs but with nonrestrictive squawking and gobbling freedom. Walking is precarious, so watch your step on the uneven flooring of cement, dirt, or wooden planks. Your imagination grows wild here. Women become witches and their *cazuelas* become cauldrons. Stews become concoctions of who knows what. Take the whole experience in by sitting down someplace and having a bottled soda. Watch how the ancient bartering system works. Three kilos of carrots for a lunch special? Sure. Scrub your bench for a tamale? Why not? A liter of *mole* for a liter of chipotle chile salsa? Good deal. Farther along, tentlike canopies appear, followed by bright sun, then the street emerges and pushcarts scamper in every direction.

The heat and humidity of Veracruz is even more apparent in the marketplace; you never feel the slightest breeze except if you stand in front of someone's table fan. Wear your lightest clothing and take your time strolling through chiles, bananas, sugarcane, pineapples, and coconuts. Autumn marks the end of mango season, but December introduces silvery-gray tree moss at every other stall. Tree moss, along with live, bright green (some painted) ground moss, is used under everyone's artificial Christmas tree as "grass." Reddish air plants with tiny lavender flowers are natural ornaments, as are tangerines, piled in streetcorner carts. These classics contrast with multicolored mini-lights twinkling merrily along while keeping beat with their squeaking pop carols.

Coconuts. Carmen Rodríguez's coconut (Cocos nucifera) stand is out the back door and on the alley, and offers coconuts still in their thick, green skins (great for tropical drinks). She told me they last about two months after being cut from palm trees. Then there's the coconut with its green skin removed. This type lasts only fifteen days but is easier to handle for cooking. The brown, hard-shell type (most commonly found in markets in the U.S.) lasts three months, but the liquid evaporates quickly, and the meat loses its sweetness before eventually hardening. Finally, on Carmen's counter is a tray of softball-sized coconuts (no shell, and the skin is pared to reveal soft, sweet white meat still filled with milk) that lasts only through the day.

Fondas. Not quite within the back maze, but at a rear entrance of the old market are two fondas, **Bella** and **Antojitos Isabel**. They have been preparing and selling cheap *picadas*, Veracruz's answer to *sopes* (griddle-fried tortillas with turned-up edges, topped with salsa, beans, and cheese) for years. The large wraparound counter is always full.

Mercado de Pescadería Come parched and get quenched, come hungry and get *comida Veracruzana*: a mixture of Spanish and a bit of French—a robust, gusty Creole cuisine not unlike that of New Oreleans. Seafood is the prime ingredient of Veracruz's most well-loved dishes, and rightly so. The city's proximity to the Gulf of Mexico, lagoons, deltas, rivers, streams, and lakes enriches the cuisine with an abundance of fish and shellfish. Perfumed, year-long, red-ripe tomatoes are next on the list of necessary ingredients. Then come sharp white onions (not the mellow yellow kind we usually see in the U.S.), and plenty of garlic. Green and red-ripe jalapeño chiles grown in the state of Veracruz, and its smoked version, the beloved chipotle chile, can't possibly be omitted. For the final fillip, add Spanish green olives, and Spanish capers, then sauté everything together with Spanish olive oil.

Mercado de Pescadería, Veracruz's old fish market, is just a few blocks off the *zócalo* and close to the docks between Serdán and Arista. (But there is talk of moving the market to larger quarters in another central-city location at Montecino and Bravo.) Enter on Landero y Coss, one block east of Zaragoza, by climbing one flight of stairs in between the line of seafood cocktail bars. Fish is to your right and the selection varies by the hour. Early mornings, as always, are best but not quite so important as in other cities because fresh fish seems to be carried in regularly until noon. You'll see huge pompano and six-inch *pompanitos* gutted and slashed on each side. Once taken home, they'll be sautéed quickly in hot butter. Large white-fish, called *pluma*, are cut into thick steaks for panfrying, or are used in soups. *Cozón* (small sand sharks), no longer than thirty inches, are sold in fillets and steaks (the meat prized for tacos); the eggs and intestines are also for sale. Bony *mojarra tilapia* are plentiful and cheap; whole fish (eight inches) are served at low-cost lunch specials around town: *Yeguas* (also called *espadines*, or *cintillas*—"small tapes") are not small at all but yard-long and very thin, bright, silver fish used mostly in *ceviche* with *sierra* and *peto*, similar fish of the mackerel family. The sea bounty seems endless: The Gulf's famous *huachinango* (red snapper) glows because of its coral-red color; *rubia* is pale pink with shimmering gold stripes; huge sea bass; manta ray wings cut into *mantazaya minilla* (small dice) or *chan-chan* (large dice) for Exotic Seafood Tacos (page 293); live lake, river, gulf, and ocean shrimp; langostinos; various snails, clams, and octopi; live blue crabs tied in bundles and hung next to hanging bags of empty, cleaned crab shells ready to stuff for *Jaibas Rellenas* (page 189).

Fondas. The fondas are located on the third floor, above the fresh seafood. All day long from dawn to evening the fondas feed fishermen and marketgoers with good seafood at rock-bottom prices. Since so many lives run on different clocks around here, fondas serve their entire menu all day.

Shrimp *mojo de ajo* at 7:30 A.M? Sure. Eggs over easy with toast and coffee at 4:45 P.M? Of course.

Seafood cocktails. Seafood cocktail bars are lined up, outside, on the Calle Landero y Coss side. **Neveria Aroporit** is on the corner selling coconut milk straight from fresh coconuts (to drink with a straw from huge green, natural containers) before you see the seafood counters. At **La Cría**, have one of the best and cheapest shrimp, crab, octopus, oyster, crab, or snail cocktails anywhere in the world. Cocktails here, as everywhere, come in two sizes, *chico* and *grande*. The counterman fills your sundae-style glass halfway with perfectly cooked seafood, then adds broth, hot sauce, tomato sauce, freshly squeezed lime, chopped onion, cilantro, flat-leaf parsley, and avocado slices. Sure, you have room for another. The sauce here is a bit thicker and not quite so sweet as in Guadalajara's market. Cocktails in Mérida and the port of Progreso are about the same as in Veracruz, but the Yucatán's habanero chile packs that sauce with gusto. Other winning treats at La Cría are piles of fresh, boiled-in-their-shells shrimp to peel and selections include: *blanco* (white, from the Gulf); *río* (black, from freshwater lakes and rivers); and *lago* (gray, from lagoons). Have a taste-off and choose your favorite.

✹ PLACES TO GO AND THINGS TO EAT ✹

Tamales. Dulce María de León, a *tamalera*, has a spot in an open doorway on Morales between 5 de Mayo and Independencía on the south side of the street near the walkstreet. You'll see cars double park, and their drivers jump out and order a dozen to-go, which Dulce María wraps in a flash. She sells a large banana leaf-wrapped tamale made with finely hand-ground *masa* steamed with *acuyo* (*hoja santa* in other parts of Mexico) and chipotle chile. Her other famous, fabulous corn leaf-wrapped Tamale (page 193) is made with fresh corn. It's a bit sweet, which blends perfectly with spicy chipotle chile and the slight anise flavor of *acuyo*. The combination of freshly hand-ground corn and coarse-ground *masa* makes for absolutely perfect *masa* texture.

Tamales Cernidos. Pushcarts are found throughout the city center, especially between the *zócalo* and the market in the evening from 6 P.M. to 9 P.M. There's usually one at Cinco de Mayo and Mario Molina, another at Cinco de Mayo and Arista. Look for steamers attached to carts made from bicycles and filled with three types: sweet with raisins (Although popular throughout Mexico, sweet tamales are virtually unheard of in the U.S. What a shame, their muffinlike tastes and textures are well worth exploring.); bits of shredded chicken in a light *mole*; and strips of fresh chile. These are typical northern-style, small, coarse *masa*-in-corn-husks tamales. Around town, especially near the markets in the morning and evening (after 8 P.M.), you'll see tamales with chicken *barbacoa*, but they're best known as a Sunday night tamale. *Tamales mollotes* are bite-sized babies, their husk pieces filled with various flavorings.

Pambazo. A Veracruz sandwich is a *pambazo*, sometimes *bambaso* (as at the bakery, Panadería y Pastelería Colón). The difference is the roll (like Puebla and Cholula's *cemita*) and again, both roll and sandwich have the same name. This time around, it's a soft hamburger bun dusted with flour or sprinkled with sesame seeds. *Pambazos*, found all over town at stand-at-the-counter-and-eat places, are first spread with black beans, then stuffed with the usual *Torta* stuffings (page 120). Small wrapped versions are for sale in bakeries.

Bakeries. Panadería y Pastelería Colón located at S.A. de C.V., Independencia No. 1435, tels. 32-38-41 and 32-36-67. Open Monday through Saturday 6:30 A.M. to 9 P.M. Closed Sunday. The stars here are definitely cakes: layer cakes with icing and fruit, birthday cakes, wedding cakes, you-name-it cakes. Famous *concha pan dulce* "shells" of Mexico are called *bomba* here.

Panver located on the corner of 16 de Septiembre and Doblado, tel. 31-27-97, is open every day 8 A.M. to 9 P.M. Where Colón specializes more in cakes, Panver does best with breads, sweet rolls (best in town), and *volovanes* (puff pastry street snacks), but here they're brought to their height in taste and texture.

Volovanes. Flaky, rectangular pastries filled with ham, cheese, crab, pineapple, chicken, tuna, beans, or sweet fruit paste are sold throughout the central city all day from vendors' baskets. People buy them for on-the-go breakfasts, quick lunches, and late-night snacks.

Corn cake. *Postre de elote* is sold on street corners throughout Mexico, day and evening. Veracruz boasts one of the best—try the vendor at Independencía near Canal. Hers is a not-too-dense cake made with fresh corn kernels, and the corn flavor comes through loud and clear.

Turrón. *Turrón* is creamy, off-white, nougat candy sold on the *zócalo* in evenings. Vendors' card tables are set up near the cathedral. You can buy *turrón* in different sizes from teeny tastes to huge blocks.

Nieve. Centro Nevero Malecón, located at Zamora No. 20 (walkstreet) near Landero y Coos, open every day from 9 A.M. to midnight, or sometimes earlier when chilly northers blow in December, or sometimes later when the temperature is still suffocating at midnight in May. Strictly take-out, but there are plenty of benches and sitting areas nearby and on the breezy Malecón, just past the long row of souvenir shops. Other places sell *nieve*, but none has the lineup of intense flavors made by Elisa and Rosendo Félix L. Ballesteros. Veracruz's sherbet and ice cream are some of the very best in Mexico—and thank goodness—with the sticky-sweaty weather along the Gulf.

Fresh Fruit and Nieve. Cayetano, located at Mario Molina No. 88, a block south of the *zócalo* on pretty Álvaro Obregón park, tel. 32-93-23, is open every day, all day long. Cayetano's is a fruit and *nieve* institution in Veracruz. *Aguas Frecas* (page 73) and *Licuados* (page 138) with mixed fruit, or fruit and milk combinations, are sublime. Fruit salads are refreshing meals on balmy evenings. Try *chintul*, a seafood cocktail look-alike, made with chopped fruit in a tall soda fountain glass, topped with *nieve de guanábana*, or lime.

Neveria Aroporit, located on the corner of Landero y Coss and A. Serdán in the fish market building, is open every day from 7 A.M. to 11 P.M. You'll recognize Neveria Aroporit with its pile of fresh coconuts in the middle of the floor ready to be opened with a machete before your eyes. Fruit salads are ambrosial with *nieve* on sweltering days.

Liquor. The state of Veracruz produces some very interesting booze. Sugarcane alcohol comes in various qualities from many manufacturers, including places where you bring in your own jug and they fill it (try the large liquor store at Arista and Bravo and notice the huge No Smoking sign). One of Veracruz's best known brandies is made in the city and is known as 1930 (best prices are at the above store). A vanilla-flavored cordial (vanilla beans are processed in the northern part of the state around Papantla), Xanath, is heavenly, and you can also buy it here. *Toro* (page 210) the beloved milky drink, is a bit like eggnog in texture but can be bought fresh only in Boca del Río, just south of the city of Veracruz. Bottled, you'll see it occasionally around Veracruz City in one or two flavors, close to Christmas. Rompope is similar and is sold in the U.S. Vino Jerez La Lupe is a sweet, heavy wine, that chefs like to use in old recipes.

Coffee. Café de la Parroquía, on Insurgentes (known as the Malecón) at the corner of 16 de Septiembre, at the port, is open every day from 6 A.M. to 1 A.M. (The old, famous *zócalo* location is closed now; the new name is El Gran Café del Portal.)

Why aren't there shops with good strong coffee like this all over coffee-growing Mexico? Veracruz's beloved coffee institution is Mexico's most famous coffeehouse because of its long history of great coffee, and the ritualistic custom of clanking spoons on the sides of thick glasses to call over the man who dispenses hot milk after the waiter has delivered your foamy espresso (order *un lechero*, espresso with hot milk). Café de la Parroquía is a nonstop action scene, with people darting everywhere and, of course, this is Veracruz so it's all choreographed to live marimba music. Sweet rolls, a few egg dishes, and fruit salads are good breakfast choices. Or have oatmeal topped with vinegared onions and jalapeño chiles (talk about an eye-opener). You can buy their coffee beans in kilo (two-pound) burlap sacks to take home.

La Merced, located at Independencia at Rayón, on the ground floor of the National Bingo Building (actually, the lottery building), is a good place for a coffee break after market exploring. La Merced is a direct copy of Café de la Parroquía, with spoon clanking and all, but doesn't have its soul. The mix of people, ever-present marimba band, and historical feel aren't here, but the coffee tastes great and the caffeine works wonders when you're dragging after shopping.

Parking. Estacionamiento del Central, located at A. Serdán No. 778 between Cinco de Mayo and Madero is open every day. Hours: Monday to Saturday 7:30 A.M. to 11 P.M.; Sunday 11 A.M. to noon, and 7:30 P.M. to 11 P.M. Francisco Javier Jiménez Rodríguez, the owner, speaks English. He goes out of his way to make your trip comfortable and enjoyable.

RESTAURANTS

Ostionería La Cría. Inexpensive. Has three locations in Veracruz: the oldest (and my favorite) is in the fish market, Mercado de Pesadería, Landero y Coss, Locales 37, 38, y 17, tel. 32-66-66. Open every day 8 A.M. to 8 P.M. The other two are: Cría Tito, Americas 1338 at the corner of Fernando Siliceo, tel. 35-52-66. Open from 8 A.M. to 8 P.M. every day; and Cría Tito, Jr., Urano No. 19, tel. 21-36-00. Open every day from 10 A.M. to 7 P.M. At the old fish market La Cría, you enter the tiny restaurant by passing through a counter of the outdoor seafood cocktail bar, and ducking your head through a low passageway, to enter the back room. Welcome to the world of some of the best seafood east or west of who-knows-where because María Alejandra Molina Rivera is a master Veracruzana cook. Here's the funkiest-looking joint (with a TV forever blasting out soap operas) with the most scrumptious seafood in town, like *Camarones Enchipolado* (page 204), *Camarones al Mojo de Ajo* (page 199), and *Jaibas Rellenas* (page 189).

El Pescador. Zaragoza 335, between Arista and Morales. Tel. 32-52-52. Open 11 A.M. to 7 P.M. every day. An old, and old-fashioned, seafood house (over fifty years) with an impressively long menu. Sit toward the rear and be surrounded by the biggest ship models you've ever seen. This is a classic place to try *huachinango veracruzana* (page 203) but the waiters, who have all been there forever, patiently explain other interesting-sounding dishes. The list of squid and octopus preparations reads like a who's who of eight- and ten-armed creatures: *al ajillo*, *al mojo de ajo*, *enchipotados*, *fritos*, *encebollados*, *rellenos de mariscos*, *Veracruzana*, *en su tinta*, *a la marinera*, *a la mexicana*, *Gabardina*, *en salsa verde*, and *a la mostada*. *Comida corrida* is a bargain lunch special—quality at a low price.

Cochinito de Oro. Zaragoza No. 190, tel. 32-36-77. Open every day from 7 A.M. to 5 P.M. The spotlessly clean coffeeshop, which still calls itself a fonda, has been around since 1940, and since 1950 in this location. It's a morning institution to have *gordas de dulce con café solo* (sweet *gordas* and coffee without sugar) at Cochinito de Oro served by motherly women dressed in white with caps or hairnets. *Picadas* are the Veracruz version of *sopes*—thin tortillas with their edges turned up ever so slightly, fried, then smeared with a tomato, green tomato, or light *mole* sauce and capped with crumbled cheese and a few raw onion circles. *Picadas* almost never contain meat unless you request them made wih *trocitas* (pieces) of beef. A fried egg often tops breakfast orders. *Gordas* (small examples are *gorditas*) are hand-formed tortillas fried to puffiness, and they come three ways: *blanca* (*masa* with a touch of bean paste), *negra* (with black beans in the *masa*, see page 215), and *dulce* (a bit sweet).

Bar Palacio. Located next door to the Hotel Colonial on Plaza de las Armas and under the *portales*, is the best beer bar in town for watching *zócalo* goings-on. It's not really a full restaurant but it does bake *pierna de puerco en adobado* (fresh, whole pork leg rubbed with a dry chile marinade and roasted) and mounds generous quantities onto French rolls for toothsome sandwiches. Vinegared onions, carrots, and jalapeños are served alongside. Another great *portales*-area drinking snack is offered at the café next door—a generous plate of Spanish Serrano ham hand-cut and served with sliced French rolls and pickled vegetables. Go for it, or order a plate of crispy, fried plantain slices with your beer or rum.

Boca del Río The restaurant-rich town sits where the river dumps into the Gulf south of Veracruz City and Mocambo Beach's big hotels. The whole village caters to people who like good seafood served in low-key-open-to-the-air sort of places. A few restaurants are more upscale, such as famous Pardiño's on the *zócalo*.

RESTAURANTS

Restaurant Boulevard. Moderate. This casual dining spot is on the waterfront road just where it curves. Open every day from noon to 9 P.M.-ish. It's large, airy, open to the river, easy to find, and has a thatched roof. The waitresses wear pretty, traditional dresses, a marimba or mariachi group is always playing, drinks are wet and tall, the fish is plentiful and of excellent quality, and the menu is perfect for the setting cha-cha-cha. This is exactly the type of place to go and feel you're *really* on vacation. Sunday seems to be the big day for large groups enjoying lingering for hours. Don't arrive much past 1:30 P.M. if you don't want to wait, but, again, sunset is magical.

Restaurant El Varadero. Inexpensive to Moderate. El Varadero is located at Zamora and Orizaba at the end of the waterfront road, tel. 86-17-87. Open every day for lunch and dinner. More or less the same view as Restaurant Boulevard, but more low-key, and the prices are cheaper. If you're lucky, local kids will be fishing off the narrow concrete slab in front of the restaurant and they'll show you how to fish with a hook, line, sinker, and beer-can reel (they do quite well, thank you). Morris, who's an avid fisherman, couldn't take his eyes off the young experts, it was as if he paid a fortune to learn secret techniques from the pros.

Toro. The very best solution to tasting *Toro* (page 210) is to try it firsthand at the source, on Revolución No. 410—look for the Corona sign with *Toro* on one side and *Torito* on the other. Open every day from 7 A.M. to about midnight. After a seafood lunch, stroll over to the tiny bar for a liter bottle (*toro*) to share, or plastic cup (*torito*). It's an outrageous dessert, and you'll be doing your part to keep up an old Boca del Río tradition.

Mandinga A seafood lover's paradise south of Boca del Río by a couple more miles. Take the road toward Antón Lizardo (just after the bridge) and turn right at the sign into Mandinga. Driving into the village you'll see seafood places lined-up in the distance, downhill, to your right. This dirt road pueblo's claim to fame is its assortment of cheap and casual, lagoon-fronted, thatched-roofed, semi-shacks that are sadly becoming more upscale every year.

Restaurante Mandinga is the first place you'll see, on the left side of the row of joints as you drive toward the water. It's open every day for long lunches as are the other five or six places to the right. **El Paisa** is at the other end, and also very good. Both are large restaurants with some swell waterside views of a tiny island a stone's throw away and accessible by a rope bridge. Fresh shrimp, snail, octopus, or crab cocktails can't be beat in a setting like this (and there's no need to ask for additional hot sauce—wow). Any shrimp dish should be your first choice, but the piquant *Chilpachole de Jaiba* (page 188) is a temptation.

La Laguna Miles of pineapple plantations run along highway 180, across Lago Mandinga Grande from Mandinga, at La Laguna. Dozens of roadside thatched-roofed stands strung with fresh pineapple decorations sell delectable pineapple juice. Bring your own bottle of rum and have a party during daylight hours. Locals say this isn't the safest stretch of highway after sunset.

Tlacotalpan Tlacotalpan, an entrancing town, is an hour south of Veracruz, along the Gulf, and ten miles inland. In the eighteenth and ninteenth centuries, ships from Europe stopped at this river-mouth port before heading up the coast to Veracruz. Europeans left their stamp of lovely, colonnaded buildings (still painted various pastels) furnished with antiques of the era. Today, miscellaneous restaurants and talapa-roofed seafood bars line the riverfront and all are within walking distance of the exceptionally tidy *zócalo*.

Hotel Doña Lala, Carranza No. 11, tel. 288-42-580, boasts an excellent dining room (see pages 201 and 206) and there are many seafood huts along the riverfront for low-key munching fun.

Lake Catemaco The lake, about three hours south of Veracruz, is crowded in summer and during Mexican school vacations, but you won't see many foreign tourists here. Lakefront restaurants like **La Ola** offer freshwater fish and seafood from the coast, which is only a few miles away. On your way out of Lake Catemaco and toward Tabasco, stop for lunch along the main road in Acayucan. Just off the toll road there's a succulent, slightly smoky, grilled, chicken awaiting your arrival. You'll see a huge Corona beer sign stating, **Pollos Asados y Ahumados**. A thatched-roofed, open-sided building with scattered picnic tables is the dining room. Fresh salsa made with tomatillos, avocado, habanero chile, onion, cilantro, and lime is brought to your table for spooning onto some of the best handmade tortillas in all of Mexico. *This* is roadside dining.

Restaurant El Varadero's

Adereso *Creamy Pumpkin Seed Salsa (or Spread)*

THE SEAFOOD RESTAURANT EL VARADERO IS IN BOCA DEL RÍO just south of Veracruz City and right on the Gulf of Mexico. The entire town is a seafood paradise offering dozens of places serving regional fish, such as *huachinango* (the Gulf's famous red snapper), grouper, pompano, *robalo* (sea bass), and shellfish specialties.

As soon as you place your order at El Varadero a waiter brings over a basket of tortilla chips with this version of tartar sauce Veracruzana. *Crema* and mayonnaise are mixed with smoky chiles and ground pumpkin seeds to make a spread that could easily become your favorite for almost any sandwich.

Yield: about 1½ cups

- 4 to 6 dried serrano chiles (dried, smoky, Veracruz style) or 2 to 3 chipotle chiles, soaked for at least 1 hour in hot water with stems and seeds removed, or use canned chipotle chiles en adobo, dried in paper towels
- ¼ cup raw, shelled pumpkin seeds (green "pepitas")
- 1 Tablespoon vegetable oil
- 3 heaping Tablespoons mayonnaise
- ¼ cup chicken broth or water, as needed
- 1 cup "Crema" (page 80), sour cream, or crème fraîche

1. Fry the chiles with the *pepitas* in oil for 2 to 3 minutes, until the chiles change color.

2. Put the chile mixture in a blender container with the mayonnaise. Purée until smooth, adding broth or water if needed to thin the sauce.

3. Add the *crema* and purée again. Serve at room temperature.

Julia García de Cruz's

Chilpachole de Jaiba *Spicy Crab Soup*

SEÑORA GARCÍA DE CRUZ HAS A TWO-TABLE FONDA in the southern end of Veracruz City not too far from Plaza Mocambo. Julia makes *chilpachole de jaiba* two ways: either with fresh jalapeño chile, or with the jalapeño's smoked version, chipotle chile, for more assertive flavor. The spicy crab soup is a warming winner best on winter days; on a hot day, so much sweat drips off your chin it oversalts the broth.

Yield: 8 servings

- 4 pounds live blue crabs (about 16), rinsed well
- ⅓ cup delicate "masa," or "masa harina" prepared per package directions, for thickening the broth
- 4 pounds tomatoes
- 2 large white onions, quartered
- 1 garlic head, separated into cloves and peeled
- 2 Tablespoons fruity olive oil
- 2 sprigs "epazote"
- 5 fresh jalapeño chiles, or 3 canned chipotle chiles, stemmed and finely chopped
- 4 limes, quartered in wedges
- salt, or Knorr's chicken bouillon, to taste

1. Heat 5 quarts water in a large deep pot and bring to a boil. Add the crabs, cover the pot, and bring to a boil for 5 to 6 minutes, or until the crabs are bright red. Remove the crabs and set the broth aside.

2. Remove the crab bodies from the shells by breaking off the claws and legs first, then pull back the pointed flap, known as the apron, on the crab's underside, and pull it off. Put the claws in a bowl. Separate the shells from the bodies and put the shells in the cooking liquid with the aprons and legs. Discard the hairy gills attached to the bodies. Break the bodies in half, pick out the lumps of meat, and put the meat in another bowl. Save any orange roe and add it to the body meat. Put the picked bodies in the pot with the liquid.

3. Cook the liquid and shells for 30 minutes, then strain the broth, discard the shells, and rinse the pot.

4. Mix the *masa* with 1 cup of the broth.

5. Toast (page 16) the tomatoes, onion, and garlic. Put the tomatoes in a plastic bag to "sweat" a few minutes. Peel, core, and put them in a blender container with the toasted onion and garlic. Purée.

6. Heat the oil in the rinsed pot and pour in the purée (it splatters!). Cook for a minute, then simmer for 10 minutes, uncovered. Add the cup of *masa* water, *epazote*, chiles, and broth and simmer, covered, for 30 minutes. Salt to taste. Remove the *epazote,* then add the crab claws and meat. Stir the crab in the hot broth for a minute. Serve immediately with broth, claws, and meat, and with lime wedges on the side. Pass huge napkins, shellfish crackers, and pickers.

María Alejandra Molena Rivera's

Jaibas Rellenas *Stuffed Crab Shells*

MARÍA ALEJANDRA'S STUFFED CRABS ARE THE PURE ESSENCE OF VERACRUZANA-style cooking with flavors of tomato, onion, capers, olives, and olive oil coming through loud and clear. Her fonda, La Cría, uses cleaned blue crab shells for stuffing; it's traditional and makes a charming presentation. Upstairs in the old fish market plastic bags hang over fish stalls—they're right next to the live blue crabs, which are also hanging and all tied together in raffia. You can substitute clam or scallop shells if you don't have access to blue crab shells. You could also substitute with one large casserole. Blue crabs are used in Veracruz, but try this recipe with any crabmeat available at your seafood counter. Serve either hot or warm. *Yield: 12 stuffed crabs (using blue crab shells)*

For the stuffing

- 4 Tablespoons olive oil
- 5 pounds ripe tomatoes, chopped
- 2 pounds white onions, chopped
- 4 ounces pitted green olives, chopped
- 1 Tablespoon capers, chopped
- ½ cup fresh Italian parsley, chopped
- 2 pounds crabmeat
- 2 Tablespoons additional olive oil

1. Heat the olive oil in a deep pot and add all the ingredients except the crab and additional olive oil. Sauté until the onions are golden, then simmer, uncovered, for 30 minutes.

2. Add the crabmeat. Stir and simmer for about 3 minutes. María Alejandra says this is an important step because the dish needs to be slightly moist (not wet) at this point—don't cook down all the liquid. Add 2 tablespoons olive oil for flavor and added moistness. Remove the pot from heat.

To assemble

- 1 cup coarse bread crumbs made from stale French bread
- 2 Tablespoons, plus additional olive oil

1. Preheat the oven to 400°F.

2. Combine the bread crumbs and olive oil and mix to soften the crumbs.

3. Rub olive oil over each shell. Form 12 balls of equal size with the crab mixture, place one in each of the shells, and press down a bit.

4. Cover the crab with bread crumbs. Place the shells on a baking sheet, the casserole on a rack in the center of the oven, and bake only until the bread crumbs are light brown—not a moment longer or the mixture will become too dry. You will need to stay near the oven and check regularly.

Josefina's

Huevos Tirados *Scrambled Eggs with Black Beans*

YOU'LL SEE ALMOST EVERYONE EATING A PLATE OF *HUEVOS TIRADOS* for breakfast at Café de la Parroquía, Veracruz's best coffeehouse. Scrambled eggs with black beans (let me warn you that this dish will look unappetizing) appears to be the café's most popular morning meal. *Huevos tirados* is also standard morning fare at the fondas in Mercado Unidad Veracruzana's labyrinth. I wrangled this recipe by watching an elderly woman prepare the dish at one of the plastic-roofed fondas. Make this recipe when you have leftover black beans.
Yield: 2 servings

- 2 Tablespoons butter
- ¼ cup finely chopped onion
- ½ cup cooked black beans
- 4 eggs

1. Heat 1 tablespoon butter in a skillet and sauté the onion until lightly brown.
2. In a small bowl, stir together the beans and eggs.
3. Add the remaining tablespoon butter to the hot skillet with the onions. Pour in the egg mixture. Stir until cooked the way you prefer your eggs. Serve it formed into an oval shape, like a French roll, on a plate.

Veracruz's Mercado de Pescadería's Fonda's

Torta de Mariscos *Seafood Frittata*

TORTA DE MARISCOS IS ALWAYS MADE FOR ONE PERSON like an individual Italian frittata filled with seafood at the fondas on the old seafood market's second floor. At home, you don't need to make the full mixture of shrimp, octopus, clams, sea snails, and crab often thrown together in "Seafoodland," but combining a few adds authenticity.
Yield: 1 serving

- ¼ medium onion, finely chopped
- 1 Tablespoon vegetable oil
- 1 jalapeño chile, chopped
- 3 large eggs
- ½ cup mixed, cooked seafood
- 1 Tablespoon chopped parsley
- 1 Tablespoon butter

1. In a small skillet, sauté the onion in the oil until it's transparent. Add the chile and sauté 2 minutes more.
2. In a medium bowl, beat the eggs. Add the sautéed onion and chile, seafood, and parsley to the eggs and mix.
3. Heat the butter in the same skillet and add the egg mixture. Cook until firm. Put a plate on top of the *torta*, upside down. Turn the *torta* over, onto the plate.

Instituto Internacional de Belleza's

Plátanos Fritos con Crema y Queso

Fried Plantains with Cream and Cheese

THIS HAS TO BE JUST ABOUT EVERYONE'S FAVORITE HOME-STYLE DISH in Veracruz. Everybody loves cooking plantains filled with *crema* and topped with cheese. Countless people wanted to share a recipe, saying that theirs was a family favorite and was passed down from Grandmother. One afternoon I found myself chatting with Carmen Córdoba, a cosmetology student, and she insisted I come to her school and talk with the adult students who "yap about food all the time—and they're great cooks, too." This recipe is a group effort by women studying and working at Instituto Internacional de Belleza, a cosmetology school in the city of Veracruz. Needless to say, the good-natured bickering back and forth between the women before coming to a communal conclusion was fun for all and resulted in the best of everyone's kitchen. All the women unanimously agreed, "Serve with anything, anytime you want—we love *plátanos fritos con crema y queso.*"
Yield: 4 servings

- ½ cup vegetable oil for frying
- 4 plantains, black and ripe, peeled
- 1 cup "Crema" (page 80), crème fraîche, or sour cream
- ¼ cup grated "queso añejo" or Parmesan cheese

1. Heat the vegetable oil in a deep skillet to 365° F, or until the surface ripples. With a long-handled spoon, carefully place each whole plantain in the hot oil. Fry, turning, until each is medium-to-dark brown. Remove the plantains from the oil and place on a stack of paper towels to drain.

2. When the plantains are cool enough to handle, make a slit lengthwise down the center of each, being careful not to cut all the way through.

3. Serve hot, warm, or at room temperature, stuffing each with 3 tablespoons *crema* and sprinkling with grated cheese.

Eva Camarero Ocampo's

Plátanos Rellenos *Plantains Stuffed with Cheese and Chile or* Picadillo

EVA IS ADAMANT ABOUT USING A CERTAIN COLOR and ripeness for her plantain dish—golden yellow only with some black splotches, never with green areas, and never fully black and ripe. *Plátanos rellenos* are made with mashed plantains stuffed with either cheese and chile or *picadillo* (page 196) and panfried in oil. Eva likes hers with a spoon of *crema* and a green salad for a complete meal. She knows tasty *picadillo* or melted cheese *plátanos rellenos* are home-style Veracruzana recipes at their best. In a few of the fancier restaurants around Veracruz, plantains are stuffed with mixed seafood, and the bit of bland, dried-out fish mixture can't stand up to the assertive flavor of fried banana.

Yield: 4 servings

- 4 plantains, golden yellow skins only, peeled and cut in half lengthwise
- ½ teaspoon salt
- 1 cup "picadillo" or 4 pieces "quesillo de Oaxaca" or mozzarella, cut into ¼ x ¼ x 1½-inch pieces
- 1 jalapeño chile, stemmed and quartered
- vegetable oil for panfrying

1. To peel plantains: Cut the two ends off about ½ inch into the flesh. Make four vertical cuts, into the skin and just barely into the flesh. Peel away the skin, from top to bottom, one strip at a time. The riper the plantain, the easier it is to peel, so these will be a bit difficult.

2. Put the peeled plantains and salt in a pot with water to cover and bring to a boil. Boil the plantains until they are soft, 30 to 45 minutes. Use a fork to test for doneness. Drain and set aside to cool. Mash the plantains. When cool enough to handle, divide into 4 parts.

3. Oil your hands. Put one part in a hand and pat it into an oval shape with your other hand, about ½ inch thick. Place 2 tablespoons *picadillo* (or 1 piece of cheese and a chile strip) on the oval. With both hands, enclose the filling with the edges of the oval. Mold into a tiny watermelon shape. Set aside on an oiled plate. Repeat with the other 3 pieces.

4. Heat about ¼ inch of vegetable oil in a deep, small frying pan to 365°F, or until the surface ripples. With a long-handled oiled spoon, carefully place each plantain piece in the hot oil. Panfry, turning to brown them evenly, for 10 to 12 minutes, until the cheese inside has melted and/or the meat is sufficiently hot. Drain on paper towels. Pass a bowl of *crema* at the table.

Dulce María de León's

Tamales Veracruzana

Corn-Leaf-Wrapped, Fresh Corn Masa *with* Acuyo, *Pork, and Chipotle Chile*

A SWEET WOMAN WITH A SWEET NAME, DULCE MARÍA, has been selling her fabulous tamales out of the same doorway in Veracruz for more than twenty years. And before her, her mother did the same for thirty-five years. The large tamales (about eight inches long) are made with hand ground fresh corn and coarse yellow *masa*, and flavored with chipotle chile. A piece of *acuyo* (*hoja santa*) herb is wrapped around each *masa* bundle before it is packaged in corn leaves and steamed. Dulce María usually adds a few small pieces of pork to the filling, but she said this is optional.

Fresh corn in the U.S. is generally smaller than Mexican. Getting leaves big enough to duplicate Dulce María's tamales exactly is a problem. These tamales turn out half the size of her beauties, but their outstanding flavor is not compromised. Hers are, truly, some of the best tamales in Mexico. But, like all good things, her recipe is labor intensive. To achieve the same texture, hand-grinding both the *masa* and fresh corn is necessary. Extra-coarse *masa* can sometimes be special-ordered from a tortillería, but the fresh corn cannot be chopped in a blender or processor.

The best way to experience one of these temptations is a trip to Veracruz. Bring back a bunch of tamales without pork (page 193) in an insulated cooler for an authentic feast (for Dulce María's location, see page 181). Making this recipe can take hours of very hard work. If that's more time than you have to invest, just reading the recipe is interesting to see how much effort it takes to make outstanding traditional tamales. A tamale party would be a good reason for making this many (with Veracruzana *jarocho*, or marimba music, of course!), or the recipe can be cut in half. *Tamales veracruzana* also freeze well, as do most tamales. *Yield: 75 tamales (about 150 small tamales)*

For the salsa

- 3½ ounces chipotle chiles (about 30 chiles)
- 1 garlic head, separated into cloves and peeled

Soak the chiles for 2 hours in hot water. Remove the stems and seeds. Put the chiles in a pot with 2 quarts water. Bring the water to a boil, then turn off the heat, and cover. Let the chiles cool to room temperature, about 3 hours; then drain. Purée the chiles, garlic, and ½ cup water.

For the meat (optional)

- 2 pounds pork leg or loin

Put the pork in a pot, add water to cover, and bring to a boil for 30 minutes. The meat should not be completely cooked because it finishes cooking in the steamer. Cool until it's cool enough to handle, then shred it into small pieces with a fork, with the meat's grain.

(Continued)

For the "masa"

10 pounds extra-coarsely ground yellow (not white) "masa" made from 6 quarts dried yellow field corn kernels and 8 Tablespoons lime, calcium hydroxide, or slaked limestone bought in a building supply store or "cal" from a tortillería

1. Rinse the dried corn kernels in a colander to remove the chaff. Add the lime to 8 quarts water and dissolve the lime, stirring. Add the corn and bring to a boil. Reduce the heat and simmer for 15 minutes, covered. Remove from the heat and let sit 2 to 6 hours, covered.

2. Put a large colander in the sink. Pour the contents into the colander. Running water over the corn, rub the kernels between your palms and the hulls will come off—let this debris wash away.

3. To get the same grind (not unlike the texture of coarse bran muffin dough) as Dulce María's *masa*, hand-grinding with a *metate* is a necessity. The best alternative is to have a tortillería special-grind extra coarse *masa* for you. You could also try a food mill.

For the tamales

25 ears corn (20 cups kernels). Choose the largest ears so the leaves are large.

10 pounds fresh, extra-coarsely ground "masa" (20 cups)

3½ cups fresh lard (page 18) or purchase fresh lard from a pork butcher who makes "carnitas"

1 cup sugar

4 Tablespoons salt

2 cups meat cooking broth or Chicken Broth (page 19)

1. Cut off 1 inch of the bottom of each ear of corn. Shuck the corn saving the largest leaves; discard the silk. Cut across each leaf at the widest point with sissors. Set the leaves aside with a weight to press them, curled side down. Continue with the rest, stacking the leaves in piles with weights (large cans of food work well). You should have 175 to 300 leaves, depending on size.

2. Scrape the kernels off the cobs. Using a heavy knife on a baking sheet with sides helps control flying kernels. Hand-grind the fresh corn with a *metate*, or with a food mill set at a coarse grind.

3. Put the *masa* that you made from the dried corn in a very large stockpot. Add the lard, a few cups at a time, mixing with your hands. Add the sugar and salt. Continue until all the lard is incorporated (by this time the *masa* will feel lighter), about 10 minutes more. Add the ground fresh corn and continue mixing for 5 to 10 minutes (you can see and feel pieces of corn in the *masa*).

4. Add the broth, 1 cup at a time, until it is incorporated and the *masa* feels very light, about 5 minutes. The total mixing time is about 30 minutes.

Finishing the tamales

the fresh corn leaves
10 to 12 "acuyo" ("hoja santa" or "momo") leaves, or 1 cup dried and crumbled leaves
the salsa

1. Overlap 2 corn leaves by at least 1 inch, pointed ends outward, with the leaf edges naturally curling inward. If the leaves are small, use 4 overlapping leaves, 2 on each side.
2. Cover with ⅓ cup *masa*, in an oval shape, positioned lengthwise over the leaves. Place a 1-inch square piece of *acuyo* (½ teaspoon dried) on the *masa*. Add 1 or 2 small pieces of optional pork. Top with a teaspoon of sauce.
3. Fold the lengthwise corn leaves inward, then fold over the ends to make an envelope. Continue with the others. If the tamales are made with small leaves, tie them closed with "ribbons" made from strips of leaves, about 6 inches long.

Steaming the tamales

1. Use a tamale steamer (see Glossary). Spread the rack with any remaining leaves to cover and stack the tamales horizontally, in overlapping layers so steam can pass easily through the pile. Cover the pot, turn the heat to high, and steam for 1 hour, checking the water level after 45 minutes (do not remove the lid for 45 minutes). You will have to steam the tamales in 2 or 3 batches, depending on the size of your steamer.
2. Open a tamale. It's ready when the *masa* does not stick to the leaf. If the *masa* sticks check the water level and continue steaming. The green leaves turn gold after cooking. The tamales may be cooled then refrigerated and resteamed, or frozen and resteamed. Remove and discard the leaves before eating the stuffing.

Dulce María de León.

Hint: Drop a coin into the water before inserting the steamer rack. You know there is water in the steamer as long as the coin rattles.

Note: Leftover and refrigerated, these are sensational for breakfast: Peel away and discard the leaves, cut cold tamales into 1/2-inch slices on a diagonal, heat butter in a skillet, and brown on both sides. As Susan Sarandon responded to Kevin Costner's classic speech in the film *Bull Durham*, "Oh, myyyyy." Who said food can't be as good as sex?

Taco Paco's

Chiles Rellenos de Chipotle con Picadillo

Chipotle Chiles Stuffed with Picadillo, Battered and Fried

LOCALS LOVE TO SIT AT THE BUSY COUNTER (page 178), right in the center of bustling Mercado Hidalgo, and feast on *picadillo*-stuffed chipotle chiles. The *picadillo* stuffing is made with shredded beef, *panela*, and raisins. The classic sweet-spicy combination reaches its zenith at Taco Paco's. By one o'clock the last one is gone, so be sure to get there early. Once, when I was next on line, a woman ahead of me bought every single *relleno*—to go. Talk about an unhappy soul. I drank away my frustrations at the fruit bar directly behind Taco Paco's—tears spilling into a chilled, frosty mug of freshly squeezed pineapple juice.

The owners wouldn't give up their "secret" recipe. No matter. These *rellenos* are so good I must have sat at that counter five times before working out this formula. I also noticed that their combination was not exactly the same every day. Some days raisins, other days none; one day a bit sweeter, another obviously more onion. Unlike northern-style, or cheese-stuffed *rellenos*, *chiles rellenos de chipotle con picadillo* aren't served with tomato sauce. Taco Paco's serves the intensely flavored favorites on a plate, or wrapped in a tortilla, with or without guacamole to cut the heat. And, these are spicy. A bowl of *crema*, sour cream, or throat-cooling yogurt is appreciated by new-to-spicy-chile eaters. You'll pour all three quarts of María del Carmen's refreshing Cucumber Drink (page 126) to calm the chipotle chile's heat.

Yield: 15 to 20, depending on the size of the chiles

- 15 to 20 chipotle chiles (dry, not canned in adobo)
- 1 cup "panela" or dark brown sugar
- 2 teaspoons salt

1. Wash the chiles and put them in a large bowl. Pour 2 quarts hot water over the chiles. Add *panela* and salt and dissolve. Soak the chiles. Soaking time will be determined by the age of the chiles. Retain the soaking water.

2. Using a small, sharp knife or scissors, make a small horizontal slit just below the chile stem. Then make a slit down the side to almost the bottom point (the stem stays on). Using a teaspoon, carefully remove the seeds and large veins without breaking the skin.

3. Pour the soaking water into a pot and bring to a boil, then reduce the heat. Add the chiles and simmer for 15 minutes. Remove the chiles from the liquid and cool.

For the picadillo

- 1 pound beef chuck, skirt steak, brisket, or flank
- 1 small onion, quartered
- 5 plum tomatoes
- 1 onion, peeled and halved
- 2 garlic cloves, peeled
- ¼ cup finely chopped blanched almonds
- 2 Tablespoons vegetable oil
- 1 cup "panela" or dark brown sugar
- 1 three-inch "canela" stick or ¼ teaspoon ground cinnamon
- ¼ cup raisins
- 1 small lime, juiced
- salt and freshly ground pepper

1. Bring 2 quarts water to a boil and boil the beef and small onion, skimming and discarding any scum that forms on the surface. Partially cover the pot and simmer beef 1½ hours, or until tender depending on the cut.
2. Remove the beef from the water and let cool. When the meat is cool enough to handle, shred it into a large bowl. Chuck is easier to shred than the others. Skirt steak is a popular cut in Mexico for shredding. Stringy brisket and flank will take a bit more cooking time and will possibly be more difficult to shred. Their flavors are all excellent. Shred with a large fork with the meat's grain.
3. Toast (page 16) the tomatoes. Put them in a plastic bag to "sweat" for a few minutes so the peel comes off easily. Peel and put the tomatoes in a blender container. Toast the onion and garlic. Chop coarsely and put them in the blender with the tomatoes. Purée.
4. Toast the almonds to light brown.
5. Heat the oil in a deep pot. Carefully add the tomato mixture (it splatters!). Turn down the heat to a simmer, add the *panela*, and continue cooking and stirring for 10 minutes. Add the beef, *canela*, raisins, almonds, and lime juice. Continue cooking, and stirring for another 10 minutes. Continue cooking until the mixture forms one large mass. Remove from the heat. Salt and pepper to taste.
6. Stuff each chile loosely with *picadillo* and close with a toothpick. The chiles may be prepared to this point and refrigerated.

Battering and frying the chiles

- 4 large eggs, at room temperature
- ¼ teaspoon salt
- ¼ cup flour, in a shallow bowl
- vegetable oil to cover the bottom of a skillet by at least ¼ inch
- the stuffed chiles

1. Separate the eggs. Put the whites in a large bowl and the yolks in a small bowl. Add the salt to the whites and beat them with an electric mixer or wire whisk, until they hold medium-stiff peaks. Slowly beat in the yolks and the flour.
2. Heat the oil to 375°F, or until the surface ripples (cooler oil guarantees greasy *rellenos*). Gently lower the chiles into the hot oil being careful not to crowd the skillet. When the bottoms of the chiles are golden, turn them over. Remove to paper towels. Repeat with the remaining chiles. Move all the chiles onto clean paper towels and drain again so they don't re-absorb the oil in the towel.

María Alejandra Molena de Rivera's

Filetes de Pescado al Mojo de Ajo *Fish Fillets in Garlic*

GARLIC LOVER'S ALERT! There are two ways to prepare wildly popular *mojo de ajo*: one is to cook garlic purée slowly in oil until it becomes sweet and creamy, then pour it over seafood; the other, unabashedly my favorite, is to cook sliced garlic in olive oil until it becomes golden brown and chewy, then pile it on seafood that's been rubbed with garlic purée and sautéed. What a double garlic whammy! Fonda La Cría (page 184) makes *mojo de ajo* exactly the way I like this dish best, and here's María Alejandra's recipe, which she serves with white rice and handmade tortillas.

María Alejandra told me, "Be sure you tell everyone to clean their skillets completely of those little brown garlic bits that fall off the fish into the oil; these get black and turn bitter when cooked again with the sliced garlic."

Yield: 2 cups

For the sliced garlic

- 6 to 8 heads garlic, depending on size
- 2 cups olive oil

1. Trim off the hard ends of the garlic cloves, smash the cloves slightly (to make peeling easier), then peel and slice as thinly as possible. If you have sensitive skin be sure to wash your hands after every dozen or so cloves—probably at the same time your knife gets sticky and needs a soapy washing. You can also use the thinnest slicing blade of your food processor.

2. Place 1 cup of the oil in a large skillet and bring to medium heat. Add the garlic. Cook, stirring, for about 15 minutes, until the garlic turns pale golden.

3. Remove the skillet from the heat and spoon the garlic and oil into a quart-glass jar. Add the second cup of oil to cover the garlic. Oil preserves the garlic and if the garlic is not covered completely it gets moldy. Cool to room temperature, then screw on the lid. The garlic oil may be stored at cool room temperature for a week; refrigerate if kept longer.

For the fish fillets

Yield: 4 servings

- 1 head garlic, about 12 cloves
- 4 six-ounce fish fillets, such as grouper, red snapper, rock cod, or flounder
- ¼ cup white flour
- 3 Tablespoons vegetable oil
- ¼ cup chopped flat-leaf parsley (for garnish)
- 2 fresh limes, quartered

1. Peel the garlic cloves, then put through a garlic press and into a small bowl.

2. Coat the fillets with flour and shake off any extra. Rub each fillet on both sides with one quarter of the pressed garlic.

3. Heat the oil in a large skillet and put in the fillets. Cook for 2 minutes and carefully turn them over with a spatula. Continue cooking until done (when you make a small cut in the thickest part, the fillet should be opaque throughout; cooking time depends on the thickness of the fish). Remove to a warm plate with a slotted spatula so very little cooking oil goes on the plate.

4. Remove any dark garlic bits from the pan, then spoon in 6 to 8 rounded tablespoons of the cooked garlic from the jar, without extra oil, and heat until sticky and caramelized, about 2 minutes. The color quickly changes from pale to golden brown.

5. Cover each fillet with 2 rounded tablespoons of the carmelized garlic. Sprinkle with chopped parsley and serve with lime wedges.

Variations:

Camarones al Mojo de Ajo *Shrimp in Garlic*

Yield: 4 servings

- 1½ pounds large shrimp
- ½ cup white flour
- 3 Tablespoons olive or vegetable oil
- ¼ cup chopped flat-leaf parsley (for garnish)
- 2 fresh limes, quartered and arranged on plates

Prepare the browned garlic and garlic purée as above.

1. Either leave the shells on the shrimp or remove and devein, leaving the tails intact. Pat the shrimp with flour and then shake off. Rub with the garlic purée.

2. In a very large skillet, sauté the shrimp in olive or vegetable oil just until they turn completely pink. With a slotted spoon, put the shrimp on a warm plate.

3. Remove any dark garlic bits from the pan, then spoon in 6 to 8 rounded tablespoons of the cooked garlic from the jar, without extra oil, and heat until sticky and caramelized, about 2 minutes. The color quickly changes from pale to golden brown.

4. Cover the shrimp on each plate with 2 tablespoons of the carmelized garlic. Sprinkle with parsley and serve with lime wedges.

(Continued)

Pescado al Mojo de Ajo *Whole Fish in Garlic*

Yield: 4 servings

- 4 whole, 1 pound or less, fish such as pompano, snapper, perch, or rock cod
- ½ cup white flour
- 4 Tablespoons vegetable oil
- ¼ cup chopped flat-leaf parsley (for garnish)
- 2 fresh limes, quartered and arranged on plates

Prepare the browned garlic and garlic purée as in Fish Fillets in Garlic.

1. Clean and scale the whole fish and make 2 or 3 diagonal cuts in the meat on both sides, almost down to the bone. Pat the fish with flour and then shake off before rubbing with one quarter of the garlic purée.

2. In a very large skillet, or 2 skillets, sauté the fish over high heat in vegetable oil, about 6 minutes total. The exact time will depend on the thickness of the fish. Place a fish on each of 4 warm plates.

3. Remove any dark garlic bits from the pan and spoon in 6 to 8 rounded tablespoons of the cooked garlic from the jar, without extra oil, and heat until sticky and caramelized, about 2 minutes. The color changes from pale to golden brown.

4. Cover each fish with 2 rounded tablespoons of carmelized garlic. Sprinkle with chopped parsley and serve with lime wedges.

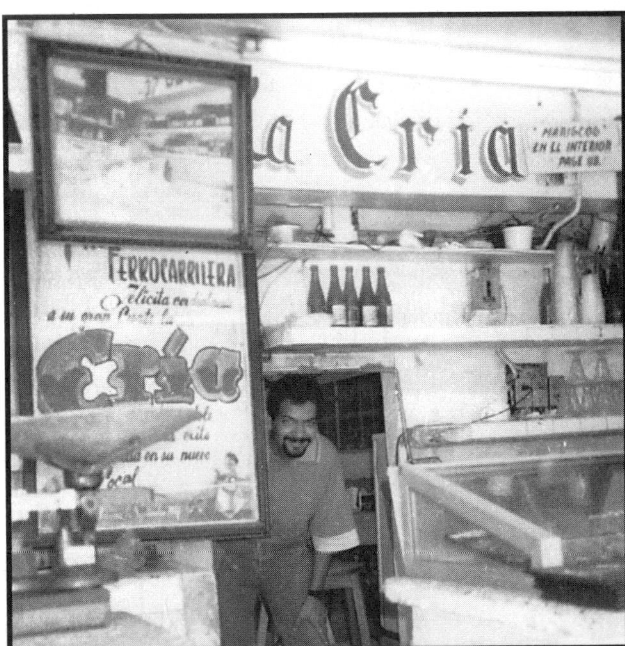

Carlos Hernández Estrada leaves the "back room" of La Cría.

Carlos Vives Iñíguez's

▲▼▲

Langostinos o Camarones al Ajillo

Langostinos or Shrimp with Garlic and Chile

IN SOUTHERN VERACRUZ WHERE THE PAPALOAPAN RIVER EMPTIES INTO LAKE ALVARADO before making its way to the Gulf, the pastel-painted town of Tlacotalpan sits in wait with her shrimping nets at the ready. Giant langostinos come from this fresh water as do the black river shrimp and gray lagoon shrimp you see in the town's market. One of the most popular ways of serving langostinos in the area is *al ajillo*, the name derived from *ajo* (garlic) and guajillo chile. Mild guajillo chile has a distinctive citrus-with-fruit taste that works perfectly with seafood.

Chef Carlos Vives Iñíguez serves platters of *langostinos al ajillo* in the Hotel Doña Lala's dining room. Small seafood places along the riverfront, right across from the hotel, are other options if budget is a constraint. They may not have the more expensive *langostinos,* but huge shrimp are on every menu as are small whole fish, fillets, squid, and octopus *al ajillo.*
Yield: 4 servings

- 1½ pounds langostinos or very large shrimp
- 3 Tablespoons olive oil
- 12 garlic cloves, peeled and thinly sliced
- 3 six-inch guajillo chiles, washed and dried, stem and seeds removed, sliced across the length into ⅛-inch rings
- 4 Tablespoons flat-leaf parsley leaves
- 2 limes, quartered
- sea or kosher salt to taste

1. Preheat a broiler to hot. Split the langostinos lengthwise. Brush with 1 tablespoon of the olive oil and broil, cut side up, for 3 to 4 minutes, or until cooked through.

2. Meanwhile, in a small skillet, heat the other 2 tablespoons olive oil, with the garlic and the chile. Cook, stirring, until the garlic is light brown.

3. Place the *langostinos* on serving plates or on one large platter and pour the sauce over them. Garnish with chopped parsley and lime wedges. Sprinkle with salt to taste. Serve with white rice.

Note: if using shrimp:

1. If large shrimp are fresh, keep them whole. If they were once frozen and without heads, either use as is, or shell and devein, keeping the tails intact.

2. Heat the oil in a large skillet. Sauté the garlic and chile over medium heat until the garlic is pale gold. Add the shrimp and sauté, turning, until they are all pink and cooked through. The garlic should be medium brown.

Carmen Córdoba's

Pulpos Encebollados *Octopus with Stewed Onions*

CARMEN TOLD ME THAT OCTOPUS IS EQUALLY ADORED cooked two ways in Veracruz: in its own ink and with onions, which is her favorite. She said, "The recipe seems like it calls for tons of octopus, but it shrinks like crazy during cooking, and you use only the tentacles."

You can try both variations in Veracruz at fondas in the great, old fish market. Better yet, in Boca de Río (page 185) or at any thatched-roof seafood shack in Mandinga (page 186).
Yield: 4 servings

- 6 pounds cleaned and tenderized (usually sold frozen), thawed octopus
- 1 pound large, white onions, cut into ⅛-inch-thick slices
- 2 garlic cloves
- 5 bay leaves
- ¼ cup olive oil
- 4 jalapeño chiles, stemmed and cut into round slices, with seeds
- salt or Knorr chicken bouillon

1. Put the octopus in a large pot with enough water to cover. Add a quarter of the onion slices, 1 garlic clove, and 3 bay leaves. Bring to a boil, reduce the heat, and simmer for 1½ to 2 hours, uncovered, or until the octopus is tender. Overcooking causes mushiness. Do not add salt at this point or the octopus will get tough.

2. Remove the octopus from the water and cool enough to handle. Cut the tentacles from the body and discard the body. Scrape the purple skin from each tentacle with a paring knife and discard. Cut the tentacles into bite-sized pieces.

3. Heat the olive oil in a large skillet and add the remaining onions, garlic, bay leaves, and the jalapeño chiles. Sauté until the onion is just starting to brown. Add the octopus and sauté for 5 minutes longer, to heat through and blend flavors. Season with salt or bouillon powder. Serve with white rice.

Leticia Delgado de León's

Pescado Veracruzana

Fish with Tomatoes, Capers, Olives, and Onions

LETICIA'S RECIPE FOR VERACRUZ'S MOST FAMOUS DISH is usually made with red snapper and entitled *huachinango veracruzana*, but any nonoily, mild fish works except those that are very finely textured and fall apart, or don't stand up to assertive flavors. Grouper, cod, bass, halibut or the like are fine. Whole fish, six pounds and more, are fabulous party fare, just be more particular with garnishes. Spanish flavors of olive oil, capers, and green olives give the dish its character with an unparalleled boost from Veracruz's own jalapeño chile.

This recipe uses fine bread crumbs to thicken the sauce, which you won't find in restaurants, but it's the way home cooks prepare this classic. Leticia suggests using only large capers available in any Veracruz *supermercado.* Their flavor is imperative to a tasty *pescado veracruzana.* Serve the fish with traditional white rice molded in a custard cup after steaming, sautéed plantain slices, and a green salad.

Yield: 6 servings

For the sauce

3 Tablespoons olive oil
2 large white onions, chopped
3 garlic cloves, chopped
3 jalapeño chiles, chopped
3 large tomatoes, chopped
½ cup chopped parsley
6 large capers
10 large green olives, pitted
3 bay leaves

1. Heat the oil in a very large skillet and add the onions and garlic. Sauté until the onion is golden.

2. Add the chile, tomatoes, parsley, capers (plus 1 tablespoon juice from the jar), olives, and bay leaves. Simmer for 15 minutes, uncovered, until the flavors are blended.

For the fish

6 red snapper fillets about ½ inch thick, or similar fish (2¼ pounds total)
3 Tablespoons fine bread crumbs
¼ cup chopped cilantro (for garnish)
limes

1. Slide the fillets into the sauce and cover the skillet. Cook for 5 minutes.

2. Scatter the bread crumbs over the sauce. Simmer for another 2 minutes, delicately stirring, to thicken. The fillets should be cooked and flake when pressed.

3. Remove to serving plates. Place a cup of molded white rice on each plate and spoon on any remaining sauce in the skillet. Scatter the cilantro over, and place a few lime wedges on each plate.

María Alejandra Molena de Rivera's

Camarones Enchipolado *Shrimp in Chipotle Chile Sauce*

MARÍA ALEJANDRA'S VERACRUZ FONDA, LA CRÍA (page 184), has quite a following of aficionados at her three locations because everyone in Veracruz has at least one on his "best" list. None is fancy, but all deliver superlative seafood at reasonable prices. When you're sitting at my favorite branch, in the old fish market building, start your meal with a crab cocktail before moving onto this gutsy, glorious plate of real food.

Back home, serve yours with a green salad, steamed rice, and tortillas to absorb the splendid sauce. This is one of the best sauces in Mexico, bar none—smoky chipotle chile makes all the difference. *Camarones enchipolado* is finger-licking good, but still pass around oversized napkins.

Yield: 8 servings

For the "enchipolado" sauce

- ½ ounce (about 6) chipotle chiles (dried, not in adobo)
- 8 ripe tomatoes (2 pounds)
- 2 white onions, chopped
- 8 bay leaves
- ½ teaspoon thyme
- 1 head garlic, peeled
- 2 Tablespoons water
- 3 Tablespoons vegetable oil
- 2 teaspoons freshly ground black pepper
- 1 Tablespoon sugar

1. In a medium pot, bring 1 quart water to a boil with the chipotle chiles. Boil the chiles for 15 minutes. Drain and cool enough to handle. Remove stems and seeds.

2. Put the tomatoes, chopped onions, bay leaves, thyme, and garlic in a blender with the 2 tablespoons water and purée. Add the softened chiles and purée again. Scrape down the blender's sides and purée one more time.

3. Heat the vegetable oil in a deep pot. Carefully add the blender mixture (it sizzles!). Taste and season with pepper. Add the sugar if your tomatoes are acidic. Simmer the sauce, uncovered, for 30 minutes. The sauce can be made ahead and refrigerated for a week.

For the shrimp

- 3 pounds large shrimp
- ¼ cup vegetable oil
- 1 pound white onions, sliced

1. Clean the shrimp. María Alejandra buys live shrimp and cooks them whole. You may keep the shells on or remove them and devein, keeping the tails attached.

2. Heat the oil in a large skillet and lightly brown the onions. Add the shrimp and sauté just until they turn pink—not a moment longer. Quickly add the sauce to the shrimp and stir for 30 seconds.

María Alejandra Molena de Rivera's

Puerco Enchipolado *Roast Loin of Pork in Chipotle Chile Sauce*

MARÍA ALEJANDRA ALSO LIKES HER *SALSA ENCHIPOLADA* WITH PORK, which she sometimes does at home (her Veracruz fonda, La Cría, is strictly a seafood restaurant). She says the pork is classically served with black beans and corn tortilla chips. You'll also need plenty of French bread or tortillas to soak up every delectable drop of sauce (what more southernly Mayans call "making *chuc*").

Yield: 10 servings

- 1 five- to six-pound pork loin or four-pound boneless boned-and-tied double loin
- 3 garlic cloves, peeled and thinly sliced
- 1 teaspoon freshly ground black pepper
- 1 teaspoon salt
- "Salsa Enchipolada" (page 204)

1. Using a sharp paring knife, cut slits in the pork large enough to insert slivers of garlic. Rub the meat with ground pepper and salt. María Alejandra covers the roast with fresh lard or pork fat. Tell your butcher to keep a thin layer of fat on the roast when trimming. Bake at 350°F for 2 to 2½ hours, depending upon cut and size. Internal temperature should be 160°F.

2. Slice and serve on a huge platter with the warmed sauce poured over, family style, that is, Mexican style. Or, of course you can put a few slices on individual plates and cover with the sauce.

Carlos Vives Iñíguez's

▲▼▲

Tapado de Jolote

Fish Steaks Covered with Acuyo (Hoja Santa) Herb Sauce

HOTEL DOÑA LALA'S DINING ROOM BOASTS AN EXCELLENT RESTAURANT, thanks to chef Carlos Vives Iñíguez. Try his *jolote*, a scaleless freshwater fish caught only in the waters around Tlacotalpan, that is, in southern Veracruz, where freshwater rivers empty into lagoons, then, in turn, into the Gulf of Mexico. Carlos prepares *tapado de jalote* with half-inch steaks (*tapado* means "covered"). He says to be sure to use the lard instead of olive oil because of the specific flavor it imparts. Serve with steamed white rice, molded in oiled teacups, as is typical in Veracruz, and garnish with lime wedges.

Yield: 4 servings

- 2 "acuyo" ("hoja santa") leaves (about 8 inches in diameter) without veins, roughly chopped, or 4 Tablespoons dried, or ¼ teaspoon fennel seeds, crushed
- 4 garlic cloves, peeled
- 1 medium white onion, peeled and quartered
- 3 jalapeño chiles, stemmed
- salt and freshly ground black pepper to taste
- ⅓ cup fresh lard (page 18) or olive oil (see additional text above)
- 4 "jolote" steaks, or substitute a mild ocean fish such as bass or halibut, cut ½ inch thick
- 2 limes, quartered

1. Put 1 cup water in a blender with the *acuyo*, garlic, onion, and chiles; purée.

2. Heat 2 tablespoons of the lard in a deep pot. Carefully pour in the sauce (it sizzles!). Reduce the heat and keep it at a simmer, uncovered, while the fish is cooking. Season to taste.

3. In a large skillet, heat the remainder of the lard and brown the fish for about 2 minutes on each side.

4. Carefully remove the fish from the lard and slide it into the simmering sauce. Cook for 4 to 6 minutes more (check for doneness at 4 minutes). Put on plates and cover with sauce. Garnish with lime quarters.

Restaurant Tlacotalpan's

Salpicón de Jaiba *Stir-Fry of Crab with Onion and Chile*

IN FONDAS AND SEAFOOD BARS ALONG THE GULF in the state of Veracruz, *salpicón de jaiba* (literally a "spill" of crabmeat) is similar to the recipe for *Jaiba Rellena* (page 189). It's flavored with olives, tomatoes, and capers, but there's no bread crumb coating so it's a moister dish. But, in the joints along the river in Tlacotalpan, an hour south of Veracruz City, *salpicón de jaiba* is a quick stir-fry of flaked blue crab with chopped onion and fresh chile. This fast and easy recipe is foolproof if you are fortunate to have lots of crabmeat. Serve with homemade tortillas or warm tortilla chips, *Adereso* (page 187), and a mild tomatillo salsa.

Yield: 4 appetizer servings, or 2 to 3 main course servings

- 2 Tablespoons olive oil or butter
- 1 large white onion, chopped
- 2 jalapeño chiles, stemmed and chopped
- 1 pound cooked, flaked crabmeat
- 2 Tablespoons chopped fresh Italian parsley

1. Heat the oil or butter in a skillet and add the onion.

2. Cook the onion, stirring, for 2 minutes, then add the chile. Continue cooking until the onion is golden-brown.

3. Add the crabmeat and parsley. Stir only long enough to heat the crab. You will not need additional salt with the crab.

Note: The recipe is delicious and less expensive with a mixture of crab and a chopped mild fish. Monkfish's lobsterlike texture is an exceptionally good choice.

Concepción's

Mojarra Asada *Panfried Whole Fish with Tomato-Chile Sauce*

LAKE CATEMACO, ABOUT THREE HOURS SOUTH OF VERACRUZ, is crowded in summer and during school winter vacations with Mexican families, but you won't see many foreign tourists here. Its setting is a large lake with islands to explore by boat, all surrounded by handsome mountains and bougainvillea-covered homes. The nondescript town of Catemaco offers many modest motels lakeside. A tiny market houses inexpensive fondas—one even provides microscopic lake views.

Lakefront open-air restaurants like La Ola offer freshwater fish and seafood from the coast, which is only a few miles away. *Mojarra* is a small, bony Gulf fish (porgy that's wildly popular because it's sweet, plentiful, and cheap). It goes well with aggressive sauces such as Concepción's favorite, this simple tomato, chile, garlic, and onion blend. You can substitute other whole saltwater fish such as snapper or rockfish, or use steaks or fillets from a not-too-delicate fish. Serve with white rice and tortillas. Shredded cabbage coleslaw is a good match.

Yield: 2 servings

- 5 small tomatoes
- 4 de árbol chiles, or 1 chipotle chile for a smoky flavor
- 4 garlic cloves
- 1 white onion
- 1 Tablespoon plus ½ cup vegetable oil
- 2 small mojarras (10-inch perch) or other whole, cleaned fish such as snapper, rock cod, or bass
- 3 Tablespoons flour
- 1 lime, quartered

1. Toast (page 16) the tomatoes, dried chiles, garlic, and onion until they change color and blister. Put the tomatoes in a plastic bag to "sweat" for a few minutes so that the skins will loosen. Peel. Stem and seed the chiles then soak in hot water for 5 minutes. Cool slightly and peel the garlic and onion. Put the ingredients in a blender and purée.

2. Heat 1 tablespoon of the oil in a skillet, carefully pour in the mixture from the blender (it sizzles!), lower the heat, and fry the sauce over medium heat for 2 minutes. Reduce the heat and simmer.

3. Meanwhile, in another skillet, heat the remaining ½ cup oil to 360°F, or until the surface ripples.

4. Add the fish and cook for about 3 minutes on each side (cooking time depends on the thickness of the fish). Remove from the oil with a spatula, draining off any clinging oil. Put the fish on a plate and cover with sauce. Garnish with lime wedges.

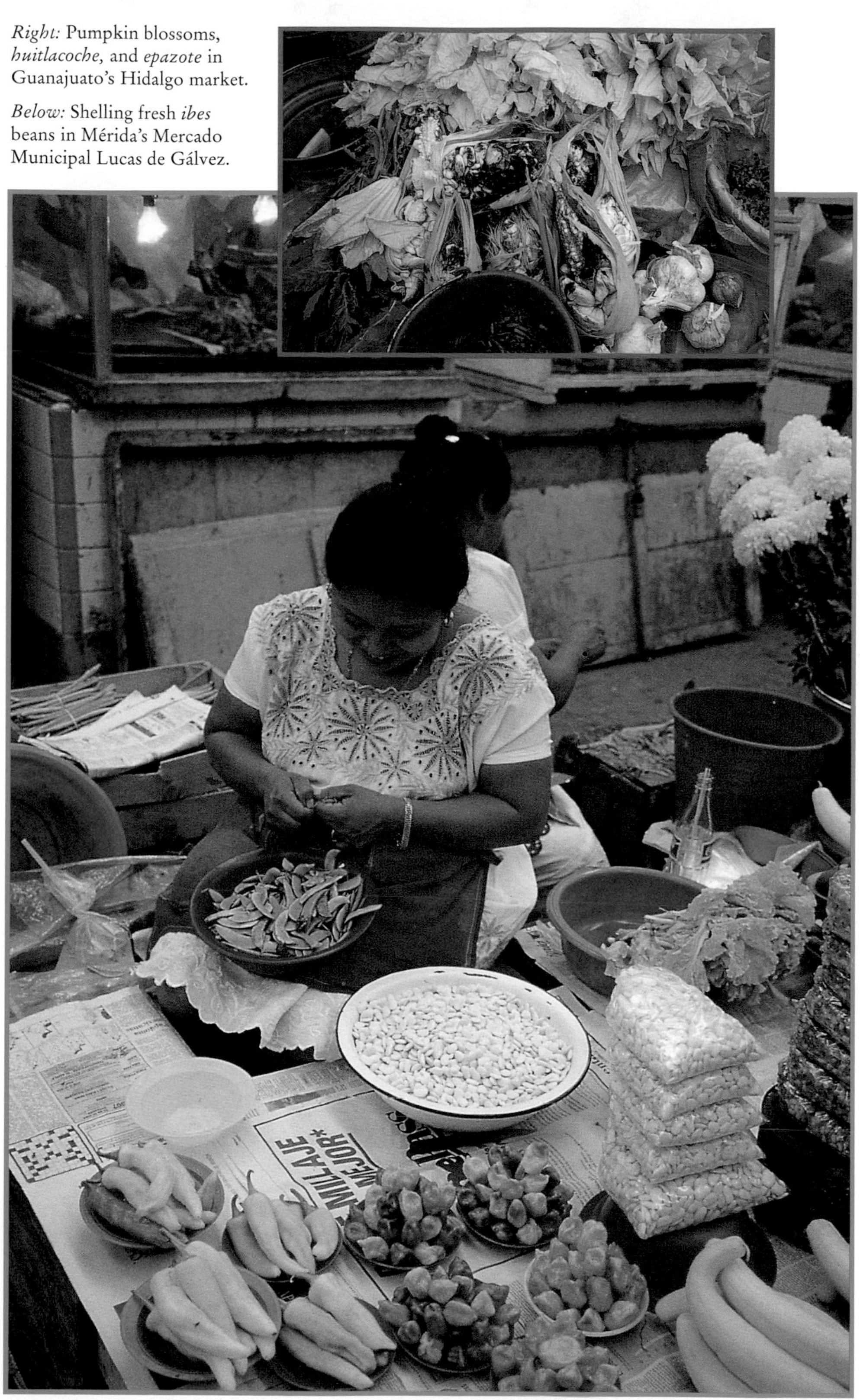

Right: Pumpkin blossoms, *huitlacoche,* and *epazote* in Guanajuato's Hidalgo market.

Below: Shelling fresh *ibes* beans in Mérida's Mercado Municipal Lucas de Gálvez.

Fresh Chiles

Clockwise from top left: Anaheim (2); Poblano (3); Serrano (6); Jalapeño (red-ripe) (6); Jalapeño (6); Güero (a.k.a. Banana or Hungarian) (2); *Center:* Habanero (5).

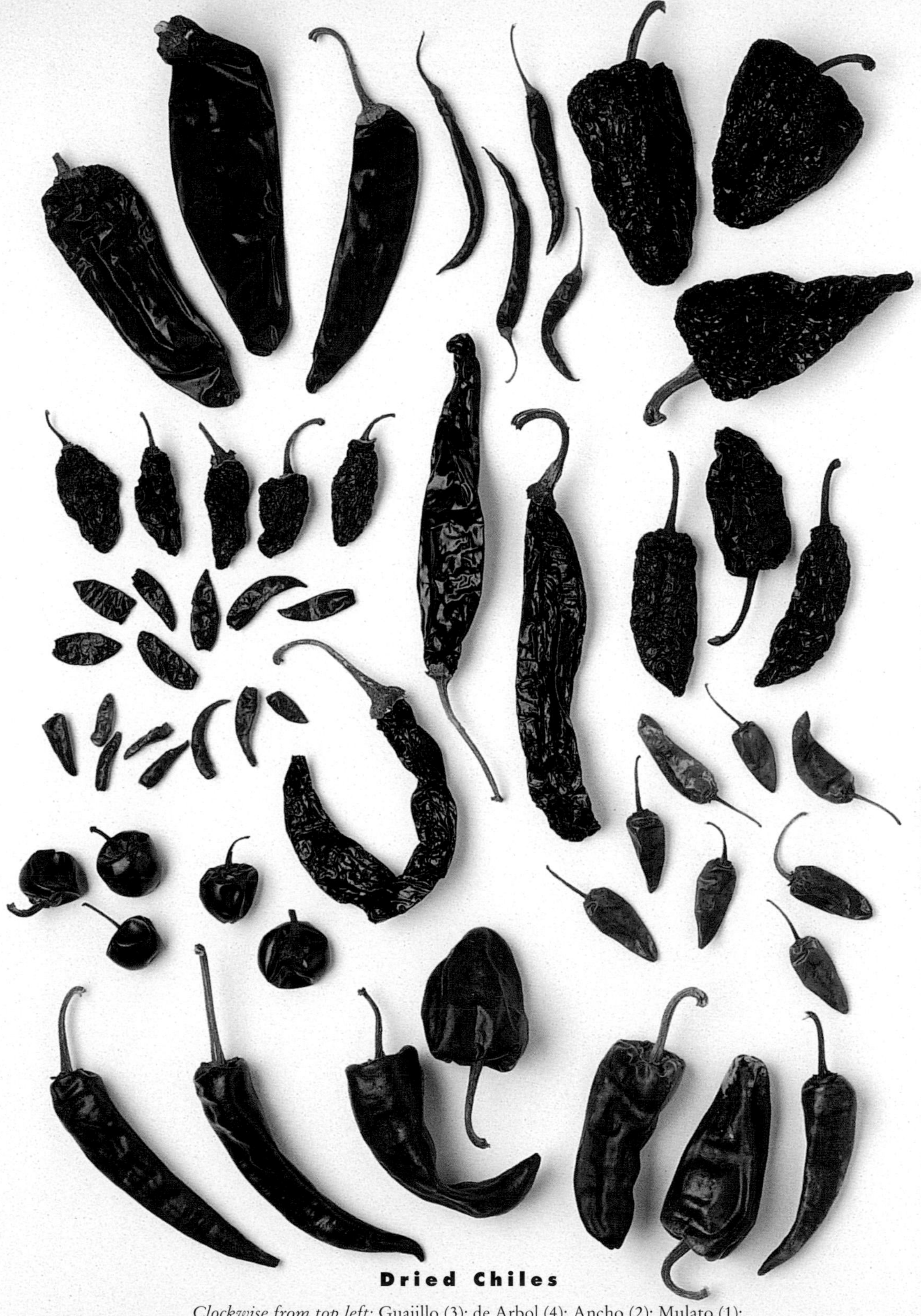

Dried Chiles

Clockwise from top left: Guajillo (3); de Arbol (4); Ancho (2); Mulato (1); Pasilla de Oaxaca (3); Costeño (8); Chilhuacle amarillo (3); Chilhuacle rojo (2); Chilcosle rojo (2); Cascabel (5); Serrano seco (8); Morita (7); Chipotle (5); *Center:* Pasilla negro (3).

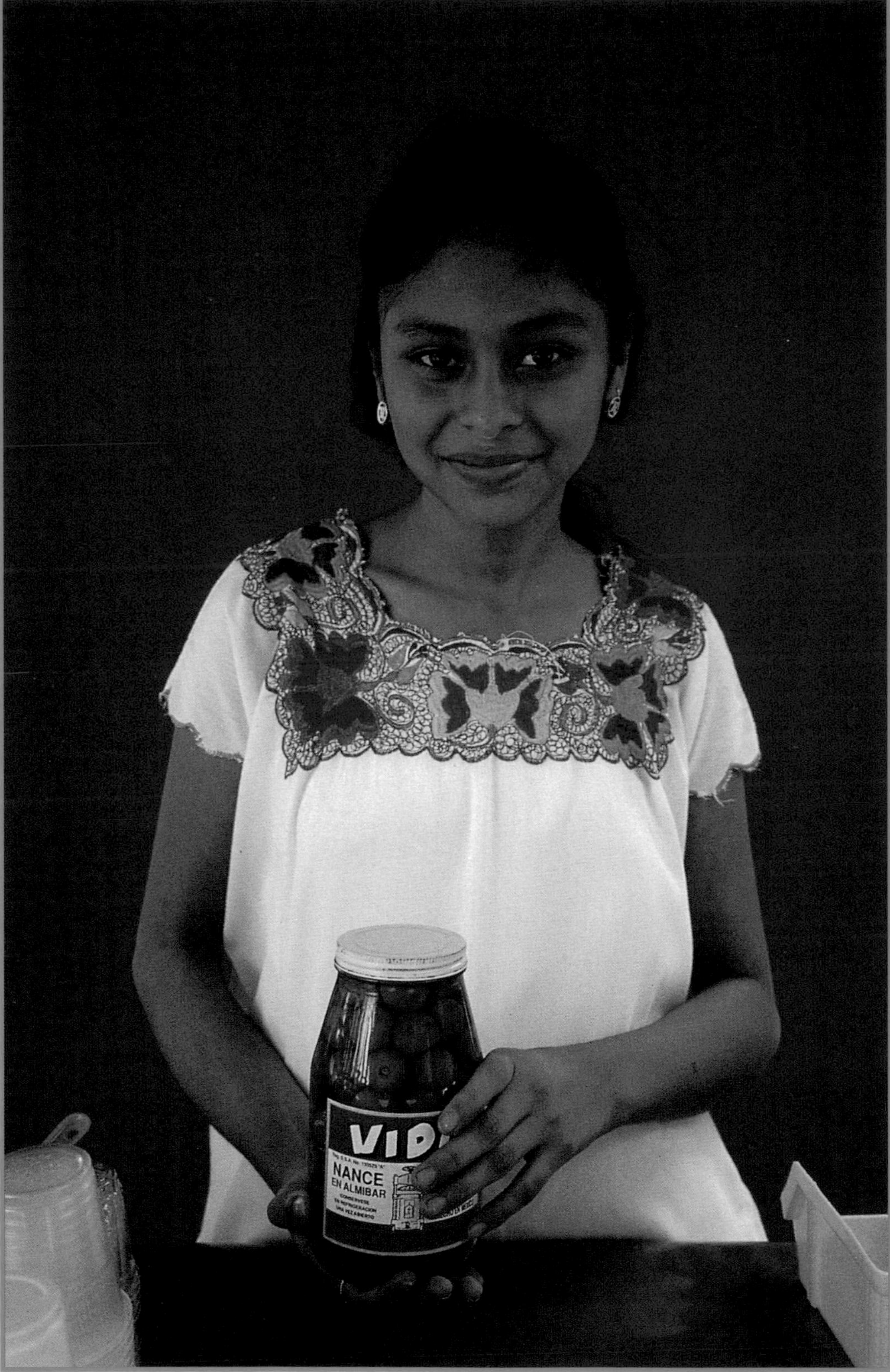
VID
NANCE
EN ALMIBAR

Opposite: Nance fruit packed in sugar syrup is sold in Mérida, Yucatán.

Above: Juice bar in San Miguel de Allende, Guanajuato.

Right: Piñatas decorate produce stalls in Cordoba, Veracruz's market.

Above: A garden table in San Miguel de Allende.

Left: Pottery selection in the Cuernavaca market.

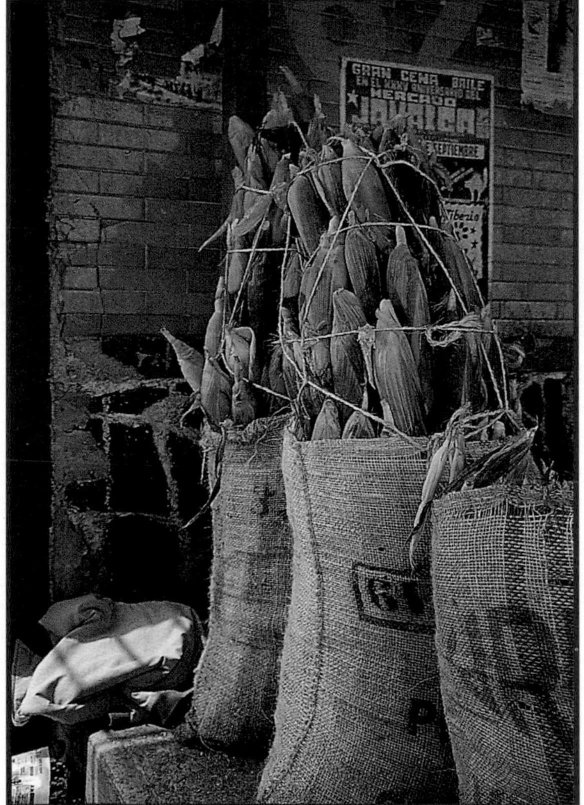

Above: Crisp *chicharrón* for sale in Oaxaca.

Right: Corn waiting for unpacking at Mexico City's Jamaica market.

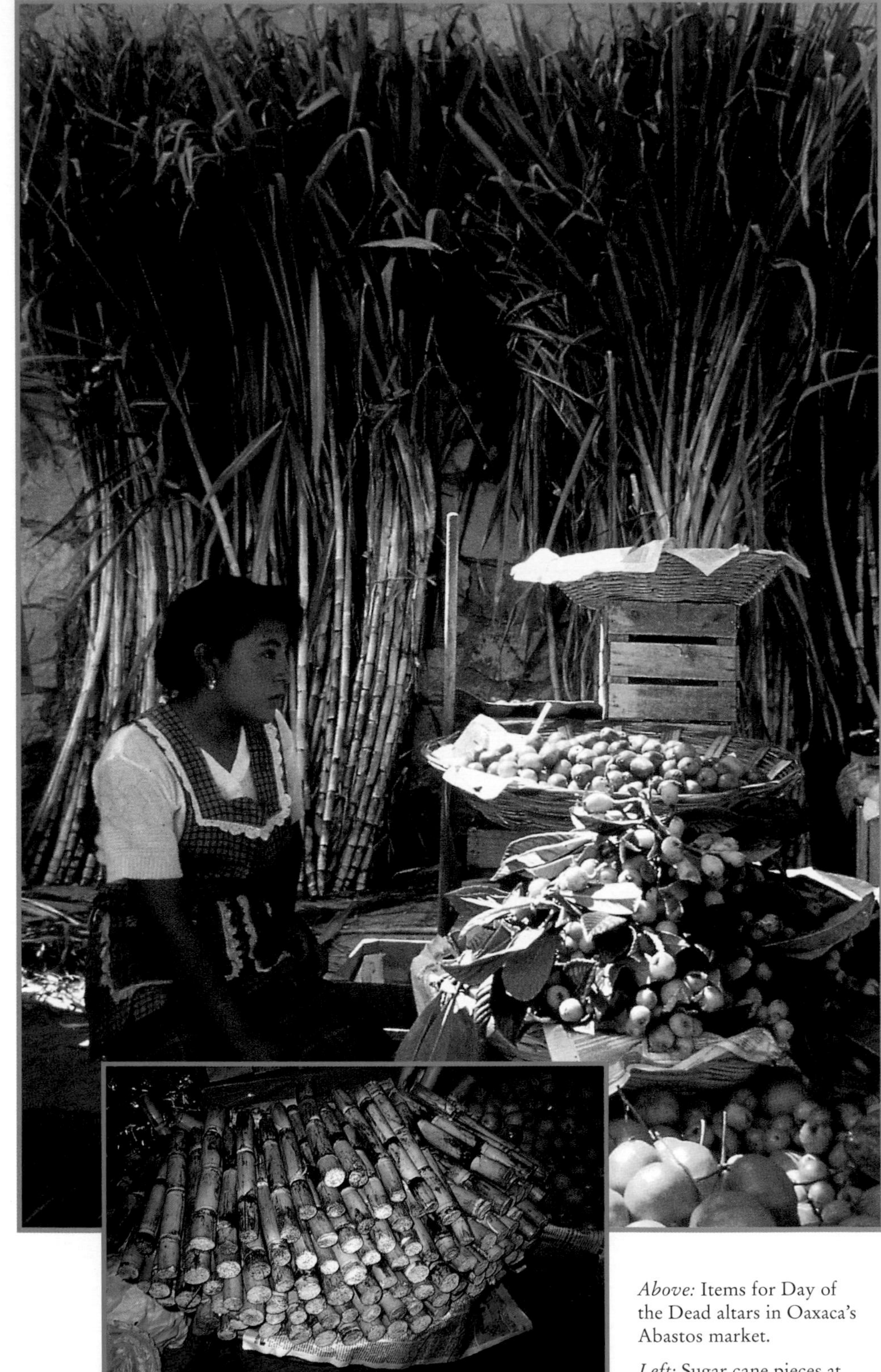

Above: Items for Day of the Dead altars in Oaxaca's Abastos market.

Left: Sugar cane pieces at Xalapa's Jaurecul market.

Carlos Ramón Hernández Estrada's

Camotes con Piña *Mashed Sweet Potato with Pineapple*

COOKED SWEET POTATOES SWEETENED WITH PLENTY OF *PANELA* (*piloncillo* in the north) are found all over Mexico from Tijuana to Mérida. The ancient tuber is a market mainstay sold both raw and cooked—ready to nibble on the spot. You'll see prepared pale yellow, gold, red, and purple sweet potatoes basking and glistening in their sugar syrup glazes, usually with tiny bees buzzing around. The city of Puebla is known for its unusual cigar-shaped sweet potato candies wrapped in papers and boxed like fancy salt water taffy (page 167). Pineapple is a mainstay of Veracruz because plantations line the highways just south of the city, and the luscious fruit is available year-round. You'll see pineapple juice bars in Mercado Hidalgo, plus street vendors squirting juice into plastic cups from bizarre, pineapple-shaped containers carried on their backs.

Friend and superb market guide Carlos, a law student and tourist office employee, provides this sweet potato recipe that's eaten as a homey dessert, or comfort-food snack, by everyone in Veracruz.

Yield: 4 servings

- 2 large sweet potatoes
- 1 ripe pineapple at room temperature
- ¼ cup "panela" or dark brown sugar
- light cream, half-and-half, or lightly whipped heavy cream, sweetened to taste with honey, if desired

1. Wash the sweet potatoes and cut them into 2-inch pieces. Put them in a pot with water to cover by 1 inch and bring to a boil. Cook the sweet potatoes until they are soft, about 20 minutes, testing with a fork. Drain and cool until easy to handle.

2. Meanwhile, clean the pineapple. Remove the leaves, rind, base, and tough, center heart. Finely chop the fruit, reserving any juice.

3. Remove potato skins and put the potatoes in a large bowl. Mash with a potato masher or large fork. Add the chopped pineapple and juice and thoroughly mix together until the color is even.

4. Taste for sweetness. You may want to add some sugar, especially if the dish is served as a dessert. Or pass sugar or honey at the table with the cream to be poured over *camotes con piña*, which is served in bowls.

Rosa María Inglesias Lachata and Rosario Ichata Inglesias's

Toro *Milk, Fruit, and Sugarcane Alcohol Drink*

TORO IS A RICH AND CREAMY ALCOHOLIC DRINK made with fresh fruit, milk, sugar, and sugarcane alcohol. You'll recognize its similarity to eggnog. *Toro's* texture is also akin to a famous Mexican drink, Rompope, commercially bottled and sold in liquor stores and markets all over the country.

In Boca del Río (page 185), you get the fresh, very real, thing. Two *toro* "girls" sure know how to turn a town into a party! Rosa and Rosario's family *toro* bar has been in Boca del Río for more than fifty years selling the natural, fresh fruit beverage to happy imbibers.

Each day there's a list of flavors, from peanut to fresh strawberry (year-round), to coconut (with teeny pieces of fresh coconut meat for texture). A few unusual tropical fruit flavors are on the list as well, such as *nanche* and *guanábana*. The alcohol is pure cane alcohol made from sugarcane fields in the surrounding hills.

Consider fresh fruit *toro* for your next party punch—peanut butter's tantalizing; strawberry's a blissfully bright pink; summer peach is heaven; and any frozen, defrosted fruit works just fine.

Yield: about 2 quarts

- ½ pound smooth peanut butter without salt (freshly ground, if possible), at room temperature, or ½ pound fresh fruit pulp (about 15 very ripe strawberries)
- 1 cup sugar
- 1 quart rich milk
- 1½ cups sugarcane alcohol (or substitute vodka)

1. Put the peanut butter, or fruit, and sugar in a blender container. Add 1 cup of the milk. Blend. Add, cup by cup, as much milk as fits comfortably in the blender. Purée.

2. Pour the mixture into a container with a tightly fitted top. Add the remaining milk and alcohol, stirring to blend. *Toro* keeps for 1 week, refrigerated.

Rosa María Inglesias Lachata and Rosario Ichata Inglesias.

◆ Córdoba ◆

✱ MARKET ✱

CÓRDOBA LIES AN HOUR INTO the lush hills west of Veracruz City on fast toll highway 150, and offers splendid views of a snow-capped volcano, Volcán Pico de Orizaba, looming straight ahead.

Mercado Revolución Located about four blocks from the *zócalo* between Avenidas 8 and 10 and Calles 7 and 9. Parking a few blocks off in any direction is the easiest solution—try Avenida 4 near Calle 7. Vendors encircling the market building streets sell the cheapest, and often the most interesting, locally grown produce and flowers. Huge bouquets are yours for a song. The market is divided in half with food on one side and household goods, clothing, piñatas and hardware on the other. At least five big juice bars specialize in *licuados*, blender drinks—no need to be thirsty in Córdoba.

Bread. *Pan de panela*, a 12-inch diameter and 1½-inch-thick loaf made in other surrounding cities is the market's popular bread—each "branded" with a bull logo before it's finished baking. Buy one of the molasses-tasting, coarsely textured loaves from any bread stall, then walk to a coffee bar and dunk a hunk into rich brew from beans grown within kilometers of your stool.

Chicken and Meat. The only place for fresh chicken is **Pollo La Nueva Gloria**, and crowds at the counter are staggering just before the afternoon meal. Butchers are lined up on two outer rows and against one you'll find lamb *barbacoa* places offering tastes before you buy to roll in handmade tortillas conveniently sold a few feet away, out of baskets.

Gordas. Toward the Avenida 10 side of the market are triangular-shaped *gordas* filled with *epazote* and chile-flavored black bean paste. They're across from herb vendors, who have everything for *curanderos* (traditional-medicine doctors) and *brujas* (witch doctors), including a spell-binding mulato chile stuffed with shell pieces, trinkets, herbs, and seeds, then sewn up with coarse black thread. Throw *that* into your pot and stew it.

Fresh banana leaves for sale at Córdoba's Mercado Revolución.

◆ Xalapa ◆

✷ MARKET ✷

THE ROAD FROM CÓRDOBA travels north through Huatusco's sugarcane fields and misty coffee-growing Coatepec, then reaches Xalapa (also spelled Jalapa), the capital and bustling university town of the state of Veracruz. An ever-changing landscape adds to the area's physical excitement when driving from one archaeological landmark to the next. Thanks to its fabulous archaeology museum, Xalapa attracts international travelers to the otherwise tourist-free, picturesque, and hilly university city often hidden in a layer of mist.

Mercado Jaurecui A few blocks north of the *zócalo* (uphill) on Revolución at Altamirano. It's clean and tidy and can easily be explored in an hour. This is the perfect place to buy burlap bags (half or kilo size) of the famous coffee grown around Xalapa and neighboring Coatepec. Chipotle chile, the dried and smoked jalapeño chile, is a best bet here, and you'll see various sizes. If any produce vendors are offering samples of exotic *guanábana*, don't miss the opportunity. Mezzanine fondas are the town's cheap-eat hot spots and favorites with market workers and Xalapa's huge college student population.

Bakery. Dauzón is very good and well-visited—so good there are branches all over town. People stop in and grab a *volovane*, a flaky crabmeat or ham-and-cheese puff to munch on the street. Or try a *ratero*, a dark chocolate-coated "rat" bonbon tasting like anything but.

Restaurant. La Casona del Beaterio, Inexpensive. Located at Zaragoza No. 20, is a popular restaurant with a few rooms off to one side of a pretty courtyard. Traditional dishes such as regional *moles*, shredded beef with pickled vegetables, robust pumpkin seed-chile sauce over broiled chicken, all types of *tortas* for quick, tasty lunches, and *chiles rellenos* are good here, as are the soups in a town well known for chilly nights where you can see your breath in winter months. Take along a heavy sweater and light rain gear if you plan to spend much time. And to think Xalapa is only an hour and a half northwest of the hot, humid port of Veracruz.

Truffles. On highway 140 west of Xalapa is **Perote**, home to elusive (and very unknown) Mexican truffles. Once they are harvested from beneath oak trees in this off-the-beaten-track area, the pricey, prized fungi are exported immediately out of the country. Japanese and French companies have concessions to collect the precious jewels, therefore nothing stays at home. *¡Que lástima!*

Dolores Ramón's

Salsa de Chile Chipotle *Cooked Tomato Salsa with Chipotle Chiles*

XALAPA'S MARKET IS A GOOD SPOT TO BUY CHIPOTLE CHILE, especially in late January through March, when the season's largest specimens are available. They can be bought whole or seeded, and they're as soft and pliable as fruit leather.

Dolores was born and raised in Xalapa, and now feeds her children traditional recipes her mother and grandmother, from nearby coffee-growing Coatepec, passed down to her. For Dolores's fat-free table salsa she toasts the vegetables then slow-cooks them, but doesn't fry the sauce as with most other cooked salsas. *Salsa de Chile Chipotle* can be made in advance; it keeps for a week, refrigerated, and it's absolutely delicious when served at room temperature. Try the very smooth salsa with other dried chiles for regional taste variations. *Yield: about 4 cups (the recipe may be cut in half)*

- 6 dried chipotle chiles (do not substitute canned chipotle chile en adobo)
- 20 dark red-ripe plum tomatoes
- 4 medium white onions, peeled and quartered
- 12 garlic cloves, peeled
- 2 limes, juiced
- ¼ cup sugar
- salt to taste

1. Wash the chiles then soak in hot water for 1 to 2 hours to soften (very hard ones will take up to 24 hours). Once they are soft, avert your eyes because of strong fumes, and remove the stem, the hard area around the stem, and the seeds.

2. Toast (page 16) the tomatoes. Put them in a plastic bag to "sweat" for a few minutes. Then peel. Put in a blender container and purée. Pour the puréed tomatoes into a deep pot and simmer.

3. Toast the quartered onions and the garlic cloves until they are browned. Put a third of them in a blender with the lime juice and purée. Add a third more and purée again. Add the remainder and purée.

4. Add the chiles to the blender and purée with the onion mixture until the sauce is smooth.

5. Add the blender ingredients to the simmering tomatoes. Add the lime juice and sugar. Simmer, uncovered, for 1 hour. The thick sauce will bubble and splatter so be sure your pot is deep.

6. Remove the salsa from the heat and cool for 30 minutes. Add salt to taste. Purée one last time until it is very smooth. Serve at room temperature in a small bowl. Pass hot, fresh, tortilla chips sprinkled with salt and lime juice.

Rosa Sánchez Namorado's

Tlatonile *Toasted Seed, Nut, and Chile Paste*

THE ROAD FROM CÓRDOBA TO XALAPA IS SELDOM TRAVELED BY TOURISTS, and is the quintessential Mexican back road, boasting jagged peaks, snow-capped volcano views, tropical vegetation, oxen-plowed fields, and crisp blue skies. Huatusco is a market town, and its market building, on two floors, is impressively large for the town size, but then you *do* need lots of room for all those bananas!

Tlatonile, a pre-Columbian *pipián*, is made here exactly as it was five hundred years ago. Upstairs, on the mezzanine, you'll see Rosa Sánchez Namorado's ancient-looking Fonda Huatusqueña where she still hand-grinds seeds and nuts on a *metate* (lava rock grinding slab) as she has been doing for the past fifty-something years. She says a blender just won't do for *her* smooth paste. Rosa uses shelled pumpkin seeds, as does Javier Martínez Orozco, who lives on the Pacific coast just north of Puerto Vallarta in the state of Michoacán (page 52). Theirs are in contrast to the *pipiáns* of Oaxaca and Chiapas, where unshelled seeds are necessary for coarse texture. *Tlatonile* is delicious thinned down with chicken broth and generously poured over Mexican Rice Pilaf (page 66). With a piece of chicken it's a full fonda plate—with or without black beans. It's also an excellent vegetarian meal when thinned with vegetable broth. *Tlatonile* makes the perfect all-around dipping sauce.

Yield: about 3 pounds (recipe may be cut in half)

- 6 chipotle chiles
- 6 ancho chiles
- ¼ cup vegetable oil (Rosa uses peanut)
- 1 pound toasted (page 16), green pumpkin seeds ("pepitas"), shelled
- 1 pound toasted white sesame seeds
- 1 pound toasted peanuts, shelled and skinned

1. Wash the chiles, put them in a large bowl, and pour boiling water over them. Soak for 1 hour then dry.

2. Stem and seed the chiles. Put them in a blender or processor with the vegetable oil. Blend. Add the pumpkin seeds and blend, pushing down on the blender sides with a rubber spatula from time to time. Add the sesame seeds and blend, pushing down with the spatula. Add the peanuts and blend, pushing down. If the paste is too thick you may add more vegetable oil.

3. Put the paste in a clean, dry, large, glass jar with a tight lid. Refrigerate the paste just like preservative-free peanut butter. Stir well before each use.

Carmen Ramírez Degollado's

Gorditas de Frijol *Masa and Puréed Black Bean Puffs*

GORDITAS ARE SOLD ALL OVER THE COUNTRY, but none is so delicate or so puffed as Carmen's. Today they are standbys of Veracruz, but their origin is said to be of Yucatán descent (note sieved black beans). Most of the *gorditas* you see as street food or market snacks in central and western-central Mexico are made from very heavy, coarse, yellow *masa* patted into disks about 4 inches x ½-inch thick. Sometimes they're topped with beans, shredded meat, vegetables, pickled vegetables, etc. Other times stuffings are flavorings—they're pulled apart (English muffin-style) and filled before eating like a sandwich. Fabulous, coarse *gorditas* of San Miguel de Allende come to mind; everyone in town knows the women who sell delicious examples under the Canal Street bridge.

Carmen, a Veracruzana living in Mexico City, offers *gorditas de frijol* on her El Bajío Restaurant menu along with a few more dishes from the hills around Xalapa, her home base. Carmen especially enjoys serving these delicate *gorditas* with a chipotle chile and garlic salsa as appetizers with drinks. *Gorditas de frijol* are last-minute preparation items. She says the rounds of *masa* may be formed ahead, but only right before serving may they be flattened into disk shapes and fried. It's important that the puffs are fried in very hot oil and served immediately. In Veracruz City, Cochinito de Oro is the classic place to eat *gorditas*. Try a few for breakfast, or *merienda* (late afternoon snack) as does everyone else.

Yield: 30 gorditas

- 2 pounds "masa" for tortillas (not too coarse), or "masa harina" to equal 2 pounds, prepared
- ½ cup heavy cream
- 1½ cups black beans, cooked and sieved or puréed Yucatán style (page 250)
- 5 to 8 Tablespoons flour
- 1 teaspoon salt
- 2 cups lard (page 18), or vegetable oil

1. In a large mixing bowl, combine the *masa*, cream, beans, 5 tablespoons of the flour, and salt uniformly until the mixture is smooth. If the dough is too moist, add the additional 3 tablespoons flour and knead again.

2. Divide the dough into golfball-sized balls (that later flatten into disks 3 inches by ⅛ inch, with squared-off edges), and put them on a traditional banana leaf or plate and cover with plastic (so they don't dry out) while forming the rest. They may be made a few hours ahead to this point.

3. Heat the lard or vegetable oil to 365°F, or until the surface ripples, in a large, deep skillet. Flatten each ball to a disk shape and slide it into the hot fat. Do not crowd the pan. Cook for about 2 minutes, until lightly browned and puffed. Drain the *gorditas* on paper towels and serve while they are very hot and still puffed.

Carmen Ramírez Degollado's

Tamales de Misantla

Banana-Leaf-Wrapped Tamales Filled with Chicken in Adobo

CARMEN CRUSHES THE ANISE-FLAVORED HERB *ACUYO (HOJA SANTA* OR *MOMO)* and mixes it into *masa* at her Mexico City restaurant, El Bajío. *Tamales de Misantla* (a town near Xalapa) are wrapped in banana leaves for additional southern flavor, and filled with shredded chicken in *adobo*. These tamales are similar to *Vaporcitos* (page 313) but are made with coarser *masa*, their size is slightly smaller, and the *adobo* filling is different.

Serve the tamales with *Atole* (page 126), and fresh tomato or tomatillo salsa made with chipotle chiles in the evening, or for a special breakfast.

Yield: about 24 tamales

For the "masa"

- 3 "acuyo" ("hoja santa" or "momo") leaves, chopped, or 6 Tablespoons dried, or 1 teaspoon toasted and crushed aniseseed, or ½ cup chopped fennel leaves
- 2 pounds "masa" for tamales, from a tortillería (about 4 cups)
- 4 quarts Chicken Broth (page 19)
- 6 cups fresh lard (page 18), or substitute vegetable shortening

1. In a very large pot, mix the *acuyo* into the *masa*.

2. Over low heat add the broth, stirring. Increase the heat and slowly bring the mixture to a boil. Add the lard, reduce the heat to a simmer, and cook the dough to a soft consistency, about 30 minutes, stirring. The final texture is thinner than that of polenta. Remove from the heat and cool to room temperature.

For the adobo filling

- 3½ ounces guajillo or ancho chiles, or 1 ounce chipotle chiles (for different regional "adobo" flavors)
- 3 garlic cloves, coarsley chopped
- 2 pounds tomatoes, coarsely chopped (about 6)
- 2 Tablespoons vegetable oil
- 1 whole, large chicken breast, boiled, skinned, and shredded

1. Clean the chiles with a damp towel and remove the stems, seeds, and veins. Soak the chiles in hot water for 1 hour to soften (up to 24 hours for old, hard chipotles).

2. Put the chiles in a blender container, reserving their soaking liquid. Add the garlic and tomatoes. Add about ¼ cup soaking liquid and purée. Scrape down the sides, add more liquid, and purée again. Repeat if necessary to make a thin paste.

3. Heat the oil in a deep pot and carefully pour the sauce into the pot (it splatters!). Reduce the heat and simmer the sauce, uncovered, for 30 minutes. Add more chile soaking liquid if it gets too thick. Remove the pot from the heat. Add the shredded chicken to the *adobo* sauce and stir.

To assemble

6 precooked, whole banana leaves (most come this way)

1. Cut any hard, center veins out of the banana leaves. Cut each leaf into pieces about 8 inches x 8 inches and put them to the side, in a pile. There should be at least 24 pieces. There will be wastage and many leaves will tear. When this happens, cut a smaller piece and put it over the tear, as a patch.

2. For each tamale, break off a golfball-sized piece of *masa* and spread it on the more textured side of a leaf centered, in a rough circle about 5 inches in diameter. Top with ¼ cup shredded chicken in *adobo*, and spread out, keeping it ½ inch away from the *masa* edge.

3. With two hands on the banana leaf, pick up one side and flap one third of the tortilla over. Put the banana leaf back down (the tortilla will still be flapped). With two hands, pick up the other side of the banana leaf and flap one third of the tortilla over the other flapped part, keeping the banana leaf in place (don't lay it back down). Pick up the first section of leaf and flap it on top.

4. Tuck the two sides under. The finished size is about 4 inches x 3 inches. Decorate the tamales by tying "ribbons" of banana leaf (⅛ inch x 24 inches) around the packages, ending with a "bow," if desired, for a delightful presentation.

To steam

1. Use a tamale steamer (see Glossary). Lay the tamales on the steamer rack or plate. They should overlap diagonally to let steam pass through the pile easily. Cover the pot.

2. Bring the water to a boil in the steamer and cook for 1 to 1½ hours. Check the water level after 45 minutes and from time to time to be sure it never runs dry.

The Land of Ancient Tradition

Oaxaca

OAXACA CAPTIVATES WITH ITS GREAT CHANGES OF SCENERY, *climate, and culture—from coastal palm-lined beaches known for world-class sunning and surfing; to dense tropical jungles still hiding undiscovered Mayan temples; to the Sierra Madre del Sur mountain range where maguey plants for mezcal cover undulating hills. The southern state is still primarily Indian; sixteen indigenous tribes still speak their own languages (with ninety dialects), practice ancient ways, and keep those traditions with little noticeable modern influences. Corn remains the primary crop as it has for centuries. Mexico's most exotic chiles are grown for demanding cooks—their specialties are* moles, *glorious sauces made from seeds, nuts, herbs, spices, fruits, and cocoa beans. Hot Mexican chocolate reaches its pinnacle in Oaxaca, where purists grind their own blends of cocoa beans,* panela, *almonds, and sugar.*

Left: Tropical fruit sherbet at the plaza in front of Oaxaca's Basílica de la Soledad.

◆ Oaxaca ◆

Fruit vendor at Mercado Central de Abastos.

OAXACA CITY LIES IN A HIGH (5,070 feet, 1,550 meters) valley overviewed by its ancient predecessor, Monte Albán. The Colonial City, founded by the Spanish in 1529, along with Taxco and San Miguel de Allende, is designated one of only three national monument towns by the Mexican government. Architecture in the central area is colonial—old government buildings now house museums, galleries, restaurants, the university, plus a music-filled *zócalo* lined with cafés under *portales.* The capital's renowned Saturday market is a magnet for colorfully dressed natives with salable items—whether homegrown fruit, handthrown pottery, or handmade tortillas.

✸ MARKETS ✸

Mercado Central de Abastos

Mercado Central de Abastos is also known as Mercado Sábado (Saturday market). The main market entrance is through a brick-fronted building with arches on Prol. G. de las Casas, across from the second-class bus station, but entrances are everywhere along surrounding streets. Hours: Open every day from 7 A.M. to 8 P.M. Behind the main building are additional buildings with their own specialties. Behind them is a *tianguis* (Indian market), which is especially grand on Saturday.

Although bustling all week, Oaxaca's Saturday market is famous throughout the country because it's on this day that Indians leave their mountain perches and come down to sell, swap, and barter. The government built Mercado Central de Abastos at the western end of the city in the 1970's to relieve congestion in the bustling center's Mercado Benito Juárez. It took a long time to catch on with traditional-minded merchants, but now the place jumps every day. Tenants are conveniently situated by product: tortilla vendors in one section; butchers in another; cheese stalls are all together; fruit here; vegetables there. Besides produce of unequaled quality and variation, regional Indian crafts, renowned throughout the world, are everywhere. You'll hear not only Spanish but also Indian dialects both inside and outside in the open air.

Oaxaqueños generally eat only black beans, not the more familiar pink, or pinto, beans. Burlap sacks, barrels, hills, and mountains of the black beauties dominate the market along with dried corn waiting to be turned into *nixtamal* for *masa*. *Nopales* (cactus paddles), cleaned, cooked, and ready for salads, are time-savers. Beautifully arranged piles of the fresh, regional de agua chile are show stoppers. Unusual fresh herbs, yardstick-long garlic braids, and dried fish and shrimp are all products of the agriculturally lush state.

Amid the zillion fruit and vegetable stalls are natives in traditional dress and selling crafts. Weavers, needleworkers, basketmakers, and potters crowd every empty space. Oaxaca's famous black pottery, actually from the nearby village of San Bartolo Coyotepec, floods the pottery building. Atzompa's green-glazed pottery is also featured down the same aisles. Tuesday, Friday, and Saturday are the best days because on those days most Indians bring their booty to town (also look in the clay area at the southwest end of the market). Teotitlan del Valle's hand-loomed wool rugs are piled by size, but also hang on every available wall space in the weavings area. Mitla's lightweight wool and cotton weavings make superb tablecloths, and Santo Tomas Jalieza's table runners and placemats make perfect complements to a delicious Oaxacan meal.

Fondas. There is no separate fonda building at Mercado Central de Abastos, but you'll see fondas everywhere—especially near the bread building, around the corner from Mayordomo's market location for freshly ground chocolate—and fondas encircle open courtyard areas. Be sure to arrive early for breakfast, when excellent hot chocolate tastes even better than its enticing aroma smells. Or, for more authenticity, try steaming cups of thick *atole*, made from *masa*, *canela*, and *panela* (*champurrado* is *atole* with chocolate; *blanco* is sugar only; and *leche*, with milk). Ask around for *atole de granillo* at these fondas—it's the way *atole* should be made, with hand-ground *masa* that leaves a gruel at the bottom of your bowl. *Atole de granillo* and tamales (flavored with the herb *chepil* in the *masa*, or filled with black beans, or *mole*) is an honest-to-goodness, pre-Columbian breakfast.

These same fondas offer *mole negro* with rice and tortilla lunches, with or without chicken. *Pipián* is popular, soups are always available, and daily specials bubble away on every stove.

Bread. A stop at market bread stalls is mandatory. *Pan de yema*, a special-occasion egg bread, looks enticingly rich but isn't. It's a natural for dunking in hot chocolate at one of the market fondas. *Pan amarillo*, a hard-crusted, five-inch round loaf, is simply delicious, especially warm. *Pan marquesote* is a square, very soft, sweet bread with a texture like sponge cake. It's so special that in some Zapotec villages it is served only at weddings.

Chiles. Oaxaca is known as "Land of Seven *Moles*" for the region's *mole* pastes made from chiles, spices, nuts, seeds, fresh and dried fruits, and sometimes, chocolate.

Besides these basics, there are hundreds of variations on the seven *mole* theme. Homemade *mole* recipes have ingredients' lists as long as *ristras* (decorative chile braids). Oaxacan chiles are some of the most interesting and flavor packed in Mexico. Dried varieties travel well and can be taken into the U.S. (see page 349).

Señor Ramírez Hernández, at No. 4, *zona tianguis*, in the dried chiles aisle, has one of Oaxaca's most comprehensive selections, and clean sacks are clearly marked with each chile's name. He has all of Oaxaca's esoteric chiles for the seven *moles*, plus some. One aisle over, gentlemen sell pasilla de Oaxaca chiles, by hundred units, all by size. Feel them and choose those with a texture of pliable fruit leather, neither stiff nor hard. They make big, gorgeous *Chiles Rellenos de Chipotle con Picadillo* (page 196), substituted for Veracruz's chipotle chile.

Tortillas. Some of the most famous tortillas in Mexico are sold at Mercado de Abastos. Two lines of Indian women with tall baskets in front of them stand outside, near the bread building. Their baskets hold handmade corn *clayudas*, wide, chewy, pale gold favorites for topping with avocado, chiles, and grilled meat. *Blandas*, or *blanditas* (smaller), are amazingly thin, handmade tortillas sold from baskets around fondas (fonda owners buy them warm for their customers). They're delicate and made from white corn.

Drinks. Thirsty? A favorite is *texate* (sometimes spelled *tejate*), the painstakenly tedious regional recipe few people master. Back at home the night before, market women grind *masa* by hand, then mix it with toasted cocoa flowers and *mamey* fruit seeds in a made-for-*texate*, huge, green-glazed bowl. In the market, gallons of water are dumped on the mound of mixed ingredients all at once, then the resulting liquid is vigorously beaten for half an hour until frothy. An unusual flower pattern foam forms on the surface, the prized portion. Thirsty locals actually hunt down *texate* with the thickest top foam. They sip the delicate drink from traditional bowls made from dried gourds painted bright red with birds and flowers. Be careful of the water (and ice); if it comes out of a hose, run.

Pulque and Tepache. Beatriz does a brisk business in plastics: bags, tablecloths, and multicolored straws. Look for her sign, **Plásticos Bety**, at Beatriz López Mateo's booth, No. 103, Sector One. But the true attractions are two large terracotta pots filled with *pulque* and *tepache* that sit on her counter. These ancient drinks are becoming more and more difficult to find throughout Mexico. After some serious shopping, use the excuse of "historical research" to sample these fermented, cool and slightly alcoholic brews. Needless to say, hanging out at Beatriz's booth can be great fun.

Tepache is made from pineapple rind (no juice), water, and *panela*, and takes three days to ferment. Beatriz makes it today exactly as her Zapotec ancestors made it. This is no touristy restaurant drink. Meanwhile, you'll just have to try *pulque*—all in the name of research, of course. *Pulque* is made from 100 percent *agua miel* (honey water), which is made from the juice of the maguey plant (*Agave*

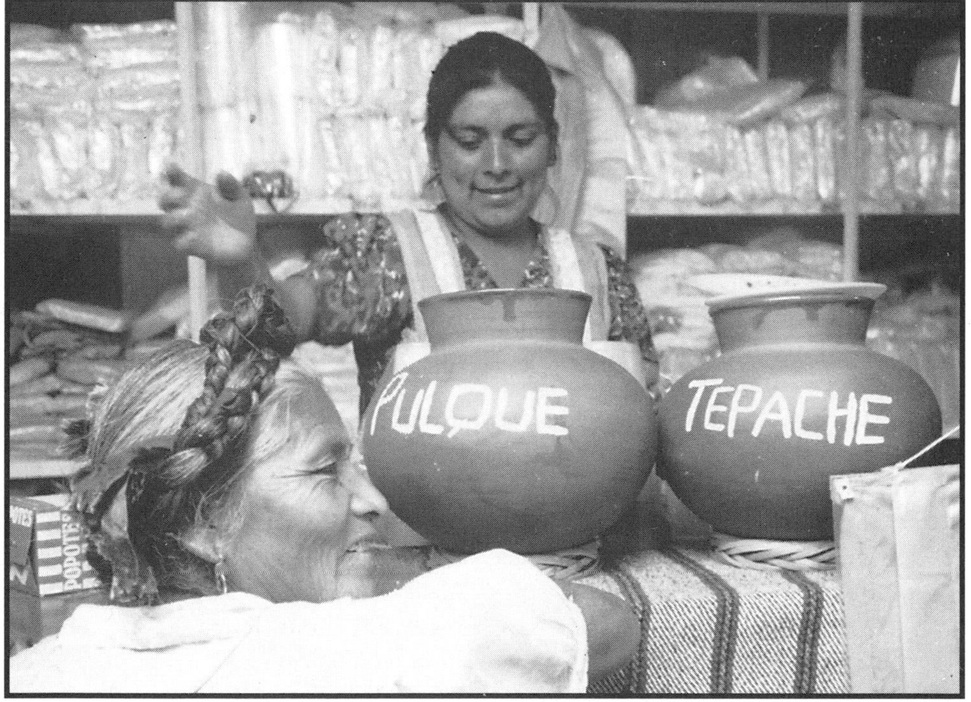

Beatriz López Mateo and her mother offer "pulque" and "tepache" at Mercado Abastos.

angustifolia). The juice takes two to three days to ferment and turn to *pulque*. *Pulque* must be made in spotless containers (even a drop of water could ruin the entire batch), which means the ancient, pure potion is okay to drink from Beatriz's plastic cups.

Flowers. The flower aisle is at the south end of the market, across from the *barbacoa* fondas. Locals know flowers are always a bit pricier on Saturday, the busiest market day.

Barbacoa. Directly across from the flowers is a line of *barbacoa* places—choose lamb or *cabrito* (kid). Wrap a few tortillas around delectable meat jazzed up, as you wish, from bowls of vinegared vegetables and salsas on the oilcloth-covered picnic tables. Wash this all down with a not-so-traditional Diet Coke.

Mercado Benito Juárez

Mercado Benito Juárez is located one block southwest of the *zócalo* bordered by Las Casas, Aldama, 20 de Noviembre, and Bustamante. It is open every day from 7A.M. to 9 P.M. The old city-center market was completely remodeled in 1993 and the new Las Casas main entrance is known for soft, squashy baskets with pleasing designs that travel so well. To both sides are booths selling regional clothes and costumes from the entire state, including elaborate outfits from Tehuantepec. *Huipiles*, *rebozos*, folk-dancing skirts, embroidered blouses, hats, and leather items are all squeezed in the aisle. Other market items besides vegetables and fruits are medicinal and culinary herbs, cheeses, chiles, chickens, meats, fish, dried shrimp, handmade tortillas, and molds for chocolate drying.

Cheese. There are many cheese stalls selling *quesillo de Oaxaca*, prized balls of white string cheese that taste somewhat salty and acidic. The prerequisite for those sinfully fatty cheese dishes of Mexico, it melts in a flash. Sizes from marbles to softballs abound (with braided specimens available, too). Maybe you'll see a vendor uncoil cheese from a basketball-sized wholesale monster and make baseball-sized babies.

Queso fresco is the second most popular cheese with cooks. Similar to farmer cheese, it's at its best here in the marketplace, where *queso* arrives sweet and fresh every day. It's eaten sliced, with fruit, or crumbled over many dishes at any fonda.

Also sold at cheese counters are chocolate tablets (for hot chocolate and *mole*) made at Oaxacan mills that do not have city-center retail stores. Some stalls carry *mole negro* and *rojo* pastes.

Gusanos. Just above eye level dried *gusanito* (tiny worm) necklaces hang to dry at many cheese stalls. Dried grubs of the maguey plant are flavored with chile-flavored salt. The savory morsels are most often crumbled into Tomatillo Salsa (page 244). Summer months bring freshly harvested (alive and moving!) baskets full, offered by women sitting with the *clayudas* sellers at the rear entrance (across from 20 de Noviembre fondas building entrance).

Chapulines. Gourmet products are everywhere. But let the buyer beware: One of the more unusual Oaxacan specimens is *chapulines* (cooked crickets). These Jimminy critters are harvested at dawn in cornfields, boiled, then fried in garlicky oil until browned. Seasoned with salt, chile, and fresh lime, they are sold by the teeny two-inch scoop. This expensive delicacy is best in the summer during the rainy season when the tiny young buggers are no more than one quarter inch long and oh so tender.

Tortillas. Alongside the *chapulines*, at the Aldama exit, *clayudas* and *blandas* are sold by Indian women, their still-warm market favorites stacked in cloth-covered, tall baskets. Homemade from ground white (delicate *blandas*), yellow, and blue corn, these enormous fourteen- to eighteen-inchers are unavailable from commercial tortilla factories.

A small pueblo, San Juan Juquila Mixes, east of Oaxaca City up in the mountains, specializes in the *tortilla de corroso*, a coarsely ground *masa* beauty mixed with *panela* and coconut—very crunchy and slightly sweet. In southwestern Oaxaca state, similar *totopos* are famous in the city of Tehuantepec, even though most are actually made in the nearby village of San Blas. The thick, crackerlike specimens are baked in tandoorilike ovens and have holes patterened over their surfaces. They're sold at cheese counters and travel well.

Chorizo. At the Aldama exit, butchers sell Oaxacan sausages. Next to Toluca's, they're Mexico's most famous. Tiny, one-inch-diameter, dainty delights are tied on strings and strung to dry overhead.

Drinks. At **Casilda**, across from the aisle of flowers, you'll see huge earthenware pots filled with refreshing drinks. Gem-colored liquids gleam from giant glass jars that sparkle like crystal. Try sweetly tangy *agua de tamarindo*, made with tamarind pods; ruby red *jamaica* is everyone's favorite sweet-sour cooler; watermelon; cantaloupe; and exotic *zapote*. Casilda's milky white rice *horchata* (sometimes turned pink with a requested spoonful of puréed red cactus fruit, called *tuna*), topped with chopped nuts and fruit can't be beat anywhere else in Mexico. All drinks are made with purified water including the ice.

Nieve. Chaqüita, next to Casilda, is the best *nieve* (fruit sherbet, or noncreamy ice milk) stand in Mercado Juárez, and its intense flavors are the reason. Sure, the place is plastered with typical celebrity photos and newpaper testimonials, but they do have unbeatable flavors: *aguacate* (avocado), *arroz con leche* (sweet rice), *piña* (pineapple), *coco* (coconut), *limón* (lime), *leche quemada* (burnt milk that imparts a caramel flavor). *Tuna*, made from a red-pulp cactus fruit, is the prize catch. The next counter over may scoop up slightly larger servings, but the flavor is just not there—have a blast at your own taste-off. Ask for two flavors in your dish. Everything is made with purified water.

Tamales. Mornings, behind the wall just in back of the flower aisle, women sit on straw mats and sell fresh herbs and tamales from cloth-covered baskets. *Tamales dulces* (sweet) with *cochilla grana* are "*muy pueblito, muy cerca*" (very home-style), says my friend Carmen Ramírez Degollado, owner of Mexico City's El Bajío Restaurant. You'll see a red line made of *grana* (dye) from *cochinillas* (bugs) found in cactus paddles. The same market vendors also have banana leaf-wrapped specimens containing a finer *masa* and filled with *mole* (with or without chicken); *mole verde* or *pipián* with pork; coarse *masa* with *rajas de chile de agua* (chile strips). There are countless others to discover. The women also sell fresh wild and cultivated herbs, picked daily.

Eggs. Out the Aldama side of Mercado Juárez, and across from the entrance to Mercado 20 de Noviembre, are the city center's freshest eggs in a tiny shop that's open every day from 8 A.M. to 9 P.M.

Seafood and Poultry. Just to the left as you walk out the exit onto Aldama, you'll notice the intense odor that comes from piles of dried shrimp of varying sizes. The fresh seafood is that, but only bought first thing in the morning and refrigerated immediately.

Kitchen supplies. Plastic tablecloths at **Plásticos Marilú**, and **Plásticos Hayde**, are located toward the Aldama side of the building. Both carry bolts of the wonderful, flowered, plastic tablecloths found only in the finest fondas. Purchase them by the meter.

Textiles. Toward the Aldama side, one aisle from the poultry and seafood, you'll find at least four vendors selling striped, cotton tablecloths in various colors to enliven any Mexican meal. You see them on top of larger, solid-color cloths all over town, set diagonally on tabletops. Sizes are one, one-and-a-half, and two meters, plus round. Prices can't be beat.

Mercado 20 de Noviembre, Fondas Building

After you've finished shopping at Mercado Benito Juárez, cross Aldama and enter the bustling Mercado 20 de Noviembre, also remodeled in 1993. It's known by locals as *las fondas,* where dozens of concessionaires sell everything from prepared snacks to full meals. Breads are also a highlight here. You won't see any gringos within a tortilla's toss; this mazelike building is the bastion of local, traditional eating. *Chiles rellenos* are so popular that many fondas sell variations of the battered and fried chiles. But watch out: tame poblano chile is unheard of here, only spicy de agua chile is stuffed into *rellenos* around these parts. As always, look around for a clean popular place, and read the posted menu signs before sitting. Immediately ask the price after deciding, as everyone else does.

Oaxaca's markets are some of the best places for traditional dishes such as *mole*, *pollo en caldo* (big bowls of chicken soup), and tamales. No early morning breakfast is better than sitting at a fonda counter sipping hot chocolate and eating Oaxaca's famous egg bread, *pan de yema*. *Clayudas con asiento* (page 264) are the first lunch choices of many hungry shoppers and they can be purchased at many fonda counters, as their menus are always clearly printed.

Street food (or *cocina callejera*) vendors. At nightfall, a slew of carts loaded with delectable *antojitos* descends all around Mercado 20 de Noviembre and Mercado Benito Juárez. *Chalupas*, quesadillas, and *molotes* (topped with *chorizo*, cubed potatoes, chile, and herbs) are all-time winners.

Fondas. La Abuelita (The Grandmother) is one of the oldest and most reliable fondas in the building. It's to the left just as you walk past a few bread stalls after entering from the main entrance across from Mercado Juárez. La Abuelita has three counters all clustered together selling exactly the same dishes. Sit at the large stainless steel table and drink *atole* or *chamurrado* in the morning, or eat *moles negro* or *coloradito* served over chicken and rice, *tasajo* and *cecina* served with beans, and *clayudas con asiento*. Soups are *caldo de res* (beef) and *pollo* (chicken). Tamales wrapped in banana leaves are usually available in the morning. I enjoy dunking *pan de yema* into bowls of hot, foamy chocolate here.

Fonda María Alejandra is located next to La Abuelita and is almost as big and flashy with its huge sign and television for attracting lone diners. If *agua fresca de guanábana* is offered, go for the refreshing drink with big black seeds but add a bit of sugar. *Clayudas con asiento* are the big draw, but *moles* and soups are popular as at most other places. Morning *atole* is served in country French-style bowls. The owner is never around, and teenage girls working behind the counter may be rude—you're forwarned.

Fonda Laurita, located at No. 173, all the way to the right as you enter the building, offers a good selection of breakfast *atoles*

María Eugenia Arroyo at Fonda Laurita.

to slurp along with tamales, and hot chocolate to dunk *pan de yema*. Both drinks are served in bowls here, too. Another favorite is *chilaquiles,* with or without chicken or meat, but always with jalapeño chiles, fresh basil leaves, and sprinkled with dry cheese. María Eugenia's *Enchiladas* (page 252) are a standout. *Chiles rellenos* are made fresh every day with spicy de agua chiles.

Butchers. To the left, past Fonda La Abuelita, is another huge, high-ceilinged room with specialty butchers lined up on both sides of a center aisle. To the immediate left and right, as you enter, people sell the necessary vegetables to grill and pile on your *clayuda,* along with the meat you'll grill yourself, right here. Walk down the aisle and notice the flat, thin, salted beef round, *tasajo*. Some piles are as dry as jerky and more salty; it must be soaked overnight before using. In the space between butchers are mesquite grills all fired up and ready to cook the meat you purchase. Look around at others and watch the process. First go back to the vegetable vendors and pick up a flat basket. Choose a bunch (about six) tiny white onions with green stems (similar to scallions) to grill, a few cilantro stems, a de agua chile (one is enough!), a tiny avocado with edible skin, and a lime. The vegetable vendor will point you to a *clayuda* seller for an enormous edible plate. Now, take it all to the butcher of your choice and ask for a small piece (about four inches square per person) of fresh beef. Put the meat on a hot grill along with the onions and chile. Yes, this is messy but so good, and so much fun. Rip off a big piece of *clayuda*, then smear on some avocado, add meat, onion, a bit of spicy chile, cilantro, and lime juice. Roll everything up and take a bite. Who brought napkins?

Mercado Democracia

Mercado Democracia (known by locals as Mercado Merced) is located between Calles Murguia and Morelos, and Casada de la República and Nicholás del Puerto. Hours: 6:30A.M. to 6P.M. every day, but Sunday is best, when the outdoor plaza is packed with vendors. A small neighborhood market, Democracia is about ten blocks east of the *zócalo*. It brims with traditional Oaxacan foods.

Fondas. Fonda Rosita is in the center patio just to the side of the Morelos entrance. The large, exceptionally clean fonda always has bouquets of gladiolas in green-glazed pots on the white tiled table. Fonda Rosita is one of the few spots in Mexico where you can try authentic, and impossibly hard-to-make, *chocolatatole*—*atole* with a huge chocolate top foam—a drink of connoisseurs. Buy a few of the small-sized rolls from Gloria Jiménez's bread table and eat them here, with *chocolatatole*. Or, for something a bit more substantial, the enchiladas and *chilaquiles* are first rate.

Bread. Ask around for **Gloria Jiménez** in the midst of the bread tables—she's next to the entranceway to the fondas (there are no signs here)—for regional *pan dulce* at its best: *pelonas* (round, with anise); *ojaldras* (oval shaped, topped with sugar); and *rejas* (pretzel shaped, sprinkled with sugar). All are made in the true traditional manner: Hard wheat flour with minimum yeast is kneaded into both large and small sizes, then baked in a wood-burning oven. These slightly sweet breads are dense and chewy, with the texture of a good Jewish deli bialy—not the bleached, white, tasteless, airy fluff found in most commercial Mexican bakeries. Get there early; by 9:30 A.M. most of Gloria's creations are cleaned out by people in the know.

Empanadas. **Antojitos La Güerita** is located near the market entrance on Nicholás del Puerto. Hours: 8 A.M. to 2 P.M. every day. Run, don't walk, to a Oaxacan eating experience you'll never forget. Olivia Castro has been at this same location for more than twenty years making fabulous *Empanadas* (page 256) at her stand-up-only counter.

Tamales. Morning tamales are made and sold by **Leticia Quevedo Noriega**. She's at her counter inside the building, directly across from the breads, Tuesday to Saturday, 7:30 A.M. to 10 A.M., and Sunday 7:30 A.M. to noon. Tamales are in the family—her mother had the concession for thirty years before Leticia. The lineup includes: *mole colorado* with chicken, wrapped in banana leaves; two sweet types—pineapple or raisins; *rajas* and chicken with tomato; black beans with either *hoja santa* or avocado leaves; and plain *masa* flavored with the herb, *chepil*.

Mercado Zonal IV Centenario

In the block bordered by Independencia and Morelos, just west of La Soledad church. Mercado Zonal IV Centenario has some of the best *bolillos* in town—women sell them on the market's upper level near the Morelos entrance. Juice bars are here, too, where orange is cool and sweet, or fresh and foamy carrot (juiced from peeled carrots) is sold "to go" in tied plastic bags with a straw. The interesting new market was built on a hill and it has levels going downward toward the Independencia entrance, where produce and abundant flower bouquets are sold. Fondas, built on terraces, are on the market's east side. Very clean **Comedor La Económica** (obviously a pride-of-ownership place) is a good spot for breakfast chocolate and *atole*, egg dishes, *chilaquiles*, or a plate of epazote-flavored black beans and rice.

✱ PLACES TO GO AND THINGS TO EAT ✱

Nieve. The picturesque plaza in front of Basílica de la Soledad is Morris's favorite spot in Oaxaca. You'll find seven or eight stands nestled under shade trees. These vendors are Oaxacan institutions—they've been around for longer than people can remember. **Neveria Malena** has excellent coconut, *cajeta*, pecan, pistachio, rose (made with tiny pink rose petals, *Rosa de Castilla*), *guanábana*, *tuna* (prickly pear cactus fruit), or lime. *Nieve* stands never have all the flavors their signs list. Ask first what's available so you won't be suicidal after having your heart set on a *guanábana-zapote* combo and they're all out, or it's the wrong season.

White wrought iron furniture adds a touch of elegance to the casual spot. On steamy days it's the coolest place in town, not only because of the excellent *nieves,* but also because the plaza seems to catch breezes found nowhere else. Weekends at sunset are magical when strings of lights are turned on overhead, floodlights illuminate the church, and the fountain splashes to sounds of wandering guitarists.

Chocolate mills. For some *moles*, like Emilia Cabrera's *Mole Negro* (page 238), chocolate is blended from cocoa beans, sugar, *canela*, and almonds at special mills to the cook's specific proportions. Warm chocolate is then packed into molds (*los moldes*, bought at a market) and dried into tablets. Chocolate lasts at least a year. House-blend chocolate tablets can also be purchased at mills throughout the city and market. The same chocolate is used for both *mole* and hot chocolate, not for eating.

Guelaguetza, is located at 20 de Noviembre, No. 605, tel. 6-35-13. Hours: 8:30 A.M. to 8 P.M., Sunday 9 A.M. to 2 P.M. María Teresa Núñez de Gómez (Terri) is the owner of the large shop, just south of Mayordomo, on 20 de Noviembre. Her chocolate is a bit more expensive because she uses a finer-quality bean. *Choco ponch* is a shop favorite. It's powdered, very finely ground cocoa, sugar, and vanilla. For a cool, foamy drink, put 2 tablespoons in a glass of cold milk, then whirl it in a blender. Terri likes to cook and she'll be glad to help with your questions.

Mayordomo. Make a right as you exit the back door of Mercado 20 de Noviembre. Just follow your nose and the familiar aroma of chocolate will lead you to the street front shop along Calle de Mina. There are two Mayordomo shops across from each other, on opposite corners (Oaxaca's best smelling spot), another is in the second-class bus station across from Mercado Central de Abastos, and yet another shop in Mercado Central de Abastos. Hours vary at Oaxaca's biggest chocolate mill locations. Dried tablets, ready to break apart for hot chocolate, are excellent travelers. Or you can buy cocoa beans, sugar, almonds, and *canela* right here, and they will grind your proportions for *Chocolate* (page 237), popular with fastidious cooks. The proportion of cocoa-to cinnamon-to-sugar-to-nuts makes one woman's chocolate another's candy bar. Toasted cacao beans are scooped from burlap bags and weighed by the kilo, then almonds and *canela* are weighed and added. Weighed sugar is placed under the spout so when the ingredients are milled the unctuous paste flows over the sugar. Lastly, the ingredients are milled again, this time with the sugar. Or add your own treats, such as fresh and dried fruit, peanuts, chiles, garlic, plantains, etc., for *mole* pastes extraordinaire.

La Soledad. Make a left as you exit the back door of Mercado 20 de Noviembre, and La Soledad is only a few yards away, on the left. This very old, very popular mill is open every day. Women line up with baskets and pots of home-assembled concoctions to be ground into pastes. A mother-and-daughter team carry in ingredients for *chintenstle*, a *mole* made with Oaxaca's beloved dried shrimp, shelled and toasted pumpkin seeds, avocado leaves, and pasilla de Oaxaca chiles. La Soledad sells chocolate tablets and its specialty, cocoa honey. That's right. Sold in convenient-to-carry jars, it's an excellent souvenir or gift.

Molinos Antequera is located on Porfirio Díaz just south of Calle Cosijopi and north of Calle Quetzalcoatl, across the street from Mercado Sánchez Pasqua (you'll see a huge tree in the plaza at the entrance). Open every day 4 A.M. to 4 P.M. Tiny Molinos Antequera opens before dawn to grind your corn for *nixtamal*, rice for *horchata*, beans, chiles, cacao, all dried grains, and mixtures for *moles*. A true neighborhood mill.

Bakery. Panificadora La Luna is located at Av. Independencia No. 1105, tel. 6-85-08. Hours: 6 A.M. to 10 P.M. every day. Just east of Juárez on Independencia, La Luna offers central Oaxaca's biggest assortment of sweet rolls and bread (try the round rolls with sesame seeds, *camposinas*). As with most large Mexican bakeries new items arrive hot from the ovens constantly.

Pan de Yema. At Francisco I, Madero No. 38, in the small pueblo of Nazareno Etla, just north of Oaxaca, the **López Porras family** has been baking country bread in their two wood-burning ovens for more than fifty years. Their holiday specialty, *pan de yema*, is sought out by people who know and love the best of traditional foods. What makes this egg bread special and unlike those found in markets, even in Oaxaca City, is the fact that it's completely natural and contains none of the artificial colors used just about everywhere else. The warm yellow color is from egg yolks, and the bread's texture is genuine, not treated with too much yeast, which artificially inflates the loaves into appearing larger and causes airiness. And their *pan de yema* is still made the original way, without salt. *Pan de yema* is similar to Jewish challah, or French brioche, and like those other classics, it's perfect for dunking—in this case into foamy hot chocolate.

Buñuelos. During holidays or fiestas an enchanting food tradition takes place outside the cathedral. *Buñuelos*, crisp white flour pastries not unlike fried flour tortillas, are splashed with sugar syrup in ceramic bowls. After eating the *buñuelo*, tradition says to make a wish and smash the bowl on the cathedral grounds. The line of people waiting to try leads one to think it works.

Mezcal. There are liquor shops all over town and others (with tasting rooms) are located on Highway 190 near Tlacolula and Mitla. The best mezcal is made in the state of Oaxaca from *Agave angustifolia* and it's most often made behind high walls in remote pueblos, by ancient methods. Maguey cactus hearts are roasted in rock-lined pits, then left to rest for five days to reach the desired sugar stage. They are then crushed under a huge stone wheel pulled by a horse or ox, to begin fermentation. Later this mash is distilled in clay or coppper stills—the condensation runs into glass jars and is later divided into bottles and sold. Quality brands are distilled again, in huge, stainless steel tanks.

One of the best is **Oro de Oaxaca**, with its bright yellow label and tiny bag of *gusanito*-flavored chile salt tied to the bottle's throat. **Pensamiento**, another good brand, has a salesroom located on Highway 190, on the left just before Tlacolula. They offer twenty different flavors. Hours: 9 A.M. to 6 P.M. every day. There is no guarantee of quality, but between Mercado Benito Juárez and the Mercado de Artisanías, on J.P. García there are shops selling all brands and styles of mezcal, many in hand-painted bottles, others are bottled in San Bartolo Coyotepec's black pottery.

Textiles. Arte Textil de Ocotlán is located at Acala No. 407-7, upstairs in the plaza across from Santo Domingo, tel. 4-42-00. It is open every day from 10 A.M. to 8 P.M. and carries handwoven, all-cotton tablecloths, placemats, and napkins from the nearby weaving village of Ocotlán, also known for its Friday market.

Aripo has two locations: García Vigil No. 809 and Cinco de Mayo No. 200. Both are open Monday to Saturday from 9 A.M. to 8 P.M., Sunday 9 A.M. to 1 P.M. These multiple-roomed craft stores offer excellent textile selections from the state of Oaxaca. Tablecloths and woven fabrics are sold by the meter for odd-sized tables. These are hand-loomed fabrics for all projects, as well as napkins and placemats—all in a good selection of colors and textures.

Yalalag is located at M. Alcala No. 104. Tel. and fax 6-21-08, and 6-98-57. Hours: 9 A.M. to 1:30 P.M., and 4:30 P.M. to 9 P.M., closed Sunday. This shop offers textiles from Oaxaca and around the country, including a good amount of Pátzcuaro's wonderful tablecloths and napkins.

Mexican cooking classes. Susana Trilling, Seasons of My Heart, can be reached at A.P. Postal No. 42, Sucursal 3, Oaxaca 68101, Mexico; or phone/fax: 951-6-52-80. Susana teaches Mexican cooking classes but also has a private, comfortable room she rents out to people who just *need* to stay a few days in the countryside, play around in a Mexican kitchen, and eat well (pages247 and 255).

RESTAURANTS

El Bice Pobre. Inexpensive. The popular restaurant has two locations: El Bice Pobre I in a less desirable spot at Triunfo de la

República No.103, and El Bice Pobre II, a short taxi ride from the *zócalo* at Calzada de la República No. 600 (close to Mercado de República). Hours 1 P.M. to 6 P.M. every day, both locations. At Bice Pobre II there are about a dozen tables plus a few more in a slightly quieter mezzanine area upstairs where business folks head at lunch. At about 3 P.M. a musical group made up of older gents strolls in and plays charming oldies. Encouragement with pesos works wonders. The best food bet here is what's known as the *botana surtida*, a platter of Oaxacan appetizers with twelve small items for each person, such as a *chile relleno* made with a stuffed Oaxacan pasilla chile, a corn husk tamale with black beans, a beef *empanizado*, a quesadilla, a guacamole taco, a piece of *carne frita*, and a slice of lean roast pork. In addition, El Bice Pobre has two soups and five specials every day.

La Olla. Inexpensive. Located at Reforma 402 behind and one-half block north of the Presidente Hotel. Breakfast and lunch daily. Emilia Cabrera's fonda has four cloth-covered tables in a spotlessly clean room right in front of her home—it's the true definition of the word fonda. Breakfasts are first-rate as are lunch tostadas piled with shredded chicken, lettuce, and tomato (yes, eat the raw veggies here, Emilia is a perfectionist about washing them in purified water for her family and customers). A bowl of very good smoky chile salsa on each table is for spooning over delicious clean tastes. Every day Emilia serves a *comida corrida* including clear soup, a small rice or noodle plate, and a meat entrée served with tortillas at rock-bottom prices.

El Topil. Inexpensive. Located at Plazuela La Bastida No. 104. tel: 4-16-17. Open every day from 9 A.M. to 11 P.M. Soledad Díaz Altamirano owns the charming spot on one of the nicest plazas in Oaxaca just to the side of the Santo Domingo church. The casually decorated and comfortable place specializes in regional dishes like *atole* for breakfast with sweet rolls, or a lunch *clayuda con asiento* (crisp tortilla smeared with fat bits that cling to the bottom of a *chicharrón* pot), topped with *quesillo* (Oaxacan string cheese)—a tasty munch to match with beer. Black beans are flavored with *hoja santa*; *chile relleno* is either a stuffed, spicy, fresh de agua chiles, or dried pasilla de Oaxaca chile. Many people think Soledad's *mole* is one of the best. A few nights a week two older gentlemen sing traditional songs and play guitar and violin—a perfect accompaniment to the classic dishes.

Flor de Oaxaca. Inexpensive. Located at Armenta y López No. 311, one block east of the *zócalo*. Tel 6-55-22. Hours: 7:30 A.M. to 10 P.M., every day. The clean, no-frills-decor restaurant has a full menu of traditional Oaxacan dishes. Service is superb—dinner waiters couldn't be more professional. On hot nights try to grab a table near a window and pray for a breeze. Lunch includes a filling, low-cost *comida corrida* popular with office workers from the government building a block away. Dinner can be something light, such as a banana-leaf-wrapped tamale—or *mole*, *amarillo*, *sopa caldosa* (soup with pasta), *tasajo* or *cecina* with enchiladas. Most dishes come with a salad, washed in purified water, on the entrée plate. The *aguas frescas* are extra good here—ask what flavors are available.

El Mesón. Inexpensive. Located at Hidalgo No. 805. Open every day breakfast to late dinner. Go for a quick lunch or late supper, but forget the all-you-can-eat breakfast buffet table, which is for kids on paupers' budgets who need a fill-up of inconsequential and cheaply made dishes. The best food here is definitely at the counter—a taco bar with sushi bar style. You receive a long list of taco (and *torta*) offerings. Check off what you want and how many. Your cook charcoal-grills lean meat, then deftly chops and mounds it on two soft tortillas before topping it with grilled onions. Huge-portion choices include *chuleta* (pork), *lomo enchilado* (pork with a chile marinade), *chorizo*, beef, and *alambre* (beef, onion, and pasilla de Oaxaca chile cooked shish-kebab-style before the cook removes the skewer and slides it all on tortillas—a fancier version includes melted cheese). Non-grilled choices come from slow-cooked stews (more typical of the area) simmered in *cazuelas*, in the back kitchen. Choices include pork with *mole verde*, diced potato and *chorizo*, *picadillo* with chipotle chile salsa, and chile strips with cheese. Ice cold beer goes down great with El Mesón's soft tacos—or try *El Suero* (page 268), a beer over ice cubes with lime. It can get mighty hot around the counter grills so don't go on a sweltering day, when not even iced beer can help.

Yu Ne Nisa. Moderate. Amapolas No.1425, Colonia Reforma, tel. 5-66-99. A short taxi ride north of the *zócalo*. Traditional dishes from the Isthmus of Tehuantepec. Unusual seafood dishes plus armadillo and iguana specialties for the adventurous.

Tlamanalli. Moderate. Located at Av. Juárez No. 39, Teotitlán del Valle (25 km southeast of Oaxaca along Rte.190), tel. 956-2-02-55 and 2-03-33, ext. 157. Open from 1 P.M. to 5 P.M. for late lunch only. Closed Monday. Five sisters run Tlamanalli (the Zapotec god of food): Abigail is the chef, Rosario the vivacious English-speaking hostess, and Marcelina, Rufina, and María Luisa keep this gem of a spot running smoothly. True, it's a schlep from the city of Oaxaca by taxi (at least $15 one-way cab fare) and its popularity has jaded the women somewhat, but the experience is wonderful and the food still first rate. Lunch after the hectic Sunday Tlacolula market is convenient because Teotitlán del Valle is a quick cab ride on the way back toward Oaxaca City. A fixed-price meal begins with a *mezcalito* (a tiny cup of mezcal with *gusano*-flavored chile salt). *Sopa zapoteca* is the restaurant's trademark squash blossom soup made with the herb *chepil.* Its accompaning quesadilla is a showstopper. Traditional, hand-ground sauces include *mole negro*, one of the best restaurant *moles* in Oaxaca. Less successful are sauces overly seasoned with the herb *hoja santa.* For dessert, *nieves* are the purest, most intensely flavorful tropical fruit sorbets you'll ever taste. Finding a taxi back to Oaxaca City after lunch can take an hour, so relax and browse the shops selling the pueblo's famous hand-loomed rugs.

SURROUNDING MARKET TOWNS

Oaxaca City's surrounding Indian market towns make the fascinating area what it is; a trip to at least one makes any visit to Oaxaca an even more memorable experience. You definitely get the feeling of being lost in time at these pre-Hispanic open-air markets. If you'd prefer to go with a guide and small tour group, check out the daily excursions arranged by the El Camino Real Hotel's travel desk. Ask for a printed day-by-day itinerary so you'll see how tours are focused on village market days.

Tlacolula Sunday is the best day to visit Tlacolula, located about half an hour east of Oaxaca City on Highway 190. Catch a city bus at the second-class station (across from Mercado Central de Abastos) or pick one up, every ten minutes or so, along the Periferico a few blocks east of Mercado de República, after visiting that market's Sunday market, where breakfast is great.

Tlacolula is the very best Indian market (Zapotec), and probably my favorite market in Mexico (that's saying a lot). Natives in exquisite dress with floral prints and head-wrapped *rebozos* spread blankets and baskets on the ground to display their produce. There are permanent market buildings, but Sunday's huge *tianguis* sprawls over acres; in fact, it spreads over most of the town. Buildings house bread stalls, meats and poultry, household products, fondas, *barbacoa* stalls, and, greatest of all, the specialty meat building with *tasajo* (beef) and *cecina* (pork) sliced very thinly, salted and aged. The airplane-hangar space is a surrealistic sight, with clouds of hazy smoke filling the air to create a dreamlike atmosphere, especially in late afternoon when smoke has had time to thicken. People buy meats from two dozen butchers and grill it right there, along with onions and chiles to eat on huge tortillas, called *clayudas*.

You'll see medicinal herbs; mounds of squash blossoms; huge wood spatulas for mixing tamale dough for a crowd; beautifully carved *molinillos* for hot chocolate; *ollas*, *cazuelas*, *comales* and other glazed (or unglazed) earthenware pottery; textiles; bolts of flowered plastic for tablecloths (near the medicinal herbs); *chapulines*, *gusanitos*, and ant eggs; *metates* with hand-painted sides and legs; even oxen yokes.

Pasilla de Oaxaca chile is a good buy here for the largest four-inch size. Bright red enameled, dried gourds, hand-painted with birds and flowers are extra nice. They are traditionally bought by women to serve their market drink, *texate*. Gourds carved with animals, painted or left natural, are superb, lightweight souvenirs. If you're not going to Teotitlán de Valle (Tlamanelli Restaurant, page 233) to roam the town's rug weaving shops (natural dyes are coming back), your best prices are here.

Zaachila Thursday is the best day to visit Zaachila, located about thirty minutes southwest of Oaxaca City by bus from the second-class bus station. Buses run about every twenty minutes. For the return trip to Oaxaca, grab a *colectivo* (shared taxi, 2 pesos) at the *zócalo*, or walk to the bus station near the animal market.

Zaachila is both Zapotec and Mixtec. Notice the women's dress and their subtle differences. The market is held on the *zócalo* and surrounding streets. Live turkeys being held by their tied feet is a typical market sight. *Comal*-roasted cocoa beans are sold for home-ground chocolate tablets, along with almonds, *canela*, and sugar. Charcoal-roasted peanuts turn everyone's fingers black, but they're worth it—they're delectable market snacks even though women buy most of them for *pipiáns* and *moles*. Candied sweet potatoes, from pale yellow to dark purple, are bought to eat on the spot, or to be carried home in plastic bags. Ten-foot sugarcane stalks are cut down to size with a machete, then cut up and peeled into refreshing walk-away chewies.

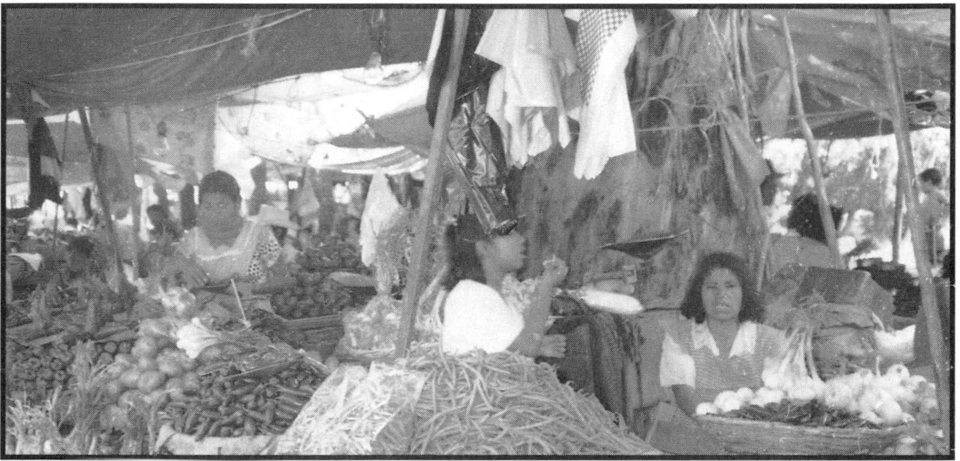

Zaachila's Zapotec and Mixtec market.

If you've got the time, a livestock market is also held on Thursday, but it's not near the *zócalo*; it's on the right just as you enter town.

Be extra careful with photography here. It's okay to take photos, just be sure to respect the personal space and beliefs of the people. If someone sees you pointing a camera in his direction and he turns his head, put down your camera immediately and shoot someone else.

Ocotlán The best day to visit Ocotlán is Friday, and it's located about 45 minutes south of Oaxaca City on Highway 175 by bus from the second-class bus station. A *colectivo* taxi back to Oaxaca is the best bet.

Like the other Indian markets, Ocotlán's goes back to pre-Hispanic days. The stunning domes of Ocotlán's church are the town's main focus. This pueblo's big sellers are reed baskets and hats. Hundreds of hats. Head over to the *portales* and if what you want isn't there, well, it doesn't exist in these parts. *Rebozos* (shawls) are big sellers, as are leather belts. Knives, machetes, and red pottery bowls are made in town and sold by various vendors. Small piles of teeny, lovely lavender beans and larger baby pinks are arranged on brown paper over hand-loomed cloth. Flowers are a big draw at this market—they're sold at stands and by roaming, giant marigold-wielding vendors, especially just before Day of the Dead celebrations.

On the road out to Ocotlán, a stop at Oaxaca's famous black pottery pueblo, **San Bartolo Coyotepec**, is a highlight. Signs to the alfarería (pottery) hacienda of **Doña Rosa** are along the roadway—it's the village's most commercial manufacturer but also the most open to travelers—it's located a few blocks off the highway at Benito Juárez No. 24. Hours: 8:30 A.M. to 6:30 P.M. Exceptionally well-made angel figures come from **Adelina Pedro** and fabulous skeletons from her brother, **Carlomagno**. It's a cinch to find the family's house, it's the first on your right as you enter town from Oaxaca. Anywhere in town when you see a large black pot outside a doorway it means you're invited in to view the artist's samples. Not all bowls and jars hold water, even if a piece is supposed to be a vase—but buy it anyway if you really like it, keeping in mind it may have to hold dried flowers. There's also a large **indoor pottery market** across from the church, on the west side of the highway, and it's open every day.

Santo Tomás Jalieza holds a Friday textile market just off the highway, so it's a natural stop on the way out to Ocotlán. The hand-loomed pieces include table runners, placemats, waist sashes, and purses.

Farther along the same road, and just outside Ocotlán, is the **Agular family's workshop** of often humorous, matte-painted, clay figures. The highly collectible pieces are, like San Bartolo Coyotepec's pottery, bargain priced here, at the source.

DAY OF THE DEAD

Oaxaca is the best place in Mexico for Day of the Dead celebrations. (People used to say Pátzcuaro, Michoacán, was the hot spot, but it's so overrun with tourists that the magic is memories.) Markets are at their most fabulous frenzied peak the week leading up to the famous celebration with mind-boggling flower displays (especially *cenpoalxuchitl*, a huge, long-stemmed marigold), mounds of specially decorated egg breads, and candy in the shapes of skulls and coffins. Skeletons made of wood, metal, or clay are brightly painted and ready to party. Private altars are set up in homes, usually made of palm leaves, sugarcane, candles, and photos of the deceased. Offerings of egg bread and other food and drink favorites of the dead are displayed. You'll also see altars around town in churches, hotels, shops, and restaurants.

October 31 is the night families pay their respects to dead relatives by offering the deceased's favorite food at his grave. People go out to cemeteries and decorate graves elaborately with sand paintings, giant marigolds, gladiolas, and four foot tall candles. To make the evening festive, families actually set up picnic tables and charcoal grills in the graveyard. You'll be offered something to eat, and certainly drink (a favorite this night is mezcal, so to be in the know, take a bottle with you to share). Cemeteries, like the two in the pueblo of **Xoxo**, are positively aglow in a surrealistic haze of smoke from thousands of candles and small bonfires. Day of the Dead is celebrated for two days, November 1 and November 2. All Soul's Day (November 2), is a continuation of the holiday spirit but quiet, with families staying at home and enjoying special foods.

Emilia Arroyo de Cabrera's

▲▼▲

Chocolate *Mexican Chocolate with* Canela *and Almonds*

A FASTIDIOUS COOK, EMILIA HAS HER OWN INGREDIENT PROPORTIONS for making Mexican chocolate (see Glossary), as does every good cook in Oaxaca. She no longer hand-grinds her own cocoa beans at home, but has everything ground for her at one of the chocolate mills near Mercado Juárez: Guelaguetza, Mayordomo, or La Soledad (page 229). Here's how you make your very own chocolate when you're in Oaxaca, thanks to Emilia.

Indigenous Oaxacans believe the "souls" or "spirits" of pre-Columbian *masa* and cocoa drinks live in the foam. To achieve the best bubbly foam when preparing Hot Mexican Chocolate (page 103), a traditional *molinillo* is used to hand-beat the liquid; electric mixers are almost unheard of. The lovely, hand-carved beaters are prized kitchen posessions and A-plus souvenirs.

This is not a recipe, but the process for making your own chocolate when you travel to Oaxaca.

Yield: about 5 pounds

- 2 pounds roasted cocoa beans (request 1 kilo)
- 1 ounce "canela" (soft Mexican cinnamon) (request 1 ounce)
- 3 ounces shelled almonds (request 3 ounces)
- 3 pounds sugar (request 1½ kilos)

1. Purchase everything at the mill counter (you'll be given a number and receipt).

2. Move over to the grinding area where you'll see your blend go into a mill.

3. Next, the ground mixture goes through again with sugar, and comes out as an unctious paste poured into a plastic bag.

4. When the chocolate cools, it will be a huge lump. Upon your arrival back home, peel the plastic away, put the chocolate in an ovenproof dish, to soften, in a very low (200°F) oven for about 20 minutes. You can then either pack it into round disks made especially for chocolate (*los moldes*, sold at Mercado Abastos, page 220), or spread it out on a cookie sheet. While the chocolate is still pliable, score lines in both directions into 2-inch squares (do not cut through). Let the chocolate air-dry for a day, then break it into pieces at your score marks. Store in a very dry, cool place, as you would all chocolate.

Emilia Arroyo de Cabrera's

Mole Negro *Oaxacan Black* Mole

STEPS TO GREAT *MOLE NEGRO*: 1. make (or buy) Mexican Chocolate (page 237); 2. make Chicken Broth (page 19); 3. make paste; 4. make sauce. You may elect to cut the paste recipe in half, which in itself is an enormous amount, enough for many huge dinners. Once the *mole* paste is made it keeps very well, unrefrigerated for weeks, refrigerated for a year, and frozen. Since the labor-intensive paste may be made far ahead and the broth a few days before, the final sauce really isn't much of a chore.

Emilia lives in Oaxaca, the dried chile capital of the world, and if you visit Oaxaca, her exacting requirements are a cinch to meet. Outside Oaxaca the chiles are hard to find. In the U.S. you can get excellent results by substituting ancho chiles for exotic chilhuacle chiles, and buy pasilla chiles (not pasilla de Oaxaca) and mulato from Latino stores, or mail-order sources. The flavor won't be absolutely identical to Emilia's, but you won't be disappointed.

Emilia's prepares *mole* feasts about four times a year for special occasions. She boils chickens or turkeys, covers the poultry with an abundance of sauce, then sprinkles toasted sesame seeds over everything. Emilia serves *mole negro* with Mexican Rice Pilaf (page 66) and tortillas. Something crunchy and fresh like a green salad, jícama slices with lime, or lightly steamed vegetables is a fine accompaniment to the exceptional dish.

Yield: about 10 pounds mole *paste, or the recipe may be cut in half*

For black "mole" paste

- 8 ounces chilhuacle chiles, or substitute ancho chiles
- 2 pounds mulato chiles
- 8 ounces pasilla chiles, a.k.a negro chile (dried chilaca chile, not Oaxacan, and not ancho chile)
- 1 cup plus 2 Tablespoons vegetable oil
- 3½ ounces shelled almonds, with or without skins, soaked in hot water for 5 minutes
- 8 ounces (1½ cups) raisins
- 9 ounces (2 cups) white sesame seeds
- 5 whole black peppercorns
- 4 whole cloves

1. Clean the dried chiles with a damp cloth, if dusty. Open the chiles flat by making a slit down one side of each. Remove and save the stems and seeds in a bowl.

2. Put 8 tablespoons of the oil in a large skillet and fry the chiles, pressing down with a metal spatula, adding more oil as needed, just until they change color and brown. Remove each from the oil immediately as it changes color using a slotted spoon. Put the chiles in a very large bowl.

3. Cook the chile seeds and stems with 3 tablespoons oil until the seeds turn black. Yes, open the window, turn on a fan, cover the smoke alarm, then burn the seeds and stems to black-black. (Charring is what makes *mole negro* black). Soak and rinse the stems and seeds carefully for at least 10 minutes. Put the seeds and stems in the bowl with the chiles. Discard the used oil.

4. Heat 3 tablespoons fresh oil and fry the almonds, raisins, sesame seeds, peppercorns, cloves, thyme, and oregano until the sesame seeds turn light brown. Put

- 1 Tablespoon dried thyme
- 1 Tablespoon dried Mexican oregano
- 1 large white onion, peeled, quartered, and toasted (page 16)
- 1 head garlic, cut into cloves and peeled, toasted

the skillet ingredients in the bowl with the chile mixture plus the toasted onion and garlic.

5. The ingredients are now ready to purée. In batches, add a few cups at a time to a blender or processor container. Pour in only enough water to facilitate puréeing. Purée to the finest texture possible. Transfer to another large bowl. Continue with the remaining ingredients. (Keep in mind the traditional method for grinding is with *metate* and *mano.*)

6. Heat 4 tablespoons fresh oil in a deep pot over medium heat and carefully (it sizzles!) pour the blended ingredients into the pot. Simmer the sauce for 1 hour, stirring. At this point there is no liquid remaining and the paste is as thick as peanut butter; if not, continue cooking and stirring. Remove the pot from the heat. The *mole* paste is now ready to cool then refrigerate, in containers.

For "mole" sauce

Yield: 12 servings

- 2 pounds tomatillos (about 12)
- 2 pounds green, unripe tomatoes
- 4 Tablespoons vegetable oil
- 2 pounds "mole" paste (4 cups)
- 3 quarts Chicken Broth (page 19)
- 9 ounces Mexican chocolate
- 3½ ounces sugar (½ cup)
- 3 cups fresh bread crumbs
- salt to taste
- 2 Tablespoons toasted sesame seeds for garnish

1. Bring 4 quarts water to a boil. Remove the tomatillo husks. Add the tomatillos and green tomatoes. Boil for 15 minutes, drain, and cool enough to handle. Remove and discard the skins from the green tomatoes only (tomatillos are never peeled) and put everything in a blender.

2. Heat the 4 tablespoons vegetable oil in a deep pot and carefully (it splatters!) add the tomatillo purée from the blender. Add the *mole* paste to the pot and stir, adding the chicken broth slowly. Add the chocolate, sugar, bread crumbs, and salt.

3. Continue simmering and stirring for 30 minutes. Generously pour the sauce over cooked poultry and sprinkle with toasted sesame seeds.

Note: Almost as famous as *mole negro* in Oaxaca are the state's banana-leaf-wrapped tamales. They are made the same way as *Vaporcitos* (page 313), except the sauce is different. Replace Adda's pork-chicken sauce with Emilia's black *mole* and shredded chicken. Oaxacans like to mix a few tablespoons of the oily top part of *mole* paste into the *masa.* They also pat out *masa* on the leaf rather than making a tortilla before adding the sauce and wrapping, as in Mérida.

Victoria Mateo's

Mole Coloradito de Pollo *Red* Mole *with Chicken*

RED *MOLE* IS ONE OF THE "SEVEN FAMOUS *MOLES* OF OAXACA": *Colorado*, or *Rojo*; *Negro*; *Coloradito*; *Verde*; *Chichilo*; *Almendra*; and *Amarillo* (see Glossary). Scholars claim there are hundreds of *moles* in Oaxaca alone, but these are the basic seven from which all derivatives sprang. Señora Mateo's family prefers *mole coloradito* over *negro*, the *mole* most often associated with Oaxaca, because *coloradito's* flavor is less intense, especially for children.

Mole coloradito has a typically long ingredients list, but don't let the length scare you. Most items are already in your pantry and the others are all within easy reach. Ancho and guajillo chiles are two of the easiest dried chiles to find throughout the U.S.

Señora Mateo makes a thickened sauce to serve with classic Mexican boiled chicken. In her family the chicken really isn't the main part of the meal—the sauce is. Nuts and seeds make the protein-rich *mole* a main event to be scooped up with hot, homemade tortillas. A small piece of chicken is but an additional enchantment.

Yield: 8 servings

For "mole" paste

- 10 ancho chiles
- 5 guajillo chiles
- 10 garlic cloves, unpeeled
- 1 medium white onion, peeled
- ¼ cup white sesame seeds
- 1 Tablespoon whole black peppercorns
- 1 three-inch "canela" stick, or 1 two-inch cinnamon stick
- 4 whole cloves
- ¼ cup fresh Mexican oregano leaves, or 1 rounded Tablespoon dried
- ¼ cup fresh thyme leaves, or 1 rounded Tablespoon dried
- ¼ cup almonds, shells and skins removed
- ¼ cup peanuts, shells and skins removed
- ¼ cup raisins
- 2 large tomatoes

1. Clean the chiles with a damp cloth, if needed. Slit them with a small, sharp knife and remove the stems and seeds. Reserve the seeds. Open and flatten the chiles.

2. Toast (page 16) the chiles on both sides to brown and release their flavors, but do not let them burn. Burnt chiles are bitter and unusable. Use a long-handled metal spatula to flatten and turn them. Put the chiles in a bowl, cover with hot water, and soak for 30 minutes to soften.

3. Toast the garlic cloves with their skins. When their color changes, remove from the heat and set aside. Cool enough to handle, remove the skins, and put the garlic in a large bowl. Toast the peeled and coarsely chopped onion to brown. Put it in the bowl. Drain the liquid off the chiles. Put them in the bowl with the onion.

4. Toast 2 tablespoons sesame seeds and set aside. Toast the remaining sesame seeds with the reserved chile seeds until they are light brown, then add to the bowl. Toast the peppercorns, *canela*, cloves, oregano, and thyme being careful not to burn them. Just cook lightly until their perfumes are released, then add to the bowl. Toast the almonds, peanuts, and raisins and add to the bowl. Mix the ingredients.

Chicken Broth (page 19), made with chicken or turkey, as needed, or water
3 Tablespoons vegetable oil
1 three-ounce Mexican, preferably Oaxacan, chocolate tablet. No substitutions, but this can easily be found in Latino markets
sugar and salt to taste
Optional broth, or water and "masa," a tortilla, or a slice of toasted bread to thicken the sauce, if needed

5. Toast the tomatoes, then put them in a plastic bag to "sweat" for a few minutes. Peel, then put them in a blender container. Add a few cups of the chile mixture and blend. Transfer to another bowl.

6. Put another 2 cups of the chile mixture in the blender with about ¼ cup broth. Blend everything to a paste, scraping the sides from time to time and blending again until smooth, adding more liquid if needed. Pour in the bowl with the tomato mixture. Continue with the remaining mixture blending with additional broth.

7. Heat the oil in a large deep pot. Carefully pour the sauce in the pot (it splatters!) stir, and lower the heat to a simmer. Break the Mexican chocolate tablet into small pieces and add it to the pot. Cover and cook, stirring often with a wooden spoon, for 1 hour. Add salt and sugar. Cook 15 minutes more. Add optional broth if the sauce is too thick. If the sauce is too thin, put ¼ cup of it in the blender with the *masa*, a shredded tortilla, or a shredded slice of toast, and blend. Add the blender ingredients to the pot and continue cooking until thickened to a paste. The paste may be kept unrefrigerated for weeks, refrigerated for a year, or frozen.

For "mole" sauce

2 tomatoes
2 cups "mole" paste
about 2 quarts Chicken Broth (page 19) or water as needed
2 Tablespoons sesame seeds, toasted, for garnish

1. To change the paste to a sauce, blanch the tomatoes in boiling water for 1 minute and remove the skins. Put in a blender and purée. Put through a strainer and mix into the paste.

2. Add chicken broth to thin the paste to the consistency of heavy cream. Continue simmering and stirring for 30 minutes. Generously pour the sauce over cooked poultry and sprinkle with toasted sesame seeds.

Ana Marina (Anita) Silva Bohorquez's

Mole Amarillo con Chochoyones

Yellow Mole *with* Masa *Dumplings*

ANITA SAYS THIS RECIPE CAN BE MADE WITH CHICKEN, TURKEY, PORK, OR BEEF—all are traditional and all are delicious. *Mole amarillo* (yellow *mole)* is a classic *mole* of Oaxaca and is prepared by good cooks throughout the state. Some (like Anita) prefer a thick, gravylike texture, while others like to serve *amarillo* as soup, in deep bowls. The dish is made with chilcosle and chilhuacle chiles in Oaxaca, so look for the special chiles when you're in the markets there.

Anita serves *mole amarillo* in shallow bowls and adds a few *chochoyones* to each bowl, then sprinkles on chopped cilantro. For her family's authentic Oaxacan condiment with this dish, slice an onion and put it in a small bowl with lime juice and sprinkle with salt. Pass at the table to stir into the stew. A dish of Vinegared Chile Strips and Carrots (page 245) makes this a complete meal served with tortillas and a pitcher of *Agua de Limón* (page 267).

Yield: 6 servings

For the meat

- 1 large chicken, about 5 pounds; ½ small turkey; 3 pounds pork leg or boneless loin; or 3 pounds beef rump or boneless chuck
- 1 head garlic, broken apart but not peeled
- 1 medium white onion, halved
- 1 teaspoon salt

1. If using chicken or turkey, cut it into pieces, removing the skin or not as you prefer. Bring a pot of water to a boil with the garlic, onion, and salt. Add the poultry and simmer 45 minutes.

2. If using pork or beef, cut the meat into 1-inch cubes before boiling for 40 minutes. Skim the broth and reserve.

For the vegetables

- 8 medium-sized red potatoes, cut into eighths
- ½ teaspoon salt
- 1 pound green beans, cut into 1-inch pieces

Cook the potatoes in 2 quarts boiling salted water for 5 minutes, add the beans, and cook for 5 minutes more. Drain.

For the sauce

- 2 cloves
- 4 black peppercorns
- ¼ teaspoon cumin seed
- 4 garlic cloves, peeled
- 5 tomatillos, husked and quartered
- 2 Tablespoons vegetable oil
- 4 each chilcosle and chilhuacle chiles (in Oaxaca), or 8 guajillo chiles and 8 de árbol chiles, stemmed, seeded and soaked for 1 hour

1. Put the sauce ingredients (except the oil) in a blender container and purée until smooth.
2. Heat the oil in a deep pot and carefully add the blender mixture (it splatters!) and cook for 5 minutes over medium heat.

For the liquid

- ½ cup (plus 1 cup for the dumplings) fresh "masa," or "masa harina" per package directions
- 10 sprigs cilantro, tied in a bunch with string

1. Put the meat and sauce in a large pot with the reserved broth and water to measure 2 quarts. Bring everything to a boil, then turn down the heat to a simmer.
2. Put 2 cups warm water in a bowl. Add the ½ cup *masa* and stir to dissolve. Add the bowl of *masa* water to the large pot. The *masa* will thicken the broth as it simmers. Add the cilantro and continue simmering, uncovered, for 30 minutes longer. Add the cooked vegetables.

For the "chochoyones"

- the 1 cup "masa"
- 2 Tablespoons vegetable oil
- ¼ teaspoon salt
- a pot of simmering water to cook the dumplings
- 3 Tablespoons chopped cilantro

1. Mix the *masa* with vegetable oil and salt. Break off a small piece, the size, as Anita says, of a robin's egg. Make a deep indentation with your finger into each piece and drop it into the pot of simmering water. Simmer 10 minutes, until cooked, then drain.
2. Ladle into bowls some liquid, meat, vegetables, and *chochoyones*. Garnish with a sprinkle of cilantro.

For optional condiment

- 1 medium white onion, sliced and broken onto rings
- 4 limes, juiced
- ¼ teaspoon salt

Mix all the ingredients in a small bowl and let it rest for at least an hour for the flavors to mingle.

Martina Guadalupe Martínez de Pérez's

Salsa de Tomatillo *Uncooked Tomatillo Sauce with* Gusanos *(or Not!)*

THIS TABLE SALSA GETS ITS TANG FROM TOMATILLOS and its unique flavor from *gusanos de maguey*, tiny grubs found in maguey plants from which mezcal is derived (it's the same worm found in some mezcal bottles). This may sound crazy but don't get turned off. "It's the secret ingredient," chides Martina, who sells the dried delicacy at a cheese booth, in Mercado de Abastos. Other Indian women sell live, fat, and frisky grubs from cloth-lined baskets during and right after the summer rainy season—truly an aquired taste. When you roam market stalls, look in cheese booths for dried "necklaces" of ready-to-wear *gusanitos*. Tiny *gusanos*, these crunchy grubs are sold pre-strung. If you're not looking for an entire choker, individual worms are very carefully removed from their strings, one by one, and sold by the one hundred pieces. The dried grubs have a subtle taste apart from their chile and salt coatings.

Naturally, you may make Tomatillo Salsa without *gusanos*. Though made with tomatillos, the sauce is not green, but beautiful brick red thanks to the chiles. The fresh citrus taste is a perfect foil for fried fish and seafood. It's addictive—you'll soon be spooning it onto chicken, steaks, cheese quesadillas, and just about anything but corn flakes.

Yield: about 3 cups

- 2 pounds fresh tomatillos (use canned only as a last resort)
- 3 dried pasilla de Oaxaca chiles (found only in Oaxaca), or 2 ancho chiles and 2 chipotle chiles, or chipotles en adobo
- 4 garlic cloves, peeled
- 12 "gusanitos de maguey," crumbled (omit if desired but substitute ½ teaspoon salt)
- ¼ cup chopped cilantro

1. Remove the outer papery husks from the tomatillos. Drop the tomatillos into a large pot of salted, boiling water and cook for 4 minutes. Remove from the water with a slotted spoon and transfer to a blender container.

2. Clean and dry the chiles. Cut off the chile stems and any hard area around the stems. Slit the chiles lengthwise and remove all the seeds. Open the chiles out flat and toast (page 16), pressing with a metal spatula, until they darken and release aromas. At the same time toast the garlic. Transfer the chiles and garlic to the blender with the tomatillos.

3. Crush the *gusanitos de maguey* (a good rule of thumb is 4 per cup of tomatillos) and add to the blender ingredients. Purée until almost smooth, keeping a bit of texture. Pour into a serving bowl and top with cilantro. Serve at room temperature.

Note: Dried *gusanos* may be brought back to the U.S.

Concepción (Conchita) Arroyo de Valencia's

Rajas con Zanahorias en Escabeche

Vinegared Chile Strips and Carrots

CONCHITA TAUGHT SCHOOL FOR THIRTY YEARS and is now retired. She enjoys cooking, weaving, sewing, and gardening, but notice that cooking is first on her list—and she excels at it. Her mother, Ofelia Cabrera Vda. Arroyo, taught her to cook the traditional dishes of Oaxaca with her other sisters, also excellent cooks. "This *escabeche* must be spicy—use hot chiles!" stresses Conchita, and rightly so. The condiment is used in the same way that table salsas or chutneys in India are used—to enliven simply cooked dishes.

Yield: 12 servings (the recipe can be cut in half)

- 2 pounds large carrots
- 4 de agua chiles in Oaxaca, or jalapeño chiles
- 1 teaspoon salt for the cooking water
- 2 medium white onions
- 2 Tablespoons vegetable oil
- 6 garlic cloves, smashed
- 1 teaspoon dried thyme
- 2 bay leaves
- 1 cup Pineapple-Apple Vinegar (page 173), or ⅔ cup cider vinegar and ⅓ cup water
- ½ teaspoon salt

1. At least three days in advance, peel and slice the carrots into ⅛-inch thick rounds.

2. Wash the chiles, stem, slice lengthwise in half and remove the seeds. Slice into ¼-inch vertical strips.

3. Bring 4 quarts of water to a boil in a large pot with 1 teaspoon salt. Add the carrots and chiles and cook 4 minutes until barely cooked and still crunchy. The carrots cannot be soft. Drain in a colander and run cold water over the carrots and chiles to stop the cooking process.

4. Slice the onions vertically about ¼ inch thick.

5. Heat the vegetable oil in a large skillet over medium heat and add the sliced onions and smashed whole garlic cloves and sauté until transparent. Add the carrots and chiles to the onions and garlic. Add the thyme and bay leaves. Add the vinegar (or vinegar and water) and salt. Bring everything to a boil, then immediately turn off the heat and cool. Marinate, covered, for at least 3 days at room temperature before serving.

Julia Manzano de Vega's

Papas en Escabeche *Potatoes in Chile Confetti Vinaigrette*

SERVED IN OVAL, TERRACOTTA-GLAZED BOWLS AT ROOM TEMPERATURE, these spicy, tiny potatoes are popular hors d'oeuvres at Julia's house. Her husband, Alberto, is a pork butcher so she also serves them as a side dish when she makes roast pork. The light, vinegary *escabeche* is a perfect foil for the meat's richness. Julia prefers to marinate the potatoes for one week in mild pineapple vinegar, but she says water-diluted apple cider vinegar is fine. The potatoes are addictive so keep a pitcher of *Licuado de Leche* (page 138) nearby to cool the chile's heat. *Licuados* are drinks made with milk and fresh fruit all blended to frothy, foamy perfection—a foil for fire that shoots from the colorful chile-carrot confetti. (This *escabeche* should be spicy, so be generous with the jalapeño chiles.)

When she doesn't have a jar-full at home, Julia chooses from among a dozen or so *escabeche* favorites from the cart that's usually parked on the corner of Alcalá and Matamoros in Oaxaca City. You'll first see a striped umbrella, then huge glass jars filled with vinegared fruits and vegetables.

Yield: 12 servings

- 3 pounds tiny (1 inch or less) red or white potatoes, peeled and left whole, or cut larger red potatoes into 1-inch rounds
- 6 green jalapeño chiles
- 6 red jalapeño chiles
- ½ pound carrots
- 2 large onions, cut vertically into thick slices
- 1 garlic head, cloves peeled and finely chopped
- 2 cups Pineapple Vinegar (page 173) or apple cider vinegar diluted with 1 cup water
- 1 teaspoon salt
- 6 fresh thyme sprigs, or 2 Tablespoons dried
- 6 bay leaves
- 1 or 2 additional chiles (optional, upon serving)

1. Prepare this recipe one week before serving. The potatoes need the full time to marinate, refrigerated. Bring 6 quarts of water to a boil and boil the potatoes for 15 minutes. They should be cooked but still firm. Drain and set the pot of potatoes aside, covered to keep them warm, while you prepare the vinegar mixture.

2. Stem, and slice the chiles into vertical strips, then dice them into ⅛-inch pieces. Add to the potatoes.

3. Peel and dice the carrots into ⅛-inch pieces. Seed if desired to cut the heat. Add to the potatoes. Add the onions to the potatoes.

4. Combine the garlic, vinegar (or vinegar and water), salt, thyme, and bay leaves in a medium bowl and mix well. Pour the vinegar mixture over the still-warm potatoes and marinate for 1 week in the refrigerator. Taste. If you'd like the *escabeche* to be spicier, add another 1 or 2 diced fresh chiles upon serving.

Susana Trilling's

Sopa de Ajo *Glorious Garlic Soup with Squash Blossoms*

SUSANA'S FROM THE U.S AND NOW LIVES ON THE OUTSKIRTS OF OAXACA CITY with her husband, kids, and dogs. Their farm is as perfect as possible, with its rolling hills and Monte Albán looming in the distance. A quick backroad drive away is Etla's charming Wednesday market. Susana likes to go early and stay for lunch at her favorite market fonda, Conchita, for *chiles rellenos* or *mole negro*. Etla is famous for production of *quesillo de Oaxaca*, string cheese wound in a ball. Here you can buy it straight off the dairymen's tables. Susana's background includes owning a Cajun restaurant in Manhattan, once popular with Paul Prudhomme and his entourage whenever they were in town. She's now giving cooking classes at her home and concentrates on Mexican foods with international touches (see page 231).

Garlic soup is one of Mexico's favorites and its long simmering transforms pungent garlic into the sweetest, most captivating taste. Susana gilds the lily by adding squash blossoms and *hoja santa* from her tree outside the kitchen door.

Yield: 6 servings

For the soup

- 2 garlic heads, cloves peeled and thinly sliced
- 1½ Tablespoons butter
- 1½ Tablespoons vegetable or olive oil
- 1 large "hoja santa" leaf, cut into strips (or dried and crumbled), or 5 crushed fennel seeds
- 25 squash blossoms, if available
- 8 cups Chicken Broth (page 19)
- 1 de árbol chile
- 3 bay leaves
- ⅛ teaspoon ground cumin
- ½ cup chopped parsley
- salt and freshly ground pepper
- Optional: 6 eggs
- 30 small slices toasted French bread (baguette-size)
- 30 half-inch cubes "quesillo de Oaxaca" or mozzarella
- ½ cup grated Parmesan cheese

1. In a large soup pot, sauté the garlic slices slowly in butter and oil for 10 to 15 minutes, until golden. Add the *hoja santa* leaf (if available), or fennel seeds and sauté 1 minute longer. Add the squash blossoms (if available) and sauté 1 minute more.

2. Pour in the chicken broth, chile, bay leaves, and cumin and simmer for 30 minutes. Add the parsley and salt and pepper to taste.

3. For the optional eggs: Crack each open and carefully drop into the simmering liquid. Poach until they are done to your liking.

4. In each of six wide, flat bowls, put 5 slices toasted bread and 5 cubes of cheese.

5. Ladle soup over the bread. Add 1 poached egg per bowl, if you are including them. Sprinkle with Parmesan cheese and serve.

Matilde Cristina Rodríguez de García and Micaela Bolaños's

Arroz Verde *Green Rice with Herbs*

GREEN RICE IS USUALLY RESERVED FOR HOLIDAYS AND SPECIAL OCCASIONS in homes, but fondas prepare it when the cook makes a dish she thinks works better with it than the more usual standbys of Mexican Rice Pilaf (page 66) or Red Rice (page 114). Matilde and Micaela have been preparing green rice every Monday at Oaxaca's Super Torta Fiesta for as long as they can remember to serve with their Monday special, Incredibly Tender Tongue in Caper Sauce (page 265). Fresh herbs and spinach turn the rice green and add great flavor to the end product, which is moister than most rice dishes.

Yield: 6 servings

- ¼ cup plus 2½ cups hot Chicken Broth (page 19)
- 2 garlic cloves, peeled
- 1 small white onion, coarsely chopped
- ¼ cup flat-leaf parsley leaves
- ¼ cup cilantro leaves
- 6 large spinach leaves, stems removed
- 1½ Tablespoons vegetable oil
- 1 cup white rice

1. Put ¼ cup broth, garlic, onion, parsley, cilantro, and spinach in a blender container and purée.

2. Heat the oil in a medium-sized pot. Add the rice and cook, stirring, for about 3 minutes over medium heat, until the rice turns opaque but does not brown. Add the blender contents to the pot, stirring.

3. Pour in the hot broth, stir once, and cover the pot. Lower the heat and simmer, covered, for 25 minutes for the rice to absorb the liquid. The rice will be, and should remain, moist.

Matilde Cristina Rodríguez de García and Micaela Bolaños.

Concepción (Conchita) Arroyo de Valencia's

Rajas de Chile Poblano y Ejotes con Huevos

Chile Strips and Green Beans with Scrambled Eggs

THE DAY CONCHITA GAVE ME THIS RECIPE WE WERE SITTING IN THE KITCHEN at her mother's Oaxacan house while her elderly mother was barking orders to the cook, jumping up to stir a pot now and then, peeling vegetables, sniffing herbs, and at the same time reciting from memory ingredients for a dish different from the one she was cooking. Children, grandchildren and their friends, plus assorted others were coming and going—passing through the kitchen as if it were Grand Central Station—and no one flinched. Before long we had a group sitting around the table suggesting favorite recipes. Good food and good times are what family meals are all about no matter where you live in Mexico.

Thick, meaty, fresh (not canned) poblano chiles are the key to this mild filling for tacos. Oaxaqueños often use spicy de agua chiles. Green beans are used by everyone in Oaxaca, but this recipe is made with cactus leaves as well, especially up north, in the central states and in Jalisco. Chile strips and green beans with scrambled eggs are delicious spooned onto tortillas for soft tacos. Squirt with fresh lime juice before biting.

Yield: 4 servings

- ½ pound green beans
- 2 garlic cloves, chopped
- ½ teaspoon salt
- 4 fresh, plump poblano chiles (or de agua chiles in Oaxaca)
- 2 Tablespoons vegetable oil
- 1 large onion, sliced vertically into ¼-inch thick slices
- 1 large "epazote" sprig
- 4 eggs
- ½ cup ranchero cheese, dry cottage cheese, or farmer cheese, crumbled
- fresh limes, quartered
- tortillas

1. Clean and string the beans, then cut them into ½-inch pieces. In a small pot, bring 2 cups of water to a boil and add the green beans and garlic with ½ teaspoon salt. Boil, covered, for 5 minutes. Drain and run cold water over the beans to stop the cooking process.

2. Char the chiles on an open flame, turning often until blistered and blackened. Put the chiles in a plastic bag for a few minutes to "sweat" and loosen their skins. Peel. Remove the stem and seeds from the chiles. Slice lengthwise into ¼-inch strips. The strips should be about 2 inches long.

3. Heat 2 tablespoons vegetable oil in a large skillet. Sauté the onion slices until they are transparent. Add the chiles and green beans. Add the *epazote*. Cook about 3 minutes, stirring, until the onion is lightly brown. Remove the *epazote*.

4. Whisk the eggs in a bowl, then add to the skillet. Add the cheese. Stir with a wooden spoon until the eggs are cooked to your liking. Serve with fresh lime quarters and warm tortillas.

Antonia Medina's

▲▼▲

Frijoles Parrados *Soupy Black Beans with Onion and Herbs*

WHAT MAKES OAXACAN BEANS DIFFERENT FROM MORE NORTHERN BEAN DISHES is an uncompromising use of black beans, the local food staple. The use of any other bean is almost considered a special occasion. Typically, the assertive taste of *epazote*, or more subtle anise-like avocado leaves, add the special Oaxacan stamp. Oaxacan black beans are always soupy—never let the liquid boil away. If more liquid is needed, add simmering water to the pot. They're impossible to serve on plates so Antonia passes around small bowls as side dishes. When you travel to Oaxaca, look in markets for the herb *yerba de conejo* (rabbit herb). Antonia says it's a popular, ancient, local flavoring for beans and not often seen in restaurants. She makes her black beans with any of three flavorings: *epazote*, avocado leaves, or rabbit herb, depending on what's fresh, and removes the sprigs before serving.

For regional variations: Yucatán's black beans are either passed through a sieve or blended then added to sautéed onion, a two-inch square of green bell pepper, and habanero chile. Sour lime juice and *epazote* are prerequisites for authenticity, but cilantro is a good substitution. Veracruz's black beans are "refried" like Jalisco's *Frijoles Refritos* (page 47) by mashing the cooked beans into hot fat but flavoring them with jalapeño chile.

Yield: 8 servings

1 pound black beans (about 2 cups dry)
6 cups water (ratio of beans to liquid is 1 to 3 here, but many Oaxaqueños cook beans 1 to 4)
2 "epazote" sprigs (2 Tablespoons dried), 8 avocado leaves, or a small bunch "yerba de conejo" (rabbit herb)
1 medium white onion, peeled and cut in half
juice of 2 key limes, or 1 large
salt

1. Pick over the beans, discarding any pebbles (this step is especially important in Mexico, where beans aren't as clean as in the U.S.), and rinse in a strainer.

2. Put the beans in a medium pot, add water, and bring to a boil. Reduce the heat and simmer, covered, for 1 to 2 hours. Add the herbs and onion 10 minutes before the beans are finished. The beans are done when their skins break easily when stirred. Time depends on the size and age of the beans. Tiny, fresh beans take less than an hour; old beans, say 2 years old, may take well over 2 hours to cook, especially if they are large.

3. Squeeze fresh lime juice over the beans and stir. Add salt just before serving to prevent the beans from toughening.

Note: See page 47.

Soledad López de Wittrock's

Pasta de Frijoles *Black Bean Paste with Avocado Leaves and Burnt Onion Oil*

THE UNUSUAL FLAVOR OF BLACKENED ONION OIL AND AVOCADO LEAVES make these beans a gourmet experience. If you live in the South and have an avocado tree you're in luck. Otherwise, ask a friend to mail some leaves; call around to Mexican markets, especially those selling black beans; or mail-order.

Soledad prefers *pasta de frijoles* with its classic mate, avocado-flavored goat *barbacoa*. She serves the beans family-style, formed into a mound on a plate, or in a wide bowl, and sprinkled with cheese as favored in her village of Matatlán, just south of Mitla.

The beans make a surprisingly special spread to serve with drinks, stuck all over with corn chips, for scooping, and Tomatillo Salsa (page 244).

Yield: 10 servings

- 10 avocado leaves, fresh or dried
- 3 de árbol chiles, stemmed and seeded
- 1 recipe "Frijoles Parrados" (page 250) without the lime juice, and 5 to 10 minutes before the beans are finished, adding 10 peeled, whole garlic cloves
- 2 Tablespoons vegetable oil
- 1 medium white onion, sliced

1. Clean then toast (page 16) the avocado leaves just as you would dried chiles, and put them in a blender container. Toast the chiles. Put them in the blender with the leaves and blend with a few tablespoons water. In batches, add the beans and purée with as little water as possible. Remove to a large bowl.

2. Heat the oil in a deep pot (nonstick if possible) and add the onion. Open a kitchen window, turn on your exhaust fan, and cook the onion until it burns. Yes, until it is black. Kill it. Remove the onion with a slotted spoon and discard. Save the oil.

3. Carefully add the bean purée to the onion oil (it splatters!). Reduce the heat and simmer, uncovered, for about an hour to form a thick paste. Stir often so the beans don't stick to the pot.

María Eugenia Arroyo's

Enchiladas Oaxaqueños *Tortillas Dipped in Enchilada Sauce and Folded*

MARÍA EUGENIA ARROYO OWNS **FONDA LAURITA NO.** 173, in Oaxaca's Mercado 20 de Noviembre food stall building, just across Aldama from Mercado Benito Juárez. She has lots of training and experience as a fonda owner and cook: Her mother had the spot before her for thirty years, and María has been here for more than ten. One late afternoon María taught me the ropes of Oaxaca's fonda politics. City market administrators permit fonda owners to prepare and sell only those items okayed by officials, and only during specified hours. These items, and these items only, are listed on signs at each fonda, which is why you'll never see every counter selling exactly the same items. Most fondas have been in the same locations throughout the city's numerous markets for more than fifty years, so any possibility of change is zero. To make sure the rules are followed, city inspectors check fondas weekly for sanitary conditions and food items sold. Heaven forbid María should ever decide to sell *menudo* (tripe soup)—which is the specialty of her neighbor's fonda. And, by the way, if you ever have a hangover (*muchas* margaritas make this easy) *menudo* is northern Mexico's classic morning-after "hangover helper" (as is a big bowl of chicken or beef soup here, in the South).

María makes Oaxacan-style enchiladas, sauced and folded, rather than filled and rolled as we're familiar with in the U.S., for her breakfast and lunch fans. Served by themselves, or as a side dish with grilled *Tasajo* (page 262)—the difference is your appetite and pocketbook. *Yield: 6 servings, 2 tortillas per person*

For the sauce

- 10 dried pasilla de Oaxaca chiles, or 5 ancho chiles and 5 chipotle chiles, stems and seeds removed
- 5 almonds, shelled
- 1 rounded Tablespoon raisins
- 5 black peppercorns
- 2 thyme sprigs, or 1 teaspoon dried
- 2 oregano sprigs, or 1 teaspoon dried
- 1 bay leaf
- 1 Tablespoon sesame seeds
- 4 Tablespoons vegetable oil
- 4 cups Chicken Broth (page 19)
- ¼ cup chopped flat-leaf parsley leaves

1. Soak the chiles in hot water for 1 hour until soft. Put the chiles in a blender container with ¼ cup water. Add the almonds, raisins, peppercorns, herbs, and sesame seeds. Purée.

2. Heat the oil in a deep pot and carefully pour the contents of the blender through a strainer into the oil (it splatters!). Press down on the sauce left in the strainer with a wooden spoon to get most of the sauce into the pot. Simmer the sauce for about 10 minutes until it changes color and becomes darker.

3. Add the chicken broth. Continue simmering, uncovered, stirring from time to time, for 30 minutes. Sprinkle with parsley.

Finishing the enchiladas

- ¼ cup lard or vegetable oil
- 12 thin corn tortillas ("blanditas" in Oaxaca)
- 16 white onion slices
- ½ cup ranchero cheese, dry cottage cheese, or farmer cheese, crumbled
- ¼ cup chopped flat-leaf parsley leaves

1. Heat the lard or oil in a large skillet. Put the tortillas in the hot oil for 10 to 20 seconds on each side so the tortilla is still pliable and not at all crunchy.

2. Holding it by upper edges, dip each tortilla in the enchilada sauce. Put it on a plate and fold in half, then in half again to make a triangle. Repeat with another tortilla on the same plate (each serving gets 2 tortillas).

3. Spoon additional sauce over the tortillas, cover with 4 raw onion slices, and sprinkle each with cheese and parsley. Repeat with the other 5 servings. Serve at once before the tortillas become mushy.

Fonda Rosita's

Enmoladas *Tortillas Dipped in* Mole *and Folded*

ENMOLADAS, ONE OF THE MOST POPULAR FONDA DISHES IN OAXACA, is prepared exactly the same way as *enchiladas*, *entomatadas*, and *enfrijoladas* in Oaxaca: dipped in a sauce, then folded without a filling. The basic difference among the four is the sauce. A favorite spot for *enmoladas* is Fonda Rosita in Mercado Democracia (page 227). Breakfast *enmoladas* are big hits here—tortillas are dipped in *mole* without first frying. Have a cup of an ancient beverage at one of the few places still making *chocolatatole* in Mexico. It's similar, but different and more involved than *champarrado* in that you start with white *atole* and add sky-high chocolate foam.

Practical home cooks prepare *enmoladas* when they have leftover *mole* on hand. Or they buy paste and add a cup of puréed tomatoes and stir in chicken broth (along with any secret additions) until the texture of light cream is achieved.

Yield: 6 servings, 2 tortillas per person

- 3 cups "Mole Negro" (page 238)
- 12 thin corn tortillas ("blanditas" in Oaxaca)
- ½ cup ranchero cheese, dry cottage cheese, or farmer cheese, crumbled
- ½ onion, sliced into ¼-inch rings

1. Heat the *mole* in a wide, medium-sized saucepan. Holding it by upper edges, dip a tortilla in the sauce. Put it on a plate and fold in half, then in half again to make a triangle. Repeat with another tortilla on the same plate (each serving has 2 tortillas).

2. Spoon more sauce over the tortillas and sprinkle with cheese. Top with 3 to 5 raw onion rings. Repeat with the other 5 servings. Serve at once.

Luisa Martínez de Aragón's

Enfrijoladas *Tortillas Dipped in Black Bean Purée and Folded*

A CLASSIC AT THE FONDAS in Oaxaca's markets, *enfrijoladas* are one of the famous dipped tortilla quartet made up of *enchiladas*, *enmoladas*, and *entomatadas*. Black beans become the sauce for tortilla dipping here; try to get *epazote* or avocado leaves to flavor yours to be delectably authentic.

As with María Eugenia's Enchiladas (page 252), Luisa's tortillas are quick-fried so they don't become mushy. Both women are adamant about including this step, but some Oaxacans absolutely never pre-fry, as they prefer a soft tortilla to absorb the sauce (see *Enmoladas* page 253). Serve alone, as a light meal, or with a salad, or with *Tasajo* (page 262) and Vinegared Chile Strips and Carrots (page 245).

Yield: 6 servings, 2 tortillas per person

For the sauce

"Frijoles Parrados" (page 250) made with "epazote" or avocado leaves, puréed, and kept hot

Chicken Broth (page 19) as needed to thin the beans to a heavy cream consistency

Finishing the "enfrijoladas"

¼ cup lard or vegetable oil

12 thin corn tortillas ("blanditas" in Oaxaca)

16 white onion slices

½ cup ranchero cheese, dry cottage cheese, or farmer cheese, crumbled

¼ cup chopped flat-leaf parsley leaves

1. Heat the oil in a heavy frying pan. One or two at a time, put the tortillas in the hot oil for 10 to 20 seconds on each side so the tortilla is still pliable and not at all crunchy.

2. Holding it by upper edges, dip each tortilla in the bean sauce. Put it on a plate and fold in half, then in half again to make a triangle. Repeat with another tortilla on the same plate (each serving gets 2 tortillas).

3. Spoon additional sauce over the tortillas, cover with raw onion slices, a sprinkle of cheese, and parsley. Repeat with the other 5 servings.

Susana Trilling's

Entomatadas *Tortillas Dipped in Tomato Sauce and Folded*

SUSANA'S COOKING CLASSES AT HER WONDERFUL COUNTRY HOME on the outskirts of Oaxaca City are filled with eager students, both Oaxaqueños and travelers (see page 231). Her tomato sauce version of the *entomatada-enmolada-enchilada-enfrijolada* quartet is "a must for a family of *tomateros* [tomato growers] because we get so many." Her husband, Eric, grows tomatoes on his thriving commercial farm.

Yield: 6 servings, 2 tortillas per person

For the sauce

- 1 three-inch "canela" stick, or 1 two-inch cinnamon stick
- 3 whole black peppercorns
- ½ teaspoon whole cumin seed
- ¼ teaspoon ground allspice
- 2 pounds ripe tomatoes (about 6)
- 5 de árbol chiles, stemmed, seeded and soaked for 30 minutes
- 1½ Tablespoons lard or oil
- 1 medium white onion, minced
- 12 cloves garlic, minced
- 1 Tablespoon "panela" or dark brown sugar
- 1 sprig or 1 teaspoon dried Mexican oregano
- 1 bay leaf
- salt to taste

1. Toast (page 19) the *canela*, peppercorns, and cumin seed until their scents are released, then put them in a blender and grind with allspice.

2. Skin the tomatoes by making an X on the bottom of each and blanching in boiling water for 1 minute. Remove from the pot with a slotted spoon and cool. Peel the tomatoes and put in the blender with the ground spices.

3. Drain and add the chiles to the blender. Blend.

4. Heat the lard or oil in a deep pot until it is smoking hot. Add the onions and fry until they are transparent. Add the garlic and, when the garlic is light brown, carefully add the tomato mixture (it splatters!) and stir. Stir in the sugar, oregano, and bay leaf. Reduce the heat and simmer for about 5 minutes, stirring, to reduce and dry the sauce. Add salt to taste.

Finishing the entomatadas

- 3 Tablespoons lard or oil
- 12 thin corn tortillas ("blanditas" in Oaxaca)
- ½ cup ranchero cheese, dry cottage cheese, or farmer cheese
- 1 white onion, thinly sliced
- ¼ cup flat-leaf parsley or cilantro leaves, roughly chopped

1. Heat a little lard in a skillet and fry each tortilla quickly until it is soft, then turn it over with tongs to fry the other side. Drain.

2. Holding it by upper edges, dip a tortilla in the tomato sauce. Put it on a plate and fold in half, then in half again to make a triangle. Repeat with another tortilla on the same plate (each serving has 2 tortillas).

3. Spoon more sauce over the tortillas and sprinkle with cheese. Garnish with onion slices and parsley or cilantro leaves. Repeat with the other 5 servings.

Olivia Castro's

Empanadas de Oaxaca *Baked* Masa *Turnovers Filled with Mushrooms*

OLIVIA'S *EMPANADAS* ARE RIGHT AT THE TOP OF MY LIST of favorite Mexican market foods. Her truly delicious "Mexican calzones" are fit for any health-conscious gourmet. Every morning she rises at 5 A.M. to prepare all her *empanada* filling mixtures: mushroom; *huitlacoche*; squash blossom and *epazote*; *rajas de chile de agua*; *médula* (intestine); and lip-smacking *sesos* (brains) before arriving at Mercado Democracia at 8 A.M.

As soon as you place your order, Olivia hand-presses a twelve-inch tortilla, places it on an unoiled (no layer of old grease anywhere in sight) earthenware *comal* set atop a wood-burning brazier. She removes it from the heat before adding ingredients and pressing the tortilla's edges together. The *empanada* is browned then placed under the *comal* in the brazier's hot "oven" to "bake." It's then put back on top of the *comal* to finish off.

Yield: 4 empanadas

For the mushroom filling

- 2 Tablespoons vegetable oil
- 1 pound fresh mushrooms, cleaned and cut in half if small, coarsely chopped if large
- 1 medium white onion, coarsely chopped
- 2 garlic cloves, chopped
- salt and freshly ground black pepper to taste

1. Heat the oil in a skillet and add the mushrooms, onion, and garlic.

2. Sauté for 5 minutes, add salt and pepper, and remove from the heat.

To finish the empanadas

- 1½ cups finely ground "masa" from a tortillería, or prepare "masa harina" per package directions
- 2 de agua chiles (as Olivia uses in Oaxaca), or 3 jalapeño chiles, or another fresh chile of your choice, toasted (page 16), stemmed, seeded, and cut into strips
- Optional: 1 cup shredded "quesillo de Oaxaca," string, or mozzarella cheese

1. Preheat the oven to 400°F.

2. Make a 12-inch tortilla (page 12). Lay it on a hot, ungreased *comal* or griddle, for 15 seconds.

3. Remove the tortilla to a lightly floured table or counter top. Turn the tortilla over so the cooked side is facing up. Put ½ cup sautéed mushrooms in the center, in a mound. Add a few chile strips, and optional cheese. Fold the tortilla over and pinch the edges closed. Cook on the *comal* for 15 seconds without turning.

4. Slip the *empanada* into the hot oven, directly on a rack, for 2 minutes. Put the *empanada* back on the *comal* for a final browning (with brown side up) for 2 minutes. Repeat with the others.

Anita Marina Silva Bohorquez's

Caldo de Gato *Chicken, Pork, Vegetable, and Smoky Chile Soup*

I'M JUST KIDDING—AND SO ARE GENERATIONS OF OAXACANS. *Caldo de gato* translates to "cat broth," but this very old recipe never included a cat; it's only a name with a bizarre, fun tradition. Bits of bony pork plus chicken pieces (cat-like?) are cooked with a slew of vegetables and smoky chiles. When served on the day of cooking, *caldo de gato* is a broth with separate vegetables and meat pieces. When the dish is reheated, tender meats fall apart, potatoes thicken the liquid, and everything becomes a thick blend. Anita serves *caldo de gato* in deep bowls; with lime wedges and tortillas it's a full meal. Meow.
Yield: 8 large servings

- 4 pasilla de Oaxaca chiles, or 3 chipotle chiles (dry, not in adobo)
- 8 tomatoes
- 2 Tablespoons vegetable oil
- 1 large white onion, quartered
- 1 small garlic head, quartered (unpeeled)
- 1 pound lean pork leg or loin, cut into 1-inch pieces
- 1 pound lean pork ribs, or another bony piece of pork, cut up
- 1 four-pound chicken, cut into 8 pieces
- 2 quarts water
- 8 medium, red-skinned potatoes, quartered
- 2 chayote squash, quartered, or substitute zucchini
- 8 large carrots, peeled and quartered
- ½ pound green beans, cut into 2-inch pieces
- 4 black peppercorns
- 2 whole cloves
- salt to taste
- ¼ cup chopped cilantro leaves

1. Clean, stem, and open the chiles flat and remove the seeds. Toast (page 16) the chiles just until they release their perfume and change color. Put them in a blender container.

2. Put the tomatoes in a pot of boiling water and cook for 2 minutes. Drain and cool enough to handle, then peel and core and put in the blender with the chiles. Purée.

3. Heat the vegetable oil in a very large pot. Add the onion and garlic and cook until the onion is translucent. Add the pork and chicken and cook, turning, for 10 minutes more.

4. Pour the blender mixture into the pot. Add the water, potatoes, squash, carrots, green beans, peppercorns, and cloves and bring it all to a boil. Reduce the heat, skim off any foam, and simmer for 1 hour with the cover slightly askew. Add salt to taste. The stew may be cooled for reheating at this point.

5. Ladle the stew into deep bowls and sprinkle with chopped cilantro.

Ofelia Cabrera Vda. Arroyo's

Estofado *Pork and Chicken Stew with Oaxacan Flavors*

DOÑA CABRERA VDA. ARROYO was born in Oaxaca and enjoys cooking traditional dishes for her family and circle of friends who parade in and out of her comfortable home (why does everyone seem to know exactly what time *comida* is served?). *Estofados* like this one, with so many ingredients, are rarely cooked out of the home; in fact, the stews in most fondas don't even resemble this dish which is *muy casero* (very home-style). Doña Cabrera Vda. Arroyo always sets her table with big soup spoons for *estofado* and serves plenty of hot tortillas, vegetables *en escabeche*, and Fresh Tomato Salsa (page 143) made with pasilla de Oaxaca chile—you may substitute chipotle chile.
Yield: 8 servings

For the meats (which are cooked separately from one another)

- 1 four-pound chicken, cut into 8 pieces
- 2 onions, quartered
- 4 garlic cloves, unpeeled
- salt to taste
- 2 pounds boneless pork loin

1. Put the chicken in a large pot with 1 onion and 2 garlic cloves. Add 2 quarts water and bring to a boil. Reduce the heat and simmer for 45 minutes, partially covered. Add salt to taste.

2. Meanwhile, put the pork in another large pot with 1 onion and 2 garlic cloves. Add 2 quarts water and bring to a boil. Reduce the heat and simmer for 45 minutes, partially covered. Add salt to taste.

For the sauce

- 25 almonds, blanched and skinned
- 8 large, ripe tomatoes
- ½ medium white onion
- 4 garlic cloves (the señora's trick: put a hole in each unpeeled garlic clove with a sharp-pointed knife so it doesn't jump around on the hot "comal")
- 1 cup crumbled dry French bread, dried in the oven if necessary
- 1 to 2 Tablespoons water
- 1 Tablespoon vegetable oil
- 1½ Tablespoons white sesame seeds
- ⅓ cup raisins
- ½ teaspoon dried Mexican oregano

1. Put the almonds in a bowl of hot water to soften for 1 hour while the meat is cooking.

2. Toast (page 16) the tomatoes, onion, and garlic. Put the tomatoes in a plastic bag to "sweat" for a few minutes. Peel the skins from the tomatoes, onion, and garlic.

3. Put the crumbled bread, into a blender with 2 tablespoons water. Chop to make soft bread crumbs, turning on and off. Put the tomatoes, onion, and garlic in the blender with the bread crumbs and purée.

4. In a small skillet, heat 1 tablespoon oil and lightly brown the sesame seeds. Add them to the blender. Add the raisins, herbs, spices, and capers plus the caper liquid to the blender and purée.

5. Heat 4 tablespoons vegetable oil in a deep pot. Carefully add the blender mixture (it splatters!) and cook for 5 minutes over medium-high heat.

- ½ teaspoon dried thyme
- ½ teaspoon powdered cinnamon
- 4 large capers
- 3 Tablespoons liquid from the caper jar
- 4 Tablespoons vegetable oil
- 5 sprigs flat-leaf parsley, tied together
- salt to taste

6. When the meats are finished cooking, add 3 cups each chicken and pork broth to the sauce (skimming fat from the surface of both broths first). Add the parsley and salt. Bring to a boil then simmer, stirring occasionally, for 15 minutes. Keep any remaining chicken broth for another use (discard the pork broth).

7. Remove the skin from the chicken. Slice the pork, or tear into chunks. Serve in large, shallow soup bowls, putting some pork and chicken meat into each. Cover the meat with large spoonfuls of sauce.

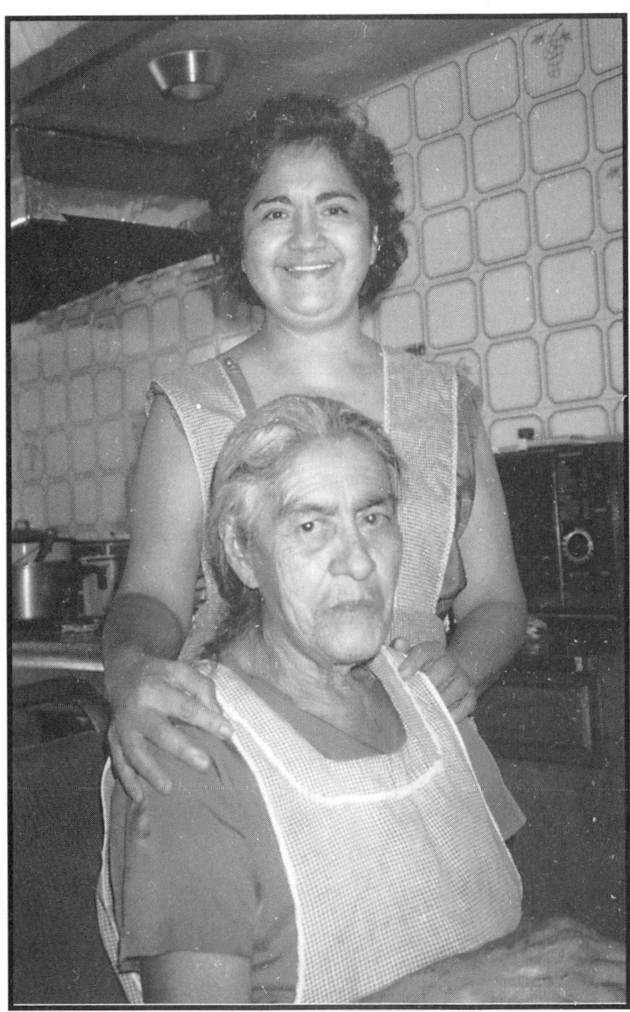

Doña Ofelia Cabrera Vda. Arroyo (sitting) and daughter, Concepción Arroyo de Valencia.

Emilia Arroyo de Cabrera's

Codorniz en Salsa de Rosas *Quail in Rose Petal Sauce*

WHEN I WAS ASKING FRIENDS IN OAXACA FOR PEOPLE THEY KNEW to be exceptionally good cooks two sources (unknown to each other) named one person as "a must": Emilia.

I've tasted many delicious dishes at Emilia's house, from sitting around her kitchen table with family at lunch, to one special culinary event where she prepared dinner for a group of U.S. foodies—and included edible flowers in every dish (at least twelve) on the buffet table. Emilia loves flowers. Next to cooking, her great joy is her cherished flower garden at a special retreat in the northernmost section of Oaxaca City. In this simple suburban neighborhood with glorious views of surrounding mountains, Emilia has a getaway pad, a house with lovely gardens and an Indian bath house. In a far back corner of the property, a small log cabin sits as invitingly as a child's playhouse. Inside, one room houses a body massage table and the other a traditional hot, dry, sauna-style bath developed centuries ago by indigenous peoples. Planted around the bathhouse are Emilia's rose bushes. Besides enjoying their beauty and perfume, Emilia cuts the blossoms for Quail in Rose Petal Sauce, an enchanting winter dish when fresh chestnuts are available.

Quail in Rose Petal Sauce is the now infamous March aphrodisiacal recipe, which sets buildings and bodies aflame in the book (and film) *Like Water for Chocolate*.

Yield: 4 servings, 2 quail each

For the sauce

- 2 garlic cloves
- 2 teaspoons butter
- ½ teaspoon aniseseed
- 12 red or pink roses with open blooms, petals only
- 1 red "tuna" (cactus fruit), or the meat of 1 large or 2 small red meat plums, such as Elephant Heart or Santa Rosa
- 12 fresh chestnuts
- 2 Tablespoons honey
- salt to taste
- ¼ teaspoon freshly ground white pepper

1. Peel and chop the garlic. Melt the butter in a large skillet and sauté the garlic and anise seed until lightly browned. Set aside.

2. Put the rose petals and *tuna* or plum in a processor or blender container. Purée.

3. Make an X over the flat ends of the chestnuts with a small sharp knife. Toast (page 16) on a hot *comal* or skillet for 5 minutes, shaking the pan from time to time. The brown shells will open. Bring 1 quart water to a boil and drop in the chestnuts. Boil, uncovered, for 20 minutes and drain. When they are cool enough to handle, peel the shells and remove the skins. Add them to the blender with the rose petal mixture. Purée while slowly adding 1 cup water.

4. Reheat the skillet containing the garlic butter and pour in the blender ingredients. Lower the heat and simmer for 10 minutes, stirring. Add the honey, salt, and pepper.

5. Put the sauce through a sieve, pushing down with a wooden spoon to get most of the sauce through. Return it to the same (wiped clean) skillet.

For the quail

- 3 garlic cloves, peeled
- 1 small white onion, halved
- ½ teaspoon salt
- 8 quail, fresh or frozen and thawed, cleaned

1. Thirty minutes before serving, bring 4 quarts water to a boil with the garlic, onion, and salt.
2. Add the quail, turn the heat down to medium, and continue cooking for 20 minutes.

Finishing the dish

1. Reheat the sauce if necessary.
2. Add the quail to the sauce and stir, covering the birds completely, for 3 minutes. Emilia serves 2 quail per person with plain white rice to absorb every last drop of the perfumed sauce.

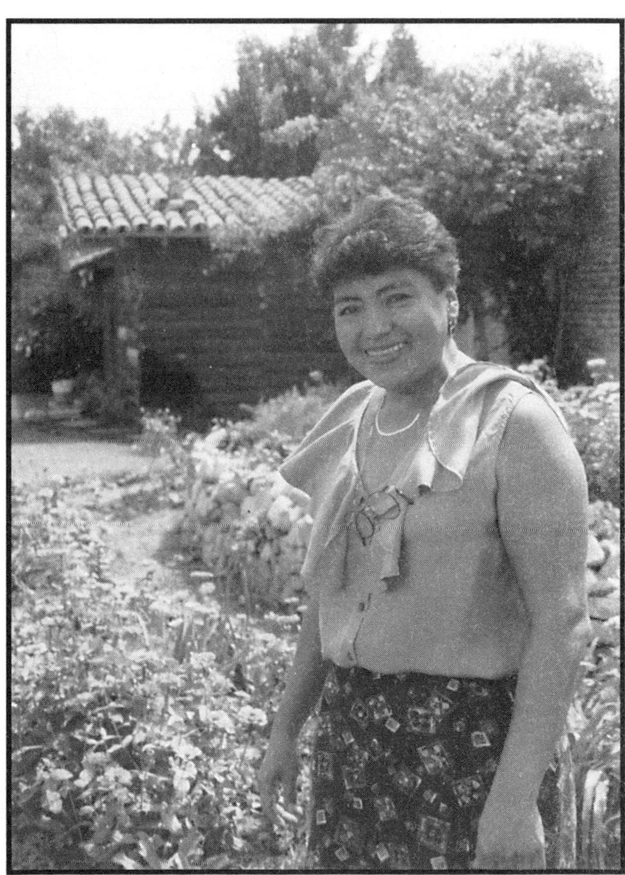

Emilia Cabrera in her garden.

Mario González's

▲▼▲

Tasajo *Thinly Sliced and Grilled Beef, Market Style*

MARIO GONZÁLEZ, A BUTCHER WHO SELLS OAXACA'S FAMOUS *TASAJO*, demonstrated this recipe firsthand when he and his wife, Gloria, invited me to their home for a Sunday picnic. After gathering around the kitchen table, laughing at Mario's cooking antics and sampling Gloria's assorted *antojitos*, we all proceeded to an oilcloth-covered picnic table in the backyard, shaded by a huge laurel tree. With their six children and various relatives clamoring for seconds and thirds, poor Mario stood over the smoky grill most of the afternoon. To my relief, he later revealed that this was his favorite way to spend his day off.

Mario likes to grill pork ribs, chicken pieces, and *tasajo*. *Tasajo* is thinly sliced beef round that's cut in one long piece by dexterous knifemanship. When you visit the 20 de Noviembre fondas building (page 226) or the surrealistic smoke-filled meat hall at the fabulous Sunday market in Tlacolula, you can watch butchers cutting one-and-a-half foot wide by three foot long strips. Then they stack the strips in piles: fresh today; marinated and salted (the salt must be washed off before using); salted and aged jerky-style (the heavily salted meat must be soaked); or *cecina* (pork) with salted chile marinade (in other regions of Mexico salted with-the-grain sliced beef is called *cecina*).

Cutting with-the-grain is an old approach to making tough beef cuts more usable. Marinating tenderizes and adds fabulous flavor. People in Oaxaca like *tasajo* very well-cooked, as most meat is in Mexico. You'll probably prefer your homemade version medium-cooked so that each bite doesn't take five minutes to chew.

Yield: 12 servings

4 pounds beef round roast, fat trimmed

1. Put the meat on a cutting board with the grain running horizontally.

2. With a very sharp long knife, slice a ¼-inch thick piece horizontally off the top, to ¼ inch of the other side, with the grain.

3. Remove the knife and starting ¼ inch below the previous cut, at the opposite end at the "hinge," begin slicing in the opposite direction, again stopping ¼ inch from the end.

4. Repeat until the entire roast is cut and you can fold out the beef, accordion-style, with the grain running the length of the strip, like flank steak.

5. On the cutting board, pound the meat with a mallet, especially at the "hinges" where it is a bit thicker.

For the marinade

- ½ cup vegetable oil
- ¼ cup freshly squeezed lime juice
- 4 Tablespoons chile powder (see page 11)
- 2 teaspoons salt

Combine oil, lime juice, chile powder, and salt for marinade. Rub into the beef and marinate a few hours or overnight, refrigerated. Cut into sizes that are easy to grill, about 4-inch squares. Cook over hot mesquite (or coals), turning with long tongs.

Oaxaca's Alcalá is a pedestrian street lined with charming colonial architecture.

Linda Ana Castillo's

▲▼▲

Clayudas con Asiento *Special Market Tortillas with Toppings*

OAXACA'S MERCADO 20 DE NOVIEMBRE (page 226), the fondas building just south of Mercado Juárez across Calle Aldama, offers the ultimate, classic, Oaxacan fonda food unavailable anywhere else in Mexico. Sit down at La Abuelita Fonda or Fonda María Alejandra, both near the entrance to the smoky (not smoked) meat area. These are two of the best known and, certainly, biggest fondas in the market. You won't be able to miss their gigantic signs and TV sets perpetually turned on to daytime soaps to attract single diners. Ask for a bean and beef *clayuda* (also spelled *tlayuda* here) and what you get is a large 12-inch, thin, rather stiff and chewy handmade tortilla smeared with *asiento* (clingy browned bits from the bottom of a *chicharrón* or *carnitas* caldron). Black bean paste is spread on next, then slices of grilled *Tasajo* (page 262), a few grilled scallions, and spicy de agua chile strips with melted *quesillo de Oaxaca* (string cheese). Pork *cecina* (marinated in chile paste) is popular as are *chapulines* (fried grasshoppers), a delicacy for the adventurous, to be sure. *Clayudas* are finger food, so rip off a piece and dig right in. They're gooey, stringy, delicious, cholestrol-laden Oaxacan pizzas. Nobody ever said this was diet food so don't get hysterical over the use of *asiento*. It's often a once-in-a-lifetime treat for travelers with a taste for Mexico's disappearing regional treasures.

Serve your *clayudas* as they do in Oaxaca, with a selection of fresh and bottled salsas, lime wedges, and salt.

Yield: 4 servings

- 4 extra-large corn tortillas
- ½ pound thinly sliced (⅛-inch) beef round (see "Tasajo," page 262)
- 8 scallions
- 2 de agua or jalapeño chiles
- ½ cup warm "asiento" from fried pork, homemade or purchased at a "carnitas" butcher (or omit)
- 1½ cups "Frijoles Parrados" (page 250), puréed without liquid
- 1 avocado, peeled and sliced
- 1 cup shredded "quesillo de Oaxaca," string cheese, or mozzarella
- salsas, fresh limes, and salt

1. Heat the tortillas in a 350°F oven, turning so they don't curl, until they become a bit stiff—but not rock hard.

2. Heat a grill until it is very hot. Cut the beef into 4-inch pieces for ease of cooking. Cook the scallions and chiles with the meat until they blacken just a bit and soften. On a cutting board, chop the beef into pieces approximately 2 inches x 1 inch.

3. Spread a few tablespoons of warm *asiento* over each tortilla. Spread ¼ cup warm beans over the *asiento.*

4. Distribute the beef, scallions, avocado, chiles, and cheese evenly over the 4 tortillas and put the tortillas on the grill to melt the cheese. Serve immediately while they are bubbling hot, with salsas, fresh limes, and salt.

Matilde Cristina Rodríguez de García's and Micaela Bolaños's

Lengua Alcaparrada *Incredibly Tender Tongue in Caper Sauce*

SUPER TORTA FIESTA IS A DOWN-HOME WORKING MAN'S LUNCH SPOT on the corner, and across from Juárez market, at Las Casas. It's a very local place, not one a tourist would easily venture into. To enter you walk through a shop selling tapes and disks. Once you enter the restaurant, you'll find waitresses bustling about with their arms laden with *comidas corridas*; a couple of kids singing their hearts out for pesos with older guitarists trying to do the same; plus, when I was there last, a TV set blasting away with Japanese cartoons competing with the music shops's contributions. Flowered oilcloth-covered tables covered yet again with clear plastic are crowded with business-suited folks and market workers who know a good, cheap meal. Super Torta Fiesta doesn't sell *tortas* (who knows why?) and most items are, truthfully, mediocre, but Monday's tongue in caper sauce is a masterpiece. In fact, just about every Monday for the past twenty years Matilde and Micaela have been making this daily special. When served with their excellent *Arroz Verde* (page 248) and washed down with *Agua de Limón* (page 267) this is mighty fine eating at rock-bottom prices.
Yield: 6 servings

For the meat

- 2 quarts water
- 2½ pounds beef tongue
- 1 medium white onion, cut into quarters
- ½ head garlic, unpeeled

1. Bring the water to a boil in a large pot. Reduce the heat and cook the tongue in simmering water, cover askew, with the onion and garlic for 2½ to 3 hours, or until it is very well done and butter soft.
2. Cool enough to handle and skin the tongue. Remove any gristle and fat from the back end.

For the sauce

- 12 tomatoes
- 4 Tablespoons large capers, plus some for garnish
- 3 serrano chiles, coarsely chopped
- 3 garlic cloves, peeled and coarsely chopped
- ½ cup vegetable oil

1. Bring a large pot of water to a boil and boil the tomatoes for 2 minutes. Drain and cool the tomatoes enough to handle, then remove their skins. Put the tomatoes in a blender container and purée. Add the capers, chiles, and garlic to the blender and purée.
2. Heat the oil in a deep pot and carefully (it sizzles!) pour in the sauce. Fry for 2 minutes, stirring. Reduce the heat and simmer for 15 minutes.

Finishing the dish

Cut the tongue into thin slices, arrange it on a platter or individual plates, and cover it with the sauce. Garnish with a few whole capers.

Hamilton Sisters'

Garbanzos con Piña, Panela y Canela

Garbanzo and Pineapple Topping for Creamy Rice Pudding

FOUR GORGEOUS SISTERS WITH THE UN-MEXICAN NAME OF HAMILTON live in Oaxaca, and each one loves to cook. At a memorable dinner in Piña's home, every course was a traditional Oaxacan dish. The grand finale was this humble mixture, an ancient regional recipe made from garbanzos, pineapple, and *canela*. It brought raves from every foodie at the table.

Oaxacan vendors, on the northeast and southeast corners of Mercado Juárez, sell this topping spooned over rice pudding, scooped from huge bowls that empty in no time thanks to a constant line of locals every evening. Various dried fruits in sugar syrup are other popular toppings.

Ladle the garbanzos over your favorite creamy rice pudding recipe (drier, baked varieties don't work here). The sauce keeps well for a few weeks in the refrigerator.

Yield: 8 servings

- ½ pound dried garbanzo beans (do not use canned)
- 1½ cups "panela," or dark brown sugar
- 1 four-inch "canela" stick, or 1 two-inch cinnamon stick
- 1 cup coarsely chopped pineapple
- prepared creamy rice pudding

1. Soak the garbanzo beans in 2 quarts of water for 12 hours, then drain. Add 2 quarts fresh water to the pot with the garbanzos. Bring it to a boil and boil for 30 minutes. Drain. Cool the beans enough to handle.

2. This step is time-consuming but important to the dish. Slip the skin off each garbanzo, putting the skinned beans back in the pot. After the first dozen or so you'll develop a system. It's a simple task that can be done in 30 minutes while you're watching TV.

3. Add the *panela*, *canela*, and pineapple plus another 2 quarts of water to the skinned garbanzos. Bring the water to a boil and boil for an hour, stirring from time to time. Cool the mixture to room temperature.

Oaxaca's Hamilton sisters.

Matilde Cristina Rodríguez de García's

Agua de Limón *Chartreuse-Colored Limeade*

ON ANY BLISTERING HOT DAY, THERE'S NO BETTER THIRST QUENCHER than fluorescent, chartreuse-green *agua de limón*. Matilde still makes this the old fashioned way—by hand—using a *chirmolera*, a ceramic bowl with grooves dug into the clay, for grating. The green-glazed bowls can be found in the Mercado de Abastos building, in the pottery aisles, and at Tlacolula's Sunday market. (I've also seen similar bowls in Japan, where they're called *suribachi*, used for grating *toro roimo*, a sticky root vegetable.) Matilde grates the zest from dark green, underripe *limones pequeños* (tiny Key limes) to obtain the best flavor and color. She serves *agua de limón* in tall soda-fountain glasses with a colorful straw. You can easily copy the drink at home, but try to find Mexican limes from a Latino food market. They do make a difference; regular limes just don't provide the color or extra sour flavor.

Not available at Super Torta Fiesta, but certainly something to add spark to your *agua de limón,* is a jigger of clear sugarcane alcohol, clear tequila, or mezcal, per serving.

Yield: 1 quart

- 10 "limones pequeños" (Key limes), underripe and dark green, not yellowish
- 1 quart water
- about ½ cup sugar, to taste

1. Wash the limes then grate their zests (no white pith) with a small-hole grater. Put the zest in a clear glass pitcher with 1 quart water and let it stand for at least 1 hour for the water to color.

2. Strain the water through a cheesecloth-lined sieve, pressing down on and squeezing out the cloth. Return the water to the pitcher and add sugar to taste. Stir to dissolve the sugar completely. Cover and refrigerate until you pour the liquid into clear, tall glasses to show off the lurid Day-Glo color.

El Mesón's Chef's

El Suero *Beer on Ice with Lime*

ONE HOT EVENING WE WERE SITTING AT OAXACA'S EL MESÓN RESTAURANT, sweat dripping down our backs, having a few at the taco counter when a cook suggested we try *el suero* with our pork and *mole verde* tacos. We tried not to lose our cool as we watched a guy pour beer over ice. We needn't have worried; the drink disappears faster than ice melts. Don't knock this creation until you've tried it on a sweltering day with Mexican, Indian, Hunan Chinese, Thai, or other spicy food.

On the other hand, once in awhile it's nice to have a bottle of wine, rather than beer, with Mexican food. One evening at our new apartment we realized that we had left our corkscrew in Puebla, just as dinner was ready. Morris decided to borrow one. No, they were sorry, they had none, but our landlady's cousin knew how to open a bottle without a corkscrew. Intrigued, but aware we were not handing over a bottle of cherished Stony Hill Chardonnay, Morris figured, why not? The guy folded a kitchen towel until it was a half-inch thick. With sharp, deliberate blows, he carefully hit the bottle's base flat against a wall, cushioned by the towel, as Morris watched in awe. Slowly, millimeter by millimeter, the cork emerged from the bottle's neck. After a dozen blows the cork was out far enough to pull with a deft twist.

Now back to *el suero*. Every one of my drink testers gave it thumbs up, even a couple of high-fives.

Yield: 1 serving

1 lime
Kosher salt or specially ground margarita salt
ice cubes
1 bottle cold Mexican lager

1. Rub a wedge of fresh lime around the rim of a tall glass to moisten.

2. Dip the glass (upside down) into a small dish of coarse salt to coat the rim.

3. Add ice cubes, a lime wedge, and slowly pour in the beer.

José and Fernando López's

Cóctel del Oro *Mezcal and Orange Juice Party Punch Cocktail*

MEZCAL IS FERMENTED JUICE OF THE MAGUEY CACTUS, and is not unlike tequila. Many mezcals continue to be made in backyard stills: grass-roots booze can be bought around Oaxaca in squat, black pottery bottles with hand painted flowers (gringos love them as souvenirs), to clear bottles without any labeling at all—let your conscience be your guide.

The López brothers are owners of Oro de Oaxaca, Oaxaca's famous brand of Mezcal. On my last visit to the López's plant in Matatlán, an ancient Zapotec village one hour south of Oaxaca City, I saw the production process. The pueblo is a labyrinth of dirt roads lined with high walls and behind each is a mezcal-crushing business: a horse or ox pulling a stone-crushing wheel, fermentation vats, and a distillery. All this homemade booze is born before being emptied into sparkling stainless steel tanks at Oro de Oaxaca.

José and Fernando gave me this cocktail recipe, which is guaranteed to make any celebration more festive. You can spot their brand easily in Mexico: It has a bright yellow label and small burlap sack containing *gusanito*- and chile-seasoned salt tied around the bottle neck. Other brands may be purchased in the U.S.

Yield: 5 1/2 quarts, or 44 four-ounce servings

- 1 liter bottle mezcal
- 1 cup sugar
- 2 cups lime juice (about 16 limes)
- 2 Tablespoons of the seasoned salt that comes attached to the Oro de Oaxaca bottle's neck, or table salt mixed half-and-half with chile powder
- 1 gallon fresh orange juice
- 1 bag of ice, about 5 pounds
- fresh limes, cut into wedges
- coarse salt

1. Stir the mezcal, sugar, lime juice, seasoned salt, and orange juice in a large punch bowl until the sugar completely dissolves. Then add the ice.

2. Rub glass rims with fresh lime wedges then dip the glasses in coarse salt, as for margaritas, before filling with the punch. *¡Salud!*

Chiapas and Tabasco

San Cristóbal de las Casas
Villahermosa

Palenque is the most sensational of Mexico's pre-Columbian archaeological sites, and it sits smack in the middle of this region. The Mayan ruin is surrounded by a jungle setting at the foot of Agua Azul, an exquisite series of waterfalls that cascade through voluptuous vegetation. This steam bath arena is also home to crops such as plantains and pineapples. Chiapas and Tabasco's fascinating tropical fruits are expensive gourmet items everywhere else *in the world. Because of hot, marshy lowlands rising abruptly to over seven thousand feet, crops of apples and pears are cultivated in the same states as coconuts and cocoa. Cocoa plantations produce much of the world's finest beans that become Oaxacan cooking-chocolate tablets as well as European chocolate bars. With both Pacific and Gulf coasts the variety of shellfish is unmatched—its local waters teem with shrimp, crab, crayfish, and turtle;* pejelagarto *is a prehistoric-looking river fish of sublimely delicate flavor.*

Left: Vendors outside San Cristóbal de las Casa's Santo Domingo Cathedral.

◆ San Cristóbal de las Casas, Chiapas ◆

Anita de la Cruz and one of her "pituales" (see page 278).

THE OLDEST CITY IN CHIAPAS, San Cristóbal de las Casas is surprisingly high at 2,100 meters (close to 7,000 feet). Many people are shocked to learn the city is almost airborne, considering it's nearly on the Yucatán peninsula. San Cristóbal de las Casas is, simply, a magical place, beautifully situated in the enchanting valley of Jovel. It is mystical, too, its atmosphere enhanced by the deeply rooted Indian religions of the surrounding pueblos and by the strong presence of *curanderos* and *brujas* (healers and witches) seen by most people regularly.

In the news for their uprising against the Mexican government, Chiapas rebels calling themselves the Zapatista Army are demanding that their homelands be returned. The 1994 New Year's Day revolution was a jolt to most of the world, unaware of the state's plight to boost its own economy, long overlooked by the government. The state's generally poor economy has been helped over the years thanks to outstanding weaving, among other industries, done on backstrap looms by women. Chiapanecans are considered Mexico's greatest weavers, and their classical patterns of stylized birds, butterflies, snakes, and cats, many thought to be Mayan in origin, have been passed down through generations. When traveling you'll be seeing variations in dress as well as weaving patterns from the various villages because each Chiapas pueblo has its own distinctive style. The market is an excellent location to admire these different weaving marvels, with artists their own models.

* MARKET *

Mercado José Castillo Dielman is located between Utrilla and Belisario Domínguez, eight blocks north of the *zócalo*, and just a few blocks north of Santo Domingo Cathedral. The market is open every day except Sunday, which is market day in neighboring San Juan Chamula. Here's where Indians come to swap and barter homegrown produce. It's the core, the very heart and soul of the neighborhood where tourists seldom venture. Fresh fruits are the market all-stars. One unfamiliar, brown blob, a *mamey*, is transformed like a frog-kissed-by-a-prince when cut open. Other princesses demanding attention are trucked-in tropical magenta mangoes, enormous papayas sold by the slice, and multiflavored guavas. Fresh local beans of extraordinary beauty are being shelled before your eyes—the only way you'd believe they were real. Thirsty? *Atole de arroz* (rice *atole*) is sold at a few of the bread stalls in the morning. Flowers play an important role because of the huge number of city and village fiestas year-round. Every month there's at least one holiday, whether national, Catholic, or Indian. Tables piled with amber-colored quartz-like copal tree (*copalcahuite*) sap for incense is the underlying scent of the entire town.

* PLACES TO GO AND THINGS TO EAT *

Tamales. Chiapas is known for its tamales, and state-wide variations are fun to hunt in the markets. (The state capital of Tuxtla Gutiérrez has a fine selection, for example.) In San Cristóbal de las Casas's market, keep an eye out for *tamales untados* in the morning. They are banana-leaf-wrapped, finely ground *masa* delights stuffed with pork, chicken, and raisins, in a mildly sweet, light sauce. Other sometimes-at-the-market temptations are *tamales de momo*, the wrappings large *momo* leaves (*hoja santa*) stuffed with vegetables and fresh beans. Another is *tamales bolas*, called *bolas* (balls) because of their round shapes. The husk-wrapped *masa* packages are stuffed with various fillings.

Bakeries. Panadería La Mercantil, located at Mazariegos No. 17-A, tel. 8-03-07, is open every day from 8 A.M. to 9:30 P.M. **Panificadora La Hojaldra,** located at Mazariegos No. 21, tel. 8-42-86, is open every day from 7 A.M. to 9:30 P.M. Both offer the best breads and *pan dulce* in town. If you happen to be in San Cristóbal de las Casas during Day of the Dead and All Soul's Day (October 31 through November 2) celebrations, their fanciful breads are fit-for-a-(dead)-king.

Smoked Meats. Jamonería Elengrane, Crescencio Rosas No. 13, tel. 8-12-44. Hours: open every day from 8 A.M. to 8 P.M. This elegant shop with an alpine atmosphere carries *butifarra* (allspice-flavored, *achiote*-colored, cooked-with-wine, dried sausage). A favorite way to serve the local salami is as an hors d'oeuvre with drinks, thinly sliced and sprinkled with a bit of lime and salt.

Coffee. Café San Cristóbal. Two locations: Calle Cuauhtémoc No. 2, tel 8-38-61, Hours: open every day from 9 A.M. to 11 P.M. Here you'll find whole and freshly ground beans. There's table service for the best espresso and cappuccino in town (ask for strong cappuccino with a little milk or you'll get the excessively milky version preferred all over Mexico). The other location at Calle Diego de Mazariegos No. 35 does not have table service, tel. 8-45-35. Hours: 9 A.M. to 2 P.M. and 4 P.M. to 8 P.M.

Ponche. The hot toddy-like potion (page 281) is sold from booths, evenings only, on the north side of the plaza behind town hall (with the tourist information office). Fresh fruit flavors are seasonal, but there's usually a mixed fruit with cinnamon or pineapple with allspice for chilly winter nights. Before a woman ladles the steaming hot, sugared fruit into a plastic cup, tell her you want "*un picate,*" which means with a jigger or so of sugarcane alcohol, known as *poche* to the locals. The sweet, thick-with-fruit-chunks, tummy-warming drinks are topped with *marquesote* (*pan dulce* crumbs) and are served with a spoon.

Candy. Regional *dulces* (sweets) are easy to find on the big plaza behind city hall, across from the *zócalo*. Stalls here have various coconut concoctions: *cocadas*, snow white and fluorescent pink; *jamoncillos*, praline-like candies made with pecans; and *cajetas,* fruit pastes to eat with a spoon from little oval wooden boxes (not the *cajeta* from Celaya).

Table linens. Casa de las Artesanías de Chiapas, Av. Miguel Hidalgo Esq. Niños Héroes, tel. 8-11-80. Call for hours. Chiapanecans are the greatest weavers in Mexico and the best examples are right here. This lovely shop run by knowledgeable people also houses a mini-museum of regional costumes with mannequins displayed in room settings. Embroidered tablecloths, napkins, guest towels, placemats, handwoven fabric sold by the meter, pillowcases, etc., all make excellent and easy-to-carry gifts.

Tour guide. Mercedes Hernández Gómez, Señora Gómez's (*Pollo en Jigo*, page 279, and *Coleto Asado*, page 280) daughter, is intensely concerned about the future of Chiapas's people. She is San Cristóbal de las Casas's premier English-speaking tour guide, and you can catch up with her any morning at 9 A.M. on the *zócalo*. Mercedes is the one with the big smile and umbrella, rain or shine. You'll visit magical San Juan Chamula's *curandero*-filled church and a nearby healer's home. Mercedes's insights into shamanism, Catholicism, sexism, and regional politics lead travelers on tours unlike any other.

Anita de la Cruz's

Cocido de Carne de Res *Beef and Vegetable Soup, Tzotzil Style*

SEÑORA DE LA CRUZ LIVES WITH HER FAMILY a few miles from San Cristóbal de las Casas, in Zinacantán, a Tzotzil pueblo. She lives in a wood house, without electricity, on a small farm where she and her husband and children have lived for twenty-five years. A few years back her husband built a tiny adobe building next to the house for her new kitchen, including a large, modern propane gas stove. Señora de la Cruz enjoys showing it off but admits she prefers the old wood-burning fireplace with clay *comal* for cooking—and it's right on the front porch, too. She generously shared some recipes from the Chiapas highlands while offering crisp homemade tortillas hot off her *comal*. As with all Mexican highland cooking, spicy chiles don't play a big part in the alpine cuisine of this area.

Señora de la Cruz's beef and vegetable soup is traditionally served on All Soul's Day, November 2. She says that tiny, regional, fresh green pico de piloma chiles are sliced and passed at the table to spoon individually into the soup. The señora serves Tamales with Fresh Beans Wrapped in Corn Leaves (page 278) at the same special-occasion meal.

Yield: 6 servings

- 2 pounds beef chuck or rump meat
- ½ teaspoon freshly ground black pepper
- 1 Tablespoon "Recado Rojo" (page 300), "achiote" paste, or annatto seeds previously ground in a spice mill
- 1 small head cabbage, quartered
- 2 ears fresh corn, cut into 2-inch pieces
- 6 medium potatoes, white or red, peeled and cut into large chunks
- 3 chayote squash, cut into large chunks, or substitute 5 zucchini
- 6 carrots, peeled and cut into chunks
- 1 head garlic, cloves broken apart and peeled (12 cloves)
- 10 stems cilantro, tied together
- 1 large mint sprig
- 4 sliced serrano chiles

1. Put the beef in a large pot and add 1 gallon water. Bring to a boil then simmer for 2 hours, with the lid askew. Spoon off any foam.

2. Mix the pepper and *recado*, *achiote* paste, or ground annatto seeds together, then add to the pot, stirring. Add the cabbage, corn, potatoes, squash, carrots, and garlic and simmer 30 minutes longer.

3. Add the cilantro and mint 15 minutes before the end of cooking, and remove it before serving. Add a bit of meat, a variety of vegetables, and broth to each bowl. Pass a dish of the sliced chiles.

Doña Amalia Burguete's

Sopa Seca de Pan *Dry Soup with Bread, Vegetables, and Raisins*

SOPA SECA TRANSLATES TO "DRY SOUP," and Mexicans consider pastas and rice "dry soups" because they cook starches the same way they cook soup, except the broth is fully absorbed. Rice is sautéed in oil (most often with onions), then cooked with broth. Pasta is treated the same way—first sautéed in hot oil then cooked until soft, and all the sauce absorbed. (Sautéing first in oil is probably why cooks all over the country insist upon cutting spaghetti into bizarre two-inch lengths.) For this Chiapas dry soup, bread slices are toasted and arranged in a large cook-and-serve pot. Vegetables and more bread layers are added, then finally hot broth for the bread to absorb.

Elegant Doña Amalia Burguete was born in San Cristóbal de las Casas more than eighty years ago and still cooks up a storm every day. After keeping her family well fed, her spare time is spent in a lovely courtyard tending orchids. Her recipe for *sopa seca de pan* is made the traditional way with both French bread and *pan de yema* (egg bread), but you can easily substitute a good challah from a Jewish deli, or richer French brioche. Other local cooks use French bread only, and add fresh peas and often prunes. Quantities of vegetables can vary greatly—use what you have on hand but be sure everything is fresh and separately cooked. Serve hot, warm, or at room temperature—it's a perfect picnic or party platter. The amount of liquid in the bottom of the cooking pot depends upon the bread's absorption qualities. Dry or liquid, *sopa seca de pan* is *muy deliciosa*.

Yield: 10 servings

- 4 day-old French sandwich rolls, about 6 inches long, or the equivalent in French baguettes plus the same amount of day-old "pan de yema," challah, or brioche (all nonsweet egg breads)
- 7 Tablespoons vegetable oil
- 2 garlic cloves, peeled and lightly smashed
- 1 large onion, sliced
- 4 large, ripe tomatoes, sliced
- 1 large, ripe (black) plantain, peeled and cut into ¼-inch slices
- 5 red or white boiling potatoes, cut into quarters (skin left on)

1. Preheat oven to 375°F. Slice the bread and lightly brown it on a large cookie sheet for about 10 minutes, turning once. Repeat until all the bread is toasted.

2. In a skillet, heat 2 tablespoons vegetable oil and cook 1 clove of the garlic over medium heat until it turns brown, then remove the garlic from the oil and discard it, keeping the garlic-flavored oil in the pan. Add the onion and sauté until it becomes transparent, then add the sliced tomatoes and cook for 5 minutes more. Remove to a bowl.

3. Wipe out the skillet and heat another 3 tablespoons vegetable oil. Add the sliced plantains and sauté until brown on both sides. With a slotted spoon, remove to a plate lined with paper towels to drain. Discard oil in pan.

- 3 carrots, peeled and thinly sliced
- 3 zucchini, peeled and thinly sliced
- 20 fresh green beans, cleaned and left whole
- 4 hard-boiled eggs
- ⅓ cup raisins
- herb mixture: ½ teaspoon dried Mexican oregano, ¼ teaspoon dried thyme, ½ teaspoon ground cinnamon, ¼ teaspoon freshly ground black pepper, and 1 teaspoon salt
- 1 quart Chicken Broth (page 19)

4. In a pot, bring 3 quarts of water to boil and a boil the potatoes for 20 minutes, or until cooked. Remove to a bowl with a large slotted spoon. In the same water, boil the remaining vegetables: first the carrots, then 3 minutes later add the zucchini, and green beans. Cook until crip-tender (not soft). Drain and put into a bowl.

5. In a pot suitably attractive for serving, like a large paella pan, sauté the other clove of garlic in 2 tablespoons vegetable oil to lightly brown, then remove and discard the garlic. Turn off the heat.

6. Arrange one layer of toasted French bread slices over the garlic oil. Arrange some of the vegetables, a few slices of hard-boiled egg, a few raisins, potatoes, and a sprinkle of mixed herbs. The next layer is *pan de yema*. Then more vegetables, egg, raisins, potatoes, and herbs. A French bread layer is next, then more vegetables, etc. A *pan de yema* layer is next, ending with a vegetable-egg-raisin-potato-herb layer.

7. In a separate pot, bring the broth to a boil. Put the pot with the bread and vegetables on medium heat and slowly pour the hot broth over. Bring to a boil and cook for 2 to 3 minutes. Let the soup rest about 10 minutes before serving. The bread will absorb most of the liquid.

Doña Amalia Burguete and her "Sopa Seca de Pan."

Anita de la Cruz's

Pituales *Tamales with Fresh Beans Wrapped in Corn Leaves*

INDIGENOUS PEOPLES OF CHIAPAS LIVE ATOP MOUNTAIN PEAKS where corn is still the major crop. The Tzotzils plant their crops on devastatingly steep, terraced cliffs. They can be spotted working their fields from what seems miles away because of their hand-loomed shirts and vests, which are dyed dazzling fuchsia to announce township affiliations. On one Sunday afternoon visit to Señora de la Cruz (see photo page 272) in Zinacantán, we saw a group of men dressed in flamboyant hot-pink-tasseled overshirts and wearing flat, wide hats with multicolored, three-foot-long florid ribbons fluttering around their heads. The sight literally took our breath away—five humans as colorful as peacocks casually strolling across the road and oblivious (thank goodness) to our stares.

As traditional as their clothing, *pituales* have been a Tzotzil culinary standard for generations. Fresh beans are mixed with *masa* then folded in fresh corn leaves. Classically, the small, triangular tamales are served for special breakfasts.

Yield: about 50 tamales

- 2 pounds coarsely ground "masa"
- 2 cups lard (page 18) is tradtional, but vegetable shortening may be used
- 2 cups fresh (not dried) beans, best ground on a "metate" or in a blender, but not to a purée
- 12 ears corn, providing about 60 fresh corn leaves

1. In a large bowl, mix the *masa* with the lard until the *masa* feels light and airy, about 10 minutes. Stir in the fresh, uncooked beans.

2. Choose the largest corn leaves, without holes or tears, and wash them.

3. Open a leaf out flat, with the edges curving inward. Put a rounded tablespoon of *masa* on the wide end. Fold the leaf over itself and the *masa*. Fold again until you have a triangle. Continue folding once or twice more, and tuck in the pointed end (the folding system is like making triangular Greek *spanakopitas*). As with all tamale-making, this is time-consuming work; if you have a friend who likes to do things like this, now's the time to call. Continue until all the *masa* and leaves are used.

4. Slightly overlap the *pituales* in a tamale steamer (see Glossary) and steam for 1 hour. Check the water level after 45 minutes and add more water if necessary. Like all tamales, these may be refrigerated and frozen.

Dora Gómez's

Pollo en Jugo de Jitomate

Chicken Stewed with Tomatoes, Canela, *Vinegar, Raisins, Almonds, and Olives*

SEÑORA GÓMEZ WAS BORN IN SAN CRISTÓBAL DE LAS CASAS to a mother who operated a fonda (in the true sense of the word—out of her house) back in 1950-57 when there were only a few hotel restaurants in town and fewer than a handful of fondas, and those all in the market. Señora Gómez learned her way around a kitchen by helping her mother, especially on Sundays, serving a dozen turkeys with various *moles*, and countless tamales to an endless line of take-out devotees.

Chiapas cooking is less spicy than that of the surrounding, low-lying areas. High elevations ensure cool, sometimes brisk weather and Mexico's cooler regions use less chile in their cuisines. "*Pollo en jugo*, the juice being tomato, is made more delicious-tasting," says the señora, "by substituting wine, either dry red or white, or, preferably, brandy. All versions are traditional and all delicious." Serve with Mexican Rice Pilaf (page 66).

Yield: 4 servings

- 1 Tablespoon vegetable oil
- 1 teaspoon "achiote" paste
- 1 four-pound chicken, cut into eighths
- 5 tomatoes
- 1 small white onion
- 5 garlic cloves
- 1 three-inch "canela stick," or 1 two-inch cinnamon stick
- 1 large stem Mexican oregano, or 2 teaspoons dried
- 10 black peppercorns
- 1 cup tomato juice, or red or white wine, or diluted brandy
- 1 cup Pineapple-Apple Vinegar (page 173), or ¾ cup cider vinegar and ¼ cup water
- ¼ cup raisins, chopped
- ¼ cup chopped blanched almonds
- 12 green olives, pitted and chopped
- 1 teaspoon sugar
- salt to taste

1. Heat the oil in a very large, deep skillet or shallow pot. Add the *achiote* paste and cook on medium heat, stirring, for 1 minute, until the paste dissolves. Add the chicken pieces and brown on all sides in the hot oil.

2. Put in a blender container the tomatoes, onion, garlic, *canela*, oregano, peppercorns, tomato juice, and vinegar. Purée and pour over the chicken.

3. Add the raisins, almonds, olives, and sugar. Cook for 40 minutes. Check the thickest part of a thigh to see if the chicken is completely cooked. If it's pink, continue cooking for a few minutes longer. Add salt to taste.

Dora Gómez's

Coleto Asado *Pork Cubes Stewed in Ancho Chile-Tomato Sauce*

COLETO MEANS "FROM SAN CRISTÓBAL DE LAS CASAS" and this regional pork specialty has been a favorite of Señora Gómez for many years. As a young woman, she helped out at her mother's fonda by preparing this dish. Now her family enjoys home cooking at its best whenever Señora Gómez continues the tradition and makes *coleto asado* with extra-lean pork cubes cooked in splendid sauce. "For the pork, use two-and-a-half pounds lean, boneless loin or leg meat. Or, if you haven't much money," Señora Gómez says with a wink and smile, "meaty, but fattier, country-style ribs work just fine."

Other people in San Cristóbal de las Casas enjoy a bit of sweetness in this sauce. If you'd like, try it with the optional one-half cup *panela* or dark brown sugar. Serve with Mexican Rice Pilaf (page 66) and a salad made from lettuce, sliced raw onion, sliced radishes, and sliced avocados.

Yield: 6 servings

- 2½ pounds lean, boneless pork loin or leg meat, or 4 pounds country-style pork ribs
- 5 ancho chiles
- 4 tomatoes
- ¼ white onion
- 6 garlic cloves
- 2 three-inch "canela" sticks, or 1 three-inch cinnamon stick
- 2 sprigs fresh Mexican oregano, or 1 Tablespoon dried
- 2 sprigs fresh thyme, or 1 Tablespoon dried
- ½ teaspoon freshly ground pepper
- ¼ cup white vinegar
- ½ teaspoon salt
- optional: ½ cup "panela" or dark brown sugar

1. Cut the pork into 1-inch cubes. Heat the oil in a pot and add the pork, frying, to sear the meat on all sides, about 10 minutes.

2. Bring 1 quart water to a boil and add the pork cubes. Return to a boil, then cover with the lid set slightly askew, and simmer the pork for 1 hour.

3. Remove the stems and seeds from the chiles and open them out flat. Toast (page 16) the chiles until they change color and release their perfume. Soak in hot water for 30 minutes.

4. Toast the tomatoes, onion, and garlic. Put the tomatoes in a plastic bag for a few minutes to "sweat," then peel and put in a blender. Peel the garlic and put it and the onion in the blender. Tear the chiles and put them in the blender. Add the *canela*, oregano, thyme, pepper, and vinegar. Purée the ingredients to a smooth paste.

5. Pour the sauce into the pot with the pork and pork liquid. Add the salt and optional *panela* and continue simmering, uncovered, for another 30 minutes.

San Cristóbal de las Casas's

Ponche con Posch *Hot Mixed Fruit Punch with Sugarcane Alcohol*

SAN CRISTÓBAL DE LAS CASAS CAN GET MIGHTY COLD IN WINTER—chimneys and fireplaces are in full use and evening strolls are out of the question if you brought only clothing for the nearby jungles of Palenque. Go ahead and buy a hand-spun-and-loomed wool vest sold by street vendors, or head over to the plaza behind town hall and look for *ponche* stands. *Ponche* is Mexico's delectable steaming-hot punch that is thick with fruit and guaranteed to make your teeth stop chattering. Fresh fruits are seasonal, but either mixed fruit with cinnamon or pineapple with allspice is usually available. Before a woman ladles the hot potion into a plastic cup, tell her you want *un picate*, which means with a jigger or so of *posch*, sugarcane alcohol. This tummy-warming drink is topped with sweet-roll crumbs. *Ponche con posch* is so thick you eat it with a spoon.
Yield: about 1 gallon

- 2 "panela" cones, or 2 cups dark brown sugar
- 4 quarts water
- 2 four-inch "canela" sticks, or 1 four-inch cinnamon stick
- 8 pears, peeled, cored, and chopped
- 12 guavas (if you can get them), peeled and chopped, or 8 apples, peeled and chopped
- 10 pitted prunes, chopped
- ½ cup raisins
- 2 two-foot stalks sugarcane, peeled and cut into ½-inch pieces to chew along with the liquid (this is traditional in San Cristóbal de las Casas—you'll be forgiven if it's unavailable)
- 1 jigger sugarcane alcohol, or substitute vodka, brandy, or wine, per portion
- 4 cups crumbled stale "pan dulce" or pound cake, in large ½-inch pieces

1. Melt the *panela* over low heat with 1 cup water, stirring to break up the cone. Add the rest of the water and *canela* and bring to a boil.
2. Turn down the heat, add the fruit and sugarcane, and simmer for 1 hour. Turn off heat and add the alcohol, or serve it on the side.
3. Ladle into mugs with some fruit. Top with ¼ cup *pan dulce* crumbs and hand everyone a spoon.

◆ Villahermosa, Tabasco ◆

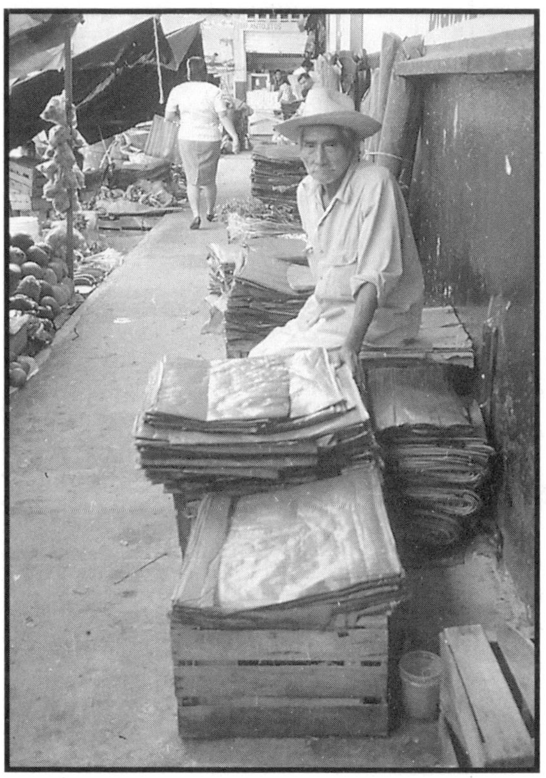

Fresh banana leaves for sale at Mercado Pino Suárez.

SUNNY, SWELTERING, AND STICKY—that's Tabasco. The state's miles and miles of humid, marshy lowlands are generally best left to fishermen and the newcomers—oilmen. Along the Gulf, seafood shacks offer interesting items such as tacos of *mantazaya minilla* (diced) or *chan-chan* (large chop) manta-ray wings sautéed with onion and habanero chile. *Piguas*, super-large river prawns split in two and grilled with garlic butter, are fired-up with salsa also made with habanero chile. There's not much better stand-up eating anywhere.

Cocoa, *Theobroma*, the world's favorite crop, is harvested from pods that cling to tree trunks grown in groves that are cut out of Tabasco's jungle. (Revered for over four thousand years cocoa beans were used by the Aztecs as currency.) Today, just about every house in Tabascan pueblos (low-lying Chiapas, too) has what looks to be a cement parking strip out front—it's not for cars but for drying cocoa beans in the sun for several days during the harvest from October to January. This method of drying is generally for home use or for selling at local markets. Higher-priced fermented beans (the European process began in Mexico only in the early 1960s) is another story altogether: Fermentation brings out intense richness so prized by chocolate lovers. Commercial blast furnaces force heat into the already sweltering, tropical forest buildings to temperatures hovering around 120°F. Vats of fresh, white, moist beans, covered with banana leaf blankets, ferment in their own juices. The beans are turned daily and become dry specimens nine days later to be shipped worldwide, roasted and blended into edible ecstasy.

✷ MARKET ✷

Mercado Pino Suárez Villahermosa's Mercado Pino Suárez, at Hnos. Bastar Zozaya between Constitución and Pino Suárez, is an exciting place to experience tastes you won't find anywhere else. What an explosion of tropical smells! Rush downstairs and hide from the heat, like a lizard hiding under a rock. The seafood area is a fine place to start, and all the ice cools this room by a degree or two. Here's your chance to buy a grilled-and-smoked-on-a-stick *pejelagarto asado*, a prehistoric fish that positively looks it. Long and eel-like with a set of teeth that'll set yours to chattering, it's deliciously sweet and caught in nearby Río Grijalva. (Look for women selling tamales stuffed with shredded *pejegarto* upstairs.) You'll also see *sietes presas* (smoked wild marsh birds) at an adjacent booth. As at all standup market dining experiences, a folding knife comes in handy.

Fondas. Upstairs at the fondas you'll see *huevos con pejelagarto* (scrambled eggs with shreds of the smoked fish); armadillo in *adobo*; and iguana dishes listed on painted wall menus. *Chalupas,* Tabasco style, are made with two tortillas sandwiching beans and one of these exotic meats. They are then fried and sauced with a simple, very spicy tomato purée.

Tortillas. Grab a few thick, handmade tortillas made from both ground dried and fresh corn (which produces a wonderfully coarse dough). Other women sell handmade *tortillas ordas*, which are even larger in diameter, thick and crisp. Next chair over are smaller, sweetened-with-*canela* tortillas, *tortillas toda poste*.

Pozole. Also downstairs, the smell of roasting cocoa beans is glorious. If you can possibly stand the thought of a hot drink, let your nose guide you to a sweet brew made with cocoa, *masa*, sugar, and water. Like the soup-stews of Jalisco and the iced *masa* drinks in Mérida's market, its name is *pozole*. The taste is more akin to *champurrado*, chocolate *atole*.

Vinegar. Down the same aisle is a good take-home item: locally brewed *vinagre mundial* (banana vinegar) in screw-top bottles. Around here it's used in *escabeches* and stews.

Chiles. You'll see piles of local *blancos* used mostly in table sauces, and *pico de perrón*, tiny red and green mouth numbers.

Cocoa. The real thing, cocoa beans from nearby Tabasco plantations, are sold raw or roasted. A few women sell beans they have darkly toasted on clay *comales* for boldly flavored drinks and *moles*. Hot, foamy chocolate made from these beans boiled with water and honey is how the drink tasted centuries ago. Unfortunately for chocolate lovers worldwide, the much more lucrative oil industry is encroaching on Mexican cocoa fields at an alarming rate. What used to be a booming industry, cocoa is rapidly becoming extinct in Tabasco.

Señora Gómez de Martínez's

Pipián *Pumpkin Seed Sauce for Poultry or Vegetables*

THIS PRE-HISPANIC SAUCE is most often served in Tabasco over chicken rather than wild turkey, and it's a fonda favorite around Villahermosa. Señora Gómez de Martínez, who cooks at one of Mercado Pino Suárez's fondas, says to be sure to use raw, unsalted, and unhulled seeds for the sauce because the hulls add flavor. The hulled variety make the dish oilier (see pages 52 and 214). Some cooks purchase preroasted seeds to make things easier. A *metate* is used for the grinding. If possible, try this ancient and still popular technique. Traditional cooks, like Señora Gómez de Martínez, swear that using a *metate* makes an enormous difference to the dish's taste and texture rather than using a blender or, heaven forbid, a processor. But, as we all know, times have changed and blenders make easy work out of once all-day chores.

Yield: 2 cups

For the sauce

8 ounces unhulled pumpkin seeds
½ teaspoon cumin seed
1 ancho chile, stemmed, seeded, and deveined
2 guajillo chiles, stemmed and seeded, or 2 chipotle chiles for a spicier, smoky "pipián"
2 garlic cloves
2 Tablespoons vegetable oil
2 "epazote" sprigs, if available
salt

1. Toast the raw pumpkin seeds, or bake them on a baking sheet in a 325°F oven, until they are lightly browned, stirring regularly. Add the cumin seed and continue toasting for another minute. Cool. Place the seeds in a blender container, or *metate*, and grind to the point where the seeds still have a bit of texture and are not a completely smooth paste.

2. Transfer the seeds to a medium-sized bowl, add 2½ cups water, and stir. Remove the husks by pressing the mixture through a sieve with a wooden spoon into another bowl, or use the medium disk of a food mill.

3. Put the chiles, with enough water to cover, in a pot and bring the water to a boil. Lower the heat and simmer for 5 minutes. Drain (reserving 1 cup liquid) and transfer the chiles to the blender jar. Add the cup of chile water and the garlic. Blend until smooth.

4. Heat the oil in a deep pot to very hot and carefully add the chile sauce (it splatters!). Stir for 3 minutes, until the sauce has reduced slightly. Pass the pumpkin seed sauce through the sieve one more time and into the chile sauce. Reduce the heat and simmer, uncovered, for about 20 minutes, stirring from time to time. Add the *epazote* during the last 10 minutes of cooking and remove it when serving. Add salt to taste.

Anita Martínez's

Chilaquiles I *Tortilla Hash*

BREAKFASTING AMONG LOCALS IN EARLY MORNING HOURS at a market is an experience you'll never forget. Workers often relax and catch a bite before the hordes arrive, so find a spot at a crowded fonda and order the same as almost everyone seated around you. In Tabasco, the usual fare will be saucy, chewy *chilaquiles*. Just remember: You're the outsider and it's up to you to be friendly. Tabascans always respond in kind.

Chilaquiles is the perfect breakfast dish of fonda cooks nationwide: It gives them a chance to use leftover tortillas (the dish is actually made with day-old tortillas because they soak up juices better than fresh). The fonda where Anita cooks is no exception; she serves twenty orders every morning at the seven-stool counter, probably because hers is one of the few places in Villahermosa making *chilaquiles* with tomatillo salsa to order. I collected five *chilaquiles* recipes from fondas—(Mazatlán to Mérida), and another four from home cooks. All were basically identical except for fresh or dried chiles and sauces. *Chilaquiles*, whether for breakfast or a light supper is one of Mexico's most popular dishes.

Yield: 6 servings

- 24 day-old corn tortillas
- ½ cup vegetable oil
- 2 cups Tomatillo Salsa (page 244), made without the Oaxacan specialty, "gusanitos"
- 1 cup Chicken Broth (page 19)
- 2 Tablespoons chopped "epazote" leaves, if available
- ½ cup crumbled ranchero cheese, dry cottage cheese, or farmer cheese
- 1 cup "Crema" (page 80), crème fraîche, or sour cream
- 18 raw onion slices

1. Stack 8 tortillas and cut through them into eighths (pie style). Continue with the rest. Heat the oil in a large skillet, fry the tortilla pieces, and drain on paper towels. They must remain chewy in the sauce so don't let them get too crisp. A chewy, almost meatlike texture is important to the dish.

2. Discard any remaining oil in the skillet, then add the salsa and broth. Stir in the tortilla pieces and *epazote* (if available). Cook, turning, for 3 minutes.

3. Spoon the mixture onto plates, sprinkle with the crumbled cheese, and serve immediately with a spoonful of *crema* and raw onion slices.

Inez Rodríguez del Agrio's

Chilaquiles II *Tortilla Casserole*

Chilaquiles is most often baked in a casserole—or *cazuela*—at home, as is Inez's family version. Most fondas don't have ovens, if they did, this would probably be the favored preparation method, too, as *chilaquiles* can easily be made in advance. As in the preceding *chilaquiles* recipe, tortilla pieces must be lightly fried before mixing with the sauce and baked. Mexicans love the chewy, meaty texture the fried tortillas provide, especially if no meat is eaten with the dish.

But you can add cooked chicken or chorizo to the sauce before mixing. The pan version is moister with the tortillas swimming in sauce; this baked rendition is drier, so it's perfect as a flavorful starch on a plate with meat or vegetables. Rather than tomatillo salsa, Inez likes a red tomato sauce (see *Entomatadas,* page 255). Casserole *chilaquiles* makes a terrific party dish, not unlike a great lasagne, so feel free to double the recipe and add more cheese if you'd like.

Yield: 6 servings

- 24 day-old corn tortillas
- 1 cup vegetable oil
- 2 cups red tomato sauce for "Entomatadas" (page 255) or Tomatillo Salsa (page 244)
- ½ cup shredded "quesillo de Oaxaca," stringy cheese, or mozzarella
- 2 Tablespoons fresh "epazote" leaves, if available
- 2 cups cooked and shredded, skinless chicken or 1 cup cooked and drained chorizo (optional)
- ½ cup crumbled ranchero cheese, dry cottage cheese, or farmer cheese
- 1 cup "Crema" (page 80), crème fraîche, or sour cream

1. Preheat oven to 375°F.

2. Stack 8 tortillas and cut through them into eigths (pie style). Continue with the rest. Heat the oil in a large skillet, fry the tortilla pieces, and drain them on paper towels. They must remain chewy in the sauce so don't let them get too crisp—the chewiness is essential to the dish.

3. Mix the tortilla chips, sauce, shredded cheese, *epazote*, and optional meat.

4. Immediately pour the mixture into a greased 3-quart shallow casserole and bake for about 20 minutes, until brown and bubbly. Scoop onto plates, topping each with a sprinkle of crumbled cheese and a spoonful of *crema*.

Inez Rodríguez del Agrio's

Horchata *Cold Rice Drink*

HORCHATA, ONE OF MEXICO'S FAVORITE TRADITIONAL COLD DRINKS, is especially satisfying, Inez tells me, when the temperature in Tabasco hovers at 110°F and the humidity hits 99 percent. I say it's best when you've just eaten lunch with one too many chiles (the two H's, *horchata* and *habanero* seem to have been made for each other). The throat-cooler is similar in flavor to a cold, liquid rice pudding.

Unlike ubiquitous bottled sodas, *horchata* is not sold at every food counter, and so often these days it's instantly made from a mix diluted with water. If you'd like to try the real thing, go to a traditional market and look around for a counter with huge glass bottles filled with colored liquids. *Horchata* is the opaque, milky white one.

Probably the most famous *horchata* counter in Mexico is Casilda's, in Oaxaca's Mercado Benito Juárez (page 223), where they'll add a dollop of *tuna* (cactus fruit purée) upon your request, and which when stirred, will turn your drink pink. Floating on top is a spoonful of crushed fruit with chopped nuts.

As always, before ordering a water-based drink anywhere in Mexico, make sure it's made with purified water; and ask for yours to be served in a plastic disposable cup.

Yield: 2½ quarts

- ½ cup white rice
- 1½ cups ground blanched almonds
- 1 three-inch "canela" stick or 1 two-inch cinnamon sticks
- 1 cup sugar

1. A day in advance, turn the rice to powder in a spice grinder or a blender set at high speed. Put the rice in a bowl and add the almonds, and *canela*. Cover with 3 cups hot water and let stand, overnight, covered with a towel.

2. Pour the mixture into a blender container and purée about 3 or 4 minutes. This is a long time, but the mixture cannot be gritty. Add 3 cups water and contine blending for another 30 seconds (in batches, if necessary).

3. Line a large strainer with a double layer of cheesecloth and place it over a large mixing bowl. Pour in the rice mixture, stirring and pressing it through the cloth-lined sieve. When it is all passed through, gather the corners of the cloth and squeeze the remaining liquid through, wringing the cloth.

4. Add the sugar and another 3 cups water. Empty the *horchata* into a large pitcher and refrigerate. Stir before serving ice cold.

The Yucatán Peninsula

Campeche
Mérida

MEXICO'S FLAT-AS-A-PANCAKE YUCATÁN PENINSULA includes the states of Yucatán, Campeche, and Quintana Roo on the east coast just north of Belize. The east coast's fame is based on crystal-clear aqua waters for snorkeling and scuba diving. Cancún and Isla Cozumel are in a league by themselves and attract an international crowd that likes to have a good time after a hard day swimming in the Caribbean. The west coast is marshy and hot; while not a tourist destination, it is home to flocks of fuchsia flamingos that enjoy wading in those blue-green lagoons (they also crave tasty crustaceans that thrive here, in the Gulf, like no place else on earth). Yucatán, home to Mayan ruins of Chichén Itzá and Uxmal, plus charming colonial Mérida, has a cuisine all its own—much more Caribbean-influenced than Mexican.

Left: Yucatán's Chichén Itzá is a wondrous spot.

◆ Campeche ◆

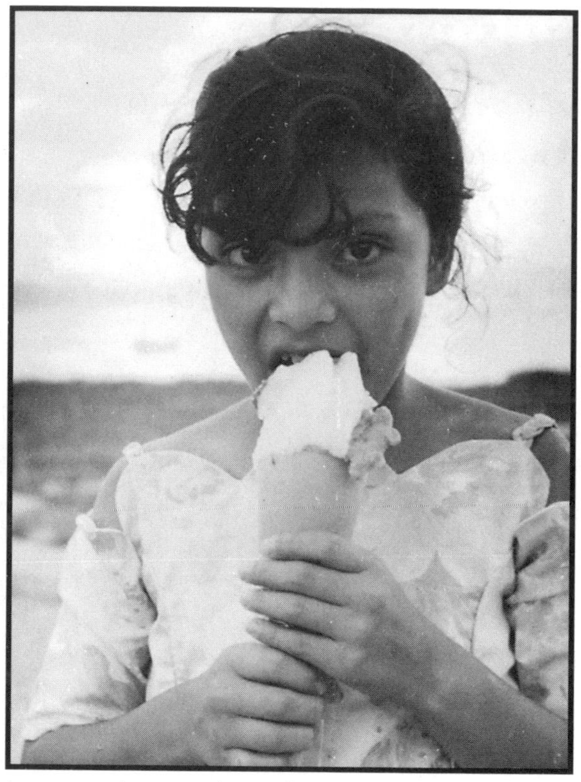

Ice cream reaches its popularity peak in Campeche.

HOT. I SAID HOT! Then throw in some chile, like everyone else, and sweat a bit more. Campeche's culinary attitude is simple: Match spicy-hot weather to spicy-hot food. Sizzle.

Located where the Yucatán peninsula bends northward in the Gulf of Mexico, the waters are perfect for shrimp. Campeche is the shrimping capital of Mexico, and that means the world. The list of restaurant, fonda, and beach shack shrimp preparations is mind-boggling. Besides cheap, wonderful cocktails at thatched-roofed huts along the coast, just north of Champotón, you'll want to try the critters at every fish place you see. Look for shrimp dishes spiced with fresh or dried chiles; *mojo de ajo* (garlic sauce); onion and sour orange sauce; stuffed with crab; grilled with pineapple juice; sautéed in *achiote* paste; or just a pile of perfectly boiled beauties to unpeel and dip in hot habanero table salsa (with various bottled brands of liquid fire on the table for your dining pleasure).

Other than shrimp, Campeche's most popular meal has to be black beans with corn tortillas and super-spicy salsa, with or without anything else (except a gallon of cold liquid in that heat—whew!). Over the centuries millions of people in southern Mexico found themselves feeling great after this simple and nourishing repast. Now we know the combination of corn and black beans (no other type of bean, except soy) makes a complete source of protein.

✷ MARKET ✷

Pedro Sainz de Barbaranda Campeche's main market, Mercado Pedro Sainz de Barbaranda, is located just SW of Baluarte de San Pedro. A *baluarte* is an old fortress, built in the eighteenth century to keep out pirates, and there are seven left in the city today that maintain Campeche's special character and entice tourists. Since it's so hot at the market, it's best to go early in the morning. Bananas are absolutely ravishing piled and hung by color and size. Black beans, sold by size, fill dozens of burlap sacks and it's here where Mexico's tiniest *bambinos* are offered; they cook in less than thirty minutes.

Yucatán's infamous habanero chile begins to make a big statement in Campeche, and you'll notice more and more piles of the green, yellow, and orange fireworks as you travel deeper into the peninsula. Chilillo chile (a variety of dried chile piquín) is coveted here, too.

Fondas. Breakfast *Chilaquiles* (pages 285 and 286) and a cold drink are top choices at the few fondas. Later in the day steaming soups are the most sought after lunch dishes, like an especially spicy, mixed fish soup made with copious quantities of habanero chiles; *chocolomo* made with beef innards, jalapeño chile, and potatoes; and a delicate-looking green onion and green habanero chile broth that's so spicy it's guaranteed to have you begging for mercy after the first slurp. Caribbean dishes like fried plantains with black beans and rice, and Cuban sandwiches are featured—they're much like *tortas* but are made on softer rolls and compressed with a weight while cooking on a griddle. The most popular filler at the market is sliced roast pork with ham, cheese, and vinegared chiles.

Pan de cazón. A small dogfish shark, the *cazón* is one of the market's most important cooked seafood items. A puffed, thick, handmade tortilla is filled with sieved black beans and *cazón,* first sautéed with *epazote.*

Seafood cocktails. A few bars are located in the market, and those on surrounding streets do a brisk business, especially those offering dirt-cheap, huge, sublime shrimp cocktails. If you're a shrimp lover, Campeche is definitely your town.

Pastry. *Campechanes* are the city's specialty—they are similar to puff pastry and made into four-inch round cookies. They are sold near the market bread tables.

Hats. *Jipijapa* hats, or Panamas, are great buys at the market. They're woven in the nearby pueblo of Becal, in large damp caves. If you plan to visit any pyramids, now's the chance to purchase a quality hat; you'll need one.

Hammocks. Hammocks are cheap because they're the standard sleeping arrangement for everyone; beds are just too hot. A state crafts store is located in Baluarte (Fort) San Carlos, at the beginning of Calle 8, with good prices, too. It's about ten blocks west of the market.

María Isabel Díaz Morales's

Enchiladas de Plátanos *Tortillas with Tomatillo Salsa and Plantains*

A WONDERFUL TASTE COMBINATION OF sweet plantains, corn tortillas, and tart tomatillos makes for one great dish. Morris and I were served these tortillas for a light, late evening supper under a backyard *palapa* (palm frond-roofed hut) in the hot, tropical air of Campeche. Though tomatillos are not often used in these parts, María Isabel has been making enchiladas this way since she was a girl and an aunt came to visit from Guadalajara with this recipe in hand, hoping to find Campeche's plantains.

Along with our supper, María Isabel and her husband, Jorge, made a *Licuado* (page 138) with watermelon. Their eight-year old daughter later proudly presented a dessert tray she had prepared of papaya, pineapple, and mango slices sprinkled with sour Seville orange juice (you may substitute lime and orange juice, half and half).
Yield: 4 servings

For the cooked salsa

Prepare Tomatillo Salsa (page 244) to step 4, except use only chipotle chile—no pasilla chile or *gusanitos*, as they're strictly Oaxacan. Heat 2 tablespoons vegetable oil in a deep pot. Carefully pour in the salsa (it splatters!) and stir, then lower the heat and simmer for 5 minutes. Add cilantro at the end.

For the enchiladas

- 3 large, ripe plantains (black), peeled
- 4 Tablespoons vegetable oil for the plantains
- 4 Tablespoons oil for the tortillas
- 8 corn tortillas, not too thin or they will fall apart in the sauce
- ½ cup crumbled "ranchero" cheese, dry cottage cheese, or farmer cheese
- ½ cup "Crema" (page 80), crème fraîche, or sour cream

1. Cut the plantains into ½-inch slices on the diagonal. Heat 4 tablespoons oil in a large skillet and fry the plantains until they are brown. Drain on paper towels.
2. Clean the skillet and heat 4 tablespoons fresh oil and fry 1 tortilla 15 seconds. Be sure not to over-crisp, as you would for corn chips. This frying is to give the tortillas strength so they won't fall apart in the sauce.
3. Immediately dip the tortilla in the tomatillo salsa and be sure the sauce covers the entire tortilla. Put the tortilla on a plate. Fold in half, then in half again to form a triangular shape. Repeat with another tortilla. Sprinkle with crumbled cheese. Place about 6 slices of plantain on the tortillas. Continue with the remaining enchiladas and plantains. Spoon 2 or 3 tablespoons *crema* on the side of each plate and serve immediately.

Fidel Torres de Mora's

Tacos de Pescados *Exotic Seafood Tacos*

MANTA RAY WINGS *MANTAZAYA MINILLA* (SMALL DICE), OR *CHAN-CHAN* (LARGE DICE), are fillings for tacos in Campeche. The bodies of the rays are never cooked, only those wondrous wings, which are skinned before chopping. There are numerous unusual seafood offerings at fast-food counters all over town; wherever you walk you're within sight of someone snacking at a stand-up bar. Another equally popular taco is *cazón* (dog shark), which is usually on the same menu with ray wings. All these tacos are quick to make with chopped seafood pieces, onion, and chile, with salsas and lime on the side. There are rarely cooking variations—variety is in the fabulous fish assortment courtesy of the Gulf of Mexico.

Fidel offers bottles of at least four different salsas at his taco counter, each made from different chiles and vinegar combinations. He also serves a home-brewed version his mother makes, but that recipe is secret, as well as her *escabeche* of tiny, fresh red chiles that bites your head off.

Yield: 4 tacos

- 8 tortillas
- 1 pound cooked manta ray meat (surprisingly similar in taste to scallops, so substitute them) or other Gulf seafood
- 2 Tablespoons vegetable oil
- 1 small white onion, chopped
- 2 jalapeño chiles, red if possible
- lime wedges, bottled hot sauces, and pickled vegetables

1. Warm the tortillas.

2. Chop the manta ray or other seafood into small or large dice.

3. Heat the oil on a griddle, cook the onion until golden, then add the seafood and chile. Stir-fry for a minute, just until the seafood is cooked.

4. Put 2 overlapping, warm tortillas on a plate and top with a quarter of the cooked mixture. Offer lime wedges, bottled hot sauces, and pickled vegetables.

• Mérida •

Black "zapote negro" fruit is offered at Mercado Santos Degollado.

MARIMBA! XYLOPHONE MUSIC catching a breeze sending the rhythm through swaying banana and palm leaves; hot days and balmy nights dining under the stars in open-roofed courtyards of old haciendas; and, of course, pulsing *mercados* with exotic fruits and spice mixtures. Ah—Mérida. Add lovely colonial buildings that had their heyday around the turn of the century when *sisal* (rope and hammock material) was king and *chicle* (chewing gum was made originally from tree sap here) was queen; clip-clop sounds of horse-drawn buggies for open-air city touring; plus nightly folk dance fests provided free by the city for everyone's enjoyment.

Mérida's, and Yucatán's, food is completely different from that in the rest of Mexico. It's a cuisine unto itself, influenced more by the Caribbean islands than by other states in the country. The Mayas first developed agriculture in the inhospitable soil of Yucatán, and corn, of course, was God. Incomparable seafood variety, wild game, including deer and turkeys, the renowned habanero chile, and *recados* (seasoning pastes) all added their special touches to the region's tantalizing dishes. Today the wild game is but a memory, but tradition runs deep in Yucatecan Mayans, who frequently prepare and savor other foods of their ancestors.

✱ MARKETS ✱

Mercado Municipal Lucas de Gálvez The city's main market is located four blocks southeast of Plaza Mayor (the *zócalo*) and bounded by Calles 56 and 56A at Calle 67, but it's not just the market building with its entrance across from the side of the post office. There are additional buildings that ramble on for blocks. Once inside the entrance, look toward your left for famous Panama hats of Yucatán (across from fruit basket displays). The very best, extremely tightly woven hats are made in the small village of Becal, just across the Campeche state line, but the selection is tops in Mérida's market, as well as in other city shops, and the prices are right, even though you are, as always, expected to bargain. These are the hats sold in New York and Paris for more than $300 in upscale stores, the kind you can roll tightly and pack in a suitcase. Buy the best quality hat you can find and afford, wear it to every open-air market and archaeological site, and you'll have a Meridian souvenir when traveling to sunny spots the rest of your life.

Also in this market area are photogenic women, wearing beautifully embroidered blouses and dresses known throughout the world, selling citrus, fresh white beans called *ibes*, vine-ripened tomatoes, and the Yucatán's habanero chile in all its glory. One interesting thing about habanero chiles is they're hotter here, in Yucatán, then the same chile grown in other states, and especially those grown in the U.S. It's not to say that any of them are bland (by a long shot!) it's just that regional items do best on their home turf.

Perfume is the key word when it comes to Mérida's fruit selection: Strange tropical beauties are perfumed with such unusually strong aromas you'll want to bottle their collective scents. More familiar papayas, pineapples, and all Yucatán's unusual sour citrus fruits make great, foamy blender concoctions. In the center and rear of the market buildings and spilling outside behind, are places to see the seasonal citrus choices. Other fruits compete: In the winter and spring months, be sure to try *zapote* (known as *mamey* in other regions, a taste of persimmon and pear) and *zapote negro* (like a round russet potato on the outside and glisteningly black inside with a soft, sweet fruit to eat with a spoon). *Nance* are small, perfumed, golden fruits you'll see both fresh and in jars with wine and sugar syrups (great to take back home).

Fondas. Upstairs just across from the entrance to **Mercado de Artesanías** (more Panama hats and hammocks and handcrafts from both Yucatán and other places in Mexico) are about fifteen fondas vying for your attention. Look for a clean place with other customers (as always, a good sign). Be sure the food you want to try is listed on a sign. Fonda owners are not above telling you they have what you want then walking over to a seedy-looking place to fill your bowl from a cauldron dripping with what looks like last week's grease. At least stop by for a *refresco* (soda) when the weather is hot and sticky. This open-air balcony is one of the few places in the market to catch the smallest breeze. And watch that your new Panama hat doesn't blow off.

Banana leaves. Steamed banana leaves are a market highlight. Folded and sold by the package (about ten leaves), they make preparing tamales much easier than picking huge leaves off your own tree and singeing or steaming each to make the leaves pliable enough for folding around *masa.* All you need to do with cooked leaves is wash and dry them before cutting to size. Market women, wearing *huipiles* (traditional white, embroidered dresses), will show you the quality of the leaves, then deftly tie your pile with "string" made from a long strand of the leaf. It's a simple and beautiful presentation centuries old.

Recados. Wandering a bit into the main building, you'll catch the scent of *recado* stalls selling the spice mixtures that make Yucatán's cooking style unique in all Mexico. Plastic tubs sit on counters filled with pastes molded into piles of brick red, olive green, and black. Small, prepacked plastic bags make perfect travelers: unrefrigerated, *recado* keeps a few months; refrigerated, up to a year. Annatto seeds are everywhere, ground, tiny pumpkin seeds fill buckets waiting to be turned into *Siquil-P'ak* (page 305), and small plastic pouches offer dried spice concoctions. Teeny envelopes of Spanish saffron threads are a good buy and travel better than you do. Buy a few tiny cans of Bijol, the Caribbean coloring condiment for Yellow Rice (page 307).

Chanchames. Mérida's *chanchames* are Yucatecan empanadas cooked like Olivia Castro's in Oaxaca (page 256) on an ungreased *comal.* The difference between Oaxaca's and Mérida's is fillings. Here the tortilla is smeared with black bean purée, then topped with raw onion, radish slices, the juice of sour oranges, and habanero chile. Around Mérida, tortilla fold-overs are called empanadas and are griddled with oil, like quesadillas everywhere else.

Drinks. Not at all like its namesake soups of the north, especially in the state of Jalisco, Mérida's *pozole* is found only in the market, on the main floor, and toward the back. The ancient Mayan *atole*-like brew is very spicy, but made with ice water thickened with a *masa* made with shredded coconut and sweetened with honey. (Both the special *masa* and the drink are called *pozole* in Mérida.) Parched imbibers first bite off half a habanero chile (!) dipped in coarse salt before drinking. (In fact, other women who sell the softball-sized *masa* rounds prepared especially for *pozole* always include a habanero chile in the plastic bag wrapping.) A friend and chef, Chris McDonald of Toronto's *Avalon* and *Zócalo* restaurants, is used to very hot chiles but once long ago bit into a "beautiful, orangey-yellow, lantern-shaped chile" when he worked in the resort town of Zihuatanejo. He had to take the rest of the day off. So, stay clear. Even without the chile I have never seen market *pozole* made with purified water. It's strictly a drink for locals, especially market workers. If you're dying to try it, buy the special *masa* and dissolve it in your own ice water.

Have a coco! Drink fresh coconut water with a straw directly from its still-green covered shell and punctured with a hole just big enough for the straw to slip through. Try to find a coco on ice—it's incredibly refreshing and, from what countless coco experts say, very healthful, and without the coconut meat's fat content.

As you would think with Mérida's heat, *atole* and hot chocolate are hardly ever sold around these parts. But in the winter months you'll see *atole* in Valladolid's **Mercado Municipal** at night, in the nearby village of Espita, and other pueblos far out in the countryside.

Butchers. Butchers are in an attached market building all their own. It's a bizarre building, to be sure, with rows of butchers lined up with carcasses and parts piled on and strung above neat counters. Each butcher has his butchered animal to sell for the day, and some specialize in beef, others pork. Everyone has all the cuts, including all the innards. Pork butchers have fresh, liquid lard for sale by the kilo in plastic bags.

Hammocks. Hammocks can be found upstairs, across from the fondas on the open-air terrace, in **Mercado de Artesanías.** Ask around and bargain hard as this is primarily a touristy spot. Buy all-cotton and get the largest hammock you can afford (see page 313). If you're ready for an adventure, go out to the pueblo of Tixcocob and watch hammocks being woven. You'll get the very best prices there, especially if buying in almost any quantity above one.

Mercado Santos Degollado Mercado Santos Degollado is a neighborhood (but still central) market having all the necessary ingredients for Yucatán's unique cuisine. It's across from the Santiago church at Santiago Parque, on Calle 59 between Calles 70 and 72. If the pulse and aromas (whew!) of the central market are a bit too much, this may be a more welcoming experience.

Tortillas. Women vendors sell handmade *arepas*, sweet tortillas made with anise then sprinkled with sugar and baked. *Ishuas* are handmade tortillas made with fresh corn, lard, sugar, and salt then cooked on a *comal*. They're Mayan cookies.

Fiambres. Soft tacos made with warm tortillas and topped with cool seafood cocktails are served at a few fondas in the courtyard. Pull up a stool to a small, glass-surrounded counter and order shrimp or octopus tacos and squirt them with plenty of Seville orange juice. Dotting a piece of spicy habanero chile across the tortilla is the custom.

Nieves. **Helados Polito**, the famous sherbet and ice milk stand in Mercado Santos Degollado is a Meridian classic and its flavors are always tropical and exotic. Order everything you've never heard of. Guanábana is a delight, as is black zapote and salmon-colored mamey. Ever-cooling is the region's famous sour lime. You'll spot Helados Polito's tropical fruit-flavored popsicle carts on the streets of Mérida—they're a sight for sore eyes in the afternoon's blazing sun.

✱ PLACES TO GO AND THINGS TO EAT ✱

Bakery. Panificadora Montejo S.A. de C.V., Calle 58 No. 489, Montejo at the corner of Calles 62 and 63 in front of the Monumento a la Bandera. tel. 27-27-01. Open every day 6 A.M. to 10 P.M. They also have a smaller shop on the *zócalo* at C-61 Avn. Costado de Catedral and Alado de Singer, tel. 23-11-74. Open every day 7 A.M. to 8 P.M. At either store you'll find the very best French bread in Mérida. Each loaf is baked with a palm frond strip running down the center, both to cut a lengthwise slit and to add a bit of local flavor. At the Montejo baking location, loaves come out of the ovens at 6 A.M., 12:30, 5, 6:30, 7, and 8 P.M. There's always a small line of regulars who know exactly what time they can take home hot bread.

Tamales. Women sell tamales outside in the evening, in front of Panificadora Montejo (Montejo location) from tamale steamers for banana-leaf- and corn-husk-wrapped varieties. Cloth-lined baskets house incredible pit-baked masterpieces. One ten-inch work of art, *pibipollo*, is *recado*-flavored chicken cooked in coarse *masa*, wrapped in banana leaves and baked underground in a *pib*. The blackened banana leaves add incredible flavor to the *masa*. *Pib espelón* is another *pib*-cooked tamale filled with fresh (not dried and reconstituted) tiny black beans. This stop is a must when you're in the neighborhood.

Linens. Embroidered tablecloths and *huipiles* (traditional dresses) are sold every day at the **Mercado de Artesanías**, which is next to the fondas, upstairs in the central market. There's a big open-air crafts market on the *zócalo* every Sunday.

Antojitos and dancing. Sunday at **Santa Lucía Park** is the place to be. Morning ballroom dancing to Latin rhythms starts promptly at 11 A.M. Dance those calories away because a few steps off are snack booths selling *polcanes*, local *masa* ovals filled with cabbage, *ibes* (fresh white beans), or *pipián*, and topped with vinegared red onion.

Antojitos and marimba. Evenings at **Tiano's** (tel. 23-71-18), in Parque Hidalgo, is a tourist attraction to be sure, with palm trees swaying to the rhythm of a marimba band. You'll be approached by at least half a dozen hammock peddlers and hat salesmen, but the place is infectious. White *guayaberas* (fancy, pleated dress shirts) and Panama hats shimmy to xylophones and maracas. This is what evening in Mérida is all about and why people travel from all over the world to be here. An order of *panuchos* is perfect light dinner fare with naughty tropical drinks.

Mazapán. Marzipan-type candy made with pumpkin seeds is sold throughout the city in shops and private homes. On occasion a woman will have a tray of the delicacies for sale in a market. The intricately made and colored candies are very similar to almond paste marzipan we see in the U.S. *Mazapán* is always special-occasion gift candy in these parts.

Pizza. This isn't traditional, or even regional by a long shot (in fact, don't tell anyone you read it here), but if you've been in Mexico for some time and long for decent pizza, try **Drive-In International** on Ave. Colón between 62 and 60. Hours: 5 P.M. to 1 A.M. Friendly waiters want you to be happy with pizza straight from a wood-burning oven. Beers are icy cold.

RESTAURANTS

Flamboyanes. Moderate. Prolong Montejo No. 374 at Calle 33, tel. 44-09-88. Hours 1 P.M. to 5 P.M. At the northern end of the famed Calle Montejo, Flamboyanes is packed at lunchtime with locals—large families and businessmen who demand excellent Yucatecan food at reasonable prices. As soon as you sit down in the air-conditioned room, an appetizer tray is placed on your table to make ordering an extra pleasant experience. *Salbutes* (page 310) and *Papadzules* (page 311) are classic starters, plus Flamboyanes's handmade tortillas are real bonuses. Very traditional dishes such as Sunday's *Puchero* (page 326); Monday's black beans with pork; *Sopa de Lima* (page 65); and turkey with various *recado*-enhanced stuffings are menu standbys. Most dishes come with rice and *epazote*-flavored black beans. Friendly waiters enjoy out-of-towners and are patient repeating the contents of unusual sounding dishes.

Los Almendros. Moderate. Calle 50A No. 493 between Calles 57 and 59, tel. 21-28-51. Open every day from 9 A.M. to 9 P.M. but can close earlier. A large, covered courtyard in the center of an air-conditioned hacienda-style building serves as the main dining room in one of the fanciest restaurants in Mérida serving traditional food. Waiters are thoroughly professional and eager to help: Newcomers to Yucatán food are given, with the menu, a brochure with color photos of the dishes to make ordering simple. Before anything, have one of their great margaritas, then share a huge appetizer portion of *panuchos* (fried tortillas stuffed with black bean purée, and topped with shredded, marinated turkey and onions *en escabeche*)—drop-by-drop adding the flavorful and spicy *salsa de habanero* that you'll find on the table. Another acclaimed starter is *longaniza asada* (charcoal-grilled sausage with Yucatán spices). *Poc-Chuc* (Grilled, Marinated Pork Steak, page 328) is not only the house specialty but was also made famous by Los Almendros. Both pork and chicken *Pibil* (pit-baked with Yucatán spices and wrapped in banana leaves, pages 320 and 322) are worthwhile choices with a side order of rice and fried plantains. All this terrific food comes with old-fashioned tunes played by a combo of gentlemen.

El Trapiche. Inexpensive. Calle 62 No. 491 between Calles 59 and 61. Open every day 7:30 A.M. to 11 P.M. An old-fashioned soda fountain-like counter with stools to match. Your view, behind the fruit drink bar, is a wonderfully hokey display of coconuts, mangoes, bananas, pineapples, and papayas smacking of palapa roof huts. Drawings of these fruits along with prices are on a menu wall to your right—any and all combinations perked up with a squirt of Seville orange is a traditional Mérida treat. Breakfasts and sandwiches are good, too.

Héctor Santiago Pérez's

▲▼▲

Recados *Red, Olive, and Black Seasoning Pastes*

BASIC TO YUCATÁN COOKING ARE *RECADOS*, SOLD IN MARKETS or made by exacting home cooks. Three main pastes are: *recado rojo*, brick-red from annatto seed, black peppercorns, white onion, toasted garlic, oregano, and allspice; *recado de bistec*, dark olive green from toasted garlic, toasted onion, black pepper, oregano, *canela*, cumin, cloves, de árbol chiles, and white vinegar; and *recado negro* (also called *chilmole*), black from burnt de árbol chiles and xcatik chiles (found only in Yucatán), blackened onions, burnt tortillas, toasted garlic, and cumin. *Recado* pastes, not unlike *mole* pastes of Oaxaca and Puebla, are made with fresh ingredients and thinned with liquid before being added to dishes. *Recado* pastes are also rubbed into meats (without thinning) as a marinade before cooking. As with *moles*, no cooks use exactly the same proportions for their *recados*, but basic ingredients are standard, with personal variations.

I was fortunate to meet Héctor in Mérida's central market while he was hunting around the *recado* stalls. A chef, Héctor makes his own *recados*, but this day he was on the prowl for unusual seasoning pastes and spice blends for Christmas. Born and raised in a pueblo outside Mérida, he learned his trade at an uncle's hotel and has been cooking at different restaurants throughout Yucatán for the past twelve years. A master of the subtleties of *recados*, he can tell what village a blend is from by color and aroma—"I guess it's my claim to fame," he smirked and shrugged.

Recado Rojo *Red Annatto Seed Seasoning Paste* (Achiote)

DEFINITELY THE MOST COMMON *RECADO* IN THE YUCATÁN. *Rojo* is generously spread over chicken and pork for the peninsula's famous *pibils*; over seafood before grilling; and in rice dishes. You'll see paste moistened with vinegar and sold in plastic bags at smaller markets. In the U.S., some markets, and all Latino markets, sell *achiote* paste in small boxes that keep indefinitely, refrigerated. Sometimes people in Yucatán add 1 de árbol chile, toasted and ground, to *recado* for a little spice.

Yield: about 1 cup

- 5 heaping Tablespoons annatto seeds (or 3 Tablespoons "achiote" paste)
- 1 garlic head, the cloves peeled
- 2 Tablespoons black peppercorns

1. Bring 1 cup water to a boil and add the annatto seeds. Lower the heat and simmer, uncovered, for 10 minutes. Let the seeds soak at room temperature in the water for 8 to 12 hours to soften. Drain.

- 2 medium white onions, coarsely chopped
- 2 teaspoons dried Mexican oregano
- 1 teaspoon freshly ground allspice berries or powdered allspice

2. Toast (page 16) the garlic cloves until they are lightly brown. Put them in a processor or blender container. Add the peppercorns, onions, oregano, and allspice and blend the mixture. Add the annatto seeds (or *achiote* paste) and blend again. Store the paste in a tightly closed glass jar, refrigerated, for up to one year.

Recado de Bistec *Olive-Green Blend Seasoning Paste*

ALTHOUGH YOU'D EXPECT THIS PASTE to be solely for smearing over a beefsteak (hence the name), it's used in countless ways, from seafood marinades to flavoring soups.
Yield: about ¾ cup

- 1 garlic head, the cloves peeled
- 2 medium onions, quartered
- 8 ounces fresh black peppercorns
- 2 teaspoons dried Mexican oregano
- 1 three-inch "canela" stick
- ½ teaspoon ground cumin
- ½ teaspoon ground cloves
- 6 de árbol chiles

1. Toast (page 16) the garlic cloves until they are lightly brown. Put them in a processor or blender container.

2. Add the remaining ingredients and blend. With a rubber spatula, scrape down the blender sides and blend again to a thick paste. Store in a tightly closed glass jar, refrigerated, for up to one year.

Recado de Negro (also known as Chimole) *Black Seasoning Paste*

STUFFINGS THROUGHOUT THE YUCATÁN ARE OFTEN BLACK. Whether for turkey, chicken, or fish, the bread or *masa* filling is particularly loved in the area around Valladolid, between Mérida and Cancún. When preparing this *recado*, open the kitchen window, turn on a fan, and be sure nearby smoke alarms are disconnected!
Yield: about 1 cup

- 6 de árbol chiles, blackened (toasted and burnt!)
- 2 medium white onions, blackened (toasted and burnt!)
- 2 tortillas, blackened (burnt!)
- 1 garlic head, the cloves peeled and toasted, but not burnt
- ½ teaspoon ground cumin
- 1 teaspoon "achiote" paste

Put all the ingredients in a processor, or blender container and blend. With a rubber spatula, scrape down the blender sides and blend again to a thick paste. Store in a tightly closed glass jar, refrigerated, for up to one year.

Rosario Chávez's

Xnipec *Habanero Chile, Tomato, and Sour Orange Table Salsa*

ROSARIO'S RECIPE FOR *XNIPEC* IS STRAIGHT FROM HER MAYAN ANCESTORS, passed down through family members. It's an uncooked salsa made with the sour juice of Seville oranges, which are popular all over Yucatán. Seville oranges are best known for marmalade in Europe. In Yucatán their particular perfume is one trademark of the peninsula's cooking; when traveling you'll quickly learn to recognize dishes cooked with the juice rather than with Mexico's ubiquitous lime or Yucatán's sour lime, *lima agria*. Rosario, who speaks fluent Mayan, laughed out loud when she told me why the salsa has such a bizarre name. "It means 'the dog's nose,' because if you add too much chile your nose will run and be wet like a dog's."

Rosario loves traditional dance performances held almost every day of the week in Mérida's parks and plazas. In fact, I met her while we were sampling *nance* (preserved tropical fruit) and *Panuchos* (page 310) while watching couples dancing the rhumba at 11:30 in the morning.

Yield: 2 cups

- 1 medium white onion, coarsely chopped
- 1 medium tomato, coarsley chopped
- ¼ cup chopped cilantro leaves
- 1 Seville orange, or ½ orange and ½ lime, juiced
- pinch of salt
- ½ habanero chile, seeds and veins removed, and cut into 2 large pieces (so you can see the fiery chile easily in the onion-tomato mixture)

1. Put the onion, tomato, and cilantro in a serving bowl. Add the juice and salt. Stir to blend.

2. Push the pieces of habanero chile into the mixture. The salsa becomes very hot thanks to the two pieces of chile. Do not eat the chile (they may be discarded before serving to be safe). Leave it at room temperature up to 3 hours, until ready to serve.

Victoria Cuesta de Carrillo's

Salsa Chiltomate *Tomato, Onion, and Habanero Chile Cooked Sauce*

LIKE TABLE SALSAS EVERYWHERE IN MEXICO this is pure joy—and pure southern Mexican when spooned on steaks or on grilled pork tacos. Its Yucatán flavor comes out loud and clear thanks to an abundance of toasted red-ripe tomatoes, onions, and the unrivaled habanero chile. Ingredients are the same as for *Xnipec* (page 302), Yucatán's uncooked salsa, except cooked *chiltomate* has no citrus juice and its texture is completely different—a purée compared to *xnipec's* coarsely chopped fresh vegetables.
Yield: 2 cups

- 6 dark ripe-ripe, medium tomatoes
- 2 medium white onions with their skins, cut into quarters
- 1 habanero chile
- ½ cup cilantro leaves
- 2 Tablespoons vegetable oil
- pinch of salt

1. Toast (page 16) the tomatoes until their skins are blackened and blistered. Put the tomatoes in a plastic bag to "sweat" for a few minutes. Peel and put the tomatoes in a blender container.
2. Toast the onion and put it in the blender.
3. Toast the habanero chile, remove the stem, and put one half (or the whole chile, to taste) in the blender. Add cilantro. Purée to a smooth consistency.
4. Heat the oil in a deep pot and pour in the mixture (it sizzles!). Reduce the heat and simmer, stirring with a wooden spoon, for 15 minutes. Add salt to taste.

Marita Vega de González's

Cebolla Curtida *Marinated Red Onion Condiment*

MARITA SELLS LARGE WHITE AND RED ONIONS, among other root vegetables, at her family produce stall in Mérida's Mercado Municipal. She says a bowl of red, mildly vinegared onions is set upon every dining table in Yucatán, whether fancy restaurant, fonda, or home kitchen. I never found her to be wrong. Serve *cebolla curtida* as a relish with just about anything: grilled or baked meats and fish, tacos, *Pibiles* (pages 320 and 322), or in *Tortas* (page 120). *Panuchos* (page 310) would be northern-style *tostadas* without the bonus of *cebolla curtida* piled atop black bean-filled crisp tortillas.
Yield: 2 cups

- 1 large red onion, 4 inches in diameter
- ½ cup white vinegar
- ½ teaspoon salt
- 1 habanero chile

1. Cut the red onion in half lengthwise; then slice it across the grain into thick, ¼-inch slices. Put the slices in a strainer and wash 2 or 3 times with cold water to be sure of mildness. Dry completely.

2. Put the onions in a bowl.

3. Pour the vinegar and salt over the onion slices and gently mix.

4. Toast (page 16) the habanero chile (or serrano chile, but the flavor will change) and put it in the middle of the bowl—this is not to eat (watch out!) but to spread its flavor and spiciness throughout the onions, to add a bit of color decoration.

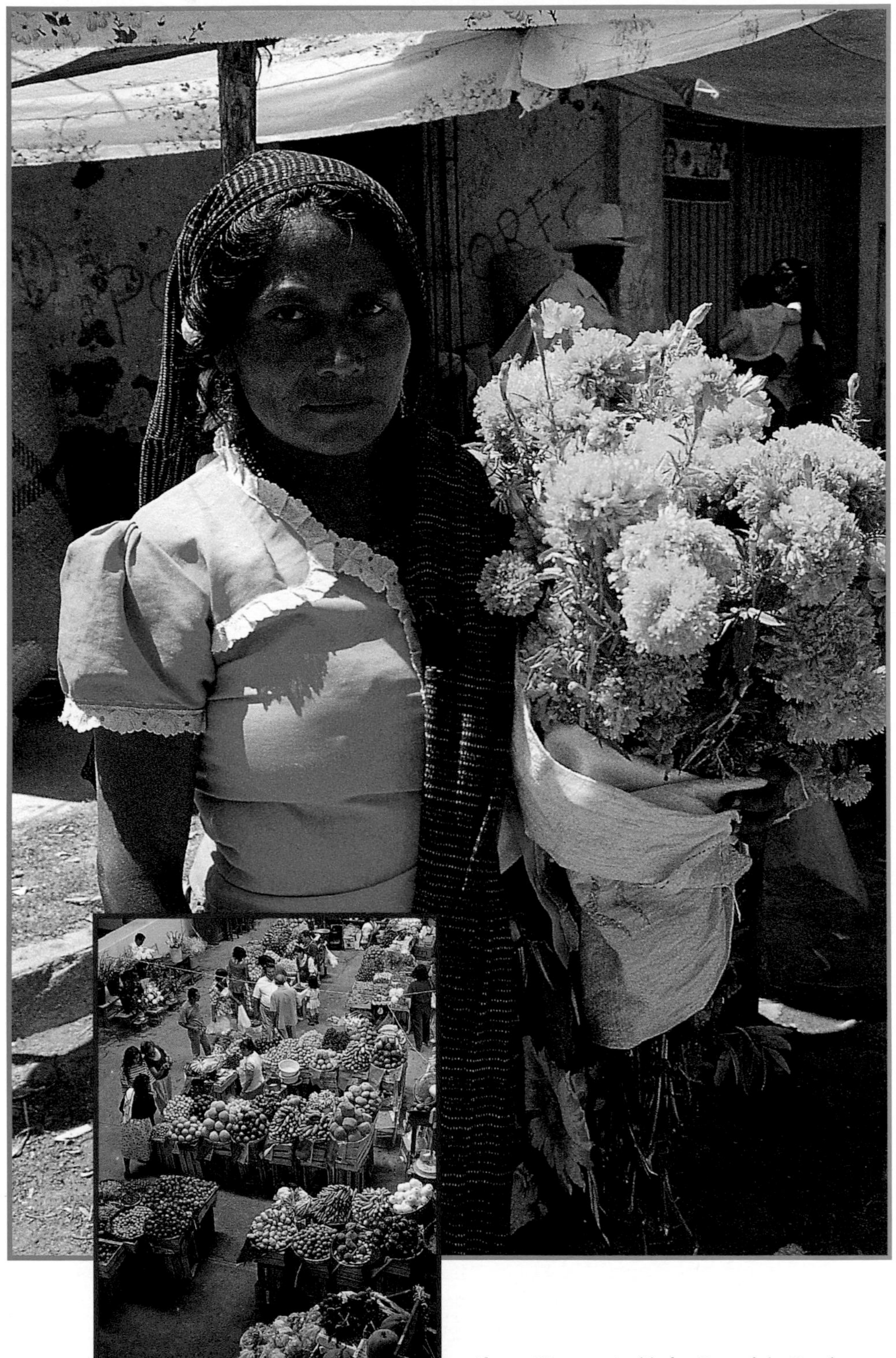

Above: Giant marigolds for Day of the Dead celebrations in Zaachila, Oaxaca.

Left: Chapala, Jalisco's indoor market.

Above: Summer's wild mushrooms at Taxco's market.

Left: Colorful piñatas brighten a stall in Veracruz's Hidalgo market.

Above: Tasajo (marinated beef) and chorizo in Oaxaca's Benito Juárez market.

Right: The ancient corn drink *texate* is freshly foamed at Oaxaca's Abastos market.

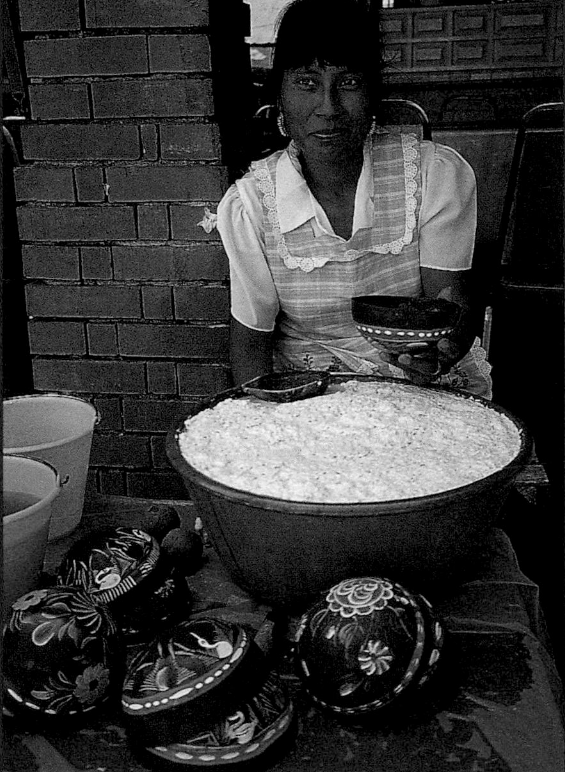

Left: Fresh beans at Huejotzingo, Puebla's Saturday market.

Above: Mole pastes for sale at Mexico City's Jamaica market.

Right: A Pátzcuaro vendor offers *atole de zarzamora* (blackberry) tamales.

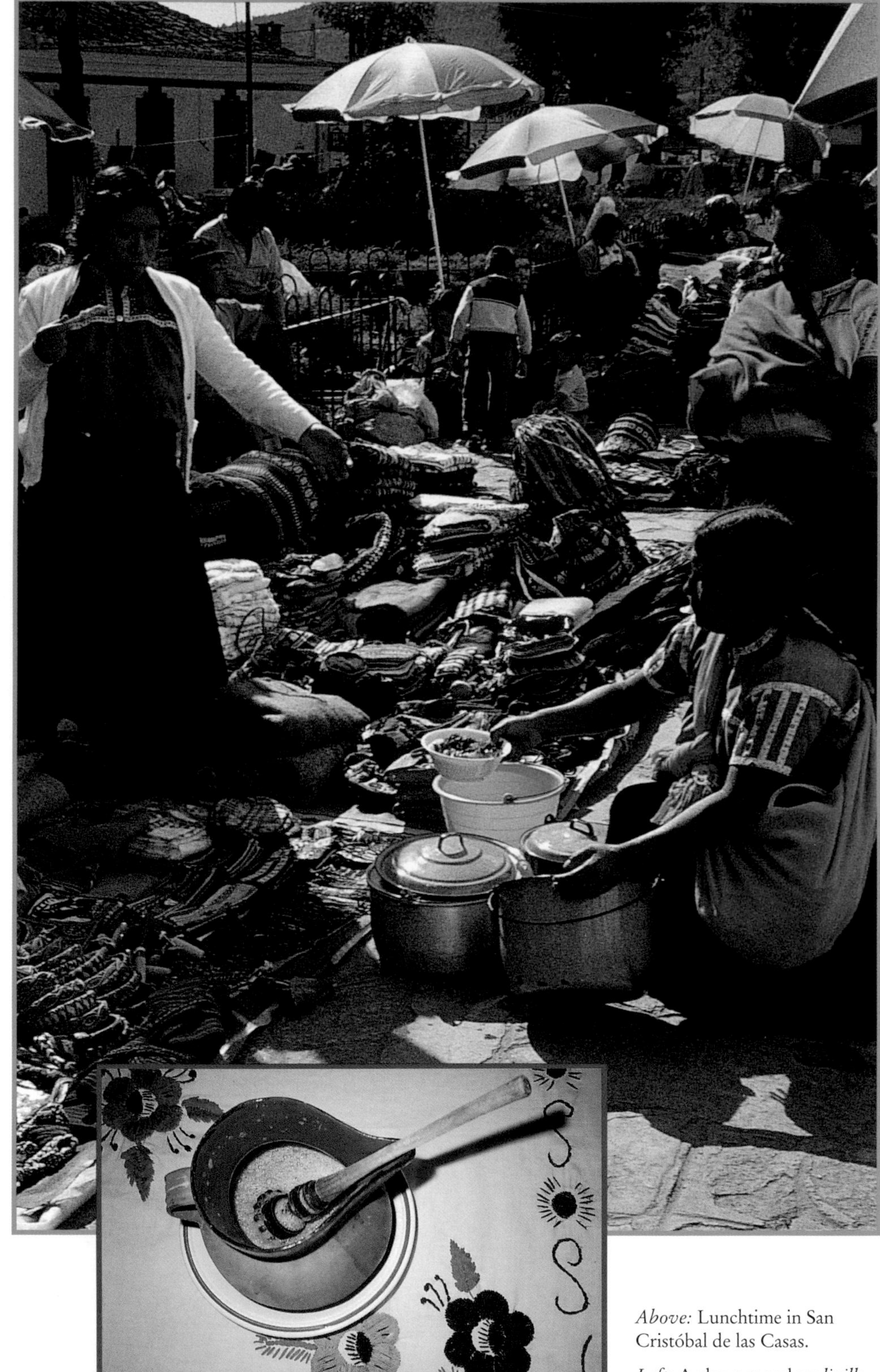

Above: Lunchtime in San Cristóbal de las Casas.

Left: A clay pot and *molinillo* for foaming chocolate.

Above: Eye-catching signage at a Veracruz seafood restaurant.

Right: Habanero chiles at Campeche's Pedro Sainz de Barbaranda market.

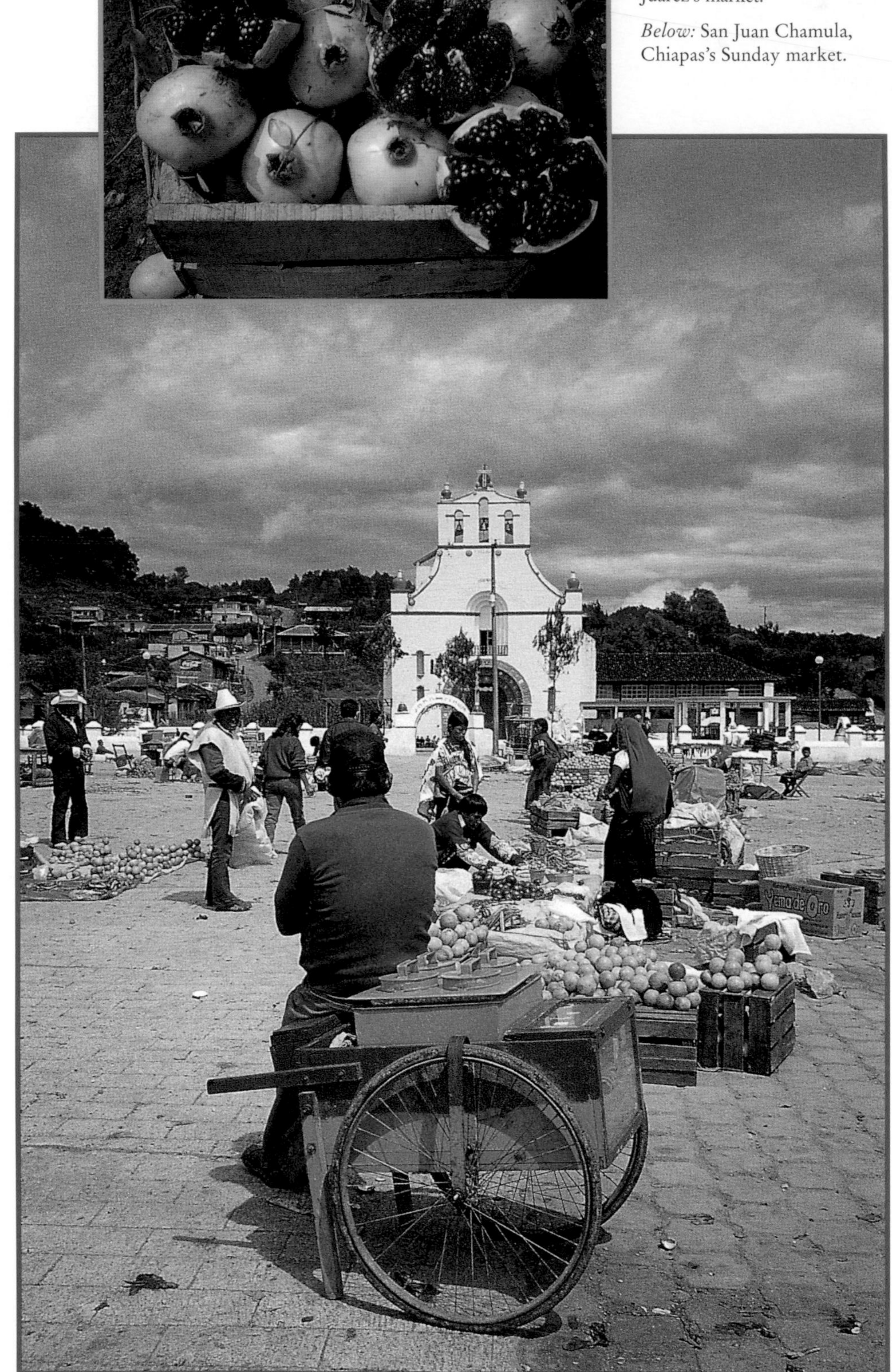

Left: Pomegranates at Toluca's Juárez's market.

Below: San Juan Chamula, Chiapas's Sunday market.

Elsie's

Siquil-P'ak *Pumpkin Seed and Tomato Spread*

ELSIE SELLS *RECADOS*, the seasoning pastes loved throughout the Yucatán, at her stall in Mérida's hot and pulsing central market. You'll see piles of pastes rising two feet from their plastic buckets ready for Elsie to scoop off a portion to weigh. They're made the same way as *mole* pastes, that is, with fresh rather than dried ingredients.

Pepitas menudas, tiny half-inch pumpkin seeds of Yucatán—their outside shells left on to achieve a nonoily texture—are toasted and hand-ground to a dry, coarse consistency on a *metate*, then sold at Elsie's booth right alongside her *recados*. A blender or processor is okay for the job but the texture just isn't the same—their blades cut rather than crush the seeds. Pumpkin seeds are larger in the U.S. and so the puréeing time must be increased. It's important to keep some texture, so don't get carried away and let your processor whip everything into a cream.

Mérida is home to a large longtime Lebanese population. In every market throughout the city you'll find bags of toasted, puffed pita breads loaded with sesame seeds, and these are delicious, healthful alternatives to fried tortillas for scooping *siquil-p'ak*. *Siquil-p'ak* is also fabulous spread on vegetable spears to accompany icy beers and tropical drinks.

Yield: about 2 cups

6 medium tomatoes
3 cups unhulled pumpkin seeds, toasted or raw, salted or not
½ to 1 yellow habanero chile to taste, washed and dried (Elsie specifically likes to use a yellow habanero chile in this recipe)
¼ cup chopped cilantro leaves
salt (if seeds are not salted)

1. Toast (page 16) the tomatoes until their skins are blackened and blistered. Put the tomatoes in a plastic bag to "sweat" for a few minutes. Peel and set aside.

2. If you are using raw pumpkin seeds, they must be toasted until they are light brown. Or, spread them out on a cookie sheet and slowly brown in a 300°F oven, turning them regularly. Set the pumpkin seeds aside and cool.

3. Toast the chile, turning it until it is blackened and blistered.

4. Put the pumpkin seeds in a blender or processor container and blend with a few tablespoons of water.

5. Stem, seed, and devein the chile. Add a ¼-inch square piece of the unpeeled chile to the blender (habanero chiles vary in extreme hotness). Add the reserved tomatoes, cilantro, and salt to the blender. Blend to a coarse consistency. Taste carefully. Add another piece of chile if you want the sauce hotter, but the important thing is the balance of habanero chile and pumpkin seed flavor.

Opposite: Elsie smiles from behind mounds of "recados" in Mérida's Mercado Municipal Lucas De Gálvez.

Rosario Chávez's

Sopa *Dry Soup with Pasta*

JUST AS TRADITIONAL AS ESCABECHE ORIENTAL (page 318) on Christmas Eve, is serving *sopa* alongside. Everywhere else in Mexico *sopa* is called *sopa seca* (dry soup). The name comes from pasta or rice totally absorbing the broth it cooks in and becoming "dry" (soup is known as *caldo* in Yucatán, to differentiate).

Sopa served with chicken or turkey *escabeche* is made with penne or bow-tie pasta, the chicken-cooking broth, and vegetables. Unlike Italians, Mexicans like their sauces to be absorbed in the pasta rather than to be poured on top after the pasta is cooked. *Al dente* is not part of the Mexican language; all pasta here is cooked pablum-soft from absorbing the cooking liquids.

Yield: 6 servings

- 4 tomatoes
- 1 teaspoon dried Mexican oregano
- ½ teaspoon freshly ground black pepper
- 2 Tablespoons vegetable oil
- 10 ounces dry penne, mostaccioli, or bow-tie pasta
- ½ small white onion, very coarsely chopped
- ½ cup very coarsely chopped red or green bell pepper (or a combination)
- 2 cups hot broth form Escabeche Oriental (page 318), or substitute chicken or vegetable broth
- salt

1. Toast (page 16) the tomatoes until their skins are blackened and blistered. Put the tomatoes in a plastic bag to "sweat" for a few minutes. Peel and put the tomatoes in a blender. Add the oregano, black pepper, and purée for 15 seconds.

2. Heat the oil in a pot. Add the dry pasta and fry, stirring, for 2 minutes. Add the onion and bell pepper and continue cooking and stirring until the onion is golden. Add the puréed tomatoes and stir.

3. Add the 2 cups hot broth to the pasta. Season with salt. Cover the pot and simmer for 15 minutes, adding another ½ to 1 cup more broth if necessary if the liquid is absorbed before the pasta is ready.

Rosario Chávez's

Arroz Amarillo *Yellow Rice*

IN MÉRIDA, YELLOW RICE IS SIMILAR TO YELLOW RICE MADE ALL OVER THE CARIBBEAN, but Meridians cook it with chunks of onion plus green and red bell peppers. Bijol, an intensely bright orange coloring agent, can be found in Latino and Caribbean stores. It gives yellow rice its golden color, and it's stirred into broth along with ubiquitous Knorr bouillon. Vivid yellow rice flecked with red and green is a knockout served on turquoise-colored plates, if you can find some, but the taste will enhance anything it's served on.
Yield: 4 servings

- 2 Tablespoons vegetable oil
- 1 cup white rice, rinsed in a strainer and shaken dry
- ¼ medium white onion, cut into 4 slices
- 3 slices green bell pepper, ½ inch by 2 inches
- 3 slices red bell pepper, ½ inch by 2 inches
- ½ medium tomato, coarsely chopped
- 1½ cups hot water
- 1½ teaspoons Knorr chicken bouillon powder
- ½ teaspoon Bijol condiment (or substitute turmeric)

1. Heat the vegetable oil in a medium pot with a lid. Add the rice and stir to coat each grain with some oil. Add the onion, green and red peppers, and the tomato, stirring, to lightly brown the rice.

2. Pour the water into a measuring cup. Add the bouillon and Bijol and mix thoroughly. Add the liquid to the rice and bring it to a boil. Immediately turn down the heat, cover, and simmer for 25 minutes.

3. Fluff the rice with a fork and let it sit, covered, for 10 minutes to dry any remaining moisture.

Rosario Chávez's

Garnachas *Corn Dough Tartlets Filled with Ground Turkey and Mashed Potatoes*

GARNACHAS ARE SMALL *MASA* TARTLETS layered with seasoned ground turkey and topped with soft mashed potatoes. They are fried in hot oil until golden brown and crisp. The trick is to keep the oil level low and never let it touch the soft potatoes.

Try to hunt down these delectable morsels when you're in Yucatán. They're known as *garnachas* or *chalupas* (don't confuse them with same-name *chalupas* found in Puebla and Chiapas); both names are correct and equally used. On rare occasions you'll see them in fondas at the Valladolid market, but never in Mérida. They're primarily homemade delicacies to have as a light evening meal. Serve while the *garnachas* are piping hot, with *Xnipec* (page 302) and/or *Cebolla Curdita* (page 304), and a bottle of hot sauce made with habanero chile.

Yield: 24 garnachas

For the meat mixture

- 1 pound ground turkey
- ½ medium white onion, finely chopped
- 1 two-inch square piece of bell pepper
- ½ tomato, coarsely chopped
- ¼ teaspoon salt
- ¼ teaspoon freshly ground black pepper
- 1 rounded teaspoon raisins
- 3 green olives, pitted and finely chopped
- 1 teaspoon white vinegar

1. Heat a nonstick skillet and add the ground turkey, stirring to break up any clumps. Cook for 5 minutes on medium heat.

2. Add the remaining ingredients and continue cooking until the turkey shows no more pink. Remove from the heat and set aside.

Rosario Chávez cutting banana leaves for her "Pollo Pibil" (page 322).

For the mashed potatoes

- 4 or 5 russet baking potatoes, depending on size
- 2 teaspoons salt
- ½ cup milk
- 3 Tablespoons butter
- ¼ teaspoon salt
- ¼ teaspoon freshly ground black pepper

1. Peel the potatoes and cut them into quarters. Put them in a pan with 2 quarts water and 2 teaspoons salt.
2. Bring the water to a boil, cover the pot loosely, and boil for approximately 20 minutes, or until the potatoes are tender when pierced with a fork. Drain.
3. While the potatoes are still hot, put them through a ricer, or mash them with a hand-held electric mixer with the milk, butter, salt, and pepper.

For the masa shells

- 2 pounds "masa" from a tortillería, or 4 cups prepared "masa harina" per package directions
- oil for frying, about 3 cups

1. Make 24 small, oval tartlet shells 2 inches by 3 inches, with ¼-inch edges (round tarts are easier, but not authentic). Cook the thick *masa* disks on an ungreased *comal* or heavy skillet until the bottom side is pale golden, about 2 minutes. Turn over and quickly cook the other side, about 30 seconds. Remove from the heat and pinch-up the sides ¼ inch all around (cooked side is on top) as for tart shells (they are hot!). Continue with the rest.
2. Gently spread 2 rounded tablespoons turkey mixture in each tartlet.
3. Very gently spread 2 rounded tablespoons warm mashed potatoes over the turkey mixture. Fill the tartlets to the top edges but not over.

Finishing the "garnachas"

1. In a large skillet, heat about ⅛ inch of vegetable oil to 365°F, or until it ripples.
2. Carefully place a few *garnachas* in the hot oil, being sure not to get oil on the mashed potatoes. Fry until the *masa* tartlets are golden brown, about 2 minutes. Drain on paper towels.

Rosario Chávez's

Panuchos *Crisp Tortillas with Black Beans and Garnishes*

MÉRIDA AND VALLADOLID'S MARKET FONDAS ARE PRIME SOURCES for Yucatán's favorite snack. *Panuchos* are enjoyed all day long with, or without, meat toppings. My friend Rosario says, "There are rich and poor *panuchos*—those with meat and lettuce piled high, and simple bean-filled tortillas for those one-peso days." Rich or poor, these are scrumptious.

Epazote-flavored, sieved black beans are stuffed into a corn tortilla. Then it's panfried in a little oil until slightly crisp and sometimes topped with *Cochinita Pibil* (page 322). Simple *panuchos* are often served alongside *pibil* for special meals. Not too many years ago the Yucatán peninsula was filled with deer herds, and venison *pibil* was as popular as chicken or pork is today. But unfortunately for everyone, the herds are depleted and venison is no longer legally hunted or sold in city markets.

Yield: 8 panuchos

- 8 corn tortillas, about 6 inches in diameter and on the thick side
- 1 cup "Frijoles Negros Yucatecos" (page 250), the paste should be warm
- 2 Tablespoons vegetable oil
- 2 habanero chiles, halved

1. Place a tortilla in a hot *comal* or skillet and heat on one side, then flip it over and heat the other side. You'll notice one side puff; this is the *ollejo* side. (An interesting note: The same thin-skinned side of the tortilla is known in the north as the *pancita*; the back side is the *esplanda.*)

2. Remove the tortilla from the *comal* and put it on a plate. With a knife, carefully cut a 3-inch slit between the tortilla and the puffed part to make a pocket.

3. Spoon 3 tablespoons of the beans into the pocket. With your hands, gently spread the beans around the pocket, almost out to the edges, being careful not to tear the fragile *ollejo*. Repeat with the remaining tortillas.

4. Heat the oil in a skillet. Carefully put one *panucho* in the oil, *ollejo* side down, and cook for only 20 seconds. Turn the *panucho* over and cook until the tortilla bottom is lightly brown and crisp, about 1 minute. Remove from the oil with a slotted spatula and place on paper towels to drain. Serve with a bowl of *Cebolla Curtida* (page 304). For authenticity, offer a few halved habanero chiles for people to wipe across their *panucho*—for flavor and spice.

Variation: Salbutes are another *antojito* just as popular as *panuchos.* Tiny puffed tortillas are deep fried and not filled with beans but always topped with meats and lettuce.

Isabella Morales de Méndez's

Papadzules

Tortillas with Pumpkin Seed Sauce, Tomato Sauce, and Hard-Boiled Eggs

ONE OF THE UNEQUIVOCAL JOYS OF YUCATÁN COOKING ARE *PAPADZULES*, tortillas dipped in pumpkin seed sauce then rolled around hard-boiled eggs and served with a light tomato sauce. You'll spot these *antojitos* on restaurant menus as first-course offerings, or as lunch and supper plates served with or without rice and beans, but always with vinegared red onions, *Cebolla Curtida* (page 304). The best *papadzules* are found in fondas where cooks whip them up first thing in the morning for unforgettable breakfasts. Go to Mercado Municipal's second-floor and simply ask who has *papadzules*—sometimes items aren't listed on the signs. Isabela used to cook at one of these second floor fondas but now sells *pipián* (hand-ground pumpkin seeds) on the market's ground floor.

Yield: 8 papadzules

For the "pipián"

- 3 cups roasted or raw pumpkin seeds, unsalted
- 1 cup water
- ½ teaspoon salt

1. Toast (page 16) raw pumpkin seeds until they are light brown. Or spread them out on a cookie sheet and slowly brown in a 300°F oven, turning regularly.

2. Put the pumpkin seeds in a blender or processor container and purée until smooth, adding the salt and water if necessary. Empty the purée into a bowl.

For the "salsa cocida"

- 6 tomatoes, cored
- 2 Tablespoons vegetable oil
- 1 white onion, thinly sliced
- 2 garlic cloves, peeled
- 3 serrano chiles, sliced
- 1 teaspoon salt

1. Put the tomatoes in a blender container. Purée.

2. Heat the oil in a pot and add the onion, garlic, and chile. Sauté until golden.

3. Add tomato purée and salt to onions. Bring to a boil then reduce the heat and simmer for 2 minutes. Remove the garlic cloves.

To assemble

- 8 hard-boiled eggs
- 8 corn tortillas
- 1½ cups "salsa cocida"

1. Peel the eggs and cut into quarters.

2. Dip a tortilla into the bowl of *pipián*, then put it on a plate. Line up 4 hard-boiled egg quarters lengthwise and roll the tortilla around the egg, placing it on another plate seam side down. Continue with the remaining tortillas and eggs. Cover with the remaining *pipián*. Surround with *salsa cocida*.

Gilberto's

▲▼▲

Huevos Motuleños *Eggs and Tortillas Stacked Pancake Style, with Fillings*

PANCAKE-STACKED TORTILLAS WITH FRIED EGGS AND ASSORTED FLAVORINGS make this a sensational breakfast treat. *Huevos motuleños* could be called Yucatán's *huevos rancheros*, but *huevos motuleños* is a much more interesting dish—the two aren't even in the same league. Gilberto, a waiter in a neighborhood *cafetería* (what coffee shops are called throughout Mexico) told me that the dish originated in Motuleño, a pueblo outside Mérida. He also gave me a layer-by-layer breakdown: first black beans are spread on a plate, next a crisp tortilla, a fried egg, cooked tomato sauce, another crisp tortilla, another fried egg, more sauce, crumbled cheese, chopped ham, peas, and fried plantain slices. Some people add diced yellow cheese—but he thinks that's going overboard (if possible).
Yield: 4 servings

4 Tablespoons vegetable oil
8 tortillas
1 cup "Frijoles Parrados" (page 250)
2 Tablespoons vegetable oil
8 eggs
2 cups "Salsa Chiltomate" (page 303)
4 Tablespoons "queso añejo" or Parmesan cheese
¼-inch slice of boiled or baked ham, diced
½ cup fresh peas, boiled
2 ripe (black) plantains, peeled and sliced on an angle ¼ inch thick and sautéed in hot oil until light brown, about 15 minutes, then drained on paper towels

1. Heat the oil in a skillet. Fry the tortillas until they are crisp and set aside.
2. Spread ¼ cup beans the size of a tortilla in the center of 4 plates. Put one tortilla over each circle of beans.
3. Clean the skillet of any remaining oil. Heat the oil in the same skillet over medium heat and fry the eggs. Place one egg on each crisp tortilla.
4. Cover the egg with ¼ cup tomato sauce. Add another crisp tortilla to the pile on each plate. Add another fried egg. Cover each with another ¼ cup tomato sauce.
5. Sprinkle each mound with equal amounts of cheese, diced ham, and cooked peas. Surround with plantain chips and serve immediately.

Adda Erosa's

Tamales Vaporcitos *Banana-Leaf-Wrapped Steamed Tamales*

ADDA LOVES *VAPORCITOS*. I know. I helped make a batch of these tamales for a gathering she was having one night. Then without much of a second thought she told me she wanted to whip out another fifty the next day for her own birthday party. So I showed up again and there she was, a voluptuous Mayan señora dressed in underwear to keep cool, preparing tamales and perspiring in proportion to Mérida's horrendous humidity. Ah, what a foodie will go through for a dazzling dish.

Later we retired to a couple of hammocks strung across an air-conditioned room. We took a siesta in adjoining "beds," and that's when I learned the subtleties of hammocks. Adda says all-cotton is best for comfort, but they sag and need to be washed often and tightened. Nylon is cheaper and never sags, but is not as comfy as cotton. The number of strings is what makes a good hammock. Always buy the biggest (widest) hammock you can afford with the most strings. For this reason, stay clear of vendors hawking ten-dollar specials around Mérida's cafés at night. The most comfortable sleeping size for one person is a large double, because the proper way to sleep is straight across at the widest spot, or at a slight angle. Most gringos assume you sleep end-to-end, but that just isn't so. Adda says in the cooler winter months she sleeps with the air conditioning off and a window open. Late at night when she begins to get too cool she'll lie lengthwise on her super-wide cotton hammock and wrap the old (about twenty years) soft weaving around her, like a blanket. The whole concept of hammocks is to have air flowing to make sleeping possible in the stickiest, hottest months. If you get a chance to visit any homes in the area be sure to notice four-inch round disks in walls about six feet up. These are hammock hook holders and almost any room can be transformed into an instant bedroom by stringing a hammock from one wall to another. Often there'll be three or four hammocks in one room at various heights and angles.

Anyway, back to *Vaporcitos*. Tamales from this region of Mexico are banana leaf-wrapped and Adda's beloved family recipe contains both chicken and pork. (When you're in Yucatán markets and spot tamales wrapped in corn husks, fonda people will undoubtably call them "northern-style.") Here, the *masa* is made into tortillas rather than patted onto a leaf, as in Oaxaca. Tamales in Mérida are served at night for light meals.
Yield: 50 tamales
(Continued)

For the chicken and pork

1 whole chicken, about 4 pounds, quartered
1 pound ground, lean pork
2 pounds ripe plum tomatoes, puréed in a blender (about 10)
2 rounded Tablespoons "Recado Rojo" (page 300), or substitute "achiote" paste
2 Tablespoons white vinegar
4 stems "epazote" (leaves only)
2 Tablespoons flour
½ cup water

1. Arrange the chicken pieces on the bottom of a large pot and heat over a high flame. Spoon the ground pork over the chicken and pour the puréed tomatoes over the meats.
2. Mix the *recado* and vinegar in a small bowl. Pour over the tomato purée. Sprinkle with *epazote* leaves.
3. When the mixture boils, reduce the heat to simmer and continue cooking, uncovered and without stirring, for 30 minutes longer.
4. Remove a chicken thigh and check for doneness; it should not be pink. Return it to the pot and cook longer, if needed. Remove the chicken from the pot. Cool enough to remove the bones and shred the meat. Continue cooking the pork in the sauce for 15 minutes more.
5. Add the flour to the water and dissolve the flour. Pour over the sauce and cook for 15 minutes more, over low heat, stirring with a wooden spoon to thicken. Combine the shredded chicken with the pork sauce. Remove from the heat.

For the masa

4 pounds fresh, delicate "masa," or follow the directions on a "masa harina" package
1 Tablespoon "Recado Rojo" or "achiote" paste
1 Tablespoon salt
1 pound fresh lard (page 18), or substitute vegetable shortening

1. Combine the *masa* with the *recado*, salt, and lard.
2. Mix together with your hands for about 10 minutes, until the *masa* feels lighter with the air that has been beaten into it, and the *recado* is mixed evenly throughout (*masa* turns a light orange color). Adda's hint to see if the *masa* is ready: Grab a golfball-sized piece of dough and flatten it to about ½ inch thick on a piece of banana leaf, then remove it. If an oil stain appears on the leaf, it's ready; if not, continue beating.

To form tortillas

the prepared "masa"
2 heavy-duty plastic freezer bags slightly larger than the surface area of the press
a tortilla press

1. Form slightly smaller than golfball-sized balls from the *masa*.
2. Put a Baggie on the bottom of the press.
3. Put a *masa* ball in the center, on top of the Baggie.
4. Center the other Baggie, on top of the *masa* ball.
5. Bring the handle over and flatten the tortilla to 5 inches in diameter.

To assemble

20 precooked (most are sold this way) banana leaves, cut into approximately 8 x 10-inch pieces. (There will be wastage and many leaves will tear. When this happens, cut a smaller piece and put it over the tear, as a patch)

1. Carefully remove the top Baggie from the tortilla and center a banana leaf over the tortilla. The smooth side of the leaf should be touching the tortilla. Turn the leaf-tortilla-Baggie over and carefully remove the other Baggie.
2. Spread ¼ cup pork sauce over the tortilla, keeping ½ inch away from the *masa* edge. Spoon 2 tablespoons shredded chicken in the center of the sauce.
3. With two hands on the banana leaf, pick up one side and flap one third of the tortilla over. Lay the banana leaf back down (the tortilla will still be flapped). With two hands pick up the other side of the banana leaf and flap one third of the tortilla over the other flapped part, keeping the banana leaf in place (don't lay it back down). Pick up the first section of leaf and flap it on top. Tuck the two sides under. The finished size is about 5 inches by 3 inches.

To steam

a tamale steamer (see Glossary)

1. Lay the tamales on the steamer rack or plate. They should overlap diagonally to let steam pass easily through the pile. Cover the pot.
2. Bring the water to a boil in the steamer and cook for 1½ to 2 hours. Check the water level after 45 minutes, and from time to time to be sure it never runs dry.
3. The tamales are ready to be served with *fresh tomato salsa* made with habanero chile, and *Cebolla Curtida* (page 304). As with all tamales, peel away and discard the leaf, then eat the filling.

Variations:

Tamales Chachaqua y Mocbipollo *Banana-Leaf-Wrapped Baked Tamales*

TAMALES CHACHAQUAS ARE MADE THE SAME WAY as *vaporcitos,* except these are baked, not steamed. *Tamales chachaquas* and *tamales mocbipollos* are exactly the same oven-baked (not *pib*, or pit-baked) banana-leaf-wrapped tamales, except the *chachaqua* is individually sized and the *mocbipollo* is a huge family-sized affair baked in a pie plate: Generously drape banana leaves over a pie plate then spread a layer of *masa* on the plate's bottom and up the sides, a filling is spread on next, the tamale is topped with another *masa* layer, then the banana leaves are folded over and baked for about two hours at 350°F.

(Continued)

Tamal Pibipollo *Pit-Cooked Banana-Leaf-Wrapped Chicken Tamale*

PIB-COOKED, BANANA-LEAF-WRAPPED, HUGE TAMALES are delights of Yucatán. Their shape is the first thing you'll notice upon spotting one for the first time, probably in a market or on a street corner in the evening. The second thing is the black color from the *pib*-charred banana leaf wrapping. And wrapped they are. Ribbons of banana leaves tie the packages together. Each tamale is about 10 inches in diameter and 2 inches thick, with straight sides. Peel back and discard the leaves before cutting the filling into slices, cake style.

Tamal de Espelóns *Banana-Leaf-Wrapped Pit-Cooked Black Bean Tamale*

ESPELÓNS ARE TINY BLACK BEANS. Cooked with *epazote* (either whole, or sieved) they fill a *masa* package in exactly the same way that chicken fills a *tamal pibipollo*. These banana-leaf-ribboned bundles of beans are blackened from the *pib*.

Tamal Colado *Banana-Leaf-Wrapped, Cooked Masa Tamale*

TAMAL COLADO IS DIFFERENT FROM ANY OTHER Yucatán *tamal* because the *masa* is cooked before the banana leaf is wrapped around it, plus steamed after. Cook a chicken in 2 quarts water for 1 hour. Heat half the broth in another pot and add *masa harina* to form a dough. Cook slowly, at a simmer, stirring with a wooden spoon. When the dough is hot, add 1 tablespoon salt. Mix in lard (3 parts *masa* to 1 part lard) to give the *masa* a thick, creamy texture. Remove from the heat. To the other half of the chicken broth, add 2 tablespoons *Recado Rojo* (page 300), 2 cups chopped tomatoes, and ¼ cup chopped *epazote* leaves. Cook for 30 minutes. Dissolve a generous tablespoon *masa harina* in 1 cup hot water and add to the tomatoes as a thickener. Cook to thicken, about 15 minutes. On an 8 x 10-inch banana leaf piece, spread out ½ cup *masa* in the center, so it looks like a pancake. Top with a piece of cooked chicken, a slice of fresh tomato, a fresh *epazote* leaf, and a piece of fresh chile. Add a spoonful of sauce and fold and steam, as for *Vaporcitos* (page 313). Serve these tamales with crisp, crackling fresh, hot corn chips sprinkled with lime and salt.

Tikin Xik *Banana-Leaf-Wrapped Baked Fish Tamale*

The Mayan *tikin xik* is a piece of *recado rojo*-marinated fish baked inside a banana leaf. There is no *masa* in this tamale.

Adda Erosa's

Puerco en Coca-Cola *Coca-Cola Pork*

ONE HOT AFTERNOON, AFTER WE FINISHED MAKING *VAPORCITOS* (page 313) and were cooling off with a couple of Diet Cokes, Adda decided she just had to make Coca-Cola Pork for Morris and me. Chuckling, she said about the recipe, "While not exactly Mayan, it's certainly old enough to be traditional Meridian." So, in the interest of research, we went back to Adda's a few nights later to pig-out on Coca-Cola Pork. We also learned how to "make *chuc*" with the sauce. "Making *chuc*," explained Adda while chuckling, "is a down-home Mayan term meaning to soak bread in sauce and mop up every drop. It's also the term used when dabbing a tortilla at a habanero chile to get a bit of its flavor and heat."

Adda's brother, Ariel Erosa Gutiérrez, a Coca-Cola executive, thinks this recipe has been around since 1945 when Coke made its splash in Mérida. He told me that the city's first day's output was 131 boxes of 24 bottles, today the same plant produces fifty million bottles a year. Serve with rice and plenty of French bread to "make *chuc*."

Yield: 4 servings

- 1½ pounds boneless pork loin, sliced ¼ inch thick
- ¼ teaspoon salt
- ¼ teaspoon freshly ground black pepper
- 2 Tablespoons white vinegar
- 1 Tablespoon vegetable oil
- 2 Tablespoons prepared mustard
- 4 Tablespoons butter
- 2 medium, ripe tomatoes
- 1 large onion
- 1 green bell pepper
- 12 ounces Coca-Cola

1. Slice the meat and marinate it in salt, pepper, and the vinegar for 30 minutes.

2. Heat the vegetable oil in a large heavy skillet over high heat. Brown the meat quickly on both sides. Remove to a plate.

3. Whip the mustard and butter together in a bowl. Spread evenly on both sides of the pork slices. Put the pork slices, overlapping, in a large pot. Slice the tomatoes, onion, and green bell pepper into ⅛-inch slices and arrange over the meat. Empty the can of Coca-Cola over the vegetables. Bring everything to a boil, reduce the heat to medium, and cook for 15 minutes.

Rosario Chávez's

Escabeche Oriental *Vinegared Chicken with Flavors of the Yucatán*

EVERY STREET IN YUCATÁN ON CHRISTMAS EVE IS PERMEATED WITH AROMAS of chicken or turkey *escabeche*. Tradition runs deep in cities and villages, and everyone eats the same meal this night: chicken if you're poor, turkey if you're rich, and both are simply delicious. *Escabeche* is a mixture of herbs, spices, and a little vinegar rubbed into poultry to produce a prized family holiday gift from the cook—with only slight variation in the recipe, depending on where you live on the peninsula (see *Variations*). The *oriental* (east, in Spanish) in this recipe refers to eastern Yucatán, not the Far East. Rosario says that for special occasions, like Christmas, poultry is served whole on a platter garnished with lettuce leaves, radish roses, and slices of fried plantain. Lastly, a cup of the onions without liquid is poured on top of the chicken or turkey breast.

Chicken (or turkey) may be cooked whole, or cut into pieces, and the skin removed, or not. After cooking a bird in water, people heat their backyard barbeques and quickly brown the chicken to bring out the *recado* flavorings; this all-important step can make or break the dish. Grilling only browns the marinade spices, it does not cook the already cooked chicken more; a quick pass over hot coals is enough.

Leftovers are revered treats for sandwiches. A slice of Bimbo bread (I'm embarrassed to write the word much less say it), Mexico's equivalent to Wonder bread (it's a wonder it's bread), is slathered with mustard. Shredded poultry is piled on top with some of the cooked onions and lettuce. Another bread slice is thinly smeared with mayonnaise and flopped on top of the lettuce. I admit, it's delectable.

Yield: 6 servings

- 1 four-pound chicken, cleaned and left whole or cut up
- 1 garlic head, toasted (page 16)
- 1 habanero chile, or 2 yellow Hungarian chiles ("chawa" or "xcakik" in Mayan), toasted
- 3 large red onions
- 4 Tablespoons "Recado Bistec" (page 301), plus additional 1 Tablespoon
- ⅓ cup white vinegar, plus additional vinegar
- 2 bay leaves, crumbled
- salt
- 2 Tablespoons vegetable oil

1. Heat 2 quarts water in a large pot and add the chicken. Add the toasted garlic and chile. Cover, with the lid slightly askew, and simmer for 1 hour.

2. Peel and thickly slice the onions. Put them in a large bowl and cover with cold water for 15 minutes. Break up into rings, then drain. Return to the bowl. In a small bowl, dissolve the 4 tablespoons *recado* in ⅓ cup vinegar with bay leaves. Pour over the onions.

3. Remove the chicken from the broth and put it on a plate, but keep the broth simmering for the onions, and for *Sopa* (page 306), if desired.

4. Put the remaining 1 tablespoon *recado* and ½ teaspoon salt, in a small bowl and dissolve in 2 tablespoons vinegar. Rub the paste over the chicken, set it aside, and marinate at room temperature. Meanwhile, heat the grill.

5. Heat 2 tablespoons oil in a large pot. Add the onions and cook, over medium heat, stirring, for about 10 minutes. The onions are to remain a bit crisp; do not cook them for so long that they become limp.
6. Put the garlic (not the habanero chile) from the chicken pot on top of the onions. With a large spoon or bulb baster, remove as much fat as possible from the surface of the broth. Slowly pour broth over the onions until they are covered with liquid. Return the remaining broth to the heat for the optional *sopa*, or reserve for another use.
7. Add ¼ cup vinegar to the onions and taste for salt. The broth should taste a little sour. Turn off the heat and cover until serving time. Serve in a large bowl with some broth.
8. Grill the chicken quickly to bring out the flavor of the *recado* marinade. Keep turning the chicken; total time is no more than 10 minutes for a whole chicken, and 5 minutes for cut-up pieces (and not much longer for a turkey).

Note: If you're cooking a 10-pound turkey begin with 6 quarts water in a very large stockpot (add more water depending on the size of the turkey). Add another garlic head, another chile or two, two more red onions, and double the ingredients for the *recado* marinade, step 4.

Variations:

Escabeche Mérida Escabeche *in the Style of Mérida*

MÉRIDA'S VERSION is the same as *Escabeche Oriental* except that *Recado Rojo* (page 300) is used instead of *Recado Bistec*. Also, Meridians like *sopa* made with bow-tie pasta.

Escabeche Valladolid Escabeche *in the Style of Valladolid*

THE CITY OF VALLADOLID OFFERS an unusual presentation. Cut 4 small onions in half, vertically. Toast them with 3 small garlic heads. After toasting, and with a very large sewing needle with heavy thread, "sew" the garlic and onion together, alternating onion, garlic, onion, garlic, etc. Tie the string around each necklace "jewel" to keep it from falling apart. Put the necklace in the chicken water with ½ cup *recado bistec* dissolved in ½ cup vinegar. Cook the necklace 15 minutes and remove. Mix ¼ teaspoon freshly ground black pepper, 1 teaspoon salt, 2 tablespoons vinegar, and 1 tablespoon oil in a small bowl. Rub the paste over the chicken after it has cooked for 1 hour. Grill the chicken. Serve in bowls, with broth, a piece of chicken, onions, and a piece of "jewel," removed from the string.

Javier Loria's

Cochinita Pibil *Oven-Cooked, Pit-Style Pork*

COCHINITA PIBIL IS YUCATÁN'S MOST FAMOUS DISH—a pit-roasted whole pig first rubbed with seasoning paste then wrapped in banana leaves. You can always find weekend-only stands along roadways selling pit-roasted pork, especially on Sunday morning, when you're in Yucatán. In Yucatán, as at the *carnitas* stands in Michoacán or Jalisco, whole pigs are cooked and you buy the pieces you want: slice of loin, chunk of leg, or particular innards. In the U.S. you'll want to make your own on a smaller scale, and this recipe tastes like the real thing. It's the banana leaves and seasoning paste that give *pibiles* their unique flavor, whether they're pit-roasted or oven-baked.

Throughout Yucatán people eat *cochinita pibil* for breakfast. In Mérida, three blocks or so south of the *zócalo*, on Calle 60 in Mercado García Rejón, you'll see people selling pit-cooked pork in the mornings—7 A.M. to 8 P.M. is best because the meat is hot, just out of the pits, and it sells out fast. Buy yours by the kilo, or made into tacos with vinegared red onions.

I was fortunate to meet Javier Loria, owner of Mérida's Corner House Restaurant. One morning Morris was jogging near our apartment and he spotted a *cochinita pibil* stand he'd never seen before. Being my number one scout, he jogged right up to the person manning the booth and began asking questions about *pibs*. One thing led to another and he jogged back (this time with money) to buy a couple *tortas* (pit-roasted pork with vinegared onions on French rolls) to bring home for an authentic Meridian breakfast. Javier happened to drive up just then to check on his new stand and he turned out to be a gold mine of *pib* information. A few days later he invited us to go with him to Ucu, a tiny village of open-sided, thatched-roof cottages, to meet Don Amalio Briceño and his son, Melchor, plus assorted family members, and get a first-hand glimpse of *cochinita pibil*-making.

Don Amalio has been in the wholesale business for more than twenty years and his backyard has thirteen pits. (Javier buys his *cochinita pibil* here for his stand so we knew just how delicious it was.) At the bottom of the pits, heat-retaining rocks are covered with wood and set ablaze. Banana-leaf-lined metal pans with tight-fitting covers containing the pork, *recado*, herbs, and spices are set over the rocks, earth is shoveled over, and the cooking process begins. Huge metal pans, sometimes containing an entire pig, are lowered into the ground at 6 A.M. every Friday for Don Amalio's weekend-only business to be removed at 5 A.M. the next morning. The process is repeated Saturday morning for Sunday's *cochinita pibil*. Javier's home-version recipe works wonderfully. Serve with *Cebolla Curtida* (page 304).

Yield: 8 servings

- 4 heaping Tablespoons "Recado Rojo" (page 300) or "achiote" paste
- 1 teaspoon salt
- ½ cup Seville orange juice, or mixed lime and orange juice
- 4-pound boneless pork leg or loin roast, deeply scored
- 2 large or 3 small banana leaves, with their nonpliable center ribs torn away
- 2 white onions, sliced
- 2 tomatoes, sliced
- 2 large "epazote" sprigs
- 1 habanero chile, or 6 serrano chiles for the spice, but much different flavor

1. Rub the *recado*, salt, and juice over and into the scored pork roast.

2. Line a large pot (with lid) with banana leaves and lay the pork roast on them. Cover the pork with the vegetables, *epazote*, and chile and wrap with more banana leaves, tucking the top leaves under the meat. Cover the pot tightly.

3. Roast in a slow oven (325°F) for 3 hours. Remove the pot from the oven and let it stand, covered, for 30 minutes. Remove the pork from the pot then remove and discard the banana leaves. Slice the pork, or shred it for tacos or *tortas* made with French rolls.

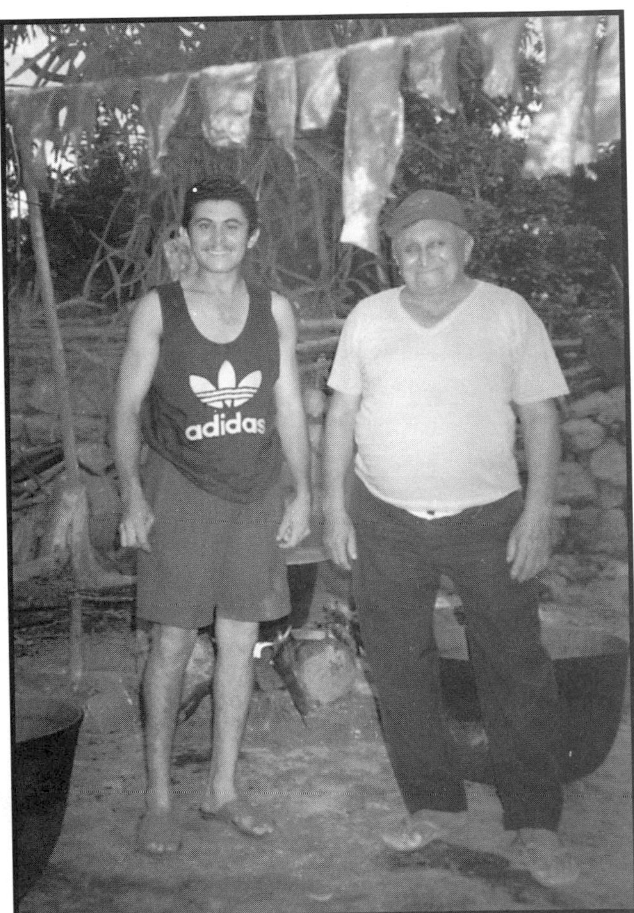

Melchor Amalio Briceño and his uncle at the family "cochinita pibil" pits in Ucu. Strips of meat are air drying in the background.

Rosario Chávez's

Pollo Pibil *Oven-Cooked, Pit-Style Chicken*

NOT EVERYONE HAS AN UNDERGROUND *PIB* (PIT) IN THEIR BACKYARD. This goes for residents of Yucatán as well. It's a cinch to buy *recado rojo* and fresh banana leaves in any market in Mérida, but you'll need to make your own seasoning paste (page 300) or buy *achiote*, and hunt down banana leaves in Latino, Asian, or Filipino stores, or obtain them by mail order. The leaves are becoming more popular all the time; markets are carrying banana leaves frozen or dried, and these work fine for *pibil*. Their subtle but important flavor, and the *recado*, are what make this dish Yucatán *pibil* rather than Hawaiian luau.

Rosario serves *pollo pibil* with traditional accompaniments: Sieved Black Beans (page 250), Yellow Rice (page 307), and *Xnipec* (page 302). *Panuchos* (page 310) make a meal an occasion. *Cebolla Curtida* (page 304) is a must.

Yield: 8 servings

- 2 chickens, 3½ to 4 pounds each, quartered and skin removed if desired
- 6 heaping Tablespoons "Recado Rojo" (page 300) or "achiote" paste
- 2 teaspoons salt
- ½ cup Seville orange juice, or mixed lime and orange juice
- 1 Tablespoon vegetable oil
- 2 large or 3 small banana leaves, with their nonpliable center ribs torn away
- 2 white onions, sliced
- 3 tomatoes, sliced
- 3 large "epazote" sprigs
- 1 habanero chile, or 6 serrano chiles for the spice, but much different flavor

1. Put the chicken quarters in a large bowl. Combine the *recado*, salt, juice, and oil and spread the mixture over the entire chicken.

2. Line a large baking pan (with a lid) or Dutch oven with banana leaves. Place the chicken pieces over the banana leaves, in one layer. If your pot is not big enough, use two layers and separate the layers with additional banana leaves.

3. Spread the onions and tomatoes over the chicken. Scatter the *epazote* on top. Nestle a whole habanero chile in the center of the pot to be removed at the end of cooking. Place additional banana leaves over the *epazote* and tuck the leaves around the chicken to seal in all the flavors.

4. Cover the pot tightly and put it in a 350°F oven and bake for 1½ hours. Remove the chicken from the pot, then remove and discard the banana leaves. Serve each person one chicken quarter.

Lilia Delgado de Rivera's

Chirmole Spicy Black Beans with Pork or Chicken

CHIRMOLE IS BLACK BEANS MADE EVEN BLACKER WITH *RECADO CHILMOLE* (page 301). "Mayans traditionally cooked the sauce with wild turkey or venison; today, chicken and pork are used for *chirmole,*" said Lilia, a local homemaker, when we chatted in one of Mérida's neighborhood markets, Mercado Santos Degollado (page 297), "and the only way to make this is the old way: cook a pot of Sieved Black Beans (page 250) for one hour, then add *recado*, meat, tomato, and *epazote*. Cook slowly for another 2 or 3 hours. That's it." Lilia serves her *chirmole* with *Cebolla Curtida* (page 304) and crisp-baked tortillas. You'll like to drink lots of beer with your pot of luscious, but outrageously colored, charcoal-gray stew. I told you so.

Yield: 6 servings

- 1 recipe "Frijoles Parrados" (page 250)
- 6 heaping Tablespoons Black Seasoning Paste (page 301), thinned with ½ cup Chicken Broth (page 19) or water
- 2½ pounds boneless pork leg, loin roast, or 4 pounds chicken thighs
- 1 tomato, quartered
- 1 large "epazote" sprig

1. After the black beans have cooked for 1 hour, stir in the thinned seasoning paste. Place the pork roast or chicken in the bean pot and cover it with the beans. Add the tomato and *epazote*.

2. Simmer the pork, covered, for 2½ hours, or until it is tender (cook the chicken for 1½ hours). Cook on a very low flame and stir the meat and beans from time to time.

Note: The favorite way to make *chirmole* is with leftover *Lomitos con Ibes Blancos* (page 324) or *frijol con puerco* (pork cooked in black beans). Add 1 or 2 thickly sliced tomatoes, 1 sprig *epazote* and 4 tablespoons *recado de chirmole* to the leftover pork and beans. Heat together and serve with oven-browned tortillas (not fried).

Adda Erosa's

Lomitos con Ibes Blancos

Pork in Tomato Sauce Over Fresh White Bean Purée

ADDA IS A GRAMMAR SCHOOL TEACHER IN MÉRIDA. She loves to cook, especially when her family comes to visit from different points in the U.S. Her high-school-aged son prefers hamburgers from Mérida's McDonald's and Burger King to traditional Yucatán dishes—what else is new? He'll learn. His mom is a good teacher.

In the state of Yucatán this dish is known by two names: *lomitos* and *puerco entomatado*—one not being more popular than the other. *Ibes*, Yucatán's fresh white beans are a rarity in Mérida, where black beans are used almost exclusively, so when November comes around each year small piles of the ½-inch pearls are found in all the markets. They are hand-shelled by women while they wait for customers. In all truthfulness, the beans taste like fresh white beans anywhere else, it's just that they are so unusual to Meridians. Adda says the dish is traditionally served with black beans at other times of the year. A very family-style trick is to put a halved habanero chile on a plate. Everyone just touches a tortilla to the chile and that smidgen adds just enough flavor and pizazz to the tortilla, which is then dipped into each person's plate of pork and beans.

The best place to eat *lomitos* outside a home is at a stand at Valladolid's Mercado Municipal (east of Chichén Itzá, on the road to Cancún). Ask around for *lomitos* and you'll be directed; only one woman prepares the classic dish as soft tacos, and everyone knows where she is. Her Mayan family has been making the specialty for generations and she will smear a bit of black bean purée on a warm tortilla, spoon on some pork, and hand it over. On the counter are small bowls of cut habanero chiles. Put a piece on your plate, then touch your tortilla to it, and you'll have a Yucatecan eating experience known by fewer than few gringos.
Yield: 6 servings

For the pork

- 2 pounds pork loin, leg, or shoulder, cut into 2-inch cubes
- 1 "epazote" sprig
- 1 habanero chile, whole
- 6 medium tomatoes
- pinch of salt
- 1 teaspoon vegetable oil, if needed

1. Put all the ingredients except the oil in a large pot, with the tomatoes on top, and bring to a boil. Reduce the heat and simmer, covered, for 30 minutes. Remove the tomatoes using a large spoon, put them in a blender, and purée.

2. Continue cooking the pork and brown the pork in its own fat. It may be necessary to add 1 teaspoon vegetable oil if the meat is very lean. When the pork cubes are brown on all sides, pour in the puréed tomatoes. Cook over medium heat for 30 minutes more, or until the meat is very tender.

For the "ibes blancos"

- 1 Tablespoon vegetable oil
- 1 small white onion, chopped
- 1½ pounds fresh (not dried) white beans, fava, or lima beans
- ½-inch piece, or larger, of a habanero chile

1. Heat the oil in a medium pot and add the onion. Sauté until lightly brown. Add the fresh white beans and piece of chile to the onions.

2. Pour water over the beans, covering them completely, and bring to a boil. Reduce the heat and simmer for 15 minutes, uncovered, or until the beans are tender. Grind in a blender, or with a hand-held mixer, or force through a sieve (not to a fine purée).

To serve

- 6 hard-boiled eggs, shelled and cut in half
- 1 chopped white onion
- ½ cup chopped cilantro leaves
- 3 limes, quartered

Spoon the puréed beans evenly in the center of a large platter and cover with the pork. Surround with hard-boiled egg halves. Put small piles of onion, cilantro, and limes on a plate, as condiments.

Adda Erosa enoys cooking at her Mérida home.

Marita Teresa Hernández's

Puchero *Three Meats with Mashed Vegetables and Broth*

WHEN I ASKED MARITA FOR A FAMILY RECIPE, she couldn't think of anything except *puchero*. The dish is served at all her family's special Sunday afternoon gatherings because it's a big amount for a big crowd (plus it's her father's favorite). About a week later she told me that her aunts were coming from Valladolid to celebrate someting-or-other and she inquired if I'd like to help the women make *puchero*? You bet.

The broth is made with three meats—chicken, pork, and beef—cooked with a ton-and-a-half of vegetables, which are later removed from the meat cauldron and mashed together. The dish is a lot of work, especially for a crowd. After everything was cooked, divided, mashed, and served, I felt like taking a nap before dinner. But we did prepare *puchero* for thirty-six people, plus a humongous pot of *Sopa* (page 306), a traditional accompaniment down Mérida way. This recipe is a smaller version using all the same ingredients and proportions. If yours is a wild and crazy group, an additional toasted habanero chile or two are always welcome. Piles of tortillas are in order here, and French bread for "making *chuc*" (sopping up the juice—see page 317). Make the whole recipe; leftovers are superb.
Yield: 12 servings

- 1 four-pound chicken, whole
- 3 pounds lean pork loin or leg, in one piece
- 2 pounds beef round or chuck, in one piece
- 1 acorn squash, quartered and seeds removed (keep skin on)
- 1 pound carrots, peeled and quartered
- 3 turnips, peeled and quartered
- 4 yams, peeled and quartered
- 6 red potatoes, peeled and quartered
- 2 plantains, golden with black spots, peeled and quartered
- 1 green cabbage, quartered
- 4 medium beets (young, with leaves), peeled and quartered

1. Put 4 quarts water in a huge pot. Add the chicken, pork, and beef. Add all the vegetables except the beets. Bring the water to a boil, then lower the heat and simmer, with the cover slightly askew.

2. Cook until the vegetables are very soft and remove them to a side pot. Remove the chicken to a side bowl after 1 hour. Continue cooking the pork and beef for another hour. Skim the surface of the broth of all fat.

3. In a separate pot, boil the beets in water until they are soft. Drain the water and mash the beets in the pot.

4. While the beets are cooking, finish preparing the cooked vegetables. Start by removing the skin from the acorn squash. Place a few cups of the vegetables at a time in a large pot or bowl and mash, using a potato masher or hand-held electric mixer. Add the beets last, once they are cooked. Mash until all the vegetables are mashed together, adding a bit of broth from time to time. They will have taken on color from the beets.

- 4 Tablespoons "Recado de Bistec" (page 301), "Recado Rojo," or "achiote" paste
- 1 pinch saffron threads, or powder
- 1 large can garbanzos (28 ounces), drained
- ½ cup raw white rice
- freshly ground black pepper and salt to taste
- 2 ripe avocados

5. Add the *recado* (thinned with a little broth) to the meat. Bring to a boil and add the saffron, garbanzos, and rice. Cover, reduce to a simmer, and continue cooking for another 25 minutes, covered. Uncover, turn off the heat, and remove the meats. Add salt and pepper to taste.

6. First serve the broth with rice and garbanzos in bowls. Then cut the meats into chunks and put them on a large platter with avocado slices (squirted with sour lime or Seville orange juice) arranged around the sides for each person to help himself. Put a bowl of mashed vegetables at each end of a family-sized table. *Xnipec* (page 302) made without tomatoes and very local *salsa de rábano* (radish condiment) both get passed around for added Yucatecan zing.

For "salsa de rábano" (radish condiment)

- 24 red radishes, chopped fine
- 1 teaspoon salt
- 8 sour "limas agrias," or 5 limes and 1 grapefruit, juiced

Mix the ingredients together in a bowl and pass at the table.

Elvira López del Castillo's

Poc-Chuc *Grilled, Marinated Pork Steak*

POC-CHUC IS ON EVERY YUCATÁN PENINSULA MENU from Villahermosa to Valladolid, with the big feeding frenzy in the center of the state. It's the region's answer to the north's *Carne Asada* (page 34).

Elvira was quietly buying pork in Mérida's main market when I boldly bombarded her with questions like, what makes *poc-chuc* so popular? Expecting a multi-ingredient recipe for a special *recado* I had never heard about, I held my breath, pencil at the ready. She couldn't believe I was so curious about this simple dish...and wondered why the hell this blond gringa had picked *her*? (I got this information later, naturally, while sharing a margarita.) It turns out that *poc-chuc* is pork steak marinated in salt water overnight and grilled. Period. It's traditionally served with a simple Mayan salsa called *Salsa Chile Kut* (recipe follows), grilled red onions, and Sieved Black Beans (page 250).

Yield: 4 servings

- 4 pork steaks, from the loin or leg
- 4 Tablespoons salt, dissolved in 1 quart water
- vegetable oil as needed
- 2 large red onions, cut in half horizontally

1. Marinate the pork steaks in the heavily salted water overnight, or for about 12 hours in a covered dish in the refrigerator. Remove the steaks from the water and pat them completely dry with paper towels.

2. Heat a grill to hot and brush the grill with vegetable oil so the steaks won't stick.

3. Brush the red onions with oil and grill them alongside the pork. Grill the steaks until no pink shows when you cut a thick section open with the tip of a sharp knife.

For the Salsa Chile Kut

SALSA CHILE KUT IS MADE FROM GROUND DE ÁRBOL CHILE, WATER, AND SALT. It's classic to serve alongside *poc-chuc* in Yucatán, and you won't see a grilled pork steak served without it northeast of Campeche, all the way to Cancún.

Yield: about ⅓ cup

- 10 de árbol chiles, stemmed
- ¼ cup water
- 1 teaspoon salt

1. Toast (page 16) the chiles (put a piece of foil over them because chile roasting fumes are very strong).

2. Put the water, chiles, and the salt in a blender container. Purée for 10 seconds. Let sit a few hours before stirring and serving in a small bowl.

Rosario Chávez's

▲▼▲

Queso Napolitano *Flan Yucatán Style*

ROSARIO LIKES HER *FLAN* SMOOTH AND CREAMY. When she was first married more than thirty years ago in her village near Chichén-Itzá, she made *queso napolitano* and it turned out a rock-heavy, pock-marked mess—she was devastated. Over the years she learned the secret to Mexico's *flans*. For a smooth *flan*, heat the ingredients slowly and simmer for about one and one-half hours. For a heavier *flan*, with more texture and air bubbles, turn up the heat to medium and cook for forty-five minutes to an hour. The best *flan* is the same *flan* as everywhere else: It's the way you remember your mother or grandmother making the custard when you were a kid.

Yield: 8 servings

- 8 eggs
- 1 can sweetened condensed milk (14 ounces)
- 1 six-inch "canela" stick or three-inch cinnamon stick
- ½ teaspoon vanilla extract
- 5 Tablespoons sugar

1. Break the eggs into a blender container. Add the can of milk. Set aside blender until step 4.

2. Tear any paper off the milk can. Half-fill the can with water. Break up the *canela* and put it in the can. Put the can on the stove and heat. When the water boils, turn off the heat. (This is Rosario's system. You may add 7 ounces water and the *canela* to a small pot, heat to a boil, then turn off the heat.) Add the vanilla.

3. Place the sugar in the top of a metal double boiler. Put the pan directly on the heat until the sugar turns dark brown and is completely melted. Move the pan so the caramel covers the bottom and goes up the sides.

4. Strain the *canela* water into the blender's egg mixture through a sieve while the water is still hot. Blend.

5. Pour the egg mixture over the caramel. Fill the lower part of the double boiler with water, put the top part (containing the caramel mixture) in place, cover, and simmer for a smooth custard for 1½ hours (check the water level after 45 minutes). Take the cover off and press a finger slightly on the surface in the center. It's done as soon as the custard is not liquid.

6. Run a knife around the outside of the *flan*. Cool at room temperature. Put a large plate on top of the pan and quicky flip the dessert over. The *flan* will dislodge along with the caramel. *Queso napolitano* is best made 1 or 2 days before serving.

Glossary and Conversion Tables and Equivalents

Achiote. Paste made from *annatto* seeds and sold by the ounce throughout markets in Tabasco, Campeche, Chiapas, and Yucatán. The seeds are mixed with other seeds and spices such as garlic, cumin, and oregano, then made into *recados* (seasoning pastes) sold in all markets of the Yucatán. In the U.S., you can buy small boxes of *achiote* paste blends at Latino markets and some large supermarkets. The intense orange-red color gets on everything and stains like crazy. Store in the refrigerator.

Acitrón. Candied cactus used in *Chiles en Nogada* and other cooked dishes. Also eaten as candy, especially in the central states.

Adobado. Cooking paste/marinade made with *achiote,* garlic, *canela,* cloves, pepper, Mexican oregano, and cumin.

Adobo. Cooking paste/marinade, either red (guajillo and ancho chiles are most popular) or green (pumpkin seeds, marjoram, thyme), vinegar, oregano, garlic, and sometimes tomatoes.

Aguas Frescas. Refreshing flavored and sweetened water, served cold and usually iced. The selection list is long—here are some favorites: ruby red from hibiscus flowers; medium brown from tamarind pods; yellow from pineapple; pale green from honeydew melon; bright pink from watermelon; peach from cantaloupe; orange from oranges; pale green from limes; neon chartreuse from green zest of tiny unripened *limones pequeños* (Key limes); neon magenta from special bougainvillea petals; almost white from cucumbers; and clear, with tiny seeds at the bottom, from chia seed.

Allspice. The whole, unripe berry of the *Pimenta dioica* tree. Its flavor is similar to a combination of cinnamon, cloves, and nutmeg. The whole berry looks like a double-sized black peppercorn. Often sold ground.

Annatto. Seeds of the *Bixa orellana* tree. Brick red, very hard seeds are ground into *achiote* paste for Yucatán's *recado* seasoning pastes.

A view of Taxco.

Antojito. Literally "little whim." It's a snack, usually made with *masa,* or tortillas. For example, a tamale eaten from a street vendor's cart is considered an *antojito,* but if numerous tamales are eaten at home, as a meal, they are no longer called *antojitos.*

Arroz. Mexicans seldom serve plain steamed rice except in the city of Veracruz and surrounding Gulf towns. Rice is otherwise sautéed in oil to coat each grain, then hot broth is poured over: *verde* (green, with herbs); *rojo* (red, with tomatoes); *pilaf* (sautéed with onion); *amarillo* (yellow, with coloring, in Yucatán) are some variations.

Asada. Literally "roasted." Often the name for a marinade or seasoning used in roasting, or meat cooked in a sauce, or meat marinated then grilled. See *Carne Asada* (page 34), *Coleto Asado* (page 280), and *Mojarra Asada* (page 208).

Asiento. Clingy pork bits that stay at the bottom of a *carnitas* or *chicharrón* kettle. Spread on *clayudas* (special tortillas of Oaxaca) for a market fonda treat.

Ate. Compressed fruit pastes, usually made with guava or mango. Latino markets carry bricks to be sliced and served, as a dessert, with a smooth cheese like cream cheese and sweet crackers.

Atole. Ancient *masa* gruel made with water or milk, with or without sugar. Mix *masa* into milk, strain, boil, then add sugar and cinnamon.

Atole con granillo. In Oaxaca, traditionally made with a special *masa* having a ricelike texture at the bottom of the mixing bowl. Some *granillo* is always scooped into the bowl when *atole* is served. *Atole* without *granillo* is not considered fine quality in Oaxaca.

Avocado. Fruit from *Persea americana*, a laurel tree family member. Hass variety is the tastiest, with the best consistency for slicing, dicing, or mashing into guacamole. Hass is usually dark green in markets, then ripens to black. The skin is very bumpy. Never refrigerate an avocado unless it is ripe and you can't use it for a few days, or it will be inedible.

Avocado leaves. Claims have been made that U.S. avocado leaves are toxic when eaten in large quantities by small animals. Mexicans have been using them for generations as a flavoring herb—they're similar to anise/bay. When you're in Oaxaca, purchase leaves from wild trees sold by Indian women in open-air markets. Their anise flavor is stronger than U.S. leaves—add fennel tops here. Dry them in your hotel room (hang them by their branches over a hanger), then remove the branches and take the leaves back home in plastic bags. They're indispensable for authentic Oaxacan *barbacoa* and some black bean dishes.

Banana leaves. Sold both fresh and frozen in Mexican, Latino, Caribbean, Filipino, and Asian markets in the U.S. Examine fresh leaves before buying—be sure they are whole and not irregularly cut pieces inside the outer leaves. They are huge, about twenty by forty inches. Frozen leaves are sold in one-pound packages. Dried leaves (to reconstitute in tepid water) are found in Chinatown. Carefully wipe off any white film with a damp cloth before using. Wash the leaves, then store between layers of moist towels to retain their moisture (and flexibility) while filling. (Purchased leaves are partially cooked for flexibility. Home-grown leaves need to be par-boiled, steamed, or singed.) Leaves stay fresh for one week, a few days longer if refrigerated. Old leaves turn brown. Banana leaves are used for wrapping and flavoring; they are never eaten.

Barbacoa. Pit-cooked lamb or *cabrito* (kid) flavored with maguey leaves in Jalisco and the central states, avocado leaves farther south around Oaxaca.

Bijol. An intensely bright orange coloring agent (corn, flour, cumin, yellow No. 5, red No. 40, and *annatto*) that gives yellow rice its yellow color. Tiny cans can be puchased in Latino markets and stores selling Caribbean products, as this is a Caribbean product, adopted by Yucatán. Substitute turmeric.

Birria. Similar to *barbacoa*, and a specialty in Mexico's central states. The meat is flavored with maguey leaves and chiles, and is not pit-cooked, but rather baked or stove-top-cooked. Usually soupy, and usually made with *cabrito* (kid), which is sometimes served separately from the broth.

Bolillos. Chewy French rolls, about 6 inches by 4 inches with pointed ends, are most often used for *tortas* (sandwiches). The short French reign of Maximilian of Hapsburg (1864-67) brought French bread to the country that claims tortillas as its own. Most Mexican markets today offer both tortillas and *bolillos.*

Botana. Light snack, such as potato chips, olives, pretzels, etc., and most often associated with drinks.

Bouillon. Southern Mexican cooks, whether in homes, fondas, or big-deal restaurants, use Knorr (the Swiss company) chicken bouillon powder when they have no homemade broth. They also use it as a substitute for salt. When you visit a *supermercado,* look for jars—they range from a few ounces (spice-shelf size) to mammoth quart-size and larger. The flavor is apparent throughout the country, and is a mainstay of Mexico's cuisine.

Cabrito. Young goat, or kid, prepared as *barbacoa,* and over coals (in the northern states).

Cajeta. Caramel candy, or sauce, made from goat's milk in Celaya, Guanajuato.

Caldo de res, o pollo. Big bowls of beef or chicken soup cherished in the south for hangovers. People claim it has the same curative effects as northern Mexico's *menudo* (tripe soup).

Canela. *Cinnamomum zeylanicum*, true Ceylon cinnamon, or Mexican soft cinnamon. Different from, and milder than, the harder stick variety in the U.S.

Cazuela. Clay casserole, glazed only on the inside, for stove-top or oven baking. Season before use by boiling water in it. Some cooks rub cloves of garlic on the outside to eliminate any too-earthy tastes; others appreciate this flavor.

Cebollitas de cambray. Tiny round onions with their green tops, similar to scallions.

Cecina. Thinly sliced chile-marinated pork or beef round (depending on region) for grilling.

Cemita. Sesame-seeded roll famous in Puebla and Cholula. It's also the name of the local sandwich served on the roll.

Cena. Light supper. After *comida corrida* (full lunch of at least three courses), Mexicans prefer a simple late meal of a tamale or a few tacos, soup, a sandwich, etc., and this often begins as late as 10 P.M.

Champurrado. White *atole* (*atole blanco*) flavored with chocolate. For each cup of milk, stir in 1 rounded teaspoon Mexican chocolate tablet, 1½ teaspoons cornstarch, sugar, and cinnamon to taste. Simmer in a double boiler for 30 minutes.

Charanda. A drink from the agave plant, like tequila and mezcal, but produced only in the states of Urapan and Michoacán.

Chayote. A summer squash with thin skin and a pear shape. Chayotes can be either light green with smooth skin or darker green with a skin full of soft "spikes." Each weighs about eight ounces.

Chepil. An herb that grows in cornfields and that is used in squash blossom soup and various rice dishes, among others. It's only now beginning to be cultivated because of increasing popularity, especially in Puebla and Oaxaca.

Chicharrones. Sheets of fried pork rind. Hot, crispy, and delectable, these are Mexico's favorite market snack.

Chiles. See page 7.

Chirmolera. Green-glazed bowl with a heavy combed texture used for grating the zest of *limones pequeños* (tiny Key limes).

Chocolate. Mexican chocolate, *Theobroma cacao* is coarser than European velvety brands like Lindt, and our Hershey. Cacao beans are always ground with sugar, *canela,* and almonds and are used exclusively for hot chocolate and mole—never eaten as candy. Have your own recipe ground at a specialty mill in Oaxaca, or buy much less impressive imported brands such as Ibarra and Abuelita. Look for the U.S. brand, Gazella, which is excellent. Store in a cool, dry place like any chocolate.

Chocolate de leche. Hot Mexican chocolate made with milk (or water, *chocolate de agua*) and whipped with a traditional *molinillo.* Drunk from mugs or bowls and often served with sweets, such as egg bread, sweet rolls, or doughnuts in the morning and at night.

Chocolateatole. White *atole* with a separately made top foam flavored with chocolate (½ foam and ½ liquid is preferred). This very special drink is difficult to prepare and is often served at weddings. Some fondas in Oaxaca still offer it at breakfast.

Chorizo. Chile-flavored sausage made famous in the markets of Toluca and Oaxaca. Chorizo casings are always removed before cooking. *Longaniza* is an untied version.

Churros. Long thin doughnuts (12 inches by ½ inch) with ridges, extruded from pastry tubes, boiled in oil, and covered with sugar. They are traditionally dipped into hot Mexican chocolate or black coffee.

Cilantro. *Coriandrum sativum* is also known as Chinese parsley or fresh coriander. The herb is always sold with its roots attached in Mexico, as it keeps longer. Use the leaves only, as the stems are bitter when cooked.

Cocina callejera. Street food cart.

Codorniz. Quail.

Comal. Cooking disk made from steel, cast iron, or unglazed earthenware (the latter extremely fragile and not a good traveler) for cooking tortillas. Toasting ingredients (see page 16) is an integral part of southern Mexican cooking and cooks keep a *comal* on the stove, in a permanent position, for this purpose.

Comedores. Food counters in big city markets, also called fondas.

Comida corrida. Very reasonably priced, fixed-menu lunch, including a simple soup broth, rice or noodles, meat, and, sometimes, beans. Mexico's blue plate special. *Comida* (lunch) is most often the main meal of the day.

Corn husks. Dried corn leaves used for wrapping tamale fillings.

Crema. Similar to sour cream and French crème fraîche. Huge variations throughout Mexico depend on brands, time of year, location, and age. Color variations from white through ivory, cream, yellow, to rich gold can be seen in markets in dairy-rich areas. Many Mexicans living in the U.S. prefer sour cream, so substituting is no problem except when the recipe calls for the *crema* to be heated or cooked. *Crema* and crème fraîche are both full-fat creams and can be boiled; sour cream curdles.

Desayuno. Light early morning breakfast, usually a sweet roll or bread and a drink. Late breakfast is often called *almuerzo*—it's heavier, with eggs, meat, or *chilaquiles.*

Epazote. *Teloxys* (formerly *Chenopodium ambrosioides*) is still a hard-to-find ingredient in the U.S., but it grows like a weed from seeds (no fertilizer and low water) in containers and in obscure garden spots. It's now found at many nurseries in 2 inch herb pots during the summer. "The taste and smell," claims a friend "is like camphor and kerosene." But it grows on you (like cilantro did, remember?), and it's the special ingredient that makes southern Mexican dishes taste regional. There is no substitute.

Equites. Corn kernels boiled with *epazote.* Served in cups from pushcarts in the evening, around the *zócalos* of Toluca, Mexico City, Veracruz, Puebla, and Oaxaca.

Escabeche. Pickled or vinegared vegetables found throughout Mexico. Served as a side relish, or condiment.

Flor de calabaza. Pumpkin blossom.

Fonda. Traditionally, a rooming house or inn, then later a room in a house (or garage) turned into a small neighborhood restaurant. Today, food counters in markets are most often called fondas, but are also called *comedores* and *puestos.*

Fry. The verb "to fry," when pertaining to a Mexican sauce, means to heat fat in a deep pot, then carefully pour in liquid (it splatters!), and "fry" the sauce before turning down the heat and simmering (see page 17).

Guanábana. Soursop. A large fruit with large black seeds and dark green cousin of the cherimoya, with a similar texture, but tarter flavor. Makes excellent *nieve,* or sherbet.

Gusano de maguey. *Aegiale hesperiaris* grubs found in maguey plants are dried and used as flavoring. They are considerd an aphrodisiac in some circles. Tiny *gusanitos* are favored in Oaxaca, where they are coated with salted chile powder and strung to dry in market cheese stalls.

Hierba buena. Spearmint.

Hierba de conejo. "Rabbit herb" used in Oaxaca for a very old, home-style way of preparing black beans.

Hierbas de olor. Herb bouquet of bay leaf, thyme, and Mexican oregano.

Hoja santa. *Piper auritum* also known as *acuyo* in Veracruz and the southern Gulf areas, and *momo* in Chiapas. Eight inch, heart-shaped, velvety leaves with an anise flavor. A good market souvenir: Buy fresh leaves, then spread them out and turn daily so they don't curl, until they're dry. Simply stack or crumble and carry home in a plastic bag.

Horchata. Cold, milky-white drink made from rice, *canela,* and sugar. A fine counterbalance for too-spicy chile dishes.

Huitlacoche. Sometimes spelled *cuitlacoche*, *Ustilago maydis* is a mushroomlike fungus that grows on fresh corn during summer rainy season. Finest quality is velvety pale gray when raw. Cooked, the color changes to charcoal-black. Often found at markets prepared with onion, garlic, and chile in quesadillas or empanadas. Eight-ounce cans packaged in Mexico by Herdez are sometimes available in U.S. Latino markets.

Jamaica. Dried flowers, a variety of hibiscus (sometimes called *roselle*) used to make a bright, garnet-red drink prized for its refreshingly sour taste.

Jímaca. *Pachyrhizus erosus* is a large tuber, usually about six inches across, with a sweet taste and the texture of water chestnuts (when old, jícamas are not sweet at all).

Limón. Tiny, yellow-green lime known in the U.S. as Key lime. Mexicans do not use yellow lemons.

Maguey. Agave succulent plants grown throughout Mexico. There are more than one hundred species.

Mamey. *Calocarpum sapota*, is a tropical, oval fruit (weighing about 1 pound when ripe) with fuzzy brown skin and orange-pink meat. The sweet fruit's flavor, a cross between persimmon and pear, is best in late summer. It is called *zapote* in Tabasco and Yucatán.

Masa. Dough, made from ground (not cut like cornmeal) dried and hulled corn kernels that have been boiled and soaked in limestone-treated water, and used for tortillas, tamales, and most *antojitos.* Texture can vary from very coarse, for some *gorditas* and tamales, to light and delicate. Typical color varies from dark gold to almost white, with blue corn *masa* popular in central Mexico. Freshly prepared *masa* lasts six hours unrefrigerated and up to two days, refrigerated, before it begins to sour, but it can be frozen for a month.

Masa harina. Dried and finely ground corn dough (*masa*) is manufactured and sold in the U.S. by Quaker Oats Company and Maseca. Maseca now produces fine- and coarse-grind *masa harina.* Fine *masa harina* reconstitutes into *masa* for delicate tortillas, fine-grind *masa* tamales, such as Mérida's *Vaporcitos* (page 313), and most other banana-leaf-wrapped tamales. *Antojitos* such as *sopes* and most tamales are made with coarse-grind. It's found in U.S. Latino markets and many large supermarkets.

Merienda. Afternoon snack, similar to English tea. Most often with Mexican hot chocolate, or coffee and sweet rolls and fruit. Veracruzanas enjoy their region's puffed *gorditas* for *marienda.*

Metate. Lava rock (basalt) grinding stone of pre-Hispanic origin. Three-legged, sloping-topped, rectangular (about 12 inches by 24 inches), and with a very heavy grinder (*mano* or *metlapilli*) the *metate* is used to grind corn, coffee, and *mole* ingredients. When it's used to grind cocoa beans or pumpkin seeds, a small fire is lit beneath to heat the ingredients so the oils run easier. Except in the smallest pueblos, these have generally been replaced by electric blenders today, and traditional food texture has suffered.

Mezcal. Alcoholic drink, similar to tequila but generally less refined. Made from the maguey plant, *Agave angustifolia.*

Milanesa. Thin slice of beef, pounded thinner, dipped in egg and bread crumbs and panfried.

Molcajete. Lava rock mortar. Three-legged bowls, often with a spout, for hand-grinding chiles and spices for sauces, with a lava rock *tejolote* (pestle).

Mole. Pronounced mo-LAY, literally translates to "sauce," and there are hundreds in Mexico, originating primarily from the states of Oaxaca and Puebla. Oaxaca claims to be "the home of seven *moles*" and the place from which all other *moles* supposedly sprang. The famous seven are:

Mole negro. The blackest *mole.* It's made in Oaxaca with chilhuacle negro chile, mulato chile, pasilla chile (the long negro chile—dried chilaca chile—not pasilla de Oaxaca, nor ancho) blackened chile seeds and stems, almonds, sesame seeds, tomatillos, raisins, *canela,* Mexican chocolate, and more.

Mole rojo. Red *mole*, sometimes called *mole colorado*, is brick red. It uses exactly the same ingredients (but there are a million variations) as *mole negro* but the chile seeds and stems are not blackened. Oaxacan cooks use red chilhuacle chile, rather than black. Many cooks add guajillo chile, and some include peanuts.

Mole coloradito. A mild red *mole* made with ancho chile and guajillo chile only. Nuts, *canela,* and raisins are always included. Many cooks add fried bread to the blender ingredients, as a thickener, along with sesame seeds.

Mole chichilo. Similar to *moles rojo* and *coloradito* but with the addition of anise-flavored avocado leaves, and *masa* as a thickener.

Mole verde. Green mole that gets its color from fresh jalapeño chile, tomatillo, *epazote*, *hoja santa*, cilantro, and flat-leaf parsley, and often thickened with *masa*. It's especially enjoyed in a stew with small *masa* dumplings.

Mole amarillo. Yellow, as the name implies, from chilhuacle chile in Oaxaca (or, a combination of guajillo chile and de árbol chile), cloves, cumin seed, and generally, tomatillos. Most often served thin, as a soup, with large chunks of vegetables.

Mole de almendra. Basically the same as *mole negro*, or *rojo*, but with a great amount of blanched almonds, which adds flavor and texture, as a *pipián*. Often only ancho chile is used, with cloves, *panela,* and, sometimes, sesame seeds.

Molinillo. Hand-carved wooden beater for making foamy Mexican hot chocolate.

Nance (spelled nanche in Veracruz). Chokecherries, often preserved in sugar syrup, sometimes with alcohol. Found beautifully arranged in large jars in Yucatán, they make fine, if fragile, souvenirs.

Nieve. Literally "snow," this is the name most commonly associated with ice cream and sherbet all over Mexico, and memorably great in Oaxaca and Veracruz. *Nieve* is made with water only for sherbet, or with water and evaporated milk for ice cream (*helado* in many places) with a granita-like, ice milk texture. Tropical fruit flavors are Mexican national treasures.

Nixtamal. Soaked, dried corn with the skins removed, ready to be ground into *masa*.

Nopales. Cactus paddles (leaves) from the *Opuntia* cactus family (*piruli* plant, in Spanish). *Nopalitos* are small, tender *nopales*. Covered with thorns, the paddles must be carefully cleaned before using. Their mucilaginous, slimy texture is similar to that of okra.

Olla. Clay pot, glazed on the inside, with a round bottom. Some have handles and a smaller top section, often with a spout, for making coffee and hot chocolate.

Oregano. True Mexican oregano is sold by Indian women in weekly markets (there are about a dozen types of wild oregano in Mexico). What is sold in jars in *supermercados* is actually marjoram. McCormick brand is Mexican oregano.

Pan dulce. There's a huge selection of sweet rolls made throughout Mexico, eaten everywhere in the country for breakfast and *merienda* (Mexican tea).

Panela. Called *piloncillo* in northern Mexico (*panocha* in Sonora), unrefined sugar is pressed into cone or disk shapes and sold in every market. To use, let it dissolve in water, or grate by hand or in a food procesor. Substitute dark brown sugar.

Parsley. Mexicans prefer *perejil*, flat-leaf parsley, over curly varieties.

Pepitas. Pumpkin seeds (or squash seeds) used throughout Mexico, especially in the southern states, to grind into *pipián* (pumpkin seed sauce). Raw, roasted, shelled and unshelled varieties of various sizes are found in all markets.

Pibil. Pork, or sometimes chicken, cooked in a Yucatán *pib*, or underground pit. The regional flavoring comes from seasoning paste, called *recado*, and banana leaves.

Picadillo. Shredded or ground meat mixed with dried fruit and nuts and usually used as stuffing.

Piloncillo. See *panela*.

Pipián. See *pepitas*.

Plantains. *Plátanos*, or *machos*, are large, ten- to twelve-inch less-sweet versions of our bananas. They are never eaten raw, but are cooked like starchy potatoes when at their green or yellow stages throughout the Caribbean and Mexico's east coast. They are usually sold green and take more than a week to turn completely black if you want to use them ripe when at their sweetest. Plantains freeze well, peeled and wrapped.

Portales. Arcades or porticoes.

Postre. Dessert.

Pozole. Soup/stew always containing a large corn kernel, also called *pozole* (U.S. grits are made from this same kernel). The soup's color varies from white to red to green, depending upon the corn's color and regional chiles used. Traditionally pork head is the meat used, but this varies considerably. Yucatán market fondas serve an ancient drink also called *pozole*. The gruel is drunk cold, with salt or with sugar and chile habanero. Tabasco market fondas offer a drink made from cocoa beans ground with *masa*, diluted with water, and served iced, and also called *pozole*.

Puesto. Market stall.

Pulque. A pre-Columbian drink made from 100 percent fermented (not distilled) sap of the maguey, *Agave salmiana*, plant and sold at *pulquerías* or roadside stands in the countryside. The milky white, mildly alcoholic drink varies in strength by age. *Aguamiel* (honey water) is pure maguey juice and a favorite of children—it ferments to *pulque* in two to three days. *Pulque* is best young and slightly effervescent—anything older is past its prime and too strong. Locals often add a splash of bottled hot sauce, a squeeze of lime, and salt.

Quesillo de Oaxaca. Mexico's premier melting cheese. It's made in long coils then wrapped into balls. In Oaxaca's Mercado Juárez, you can see vendors uncoiling giant foot-in-diameter wholesale beauties and rewinding them into smaller golfball, baseball, or softball sizes. Substitute mozzarella or string cheese for similar taste and texture.

Queso añejo. Means "aged cheese." It's aged, sharp, and crumbly, and can be grated when old. Fonda cooks sprinkle it over most dishes before any plate reaches the counter. Some types are saltier than others. Substitute Parmesan cheese.

Queso fresco. Translates to "fresh cheese." It's a fresh, milky-tasting, soft cheese but can still be crumbled and sprinkled over dishes where a sharp *añejo* would be too strong. It softens when heated, but does not completely melt. Similar to dry farmer cheese. Ranchero cheese is now popular in the U.S.

Rajas. Chile strips, usually poblano chile, and cooked with onion and eaten in tacos, quesadillas, with scrambled eggs, or as a side dish with meat.

Salsa. Sauce, either raw or cooked.

Soplador. Woven palm or rush fan used for stoking fires, and especially coals in braziers under *comales* in rural kitchens or street vendor carts.

Squash blossoms. Bright yellow bouquets of *calabacitas criollas* (pumpkin blossoms) are market favorites. They are taken home to be sauced, stuffed, stewed, fried, grilled, boiled, and baked—cooked just about any way Mexicans can think of. They can be found in the U.S. at farmers' markets and in gourmet Italian markets. Zucchini blossoms can be substituted, but their orange-green color is very different.

Tamal. Tamale to people in the U.S., is just about any food item wrapped in leaves. Most often this means *masa* lightened with freshly rendered lard (three parts *masa* to one part lard) and seasoned, or stuffed with meat or vegetables, often in a chile-flavored sauce, and wrapped with corn or banana leaves. *Tamales dulces* are sweetened with sugar, fruit, or dried fruit. Sold and eaten either in the morning, as breakfast, or at night, after 8 P.M., often with the pre-Hispanic drink, *atole*. Leaves are peeled away and discarded before eating the filling.

Tamale steamer. *Tamalerías* are large metal steamers made especially for cooking tamales. A shelf with holes for stacking tamales is placed over boiling water. An opening under the shelf, on the outside of the pot, is for adding water so the lid doesn't have to be removed during the cooking process. *Tamaleros* sell tamales from *tamalerías* in mornings and evenings near *zócalos* and markets. Before making tamales, always be sure you have a system for steaming them. Alternates if you have no *tamalería*: An Oriental bamboo steamer; or put an open vegetable steamer over one-inch of water, unscrewing the center post, if possible; or put 3 water-filled custard cups or empty tuna fish cans at the bottom of a large pot with a nonfragile plate on top (be sure there's enough room for steam to escape along the side). Add one inch water, being sure the water does not reach the plate. (Drop a coin into the water before inserting the steamer rack. You know there is water in the steamer as long as the coin rattles.)

Tamarindo. A long brown pod filled with sour-tasting pulp and eaten as a snack. Mixed with water and sugar it makes a refreshing drink enjoyed all over the country. A favorite traditional sweet when mixed with sugar.

Tasajo. Specially cut, thinly sliced beef round sold fresh, or marinated and aged, for quick grilling.

Tepache. Water mixed with *panela* and rinds of very ripe pineapple. The mildly alcoholic drink ferments in three days, then is strained and served from brightly painted, dried gourd halves in Oaxacan markets. *Tepache* turns to pineapple vinegar in fifteen days.

Tequesquite. Limestone or alkaline rocks (calcium oxide) used in the preparation of *nixtamal* for *masa*. Also called *cal*.

Tequila. Produced only from *Agave tequilana*, the Weber blue variety. Legally tequila can be produced in only five states: Jalisco, Michoacán, Guanajuato, Tamaulipas, and Nayarit, but Jalisco's is considered best. Tequilas made with 100 percent juice, no sugar or water added, are considered best. The town of Tequila is thirty miles west of Guadalajara and an excellent day trip. Recommended reading: *¡Tequila!* by Lucinda Hutson, Ten Speed Press, 1995.

Tescalate. A drink of cocoa beans ground with toasted corn and *annatto* seeds, and served cool in Chiapas and Campeche market fondas.

Texate (or tejate). Traditional cold drink from Oaxaca's markets. Corn flour, cocoa beans, cocoa powder, coconut, and *mamey* fruit seeds are all toasted first, then mixed in huge green-glazed bowls called *cazuelas verdes*. Locals look for *texate* with the thickest top foam. Foam is said to be alive and where the drink's spirit lives.

Tianguis. Open-air Indian market, usually held once a week. In towns that have a permanent market building and also a weekly market, the surrounding open-air market on that day is called *tianguis*.

Tienda. Small neighborhood grocery store stocked with daily necessities.

Toast. The verb "to toast" means to brown a vegetable, chile, seed, nut, spice, etc., on a hot *comal*, or heavy skillet, usually without fat (see page 16).

Tomatillo (or tomate verde). Physalis ixocarpa, called tomatillo in northern Mexico, areas of Oaxaca, and the U.S., is not part of the tomato family, but is still a fruit. The tomatillo has a fresh, tart taste, and is used in fresh and cooked salsas verdes and many moles. Remove the husks, but never peel the fruit before cooking.

Tortillas. See page 12.

Tuna. Prickly pear cactus fruit. Colors vary from green to pink, rose, and ruby-red. Found throughout the country but especially in Jalisco and the central states. An acorn-shaped, small, intensely red-meat variety makes Oaxaca's famous *tuna nieve* (cactus fruit sherbet).

Vanilla. *Vanilla planifolia*, is a ten-inch, skinny black bean that grows on trees around Papantla, Veracruz, in the northern part of the state. It's the fruit of an orchid and fermented before drying. Mexico's vanilla is excellent quality, but the country's liquid vanilla is usually unhealthful due to chemicals used in processing.

Verdolagas. Purslane is a ground creeper with fleshy leaves, pinkish stems, and an acidic flavor. Found in markets around Guadalajara and south to Yucatán.

Vinegar. Mild pineapple vinegar is preferred throughout southern Mexico. Substitute two-parts apple cider vinegar and one-part water.

Zapote. This tropical fruit, which is shaped like a football, is also called a *mamey*. It comes in two varieties: One is medium brown, with a fuzzy outer covering, and a pulp that is bright salmon pink-orange, and sweet; the other, called *zapote negro* (black zapote), has either a round, brown or dark green outer covering (similar to a russet potato or overripe avocado, depending on variety) and a shiny, jet-black, very sweet pulp inside. It is very delicate and does not travel well.

Zócalo. The town square. Almost every city and town has one, and it's usually right in front of the main church, and across from city hall.

Conversion Tables and Equivalents

LIQUID VOLUME

U.S.A.	Imperial	Metric
½ teaspoon (tsp.)	⅓ teaspoon	2.5 milliliters (ml.)
1 teaspoon	¾ teaspoon	5 milliliters
1 Tablespoon (Tbsp.) = 3 teaspoons	¾ Tablespoon	15 milliliters
1 ounce (oz.) = 2 Tablespoons	1 ounce	29 milliliters
1 cup (c.) = 8 oz., 16 Tbsps., 48 tsps.	⅘ cup	237 milliliters (apx. ¼ liter)
1 pint (pt.) = 2 cups	⅘ pint = 1⅔ cups	473 milliliters (apx. ½ liter)
1 quart (qt.) = 2 pints	⅘ quart = 3⅓ cups	946 milliliters (apx. 1 liter)
1 gallon (gal.) = 4 quarts	⅘ gallon	3.78 liters

U.S.A.	Imperial	Metric
⅝ teaspoon	½ teaspoon	3 milliliters
1¼ teaspoons	1 teaspoon	6 milliliters
1¼ Tablespoons	1 Tablespoon = 3 teaspoons	18 milliliters
1 ounce (2 Tbsps.)	1 ounce	29 milliliters
1¼ cups = 10 ounces	1 cup = 10 oz., 16 Tbsps.	296 milliliters
1¼ pints = 2½ cups, 20 oz.	1 pint = 2 cups	591 milliliters
2½ pints = 5 cups, 40 oz.	1 quart = 2 pints	1.18 liters
5 pints = 10 cups	1 gallon = 4 quarts	2.36 liters

TEMPERATURE

Fahrenheit = (Celsius x 9) ÷ 5 + 32
Celsius = (Fahrenheit - 32) ÷ 9 x 5

Fahrenheit	Celsius		British Gas No.
100°F	38°C (37.8°C)		
120°F	49°C (48.9°C)		
130°F	54°C (54.4°C)		
140°F	60°C (60°C)		
150°F	66°C (65.6°C)		
160°F	71°C (71.1°C)		
165°F	74°C (73.9°C)		
170°F	77°C (76.7° C)		
200°F	95°C (93.3°C)		
250°F	120°C (121.1°C)	=	½
275°F	135°C (135°C)	=	1
300°F	150°C (148.9°C)	=	2
325°F	163°C (162.8°C)	=	3
350°F	175°C (176.7°C)	=	4
375°F	190°C (190.6°C)	=	5
400°F	205°C (204.4°C)	=	6
450°F	230°C (232.2°C)	=	8

LINEAR

For exact conversion use
2.54 x number of inches = centimeters

⅛ inch = ³⁄₁₀ centimeter
¼ inch = ⅗ centimeter
1 inch = 2½ centimeters
2 inches = 5 centimeters
5 inches = 13 centimeters
6 inches = 15 centimeters
10 inches = 25 centimeters
12 inches = 30 centimeters

WEIGHT

For quick conversions 30 grams = 1 ounce; 450 grams = 1 pound; 2¼ pounds = 1 kilogram.

Below are some exact equivalents
1 ounce = 28.34953 grams
1 pound = 453.59237 grams
2.20462 pounds = 1 kilogram
1000 grams = 1 kilogram

Travel Tips for Your Own Cook's Tour of Mexico

Part of the secret of success in life is to eat what you like and let the food fight it out inside.
—Mark Twain

Water

WATER IS THE CULPRIT IN MOST CASES OF TRAVELER'S DISEASE. Bottled water is available everywhere in Mexico—maybe not at your corner store, but close enough to make getting it easy. Use bottled water, or mineral water for drinking, including brushing your teeth (and make sure you don't inadvertently drink when you're taking a shower or washing your face). If you're staying somewhere with a kitchen, bring water to a boil and boil it hard for a full ten minutes to purify it.

For washing fruit, vegetables, and dishes, chemical disinfectants are an alternative. Pure bleach (like Clorox) purifies sink water perfectly. It may smell like a clorinated swimming pool, but there won't be any telltale taste on washed food. This process can also be used to create drinking water in emergencies. Here's the American Red Cross water purification system:

Add 2 drops (4, if cloudy) bleach to 1 quart water
Add 8 drops (16, if cloudy) bleach to 1 gallon water
Add ½ teaspoon (1, if cloudy) bleach to 5 gallons water
Add 1 teaspoon (2, if cloudy) bleach to 10 gallons water

Eating precautions are few, not scary, and rather simple. In all fondas, street-food joints, and non-gringo-oriented restaurants throughout Mexico, never eat lettuce and raw vegetables served as garnish. This includes shredded lettuce, cabbage, tomato slices, and radish "roses." The food is heathful and washed, but it's the washing water that non-Mexicans can't tolerate because of the different bacteria in our waters. Now that I've said that, in areas where tourism is important nobody wants to get Mexico's number one industry sick. Most often salads and raw vegetables are safe to eat at larger restaurants.

But, as a small precaution, always ask if the salad ingredients are washed in disinfected or purified water. Health conscious Mexicans insist on this and ask the same question. Unpure water is the biggest cause of disease in Mexico to Mexicans.

Produce

PEELING UNCOOKED FRUIT AND VEGETABLES IS ALSO CRITICAL to staying healthy and avoiding "tourista" or "Montezuma's revenge." Whether this is an important step is questionable because so much of the produce we have in the U.S. comes from Mexico. Anyway, all cooked fruits and vegetables (peeled or not) are safe.

Dairy Products

MILK AND FRESH CHEESE CAN BE A PROBLEM because the bacteria in milk products is different from the bacteria in U.S. dairy items. Mexicans love cheese on everything—if it's not melted then it's dry and crumbled. Be sure that the cheese in restaurant cheese dishes is thoroughly cooked (melted all the way through). Busy cooks sometimes send out cheese dishes—quesadillas, for example—that could use a few more minutes on a *comal.* Mexican friends in San Miguel de Allende insist that locals constantly get stomach troubles from nonrefrigerated cheese. Cheese sitting in afternoon sun at open-air markets translates to "try another place."

Traveling Pointers Roundup

1. NEVER DRINK TAP WATER. Brush your teeth and rinse your brush with bottled water. Keep a bottle on the bathroom sink. Keep water out of your mouth when showering.
2. In restaurants, ask if salad ingredients are washed in disinfected water. If the waiter says he doesn't know, skip the salad, any garnishes, and uncooked salsas.
3. Don't drink fruit drinks made from unpurified water. Always ask. Ask about the ice, too. Many drinks sold in marketplaces are cooled with unpurified ice. Choose hot coffee, hot tea, beer, or canned or bottled sodas. Drinking from a can or bottle is safer than transferring the liquid to a glass that could have rinsing water left in it.
5. Peel raw fruit and vegetables or soak them in a bleach solution for 15 minutes, or follow instructions on bottles of 2 percent tincture of iodine sold in Mexican supermarkets.

If you do get sick, you will feel like hell for about 24 hours. The next day you'll be tired, have a tender tummy, but be otherwise okay. Here are a few suggestions:

1. Before leaving home, ask your doctor about a medication such as Cipro=Ciprofloxacin to use in emergencies.

2. Without Cipro, the pill form of Immodium is best (liquid can be nasty when you're feeling lousy). Bactrim tablets are widely available in Mexico. Pepto Bismol coats and relaxes your stomach, too.
3. Drink lots of bottled water to keep hydrated. Later in the day, begin eating simple French or white bread and continue with plenty of water.
4. For specific questions about traveling to remote areas, telephone the Centers for Disease Control and Prevention hot line 404-332-4559.

Prongs

ONE ITEM NEVER MENTIONED IN GUIDE BOOKS IS ADAPTERS. Not necessary, you say, because Mexico is on the same electrical current as the U.S. Correct, but there's the Prong Problem. Mexican wall outlets don't take the U.S. plugs (which your hair drier and radio probably have), but there's a simple solution. Hardware stores and marketplace hardware vendors throughout Mexico carry adapters and they're cheap, less than a dollar.

Mexican Maps and Driving

DON'T BELIEVE EVERYTHING YOU SEE. Maps often show roads and road upgrades before they are built because Mexican maps are reprinted so seldom. Our first encounter with this phenomenon was when we decided to take a road along Lake Chapala's northern shore from Ajijic to Ocotlán in Jalisco, because our pre-upgraded map ("the newest, the best") showed a good road that we assumed had some fine lake views. To this day Morris and I refer to it as "the road from Hell." Not too far out of Chapala the road got bad, but we figured it was being repaired. Kilometers later it got worse. And worse again. Finally, when we began getting panicky, we stopped a huge Coca-Cola delivery truck (in the U.S. the mail must get through; in Mexico Coca-Cola does get through). The driver said we were about halfway and, no, the road didn't get any better than this. Should we turn around? Forge ahead? The concensus was we forge ahead because that's our direction, and at five miles per hour we wanted to get somewhere before dark (driving at night can be scary on Mexico's pot-holed roads filled with assorted sleeping animals attracted to the warm surfaces). The rocky dirt road became a rock pile then a stream bed with water. To top it all off, the road climbed uphill. We closed our eyes and drove up a waterfall. Okay, it wasn't exactly a waterfall but our nerves were strung as tight as a guitar's strings and the uphill climb on slippery rocks didn't help. Then out of nowhere a kid appeared and insisted upon "pushing" the car. Just what we needed. Thank goodness we saw him in time to call him off. But the kid was thick-headed and looking for pesos, and it took some screaming (mine) to get him to move away as the car skidded left then right. Breathlessly we drove on, at the same snail's speed, past microscopic pueblos, dodging chickens and piglets all the way. Finally, close to sunset, we finished climbing a dirt road to an open vista, then headed downward toward civilization.

The tale's message: Don't always trust maps, ask three people directions (you'll be sure to get at least two answers), and ask directions before setting out—the most reliable sources are consistently policemen and gas station attendants. Mexicans have a hard time admitting they don't know directions (especially *macho hombres*). They'll give false information anytime before admitting ignorance. Don't get scared off, leave time for the unexpected, and keep in mind that Mexico demands some "creative driving." With that said—GO! and have a fabulous experience in one of the world's most exciting countries.

U.S. Customs

When you finally find that exotic herb you've been searching for in one of the indigenous markets outside Oaxaca City, remember that U.S. Customs will want to know what's in your plastic bags upon arrival back home. It's okay, don't panic, just plan ahead (you already did, you brought the freezer bags). You need to declare that you are bringing back dried plants (remember the form on international flights that asks if you are carrying plants?). The agents may ask you the names of the herbs. It's best to know their common and botanical names; for example, *epazote* is *Teloxys* (formerly *Chenopodium ambrosioides*) and *hoja santa* (a.k.a. *acuyo* and *momo*) is *Piper sanctum*.

You cannot return to the U.S. with any fresh produce, so purchase dried chiles only. You can stuff them into freezer bags and store them in the freezer when home. Many times I've hung fresh herbs over curtain rods or hangers to dry in Mexican hotel rooms and apartments. Wild avocado leaves dry this way; later strip them off their bulky branches and pack them in plastic bags. With large-leaf herbs such as *hoja santa*, which are round and about eight inches in diameter, spread a cloth on the floor and dry the leaves on that, turning them daily for about four days. Turning keeps them flat; otherwise, they curl—which is okay if you don't mind them crumbled and crumbled is easier to carry back, anyway.

All cheeses may cross the border, too. Soft, fresh cheese probably won't survive the journey, but *quesillo de Oaxaca* (Oaxacan string cheese) travels well and it freezes. Any hard, aged (*añejo*) cheese is a perfect traveler, just remember to wrap cheese tightly in double layers of plastic to keep it from smelling-up the plane!

Pork and pork products cannot be brought into the U.S. Leave all those gorgeous Tolucan chorizos behind. Prepared tamales may be brought back, except for those made with pieces of pork in the fillings (beef and chicken are fine).

These are general rules. If you have specific questions, call the U.S. Customs Cargo Desk at the international airport closest to you.

Mail-Order Sources

NEARLY EVERY U.S. CITY HAS A LATINO MARKET, and many supermarkets have Mexican sections these days. Check the international aisle of your local supermarket first, then look in the Yellow Pages under food, markets, international foods, bakeries, etc. Within a few minutes your hunt will most likely pay off with the name of a place not too far from home. The manager of Quaker Oats Company's Consumer Response Office told me, for example, that even though your local supermarket may not have *masa harina*, it is possible to order the product through the store's manager. Many other items are available this way—just ask.

Tortillerías are part of the North American landscape. Fresh plantains, avocados, chiles, tomatillos, cactus paddles, coconuts, mangoes, and papayas are seasonal standards here, and farmers' markets are supplying unusual items that people request, so if you want a certain product, make your wishes known. Dry corn husks for tamales are everyday fare; fresh, frozen, or dried banana leaves are becoming so; bottled and fresh salsas are supermarket staples. Jars of pickled chiles are probably in your neighbor's pantry, Mexican-style cheeses are now made in the U.S., and exotica such as *huitlacoche* are found in the South during the summer. Gourmet shops sell dozens of bottled hot sauces made from every chile in the world. Obscure regional dried chiles and herbs, fabulous Mexican chocolate, and blue corn *masa harina* can easily be ordered through the mail.

With the ongoing stream of Mexicans moving to the U.S., we now see products from Chiapas, Yucatán, Puebla, and Oaxaca to serve these homesick folks. Only in Mexico City would you see such a roundup of nationwide food products and liquors in one market as we do here; Mexico's tequilas, mezcals, sugarcane alcohols, rums, coffee liqueurs, and beers are stocked everywhere.

Frieda's, Inc.
P.O. Box 58488
Los Angeles, California 90058
800-241-9477 and 800-241-1771
Fax 714-816-0273

Frieda's is Los Angeles's premier specialty produce supplier, and its products are offered on a daily basis in upscale supermarkets. Frieda's mail-order division sells strictly in full-case orders, but the "availability guide" reads like a *Who's Who of Mexican Food Products*: dried cascabel, chipotle, habanero, mulato, guajillo, pasilla negro chiles, and an assortment of the last three; fresh chiles such as chilaca, habanero, jalapeño, poblano, serrano, and mixed trays; fresh and dried items including cactus prickly pear fruit and leaves (paddles), papayas, pomegranates, tamarind, a dozen winter squash varieties, chayote (white or green), corn husks, *pozole* (lime-slaked hominy), fresh (or potted) herbs, garbanzo beans, jícama, plantains, and tomatillos.

Don Alfonso Foods
P.O. Box 201988
Austin, Texas 78720-1988
800-456-6100
Fax 800-765-7373

Dried ancho, cascabel, guajillo, mulato, pasilla, de árbol, habanero, jalapeño, and chipotle chiles. Canned chipotles en adobo. Pure chile powders. *Annatto* seed, dried *epazote* and seeds, *cacahuazintle* (Mexican hominy), Mexican oregano, hulled green pumpkin seeds, tamarind, prepared Mexican *achiote* paste. Jars of chiles en escabeche, *nopalitos*, and *cajeta*. Cooking utensils such as *molcajetes*, tortilla presses, *comales*, Mexican lime squeezers, and tamale steamers. Books on Mexican cooking, chiles, and tequila.

The CMC Company
P.O. Box 322
Avalon, New Jersey 08202
800-CMC-2780
Fax 609-861-0043

Dried Mexican avocado leaves. Dried Mexican ancho, mulato, pasilla, cascabel, de árbol, chipotle, morita, and habanero chiles. Chile powders. Bottled hot sauces and salsas. Dried Mexican shrimp, Mexican oregano, *panela* (*piloncillo*), *achiote* paste, dried *epazote*, *masa harina*, canned *nopalitos* and tomatillos. Tortilla presses and *comales*.

Adriana's Caravan
409 Vanderbilt Street
Brooklyn, New York 11218
800-316-0820
718-436-8565

Dried herbs and spices from all over the world. Whole allspice, *canela* (true, soft cinnamon), cumin, Mexican vanilla beans. Dried whole ancho, chipotle, habanero, and pasilla chile. Chile powders. Canned chipotles en adobo. Canned tomatillos. Mexican chocolate tablets. Corn husks.

Herbs of Mexico
3903 Whittier Boulevard
Los Angeles, California 90023
213-261-2521

Dried *epazote*, Mexican oregano, whole allspice, *hoja santa* (called *yerba santa* here), vanilla beans. More than 750 items are included on its long list.

Gazella Mexican Chocolate
3200 Corte Malpaso, No. 108
Camarillo, California 93012
805-445-7744

The very best Mexican chocolate outside Mexico. Made in small batches with tender loving care. Call for special blends, flavors, grinds, and preparation techniques.

Mozzarella Company
2914 Elm Street
Dallas, Texas 75226
800-798-2954

Hand-made Mexican cheeses: quesillo de Oaxaca and quesillo fresco. Excellent mozzarella. Try *caciotta*, their Texas version of Monterey Jack with ancho chile.

Bijol and Spices, Inc.
2154 N.W. 22 Court
Miami, Florida 33142
305-634-9030

Bijol condiment for Yucatán's yellow rice. Bijol is also found in many Latino and Caribbean markets.

Hot Stuff
New York, New York
Mail-order only
800-WANT-HOT
Fax 212-254-6120

Dried chiles, canned chipotles en adobo, pure chile powders, chile seeds, bottled hot sauces, *epazote*, and *annatto* seeds.

Mo Hotta-Mo Betta
P.O. Box 4136
San Luis Obispo, California 93403
800-462-3220
Fax 805-545-8389

The chile-head catalog. Bottled hot sauce heaven: brands such as "Vampire Hot Sauce," "Dave's Insanity Sauce," "Hell Hot," and "I Am On Fire Ready to Die." Prepared salsas, pickled products, fresh habanero chiles, and *masa harina*. "Screamin' Meany Habanero Lollipops" for dessert. Dried chiles. Cookbooks.

Hot Hot Hot
56 South Delacey Street
Pasadena, California 91105
800-959-7742
http./www.hot.presence.com./hot/

Another catalog for chile-heads. "Habanero Hot Sauce From Hell," "Hell in a Bottle," "911 Hot Sauce," and "Ass Kickin' Hot Sauce" to name a few lovelies.

Coyote Cucina Catalog
1364 Rufina Circle #1
Santa Fe, New Mexico 87501
800-866-HOWL

A catalog filled with fun, well-designed chile gift items (posters, books, clothing, prepared salsas, etc.), also dried chiles, *epazote*, hibiscus flowers (*jamaica*), *annatto* seed, and pumpkin seeds. *Cajeta*, Mexican vanilla, and tamarind paste. The mail-order service is an offshoot of chef Mark Miller's famous Coyote Café General Store.

Los Chileros de Nuevo Mexico
P.O. Box 6215
Santa Fe, New Mexico 87502
505-471-6967
Fax 505-473-7306

Mostly New Mexican cooking fare (including decorative chile *ristras*), but some interesting Mexican items including dried chiles and powders. Blue corn products, corn husks, and prepared frozen foods.

Pendery's
1221 Manufacturing
Dallas, Texas 75207-6506
800-533-1870
Fax 214-761-1966

A mail-order company with retail shops in the Dallas-Fort Worth area. Mexican, Tex-Mex, South West—you name it and Pendery's probably has it. Chiles, spices, *jamaica*, cooking equipment, cookbooks, chile and garlic *ristras*, clothing (they have holsters for your bottled hot sauces!), and jalapeño-filled bittersweet chocolates.

Seeds of Change
P.O. Box 15700
Santa Fe, New Mexico 87506-5700
505-438-8080 Monday-Friday
Fax 505-438-7052

The seed catalog offers heirloom items not often seen: *tepany* beans from Mexico; *zea mays* Mexican sweet corn; *traditional* Mexican blue-black corn for blue corn *masa*; and *dent* Oaxacan emerald green corn grown by Zapotecs for green *masa* tamales.

Index

Page numbers in **bold type** refer to recipes.